Trekking in the Patagonian Andes

Clem Lindenmayer

D0093888

Trekking in the Patagonian Andes

2nd edition

Published by
  Lonely Planet Publications
  Head Office: PO Box 617, Hawthorn, Vic 3122, Australia
  Branches: 155 Filbert St, Suite 251, Oakland, CA 94607, USA
      10 Barley Mow Passage, Chiswick, London W4 4PH, UK
      71 bis rue du Cardinal Lemoine, 75005 Paris, France

Printed by
  Pac-Rim Kwartanusa Printing
  Printed in Indonesia

Photographs by
  Wayne Bernhardson
  Clem Lindenmayer

  Front cover: Torres del Paine National Park, Juan Pablo Lire, The Image Bank.

First Published
  April 1992

This Edition
  February 1998

Although the authors and publisher have tried to make the information as accurate as possible, they accept no responsibility for any loss, injury or inconvenience sustained by any person using this book.

National Library of Australia Cataloguing in Publication Data

  Lindenmayer, Clem
  Trekking in the Patagonian Andes

  2nd ed.
  Includes index.
  ISBN 0 86442 477 9

  1. Patagonia (Argentina and Chile) - Guidebooks.
  2. Andes Region - Guidebooks. I. Title

  918.270464

Clem Lindenmayer

Clem has long been fascinated by the wild temperate lands of the southern hemisphere, and has trekked extensively in the mountains of the southern Australian island state of Tasmania and in New Zealand. On his first trip to the Patagonian Andes in the southern summer of 1987-8, Clem found this superb mountain region the most captivating of all. Since then he has returned repeatedly to Patagonia, exploring new areas and studying the local flora and fauna. Clem's other passions include learning languages and photography. He researched and authored Lonely Planet's *Walking in Switzerland*, and has helped update its *China* and *Western Europe* travel guidebooks.

From the Author

While I was researching this update, the staff of the Chilean CONAF and Argentine APN, as well as local mountain clubs and other organisations, always received me with warm goodwill and often provided valuable information for the new edition. My particular thanks here go to the following individuals: Anselmo Palma Silva (Chilean IGM, Santiago), Jaime Ramirez (Centro Turístico Lagunillas, Laguna del Laja), Felix Ledesma (CONAF, Conguillío), Rodrigo Marin Suniga (CONAF, Huerquehue), Sarah Anderson (Torres del Paine), Oscar Bianchi (CAP, El Bolsón), Peter Hartmann (CODEFF, Coyhaique), Mariano Calvi (APN, Los Alerces), Domingo Nuñez (APN, Nahuel Huapi), Mario Guinao (CONAF, Chiloé), Hernán Velásquez and Ángel Miranda C (CONAF, Río Simpson), Ruben Oyarzo Oyarzún (CONAF, Andino Alerce), Gabriela Morales (SERNATUR, Coyhaique), Sebastián de la Cruz (CAB, San Carlos de Bariloche), Ramiro Uriarte (Refugio Hielo Azul, Comarca Andina/El Bolsón), Carlos Barria-Diaz (CONAF, Torres del Paine), Luís Briones (CONAF, Puyehue), Denis Aldrich (CONAF, Tamango), Adrian Falcone (Parque Nacional Perito Moreno).

I would also like to thank the Club Andino Bariloche, the Federación de Andinismo de Chile and Patagonia Inc for their assistance.

From the Publisher

This edition of Trekking in the Patagonian Andes was edited by Andrew McKenna. Andrew Smith coordinated the design, layout and cartography, and Adam McCrow designed the cover and was responsible for the back cover mapping. Chris Love and Tony Fankhauser assisted with the mapping, and Ann Jeffree drew the new botanical and animal illustrations.

Thanks also to David Andrew for proofreading and one of the illustrations; Tim Fitzgerald for assistance with designing the flora and fauna section, colour wraps and colour map; and Nick Tapp and Chris Klep for their assistance with editing and cartography, respectively.

Thanks

Thanks to the travellers who used the last edition of this book and wrote in with advice and their anecdotes; many readers' letters included valuable suggestions on how to improve the 2nd edition:

Katherin Achini & Andreas Kramer, Karen Beattie & David Chester, Anne Braun-Elwert, Pablo A Costa, James Garrity, Thomas Giles & Judy Cransberg, Alberto Falaschi, Malcolm Greig, Peter Hannibal, Bert Jonkers, Russel Ladkin, Terry Lamb, Campbell Mercer, Paul Nickodem, Andres Sommer, Evert Verweij, Martyn Williams, Russell Willis.

Trekking Disclaimer

Although the author and publisher have done their utmost to ensure the accuracy of all information in this guide, they cannot accept any responsibility for any loss, injury or inconvenience sustained by people using this book. They cannot guarantee that the tracks and routes described here have not become impassable for any reason in the interval between research and publication.

The fact that a trip or area is described in this guidebook does not mean that it is safe for you and your trekking party. You are ultimately responsible for judging your own capabilities in the light of the conditions you encounter.

Warning & Request

Things change – prices go up, schedules change, good places go bad and bad places go bankrupt – nothing stays the same. The southern winter of 1997 was very heavy in Patagonia, and that has possibly affected some of the trails described in this book. So, if you find things better or worse, recently opened or long since closed, please tell us and help make the next edition even more accurate and useful.

We value all of the feedback we receive from travellers. Julie Young coordinates a small team who read and acknowledge every letter, postcard and email, and ensure that every morsel of information finds its way to the appropriate authors, editors and publishers.

Everyone who writes to us will find their name in the next edition of the appropriate guide and will also receive a free subscription to our quarterly newsletter, *Planet Talk*. The very best contributions will be rewarded with a free Lonely Planet guide.

Excerpts from your correspondence may appear in new editions of this guide; in our newsletter, *Planet Talk*; or in updates on our Web site – so please let us know if you don't want your letter published or your name acknowledged.

Contents

Map Legend

BOUNDARIES

——————————————— International Boundary
——————————————— Provincial Boundary

ROUTES

Freeway
Primary Road
Secondary Road
City Road
City Street
4WD Track
Walking Track
Walking Route
Described Walk
Ferry Route
Chair Lift or Cable Car

AREA FEATURES

Park (Regional Maps)
Park (Walk Maps)
Built-Up Area
Glacier
Rocks
Reef
Beach

HYDROGRAPHIC FEATURES

River, Creek
Intermittent River or Creek
Rapids, Waterfalls
Lake, Intermittent Lake
Canal
Swamp (Mallín)

SYMBOLS

✪ **CAPITAL**	National Capital	✝	Airfield	▲	Mountain, Hill
◉ **Capital**	Provincial Capital	🏖	Beach	🏛	Museum
● **City**	City	⌒	Cave	)(	Pass
● Town	Town	🏚	Church	★	Police Post
● Village	Village		Cliff	✉	Post Office
		—500—	Contour	100	Route Number
		⋈	Gate	⁂	Ruins
		⊕	Hospital	◎	Spring
⛺	Camping Area	❶	Information	☎	Telephone
⌂	Hut (Refugio)	🔲	Lookout (Mirador)	◓	Transport

Note: not all symbols displayed above appear in this book

TREKKING ROUTES IN THIS BOOK

The Treks	Days	Standard	Season	Entry
Araucanía				
Around Volcán Antuco	3	Easy-Medium	Dec or Apr	US$2, no permit
Sierra Nevada	3	Medium-Hard	Oct-May	US$3.50, no permit
Central Huerquehue	3-4	Easy-Medium	Nov-Apr	US$2, no permit
Around Volcán Villarrica	3-4	Medium-Hard	Nov-Apr	US$1.50, no permit
Villarrica Traverse	3-4	Medium	Nov-Apr	US$1.50, no permit
Lake District				
Ascent of Volcán Lanín	3	Medium-Hard	Dec-Apr	US$5, no permit
Queñi Circuit	3	Easy-Medium	Nov-May	US$5, no permit
Puyehue Traverse	4	Easy-Medium	Dec-Apr	US$1.50, no permit
Termas de CallAo	3	Easy-Medium	Nov-May	Free, no permit
Nahuel Huapi Traverse	5	Medium-Hard	Nov-May	US$5, permit needed
Paso de las Nubes	3	Medium	Nov-May	US$5, permit needed
Laguna Fría	2	Easy-Medium	Nov-Apr	Free, no permit
Río Anay	3	Easy	Oct-May	US$2.50, no permit
Central Patagonia				
Around Cerro Hielo Azul	4	Medium	Nov-Apr	Free, no permit
Lago Krüger and Lago Amutui Quimei	3-4	Medium	Nov-May	US$5, no permit
Cerro Catedral	4	Medium	Oct-Apr	Free, no permit
Around Cerro Castillo	4	Medium-Hard	Jan-Mar	US$1, no permit
Southern Patagonia				
Tamango Circuit	2	Easy-Medium	Nov-Apr	Free, no permit
Mirador Maestri (Cerro Torre Lookout)	2	Easy	Nov-Apr	Free, permit needed
Around Monte Fitz Roy	4	Easy-Medium	Nov-Apr	Free, permit needed
Torres del Paine Lookout	1	Easy-Medium	Dec-Mar	US$12.50, permit needed
Paine Circuit	7	Medium-Hard	Dec-Mar	US$12.50, permit needed
Lago Pingo	3	Easy	Dec-Mar	US$12.50, permit needed
Tierra del Fuego				
Sierra Valdivieso Circuit	3	Hard	Dec-Mar	Free, no permit
Montes Martial Circuit	3	Hard	Dec-Mar	Free, no permit
Dientes Circuit	4	Medium-Hard	Dec-Mar	Free, permit needed

Introduction

Unique in otherwise tropical South America, Patagonia is a distinct geographical region that lies completely within the cool temperate zone at the southernmost tip of the continent. The Patagonian Andes are shared between Chile and Argentina, and have an average height and climate similar to that of New Zealand's Southern Alps or in the Coast Range of British Columbia.

Like many other countries in the New World, Chile and Argentina have an extensive system of national parks and reserves. Along the 2000km length of the mountain chain, more than 20 parks and reserves protect areas of superb alpine and coastal wilderness. Cool temperate rainforests, volcanic cones, alpine lakes and snowcapped glaciated peaks invite adventurous visitors. Patagonia is becoming increasingly popular among trekkers from all over the world, who value its

outstanding natural and scenic beauty as well as its safe and hassle-free travelling.

This 2nd edition of *Trekking in the Patagonian Andes* is a thorough update of the information contained in our original guidebook. It features some 25 detailed treks and outlines numerous other alternatives. Although much new material has been added, however, it doesn't cover all the trekking areas in the detail they deserve. With your help and suggestions, we hope the 3rd edition will be an even greater improvement.

Facts about the Region

HISTORY
Prehistoric Settlement of Patagonia

Before the arrival of the Spanish conquistadors, Patagonia was inhabited by a variety of indigenous peoples whose ancestors crossed from Siberia into North America perhaps as long as 30,000 years ago. How and when they reached the extreme south of the continent is uncertain. Archaeologists have found evidence that American Indians have lived in the southern Lake District of Chile for at least 13,000 years, and it is now believed that humans first arrived in Tierra del Fuego about 8000 years ago, thereby completing humanity's most far-reaching migration.

Indigenous Peoples of Patagonia

Among the original inhabitants, by far the most numerous were the tribes of northern Patagonia, usually referred to collectively as the Araucarians, or Mapuche. Upon the arrival of the first Spanish explorers, the Mapuche occupied lands mostly to the west of the Cordillera. Apparently attracted by wild herds of introduced cattle, by the 16th century the Mapuche had already begun to migrate eastwards from their Andean heartland to the steppes of eastern Patagonia.

Although they shared a common language, the Mapuche people were divided into numerous autonomous warrior tribes with different customs and lifestyles. In the Andean forests of northern Patagonia, the Puelche and Pehuenche ('people of the araucaria tree') were the principle Mapuche tribes. In late summer and autumn the Pehuenche would harvest the fruit of the araucaria tree (or pehuén), which formed the basis of their diet. The Mapuche of the northern Patagonian steppes were tall and nomadic. The coastal zone, including the island of Chiloé, was inhabited by the Huilliche (or Cunco) tribe. They had a more settled lifestyle, practising slash-and-burn agriculture.

To the south of the Mapuche territory, the Tehuelche people occupied the vast plains of central and southern Patagonia right down to the Straits of Magellan. At times they ventured into the Cordillera from the east along open river valleys. The Tehuelche were exceptionally tall and essentially nomadic hunters. They followed the large herds of guanaco across the Patagonian steppes, much as certain North American Indian tribes once followed the bison.

The flat northern part of the great island of Tierra del Fuego, on the southern shore of the Straits of Magellan, was inhabited by tribes of the Ona people. As well as spears, bows and arrows, both the Tehuelches and the Onas used the *boleadoras*, an ingenious device of heavy rounded stones attached to a strong cord, to trip up and bring down their quarry – mainly guanaco and ñandú. A small and largely unknown people called the Haush lived on the eastern tip of Tierra del Fuego.

The long west Patagonian coast stretching down as far south as the islands of Cape Horn was the territory of two sea-dwelling groups,

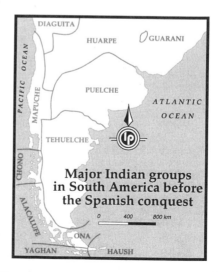

Major Indian groups in South America before the Spanish conquest

13

Ferdinand Magellan, Portuguese-born navigator and explorer for the king of Spain

the Alacalufe and the Yaghan. Living on a rich diet of seafood, they occupied one of the most inhospitable areas on earth. These hardy marine nomads travelled around the storm-battered waters of the archipelago in intricately constructed, lightweight bark canoes, which could be easily carried across the narrow isthmuses which separate the channels and fjords.

Exploration & Early Colonisation

Sir Francis Drake is now credited with discovering Cape Horn in 1578, after his ship blew off course during his circumnavigation of the world. Drake's discovery was kept a state secret by Queen Elizabeth I, apparently to protect British knowledge of a new passage to the Pacific. This closely guarded secret let Dutch mariner Willem Schouten claim all the glory for the discovery nearly forty years later. After sailing steadily southwards for some months in search of a passage to the Pacific, Schouten sighted the last land of the South American coast in February 1616. Fog caused him to erroneously chart the exposed rocky island he saw as a part of the continental mainland, and he gave it the name Cape Hoorn after his hometown in Flanders. Just three years later, in 1619, another tiny fleet arrived at the far southern

Atlantic shores of South America. The fleet was captained by the navigator Ferdinand Magellan, who, like Schouten, was seeking a safer, enemy-free trading route to India. Although Portuguese-born, Magellan was in the service of the Spanish king.

Magellan called this land 'Patagonia'. Since *pata* is colloquial Spanish for 'foot', historians have generally assumed the name to be a reference to the supposedly big-footed native inhabitants, who were almost certainly Tehuelche Indians. Another theory links Magellan's coining of the word Patagonia from the fictitious land of Gran Patagón taken from a Renaissance story, *Primaleon of Greece*. This romance of chivalry had been published in Spain several years before Magellan set sail. In 1520, as he sailed through the straits that now bear his name, the discoverer called the great island immediately to the south *tierra del fuego,* or 'land of fire', after the multitude of glowing campfires he observed there during the dark and overcast nights.

The first European expeditions into Patagonia, scarcely a decade later, were inspired by the search for the legendary Ciudad de los Césares. A sort of southern El Dorado, this was supposedly a fantastically rich city situated somewhere in the Andes of Patagonia. Jesuit missionaries, trying to convert the 'savages' to the Christian faith, also ventured deep into Indian lands and many were killed during hostile encounters with the Mapuche.

To the west of the Cordillera, the Spanish conquistador and founder of Chile, Pedro de Valdivia, began the conquest of the forested zone south of Santiago. By 1567, in spite of extremely fierce resistance from the Mapuche, many settlements had been established along the coast as far south as the great island of Chiloé. However, by the end of the 16th century the Indians' hostility reached a climax, and the Spanish invaders were unable to resist the sustained Mapuche offensives. Their cities were sacked and burnt, and the survivors withdrew to the north. Chiloé, where interracial mixing had created a loyal Creole population, was cut off from the rest of the Spanish Empire. As a result of this

Mapuche people can still be seen in traditional dress in the Araucanía

enforced isolation, a very distinctive Chilote culture developed and this was to be an important influence on settlement in the rest of Patagonia.

With such unyielding native populations and seemingly little else to offer, Patagonia was largely neglected for the next two centuries. Neither the Spaniards nor any other European colonial power made serious attempts to settle or develop the region economically. Only after Chile and Argentina won independence in the early 1800s did the two nations move to expand and consolidate their territories.

In 1833 HMS *Beagle* sailed down the coast of Argentina. On board was the young naturalist Charles Darwin, who made frequent excursions into the Patagonian interior. It was largely observations of the local biology and geology during this journey that led Darwin to develop his theory of natural selection. In a cruel irony, the Darwinian notion of 'survival of the fittest' was soon to be used as a justification for the extermination of the 'inferior' indigenous people.

'Reino de la Araucanía'

An interesting and curious episode in the history of Patagonia was the so-called Reino de la Araucanía, a 'kingdom' founded in 1859 by an opportunistic Frenchman, Orélie-Antoine de Tounens. Gaining the trust of the local Mapuche tribes, whose own *cacique* (chief) had prophesied the coming of a white saviour just before his death, Orélie-Antoine was made the Indians' monarch. The new king immediately declared the independence of the Araucanía, the Mapuche nation of northern Patagonia, and in another bold decree he annexed all remaining lands south of 42° right down to Cape Horn.

Not surprisingly, the governments in Santiago and Buenos Aires initially ignored this new self-proclaimed monarchy. After he attempted to mobilise his Mapuche warriors the following year, however, Orélie-Antoine was captured, incarcerated and eventually deported. Orélie-Antoine made several attempts to return to his Patagonian kingdom but these were thwarted.

The farcical and essentially non-existent Reino nevertheless still captures the imagination of Argentinians and Chileans of both Hispanic and Indian descent. The modern-day prince, Philippe Boiry de Araucanía y Patagonia (who ascended to the throne by a dubious series of 'hand overs' that have taken place since the first king died without an heir in 1878) toured his kingdom in the late 1980s and early 1990s. His visit aroused considerable curiosity and press coverage in Chile and Argentina. Prince Philippe has visited Mapuche and Tehuelche communities on either side of the Cordillera, and his trips have served to raise the issue of the indigenous peoples' rights and welfare.

Subjugation of the Indigenous Patagonians

Rather than save the Indian peoples of the south, Orélie-Antoine's original Reino was more a tragi-comic interlude before their almost total destruction. As in most parts of the New World, European colonisation proved to be catastrophic to the indigenous people. In the military campaigns of the late 1870s and early 1880s that were called by later historians the 'Conquista del Desierto', Mapuche and Tehuelche tribes of the southern plains of Argentina were systematically wiped out or driven onto reserves.

Similarly, the 'reconquest' of the Chilean south progressively brought Indian lands under government control, leaving the way open for a steady influx of European settlers. The Mapuche, the only indigenous people in the Americas to successfully resist the domination of the Spanish Empire, were finally subdued. The Ona of Tierra del Fuego, who once numbered 12,000, were completely wiped out by the invading settlers and gold prospectors. Disease and malign negligence have left fewer than 30 surviving pure-blood members of the Yaghan and Alacalufe tribes.

European Settlement of Patagonia

Towards the end of the 19th century, the Indian tribes of Argentina had ceased to be a menace to colonists. In 1865, immigrants from Wales arrived at Puerto Madryn, on the dry Atlantic coast of Argentina, and not long afterwards Welsh settlements were gradually established throughout northern Patagonia. As they moved up the Río Chubut, Welsh-Patagonians later founded the towns of Trevelin and Esquel in the Andean foothills. One of these newcomers, a young woman settler, wrote a literary classic of the Welsh language, *Dirngo'r Andes* ('Climbing the Andes'). Other immigrants – English, Basques and Germans – followed the coast south, moving into the drier interior along the more hospitable river valleys.

The sparse southern plains were turned over to profitable sheep and cattle grazing. The *gaucho* culture, a powerful influence in Argentine folklore, spread from the Buenos Aires *pampa* into Patagonia. Unfortunately, vast tracts of the open steppes soon fell under the control of large Buenos Aires landowners. Other small-time sheep ranchers were forced to move westwards into the foothills of the Cordillera, often taking up tracts of new land without ever establishing a legitimate title. This made the new settlers vulnerable during disputes with the large landholders, whose legal resources were hard to match.

To a lesser extent, this process was repeated on the Chilean side of the Andes, where the only available land was frequently in mountainous country or at the end of isolated fjords. Many of these smaller *estancias* were to survive little more than a generation, as low returns and isolation forced their abandonment.

Trans-Andean Border Disputes

In colonial times the Chilean-Argentine boundary had simply been the 'sierra nevada' of the Andes. Since the mountains between Santiago and Mendoza are such an obvious barrier, this seemed sufficient. As it became clear that a more precise understanding of the national border was necessary, a treaty in 1881 established the frontier line as 'the highest peaks which divide the waters'. However, in certain parts of Patagonia, the glaciers of the Pleistocene Age had left their terminal moraines well to the east of the mountains. This had diverted formerly eastwards-flowing rivers back towards the Pacific Ocean through latitudinal fractures in the southern Cordillera, and as a result the highest peaks do not always form the watershed. In some places the Atlantic/Pacific divide lies only a few kilometres from the Pacific while in other areas it is far to the east of the main line of peaks.

Under British arbitration, Argentina and Chile each established an official boundary commission. The Comisiones de los Límites sent numerous expeditions to their presumed Andean frontier lands in order to assess or assert their nations' territorial claims. During the last two decades of the 19th century all the important areas of the Patagonian Cordillera were reconnoitred. In Chile, explorers such as Hans Steffen and the geographer Luis Riso Patrón surveyed the rugged coastal areas of western Patagonia. In the service of the Argentine Boundary Commission, the naturalists Clemente Onelli and Perito Moreno (later rewarded with large tracts of

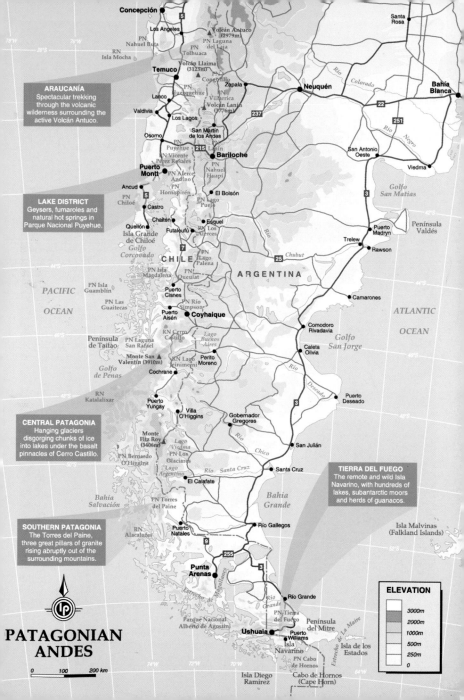

Concepción

Santa Rosa

Los Angeles

▲ Volcán Antuco (2979m)

PN Nahuel Buta

RN Isla Mocha

PN Laguna del Laja

Bahía Blanca

Temuco

Volcán Llaima (3125m)

PN Tolhuaca

PN Conguillío

PN Huerquehue

Zapala

Río Colorado

Neuquén

22

Lanco

237

Villarrica

PN Villarrica Volcán Lanín (3776m)

Valdivia

Los Lagos

PN Lanín

Río Negro

251

San Martín de los Andes

Osorno

PN Puyehue

Bariloche

San Antonio Oeste

Viedma

PN Vicente Pérez Rosales

215

PN Nahuel Huapi

Puerto Montt

PN Alerce Andino

Ancud

PN Chiloé

5

PN Hornopirén

El Bolsón

Golfo San Matías

Castro

PN Lago Puelo

Puerto Madryn

Península Valdés

Chaltén

Esquel

3

Quellón

Futaleufú

PN Los Alerces

Trelew

Isla Grande de Chiloé

Golfo Corcovado

7

Rawson

CHILE

PN Lago Palena

ARGENTINA

PN Isla Magdalena

PN Queulat

Río Chubut

25

Camarones

PACIFIC OCEAN

PN Isla Guamblín

Puerto Cisnes

PN Río Simpson

PN Las Guaitecas

Puerto Aisén

Coyhaique

ATLANTIC OCEAN

Comodoro Rivadavia

Golfo San Jorge

Península de Taitao

RN Cerro Castillo

Lago Buenos Aires

Caleta Olivia

PN Laguna San Rafael

Monte San Valentín (3910m) ▲

RN Lago Jeinimeni

Perito Moreno

Río Deseado

Cochrane

Golfo de Penas

RN Katalalixar

Puerto Yungay

Villa O'Higgins

Gobernador Gregores

Puerto Deseado

3

Monte Fitz Roy (3406m) ▲

Lago Viedma

PN Los Glaciares

San Julián

PN Bernardo O'Higgins

Lago Argentino

Río Santa Cruz

Río Chico

Santa Cruz

Bahía Salvación

El Calafate

Bahía Grande

Isla Malvinas (Falkland Islands)

PN Torres del Paine

Río Gallegos

RN Alacalufes

Puerto Natales

9

255

Punta Arenas

3

Río Grande

ELEVATION

Estrecho de Magallanes

Río Grande

Río Grande

PN Tierra del Fuego

Península del Mitre

Parque Nacional Alberto de Agostini

Ushuaia

Puerto Williams

Isla de los Estados

Isla Navarino

Isla Diego Ramírez

PN Cabo de Hornos

Estrecho de la Maire

Cabo de Hornos (Cape Horn)

ARAUCANÍA
Spectacular trekking through the volcanic wilderness surrounding the active Volcán Antuco.

LAKE DISTRICT
Geysers, fumaroles and natural hot springs in Parque Nacional Puyehue.

CENTRAL PATAGONIA
Hanging glaciers disgorging chunks of ice into lakes under the basalt pinnacles of Cerro Castillo.

SOUTHERN PATAGONIA
The Torres del Paine, three great pillars of granite rising abruptly out of the surrounding mountains.

TIERRA DEL FUEGO
The remote and wild Isla Navarino, with hundreds of lakes, subantarctic moors and herds of guanacos.

ELEVATION

3000m
2000m
1000m
500m
250m
0

PATAGONIAN ANDES

0   100   200 km

CLEM LINDENMAYER

CLEM LINDENMAYER

CLEM LINDENMAYER

CLEM LINDENMAYER

CLEM LINDENMAYER

WAYNE BERNHARDSON

CLEM LINDENMAYER

CLEM LINDENMAYER

A huge variety of wild flowers grows in the Patagonian Andes, from orchids (top left) through to wild strawberries, or frutilla de magallanes (bottom centre) and spiky cushion flowers (bottom right). When the notro (middle left) is in bloom its bright red flowers are difficult to miss, and the chilco (middle right) will be familiar to gardeners who have grown fuchsias.

CLEM LINDENMAYER

CLEM LINDENMAYER

CLEM LINDENMAYER

CLEM LINDENMAYER

The Refugio Hielo Azul (middle left) sits in dense forest in the Comarca Andina del Paralelo 42. Dense evergreen (top) and deciduous (bottom) forests of southern beech are common in the temperate rainforests of Patagonia. The gnarled arrayán (middle right) is a rainforest tree with distinctive bark and a twisted form that typically branches into multiple trunks.

CLEM LINDENMAYER

CLEM LINDENMAYER

CLEM LINDENMAYER

Altocumulus clouds (top) and striated cloud formations (bottom) provide a dramatic back-drop to the mountains of Parque Nacional Torres del Paine. In Parque Nacional Laguna del Laja, Volcán Antuco (middle) emits sulphurous gases but is otherwise dormant.

land) made extensive journeys into the Cordillera from the east.

The absurdity of seeking a purely 'geographical solution' to the frontier dispute became evident when at the instigation of its own boundary commission the government of Argentina ordered that a section of an ancient moraine wall be cut away in order to change the course of a river. This audacious piece of landscape surgery shifted the watershed westwards, allowing Argentina to successfully claim the eastern section of the lake now called Lago Buenos Aires by Argentinians.

In 1902, Chile and Argentina accepted the decision of King Edward VII of England. He drew a border across the summits of some of southern Patagonia's most prominent peaks – San Lorenzo, Fitz Roy, Murallón – and near to Cerro Stokes. The king's border also created a number of other 'international lakes', dividing Lago Palena/Vintner and Lago Cochrane/Pueyrredón between the two countries. Unfortunately, the two enormous icecaps of southern Patagonia, the Hielo Norte and Hielo Sur, were still unknown, and this provided further grounds for dispute. After an international tribunal decided in 1995 that Argentina had a superior claim of sovereignty to the Lago del Desierto region in southern Patagonia, the only remaining section of the trans-Andean border still in dispute is in the Hielo Sur.

Development & Conservation

In the second half of the 19th century, the California goldrush and the expanding settlement of the North American west coast led to a boom in maritime traffic around Cape Horn. This dangerous route via the southern tip of South America was still the only sea passage from the Atlantic to the Pacific, and of the numerous vessels that 'rounded the Horn', one in 50 was lost in the almost perpetually stormy waters. The port of Punta Arenas, founded on the Straits of Magellan to service passing ships, became a symbol of Patagonian prosperity.

Early this century work began on an ambitious project to cut a canal through the Península de Taitao at the Laguna San Rafael. The aim of the canal was to create an almost unbroken shipping lane through the naturally sheltered canals of the Chilean Archipelago, but funds and fantasy were soon exhausted. With the opening of the Panama Canal in 1915, the Taitao project was abandoned forever. From then until the discovery of oil in the inter-war period, Punta Arenas slipped into decline.

But international interest in the region was growing, and from the turn of the century Patagonia was visited by quite a number of important scientific expeditions. In 1908-9 a party led by the Swedish botanist Carl Skottsberg travelled south from Bariloche along the eastern foothills of the Andes to reach Tierra del Fuego. In the first decades of the century the naturalists William H Hudson and George G Simpson undertook scientific trips in Patagonia that took them into the Andean Cordillera. The polar explorer Otto Nordenskjöld explored the mountains around the two continental ice sheets, the Hielo Norte and Hielo Sur.

Parallel to developments in the other parts of the New World, the need to protect the beautiful yet fragile mountains from over exploitation was slowly being recognised. When in the early 1920s Perito Moreno was granted a sizable tract of land around the great lake Nahuel Huapi, he donated this back to the nation as its first national park. Soon afterwards, the first Chilean national parks were created on the west side of the Andes, with the establishment of Parque Nacional Villarrica in the Araucanía in 1925 and Parque Nacional Vicente Pérez Rosales in the southern Chilean Lake District the following year. In 1937, three more vast national parks – Lanín, Los Alerces and Los Glaciares – were declared in the Argentine Patagonian Andes.

In both countries *clubs de montaña* were set up in some of the larger provincial cities along the Cordillera. Founded chiefly by immigrants from the European Alps in 1931, the Club Andino Bariloche had became the largest mountain climbing club in Latin America. Its members played an important part in opening up new climbing and hiking routes throughout the Patagonian Andes and constructed *refugios* in the surrounding mountains. Between the wars the remarkable Italian andinist and priest Father Alberto Maria De Agostini explored much of the southern Cordillera. De Agostini (see aside) made first ascents of various important summits and published an excellent mountaineering atlas of the Patagonian Andes that even today is unsurpassed. De Agostini's work was warmly appreciated by the governments of both countries, and Chile recently named a national park in the Darwin Range of western Tierra del Fuego in his honour.

During the 1940s and 1950s all of the highest unclimbed peaks of Patagonia, such as Monte Tronador, Monte Fitz Roy, Monte San Lorenzo, Monte San Valentín and Cerro Paine Grande, were conquered by mountaineers. In the 1960s the British explorer Eric Shipton ventured into the ranges of western Tierra del Fuego and the continental icecaps. Since the war, skiing and other mountain sports have become popular activities among the more affluent Argentinians and Chileans, and many new national parks have been established.

Recent Politics

In the 1970s, military governments seized power in both Chile and Argentina. Under these brutal dictatorships tens of thousands of suspected left-wing sympathisers were murdered, tortured or sent into exile. Despite their raw political similarities, the two regimes came close to war in 1979 over the sovereignty of a few small islands south of the Beagle Channel. The conflict was later settled by Pope John Paul II, who decided largely in favour of Chile.

In Argentina, the Falklands war fiasco and economic chaos brought about the collapse of military rule and the return of civilian government in 1983. Carlos Menem, president of Argentina since 1988, has introduced sweeping economic reforms that include a large scale privatisation program and rigorous fiscal control to keep inflation low. This has produced high unemployment (well over 12% in a country that had become accustomed to almost full employment during the previous several decades). The Menem government has been rocked by various scandals, including the president's acceptance of a luxury sports car as a 'gift' from an international businessman.

In Chile, the 16-year long military dictatorship of General Pinochet ended when free presidential elections were held in December 1989. Since then a centre-left government dominated by the Christian Democrats has been in power. Under Chile's current president, Eduardo Frei Ruiz-Tagle, the economy has continued to grow at an average annual rate of 7%, consistently out-performing every other economy in the Americas. Although poverty is still widespread, there can be little argument that the situation for most Chileans has improved over the past decade. A few overly enthusiastic economists have even compared Chile to the newly industrialising economies of East Asia – a *tigre*, or Latin American 'tiger'.

GEOGRAPHY

The Andes is a relatively young mountain chain, created over the last 70 million years as the oceanic Nazca Plate was slowly pushed under the continental South American Plate. In Patagonia, the initial uplifting of the range was accompanied by intense volcanic activity. Clearly, these great volcanic eruptions must have been sudden, widespread and catastrophic for the existing vegetation. Forests of proto-araucaria and other coniferous trees were smothered below thick layers of volcanic ash. This is how the fascinating petrified forests found in the Chubut and Santa Cruz provinces of Argentina were formed. As the Cordillera gradually rose, the passage of moisture from the Pacific was blocked, drying out the land on the Andes' eastern side. Approximately two million years ago the Andes finally reached the elevation that they have today. The mountain-building continues, and as a consequence the Andes experience a high level of seismic activity.

Over the last two million years the Cordillera has undergone several periods of intense glaciation during which much of its present topography was formed. At the height of these ice ages the entire Cordillera and a considerable part of the Patagonian lowlands were covered by an ice sheet many hundreds of metres deep. The glaciers released enormous quantities of moraine debris which was washed out from the mountains and deposited over the steppes of southern Argentina.

Approximately 14,000 years ago the last (Pleistocene) ice age began to end, and the glaciers that had intermittently covered most of the Andes retreated into the Cordillera. This natural global warming allowed the plants and animals to recolonise large areas previously under ice, and probably facilitated the arrival of the first humans not long afterwards.

Definitions of Patagonia

Depending on your definition, Patagonia comprises up to one million sq km. The Patagonian region is just under one third of the land area of both Chile and Argentina, but less than 5% of either nation's population actually lives there. Chilean Patagonia is geographically very different from Argentine Patagonia. While the coast of southern Chile is a wild and wet strip of densely forested mountainous country, the greater part of Argentine Patagonia is a broad semi-arid plateau out of which rise eroded tablelands (called *mesetas*). It is only where these 'two Patagonias' meet, namely at the Patagonian Andes, that the area's continuity actually becomes apparent.

Politically speaking, Patagonia is not much more than a vague geographical area that merely forms the southern part of Chile and Argentina. Like the rest of the land in both countries, Patagonia is divided into administrative units or 'states'. In Chile these are the numbered *regiones* and in Argentina *provincias*.

In Argentina, Patagonia officially includes all the land south from the Río Colorado (at 36° S). This vast area takes in the Argentine Lake District in the provinces of Neuquén and Río Negro, as well as Chubut, Santa Cruz and the territories of Tierra del Fuego

and the Falkland (Malvinas) Islands. People who live in the so-called *provincias patagonicas* are entitled to certain tax and travel concessions from the Argentine government, which has a policy of promoting development in the area. For years governments in Buenos Aires have talked about 'argentinising Patagonia' in order to integrate it more fully into the national economy. During the 1980s there were plans – which were ultimately abandoned – to transfer the national capital to Viedma, a small city situated just inside Patagonian territory on the south bank of the Río Negro.

To the west of the Cordillera the situation is less definite. In Chile, only the strip of land extending south from Puerto Montt (which Chilean geographers call the *Sur Grande*) is normally considered a true part of Patagonia, a definition that excludes the Chilean side of the Araucanía and Lake District and usually also the island of Chiloé. Even this would come as a surprise to some Chileans, many of whom prefer to use the term Patagonia exclusively for the southern steppes of the Argentine also known colloquially as *la pampa*. However, the Araucanía and Lake District on either side of the Andes show a very high degree of geographical homogeneity, and 'Patagonia' is used loosely in this book to include all the Chilean territory south of the Río Biobío (at roughly 37°S), in addition to the 'true' Patagonia of the Argentine steppes.

The Patagonian Andes

Unlike much of South America, which has a tropical to subtropical climate, Patagonia's position at the most southerly tip of the continent produces a cool and temperate climate. Chile and Argentina share (but quarrel over) the Patagonian Andes, whose ranges lie mainly on the Chilean side. Roughly speaking, the main peaks of the Patagonian Andes have an average height of around 2000m. The climate is not unlike that found in the mountains in the west of Canada or New Zealand's Southern Alps.

Throughout their roughly 2000km length the southern Andes do not always form an unbroken chain. Rather, the mountains appear as a series of separate parallel ranges with their own unique geological characteristics running more or less in a north-south line. The extensive high plateaus that typify the Andes further to the north are completely absent. In Patagonia, the Andes' overall width diminishes to an average of less than 100km. Repeatedly interrupted by formerly eastward-flowing rivers that have been forced back through the mountains to the Pacific, in Patagonia the Cordillera ceases to be a continental divide or true geographical watershed.

The Patagonian Andes can be divided into three latitudinally arranged zones. Each of these zones is roughly 600km in length and has a relatively distinct geographical character. The mountains of Tierra del Fuego and its countless islands form an additional zone below the South American mainland.

The Araucanía & Lake District After reaching their greatest height of almost 7000m at the latitude of 30°S around Mendoza and Santiago, the character of the Andes changes in a gradual yet dramatic manner. Further south, the mountain passes and peaks become steadily lower and the Cordillera itself narrows. As rainfall increases, the dry, sparse vegetation of the north slowly changes into a fertile and perpetually green landscape of rich farming country and moist forests. Major rivers such as the Río Imperial and the Río Biobío descend from the main divide of the Cordillera through a wide and fertile valley (which Chilean geographers call *el valle longitudinal*), before breaking out through the lower Coastal Range (the Cordillera de la Costa) to meet the Pacific Ocean.

On the western side of the mountains the landscape is increasingly dominated by intense volcanic activity, and volcanoes are almost always the highest summits. Towering over the lower basalt ranges, their cones are scattered randomly along the line of the main divide between 36°S and 43°S, with one volcano roughly every 30km. The two highest peaks of this area, the extinct volca-

CLEM LINDENMAYER

Volcán Lanín from near Laguna Azul, on the Villarrica Traverse

noes Lanín (3776m) and Tronador (3460m), lie on the Argentine-Chilean frontier and form part of the Pacific/Atlantic watershed.

The centre of volcanic activity lies at the Andes' western edge, however, and for this reason most of the dormant and active volcanoes are west of the Cordillera in Chile. The perfect cone of Volcán Osorno (2652m) is known as the 'Fuji of the Andes' and is a great favourite among Chilean climbers and skiers. Small and major eruptions are quite common, and the inhabitants of towns and settlements close to volcanoes are continually on the alert. In places lava flows have dammed rivers to create large new lakes, such as Laguna de la Laja, Lago Pirehueico and Lago Caburgua.

Sudden eruptions have caused destruction and loss of life in the past, though never on the same scale as recent Colombian and Peruvian disasters. On the higher volcanoes there is the danger that an eruption may cause the rapid melting of snow and glacial ice to create a deadly avalanche of volcanic mud (known in English by the Javanese word 'lahar'). Some years ago Volcán Lonquimay had a minor yet highly spectacular eruption which continued for some four months, attracting bus loads of tourists. Volcán

Villarrica churns out smoke and gases constantly, and has erupted several times in the last generation or so. Literally hundreds of *termas*, or thermal springs, dot the countryside, most still completely undeveloped.

This volcanic belt corresponds reasonably closely to the area of Greater Araucanía, the trans-Andean territory originally inhabited by many different tribes of the Mapuche people. Today perhaps 250,000 full and mixed blood Mapuche still live here, mainly on the Chilean side of the Cordillera.

The southern part of the Araucanía takes in the beautiful Región de los Lagos, or Lake District. With more than 20 great lakes gouged into the precordilleran landscape during the last ice age, and many hundreds of smaller lakes set higher up among snow-capped peaks, the Lake District has often been promoted as the 'Switzerland of South America' – a title that very conveniently disregards the complete absence of volcanoes in the Alps!

Fertile volcanic soil and the area's mild and moist climate have made the Lake District a prime agricultural region. Lush native rainforest still covers the higher ranges and large parts of the coast, but in the Chilean longitudinal valley, situated between the Pacific and the Cordillera, most of the original forested land has been cleared for farming and grazing. The mean level of the tree line is between 1700 and 2000m above sea level, with hardy alpine grasses covering the mountainsides to the permanent snow line some 300 to 400m higher up.

On the Chilean side of the Lake District, the major lakes are situated mostly in the Andean foothills. Here, even the larger lakes are warm enough for swimming in summer (especially when compared with the chilled waters of the Pacific beaches). Chileans sometimes attribute the relatively warm water of their lakes to subterranean volcanic activity, but lower elevation (generally under 350m) is a more likely cause than thermal heating. The clarity of the water in the Chilean lakes can be surprising, often allowing visibility to depths of 15m or more. This seems to be due to the naturally low levels of

nutrients in the water, which hinders the growth of algae.

In the adjacent Argentine Lake District, the major lakes are deeper and more elevated (usually at least 750m) and, therefore, quite a few degrees colder. The Argentine lakes also tend to take a more classically glacial form, with fjord-like arms stretching westwards deep into the Cordillera. Lago Nahuel Huapi is the best example of this.

In both countries the Araucanía and Lake District are closer to the major centres than the rest of the Patagonian Andes. In Argentina, the major provincial cities of Junín de los Andes, San Martín de los Andes and San Carlos de Bariloche are connected by excellent roads that skirt the eastern shores of the large lakes. The Panamerican Highway in Chile leads north-south through the regional capitals of Temuco, Osorno and Puerto Montt. The area's splendid scenery and wildlife and its relatively easy access from the bigger cities has led to the development of a sizable tourist industry. Investment in winter sports has been particularly high. Brown and rainbow trout have been introduced for the benefit of anglers.

Virtually the entire Argentine Lake District lies within two vast national parks, Parque Nacional Lanín and Parque Nacional Nahuel Huapi. These parks straddle the eastern side of the Cordillera and are multi-use areas, with controlled harvesting of timber in certain designated sectors. There are eight or so Andean national parks in the Chilean Lake District and the Araucanía. These parks are much smaller than those in Argentina, but have complete protection. The largest are Vicente Pérez Rosales and Puyehue, two adjoining parks which front Argentina's Parque Nacional Nahuel Huapi in the southern Lake District. Nearby is another smaller park, Alerce Andino, on the coast east of Puerto Montt. Chile's other important Lake District parks are much further to the north. The national parks of Huerquehue and Villarrica are near the tourist town of Pucón, and Conguillío/ Llaima are east of Temuco. The most northerly area covered by this book, Parque

Nacional Laguna del Laja is high up in the mountains just north of the Río Biobío. You'll also find there are large expanses of semi-wilderness in the Chilean Lake District outside the national parks.

Central Patagonia South of the Chilean city of Puerto Montt at roughly 42°S the long western coastal plain begins to break up. The more or less continuous series of broad longitudinal valleys that further north are so much a characteristic of the Andes' western side now disappear completely. After dropping briefly below sea level at the narrow straits of the Canal Chacao, the Coast Range continues for about 180km as the backbone of the great island of Chiloé, before suddenly fracturing into a wild maze of narrow channels and islands below 44°S. Known as the Archipiélago de los Chonos after their original inhabitants, these rainy and windswept islands are formed by the crests of the submerged Coast Range.

The islands of the Chonos considerably shelter the shipping lanes to as far south as 47°S, where the twisted-fist shape of the Península de Taitao juts out into the Pacific and blocks any further passage. Here, at the Laguna San Rafael, the Ventisquero San Rafael descends from the northern Patagonian icecap. The Ventisquero San Rafael is the world's 'most equatorial' (ie closest to the equator) glacier that reaches the sea. At the Península de Taitao the Antarctic, Nazca and South American continental plates converge, making this remote and inaccessible peninsula a pivotal point of tectonic activity. Subaquatic volcanic eruptions occur off the coast, while on the peninsula itself the continental crust is gradually being pushed up and broadened.

Compared with areas of a similar latitude in the northern hemisphere, mean annual average temperatures on the coast are not only relatively warm, but also surprisingly constant. July (mid winter) has an average temperature of around 3°C as against the January (mid summer) average of 11°C. These climatic conditions have produced impenetrable temperate rainforests, where in places the continually cool temperatures even prevent fallen trees from rotting for hundreds of years. The coastal soils are leached and poor, and agricultural development is mostly limited to drier areas to the east that are sheltered by the coastal ranges. From about 41°S the main range of the Cordillera is increasingly dominated by hard granitic rock types. There are still isolated centres of intense volcanic activity down through the Patagonian Andes (almost entirely on the Chilean side) as far south as about 46°S, where in August 1991 Volcán Hudson erupted violently.

Until fairly recently many Chilean localities along Patagonia's central-western coast were accessible only by boat or via long and dusty overland routes from Argentina. This changed during the 1980s with the construction of the Carretera Austral, when military workers bulldozed and blasted their way south from Puerto Montt through the spectacular mountains that front the Chilean fjords. Originally conceived both as a means of promoting development in Chile's remote and sparsely settled XI Región and breaking the local dependence on Argentina, this modest gravel road was christened *huella a la oportunidad*, or 'trail to opportunity'.

As the only north-south route on the western side of the border, the Carretera Austral connects the few settlements of this region of Chile. The Argentine counterpart to the Carretera Austral is the Ruta 40, which leads south from Esquel along the eastern edge of the Patagonian Andes through the small towns of Alto Río Senguerr, Río Mayo, Perito Moreno and Tres Lagos. The Argentine national and provincial governments have recently approved funding to upgrade the Ruta 40 in order to promote tourism.

In Argentina, the central Patagonian Andes more or less correspond to the western strip of Chubut Province. In Chile this zone takes in the northernmost two thirds of the XI Región, and includes the national parks of Queulat and Isla Magdalena as well as many other large national reserves, such as Cerro Castillo, Río Simpson, and Jeinimeni. On the Argentine side there are also two national

CLEM LINDENMAYER

The view from the camp site below Cerro
Castillo (Reserva Nacional Cerro Castillo)

water draining into the sea channels from
glacier-fed rivers) and average temperatures
of around 4°C drift along the coast. Fierce
and almost perpetual storms drench and
batter the ranges in south-western Patagonia.
Miserable weather is even more common
here, and in the few isolated coastal settlements like Puerto Eden (at 49° on Chile's Isla
Wellington) two straight days without rain are
quite rare. Annual rainfall in certain areas
exceeds eight metres, the highest levels of
precipitation experienced anywhere outside
the earth's tropical zone.

The Andes of southern Patagonia are
covered by the most extensive area of glaciers outside the world's polar regions.
Situated at an average elevation of around
1500m bet-ween 46°S and 51°S, two massive
longitudinal sheets of glacial ice, many hundreds of metres thick, smother all but the
higher peaks. Mountains within these frozen
plateaus appear as rock islands (which
mountaineers call *nunataks*), their summits
projecting spectacularly from their white
surroundings. Fed by extremely heavy
snowfalls, these icecaps are kept from
melting by almost continual cloud cover.
Unlike other great expanses of glacial ice,
the Hielo Norte and the Hielo Sur move out
in all directions from the centre and have few
crevasses. Glaciologists have calculated that
each snowflake that falls on these icecaps is
trapped for 300 years or more before being
finally released at the termination of a
glacier.

The northern icecap is called the Hielo
Patagonico (or Continental) Norte, 100km
long and comprising almost 4500 sq km. The
Hielo Norte is the smaller of the two and lies
completely on Chilean territory. The 4058m
Monte San Valentín, generally considered to
be the highest peak in Patagonia (although
the 4709m Volcán Domuyo, in the far north-
west of Argentina's Neuquén province, has
a superior claim to this title), towers from its
north-eastern flank. The largest icecap is the
more southerly, the Hielo Patagonico (or
Continental) Sur. The Hielo Sur comprises
roughly 14,000 sq km and stretches about
320km from north to south. Although most

parks, Los Alerces and the smaller Lago
Puelo, while the so-called Comarca Andina
del Paralelo 42 (or the 'Andean District of
the 42nd Parallel') also offers outstanding
natural scenery.

Of the four zones discussed here, the
Andes of central Patagonia are by far the
most thinly settled. Particularly in Argentina,
transport and access are still the most difficult factors. Because of its remoteness,
undeveloped infrastructure and wet weather,
central Patagonia is rather more demanding
of trekkers. Yet the greater difficulties
involved in visiting the Andes of central
Patagonia reflect the region's much wilder
nature, and the extra hardship is well worth
enduring.

Southern Patagonia Below 46°S volcanoes
appear only sporadically and the Andes'
average height once again increases. The
climate becomes steadily more extreme and
more heavily influenced by the closer proximity of the sea. Antarctic ocean currents
with relatively low salt concentrations
(caused by the enormous volumes of fresh

CLEM LINDENMAYER

Monte Fitz Roy (right) at 3441m and Cerro Poincenot, from Laguna de los Tres

of its mass is in Chile, some parts of the southern icecap's eastern fringe edge over the frontier.

Most of the highest peaks in southern Patagonia are associated with the great icebound ranges around the two main icecaps. It is here that Patagonia's classic peaks of over 3000m are found, and names like Cerro Torre, Monte Fitz Roy and Cerro Paine Grande are known to climbers all over the world. An exception to this is the great lone massif of Monte San Lorenzo (called Cerro Cochrane in Chile), whose 3706m granite summit forms the Chile-Argentina border.

On the Andes' western side, glaciers from the inland icecaps slide down to calve in the deep fjords that extend far inland from the Pacific Ocean. To the east, huge glaciers of Alaskan proportions spill off east into enormous lakes fringing the Argentine pampa. Unlike those of the Argentine Lake District far to the north, these lakes are low-lying, with an average altitude of just 200m above sea level. The most northerly of these is Lago General Carrera/Lago Buenos Aires, the second largest natural lake in South America.

At around 47°S, Lago General Carrera and the adjacent Península de Taitao both form a botanical and climatic division between the more temperate flora zone of central Patagonia and the frigid areas of the far south.

South of the Hielo Sur, the Patagonian Andes rapidly lose height. The higher peaks average little more than 1500m and are entirely within Chilean territory, stranded on offshore islands and peninsulas almost cut off from the mainland by canals and deep sounds channelled out by colossal glaciers during recent ice ages.

Large icecaps cover some of the higher and more exposed ranges, but never reach anything like the proportions of the Hielo Norte and the Hielo Sur. It is at Puerto Natales, on Seno Última Esperanza, that the dry zone of Patagonian steppes first extends eastward right to the water line on the Atlantic coast. Below the Península Brunswick, the most southerly point on the South American mainland, the Cordilleran islands connect with the intensely glaciated ranges of Tierra del Fuego. Here, on the Fuegian Peninsula, the Cordillera Darwin has a number of 2000m peaks that soar above the surrounding wild seas.

Chile's Carretera Austral, the 'Southern Highway' leading around fjords and mountains on the Pacific coast of central-western Patagonia, currently ends at Puerto Yungay, at the mouth of the Río Bravo. The final section to Villa O'Higgins, a tiny settlement on the remote Lago O'Higgins near the Argentine border, is currently under construction and should be completed by about 2001. Southwards from here the many glaciers that descend from the southern continental icecap to meet the Pacific Ocean make any southern extension via Chilean territory unfeasible for the moment. Nevertheless, ambitious (but probably unfeasible) plans have been drawn up that would push the Carretera south around the Hielo Sur as far as the Beagle Channel, with a series of car ferries to cross the numerous fjords. South of the Hielo Sur, however, good roads lead southwards to Punta Arenas on the

Straits of Magellan. Punta Arenas is the largest Chilean city south of Puerto Montt.

In Argentina the Ruta 40 follows a zigzag route along the eastern edge of the Andean foothills from the town of Perito Moreno in northern Santa Cruz through Calafate to Río Turbio near Puerto Natales in far southern Chile. This remote road has many dusty turn-offs that lead west to small settlements or estancias (sheep ranches) close to the Cordillera. The Ruta 40 connects with surfaced roads that go to Río Gallegos, the most southerly city on the Argentine mainland.

In Chile the zone of the southern Patagonian Andes takes in the southern third of the XI Región (chiefly the O'Higgins Province) and the mainland area of the XII Región (Magallanes). On the Argentine side, this zone corresponds fairly closely to the western part of Santa Cruz Province.

Tierra del Fuego As they near the tip of the South American continent, the Andes swing around into an east-west line. For the first time in its entire length the Cordillera dips completely below sea level into the Straits of Magellan, only to surface again a little further south to meet the great island of Tierra del Fuego.

On Tierra del Fuego the mighty Cordillera Darwin (or Darwin Range), situated on a great peninsula stretching 250km west-to-east, forms the main range of the Andes. This entire Fuegian Peninsula is part of the remote Parque Nacional De Agostini, a wild area visited only by the occasional mountaineering expedition. The rugged and ice-cloaked peaks of the Chilean Fuegian Andes rise up directly from the icy seas to well over 2000m, sending numerous glaciers back down into deep fjords. Notorious for its poor weather, the Darwin Range can remain clouded in for months – seldom seen even from the passing fishing boats that trawl in the frigid Fuegian canals. To the west and south, many larger and smaller islands surrounds the Isla Grande, forming an intensely glaciated and storm-battered archipelago.

The Darwin Range peters out at its eastern end about 20km west of the Chile/Argentina

CLEM LINDENMAYER

The landscape of Tierra del Fuego offers some of the most rewarding trekking in Patagonia.

frontier. The ranges that continue eastwards into Argentine Tierra del Fuego have more modest elevations that rarely exceed 1500m. Although still exposed to winds from the south, the Argentine Fuegian Andes are somewhat sheltered from the wet westerlies. This produces a more moderate climate with lower precipitation levels, yet a decidedly subantarctic climate still prevails. Very small glaciers hang from the higher peaks and the permanent snow line lies at around 800m.

Cape Horn lies less than 100km from Tierra del Fuego, and is usually regarded as the most southerly extension of the South American continent. However, although the Cordillera continues as a deep submarine ridge that reaches south as far as the Antarctic Peninsula, the rugged and windswept Staten Island ('Isla de los Estados' in Spanish), due east of Tierra del Fuego, is the Andes' true point of southern termination. Geologically, Tierra del Fuego belongs to the Patagonian mainland, and the northern part of the island is essentially a continuation of Patagonia's arid steppes. The elongated form of Lago Kami, a deep glacial lake over 100km long, almost cuts Tierra del Fuego in two and more or less marks the halfway point between the dry flat north and the Fuegian Andes on the island's shattered southern coast.

When its numerous larger and smaller islands are included, over two thirds of Tierra del Fuego is Chilean territory. Despite this, the Argentine sector has a considerably higher population and is more homogeneously settled. Under the Argentine national government's development policies, Ushuaia on the Beagle Channel has now displaced Río Gallegos as the largest Argentine city south of Comodoro Rivadavia. Apart from a few isolated estancias along the coast and south of Lago Blanco, the southern part of Chilean Tierra del Fuego is hardly populated and virtually inaccessible. As a southern extension to its Carretera Austral, the Chilean government has approved plans for the construction of a road south across the Río Azorpardo to the Fuegian south coast.

CLIMATE

The vast, unbroken stretch of ocean to the west and south of the South American continent leaves the Patagonian Andes exposed to the saturated winds that circle the Antarctic land mass. The north-south line of the range forms a formidable barrier to these violent westerlies (known to English speakers as the Roaring Forties and the Furious Fifties), which dump staggering quantities of rain or snow on the ranges of the Patagonian Cordillera.

By Andean standards, the average height of the Patagonian mountains is relatively low, but they capture virtually all the airborne moisture and leave the vast Patagonian plains on the leeward side in a severe rain shadow. Nowhere else on earth do precipitation levels drop off so dramatically over such a short distance. In places the vegetation changes from dense, perpetually wet rainforest to dryland *coirón* tussock grasses and low shrubs in as little as 10km. Having left their moisture behind in the Andes, the now dry and cold westerly winds sweep down across eastern Patagonia to the Atlantic, drying out the already arid steppes even more. The strong maritime influence makes for highly unpredictable weather in the Patagonian Andes. Particularly in spring or early summer, fine weather may deteriorate almost without warning, as violent westerly storms sweep in from the Pacific. During such disturbances

snowfalls occur on all but the lowest ranges, even in midsummer.

As a rule, climatic conditions become steadily harsher the further south you go. This is reflected in the upper limit of alpine vegetation and the level of the summer snow line. Although there are major variations depending on many local factors such as exposure and precipitation, both the tree line and summer snow line drop dramatically the further south you go. For example, in the Araucanía of Argentina's northern Neuquén Province, the stunted high alpine vegetation reaches above 2000m in places, but around Cape Horn only species of lichen have adapted to grow above 400m. The highest average levels of permanent snow are also on the Argentine side of the northern Araucanía at roughly 2400m. In the subantarctic islands of far southern Chile snow fields come down to as low as 450m.

The severe winds for which Patagonia has become notorious arise from strong low pressure systems over the Argentine steppes. These low pressure systems build up in summer as a result of the sun's warming effect and constantly draw in masses of moist air from the Pacific. As a general rule, winds become progressively stronger the further south you go, where very strong winds are a major nuisance and a real danger to walkers and mountaineers in all high or exposed areas. Strong westerly winds are usually at their worst from November to January, but typically continue through to the end of April. Winter is surprisingly wind-free, with long periods of virtual stillness.

In the southern hemisphere, star formations appear upside down to people from Europe and North America, and the sun shines in the northern half of the sky. This generally gives north-facing mountainsides a milder microclimate than south-facing slopes. On the other hand, slopes with a southerly aspect are shady and cold, allowing snow and ice to accumulate more readily. For this reason glaciers tend to form on the south sides of ranges, and here and there glacial action has sheered out rounded cirques that also usually open out southwards.

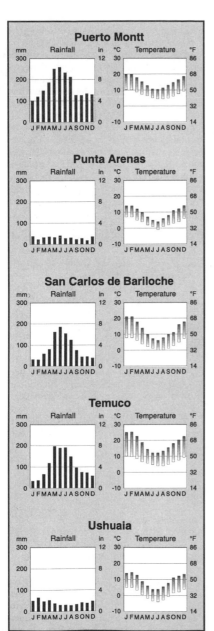

In recent years there has been considerable climatic variation in the Patagonian Andes. The (southern) winter of 1995, for example, brought extremely heavy snowfalls, and – fortunately for the alpine vegetation – was followed by an exceptionally hot and dry summer that removed much of the excess snow by late January.

Weather

Long wispy streams of high cirrus cloud known as 'mares' tails', and heavy lens-shaped or lenticular clouds called 'hogs' backs' that hover above higher peaks are a possible (but by no means definite) indication of a breakdown in the weather. Local weather is generally more stable in northern Patagonia, with less wind and longer, warmer summers. From the Lake District down to Aisén, signs of approaching bad weather often include strong, moist and suspiciously warm winds blowing in from the north. In northern areas isolated thunder storms sometimes build up in the mountains during hot summer weather. Storms of this type usually bring heavy rain but pass quickly. Areas of the Cordillera with an easterly aspect (generally on the Argentine side) also tend to have somewhat less severe weather, though frosts are more frequent because of higher valley elevations and a much more typically continental climate.

In southern Patagonia, where the climate comes more heavily under the influence of the subantarctic zone, extremely strong and incessant winds tend to blow westerly, but can vary from north-westerly to southerly. West to south-westerly winds generally indicate an approaching cold front and imminent storms. If a new westerly storm is approaching, winds may again begin to turn south-westerly and very cold after only a few days of fine weather. On the other hand a southerly airstream usually brings fine and stable conditions, although accompanied by very cold weather. Thunderstorms are unheard of in southern Patagonia.

Seasons

Patagonia lies completely within the world's

southern temperate zone. This means the year is divided into four very distinct seasons, as in North America or Europe. The seasons of the southern hemisphere are offset to those in the north by six months, which means that during the southern summer the northern hemisphere is experiencing its winter and vice versa.

Because of the peculiarities of the earth's rotation cycle, the seasons in the two halves of the globe do not have an identical pattern of daylight distribution. For example, Punta Arenas, situated between 53°S and 54°S, enjoys more summer daylight but less winter daylight than the English city of Manchester, which is located at precisely the same latitude in the northern hemisphere. Patagonia might therefore be expected to experience hotter summers and colder winters than comparable areas of Europe or North America. The enormous expanse of ocean (covering about 80% of the southern hemisphere's surface) serves to even out seasonal temperature differences and to moderate the climate of the whole region. In high summer (late December) the maximum period of daylight ranges from around 15 hours in the far north at Laguna del Laja to 19 hours in Tierra del Fuego. See also When to Go in the Facts for the Trekker chapter.

Geology of the Andes

The Andes bring superlatives to mind: the longest uninterrupted mountain chain in the world, the highest volcano, source of the longest river in the world, the oldest volcanically active chain of mountains. The Andes have also been home to devastating earthquakes and spectacular volcanic activity.

Like all mountain chains, the Andes are a result of movements at the margins of plates that make up the crust of the earth. The Nazca and the South American Plates meet along the west coast of South America, the eastern extremity of the Ring of Fire, a belt of intense seismic and volcanic activity around the rim of the Pacific. Along the western coast of South America the Nazca Plate is subducted – or drawn beneath – the South American Plate at

CLEM LINDENMAYER

The twin summits of the periodically active Volcán Llaima lie in the heart of Parque Nacional Conguillío.

around 10cm a year, which may not sound much but is dramatic in geological terms. A similar process takes place along the west coast of North America, although the lateral movement of the San Andreas Fault is more obvious.

These movements were already building the Andes in Palaeozoic times, roughly 225 to 600 million years ago, folding and faulting layers of rock and producing volcanoes, islands and ocean troughs. The build up of pressure from the two plates grinding against each other is released as volcanic eruptions, hot springs, fumaroles and geysers. A sudden break in the underground rock will be felt above ground as an earthquake. Volcanoes are nearly continuous along the Andes, although it is more than just a volcanic range, and the highest mountain (Aconcagua, 6959m) is not a volcano.

The main exogenic influences (or those factors that occur above the surface of the earth) on the Andes have been the periodic ice ages, when glaciers and icecaps covered most of Patagonia to as far north as Ecuador. The last ice age was more severe in South America than on any other continent, and glaciers gouged out lakes and fjords and deposited boulder clay, or till, a mixture of clay and rubble, on the surrounding lowlands.

The Andes are at their narrowest in Patagonia, only 100 to 200km wide, and they gradually peter out then disappear at Tierra del Fuego. The deep magma chambers that supplied lava and other molten material for Mesozoic (which came after the Palaeozoic) volcanoes are now exposed as granite batholiths, such as the Torres del Paine, along the length of the Andes. ■

Flora & Fauna of The Patagonian Andes

WAYNE BERNHARDSON

Lush rainforest bordering a rushing stream in Parque Nacional Huerquehue.

FLORA

The vegetation of Patagonia shows strong links with the plant life found in other parts of the southern hemisphere. The similarities are an indication of a common geographical past, when during Carboniferous times the earth's southern landmasses were joined together in a single supercontinent called Gondwanaland. When Gondwanaland began to break up 100 million years ago plants that had grown all over the supercontinent were left stranded on each of the newly formed continental islands. The vegetation continued to evolve in isolation, gradually developing into new species as the continents drifted apart. Visitors from Australia's Tasmania and New Zealanders in particular will notice a close resemblance to their own native flora.

Broadly speaking, the vegetation of the southern Cordillera can be divided into three main zones which extend southwards through the Patagonian Andes in more or less longitudinal bands. Vegetation zones largely reflect the climatic change as you move east from the mild wet lowland conditions to a colder and slightly drier montane environment before dropping down to the semi-arid steppes in the lee of the ranges. Because of the steadily worsening climate as you go south, the temperate rainforest and deciduous forest zones gradually occupy lower altitudes.

The zone of the evergreen temperate rainforest (often called *bosque valdiviano*, or Valdivian forest) is composed of mixed evergreen tree species and occupies all areas west of the Cordillera. This is the most luxuriant and diverse of the three zones, and includes virtually all the important species. In the Araucanía and Lake District, temperate rainforest is species-rich and grows from sea level up to about 1400m. In the far south, however, the rainforests are composed of only a few species (dominated by the *guindo* or *coigüe de Magallanes*) and are found close to sea level in sheltered locations. Temperate rainforest is generally very dense and this can make off-track hiking a very proposition.

The zone of deciduous forest *(bosque deciduoso)* is subalpine to alpine and extends from as low as 600m up to the tree line in the Lake District. In southern Patagonia it corresponds to the so-called *bosque magellanico*, or Magellanic forest. The factors favouring the distribution of deciduous forest are mainly better drainage and more severe winters, rather than just lower rainfall. There is usually no definite transition point and the rainforest zone tends to merge gradually into deciduous forest. Although very attractive, these forests have a much poorer range of species, with deciduous southern beech species (chiefly *lenga*) dominating. Especially in southern Patagonia where there is little undergrowth, mosses and herbs make an attractive 'park lawn' type landscape.

The steppes fringe the eastern side of the Cordillera and are generally sparsely vegetated. Classed as *monte* by Argentine geographers, but known more colloquially simply as *pampa*, the dominant plants found on this terrain are tough but slow-growing breeds of tussock grass *(Stipa* species) known as coirón, and thorny 'saltbush' plants called mogotes, or mata barrosa, (*Mulinum spinosum*). From a distance a field of rounded pale-green mogotes can look deceptively like a scattered herd of sheep. Isolated clusters of low trees (especially ñirre), and calafate scrub grow in sheltered places and along the river courses. Having been overgrazed for decades, today the steppes of eastern Patagonia are suffering from the steadily worsening effects of wind erosion, which has rendered some estancias unviable.

Trees

Southern Beech
The Andean-Patagonian vegetation is dominated by the southern beech.

Coigües The three evergreen species of southern beech known as coigüe (or coihue in Argentina) are mostly found at lower elevations, or where the marine influence produces a milder climate. Vigorous and highly adaptable, the common coigüe *(Nothofagus dombeyi)* has larger and more serrated leaves, grows to well over 50m and often attains a massive girth. Coigüe de Magallanes – often called by its common Mapuche name, guindo, in Argentina, – *(Nothofagus betuloides)* is at least as widespread, and can be identified by its stratified form and tiny, deep-green leaves. The distribution of these two species overlaps considerably, and novices may find it difficult to distinguish the common coigüe from coigüe de Magallanes. In the often saturated forests, experienced Patagonian mountain-goers value the dry bark of both trees as kindling to start a campfire.

A third species, coigüe de Chiloé *(Nothofagus nitida)*, has scaly, almost triangular-shaped leaves of a lighter colour. As its name suggests, its distribution is centred on the large island of Chiloé, but coigüe de Chiloé can sometimes also be found in the forests on the adjacent mainland.

Lenga Of the deciduous species of southern beech, lenga *(Nothofagus pumilio)* is easily the most common, and grows in a variety of forms. The leaves of the lenga are generally three or four cm long and have neat, rounded double indentations. In spring and early summer the leaves are a soft light-green, which gives the tree an 'airy' feel, while in autumn the leaves turn a beautiful golden red. In the mountains of the Araucanía and Lake District, lenga is rarely found below 1000m, but in the far south of Patagonia and Tierra del Fuego it often grows right at sea level. At lower altitudes lenga grows to be a full-sized tree up to 40m, but it also commonly grows right up to the timber line, forming low, impenetrable thickets. Under the extreme conditions at high altitude, lenga takes on an attractive 'bonsai' appearance.

Ñirre Ñirre *(Nothofagus antarctica, spelled ñire in Argentina)* is a small southern beech species that occupies difficult sites, from dry semi-steppe to waterlogged mallín. Ñirre only occasionally grows large enough to earn the title of a tree proper, when it is easily mistaken for lenga – particularly in autumn when its leaves turn the same golden-red hue. It is easily distinguished from lenga by its crinkled, irregular leaves and much coarser bark.

Raulí Another lovely species of deciduous southern beech found in the forests of the Araucanía and northern Lake

Evergreen coigües can form pure stands, but they are also found in mixed stands with ulmos, robles and other species.

The beautiful raulí prefers lower temperatures and well drained soils. It can grow in pure stands or in close association with related species.

CLEM LINDENMAYER

The araucaria was almost like bread to the Mapuche, who collected the nuts to eat immediately or to dry and store for winter. This tree is sometimes called the 'paragua' (umbrella) in Spanish and 'monkey puzzle' in English.

The alerce increases in diameter at the rate of only about 1cm every 15 to 20 years, so the enormous size of some specimens attests to their great age (see Parque Nacional Alerce Andino and Parque Nacional Los Alerces).

District, the raulí *(Nothofagus alpina)* rarely grows above altitudes of 1000m. Raulí has leathery, almost oval-shaped leaves of up to 15cm long and reaches a height of up to 40m. The tree prefers the zones of lower temperature, often forming pure forests or in loose association with its near relative the roble. Being relatively fast-growing, raulí is an ideal species for reforestation programs, and produces a much-prized, red-grained timber.

Roble Called pellín (or hualle in its sapling form) by the Mapuche people, the roble *(Nothofagus obliqua)* has a straight untapered trunk reaching up to 35m. The tree has a similar distribution pattern to the raulí, although it is found somewhat farther south. The tree has distinctive 'oak-like' leaves with serrations. It seems to grow best at an altitude of around 600m.

Other Trees

Alerce (or Lahuén) Reminiscent of the North American sequoia, the alerce *(Fitzroya cupressoides)* is an extremely slow-growing conifer that reaches enormous proportions and a great age. These majestic trees have green scaly segmented branchlet-leaves and a reddish, spongy bark. Once widespread even on the coastal plains of the Lake District, alerce forests are mainly limited to national parks and reserves. Interestingly, fossils recently discovered in Tasmania suggest that ancient proto-alerce species once grew throughout the great supercontinent of Gondwanaland 35 million years ago.

Alerce wood is in high demand, particularly for use as highly durable roof shingles, which can last up to 100 years! It is illegal to cut down living trees (although some clandestine felling of alerces nevertheless occurs), and therefore most of the alerce timber on sale comes from trees that fall over naturally or were buried by past landslides. The moist conditions underground preserve the wood for centuries, and so-called *alerceros* – experts who know just where to look – dig out the valuable old trunks.

Araucaria (or Pehuén) The araucaria 'pine' *(Araucaria araucana)* typifies the Araucanía and northern Lake District, and its name is inextricably linked with the Araucarian (or Pehuenche) Indians, local Mapuche tribes whose staple diet was the araucaria nut. Interestingly, the species is a close relative – virtually an unidentical twin – of the similar-looking Queensland bunya pine *(Araucaria bidwillii)*, whose nuts were also a major food source for certain Aboriginal tribes of Australia.

The graceful umbrella-like conifer has sharp-pointed leaves shaped like scales, which are attached directly to the branches. Mature trees produce a cone at the tips of their branches, about the size and shape of a pineapple, which ripens towards the end of summer. The araucaria is often called the monkey-puzzle tree, because the first Europeans to inspect it were reportedly 'puzzled' at the question of how monkeys could possibly climb the spiny branches in order to reach the fruit. There are no monkeys in this part of South America, but the araucaria does provide food for much of the forest life. A member of the parrot family, the cachaña *(Microsittace ferruginea)*, lives almost exclusively on the nuts, as do about 50 species of insect.

Essentially a montane species, araucarias thrive in the Andean foothills between 1000 and 2000m, and are often found right at the tree line. Individual specimens have been measured at 50m tall and estimated to be 2000 years old. The high commercial value of the timber has led to over exploitation of the tree in years past, but national parks and forest reserves now ensure the protection of the araucaria. The Chilean national park authority CONAF has adopted the araucaria as its official symbol.

Arrayán The arrayán *(Myrceugenella apiculata)* is a species of myrtle (belonging to the family of *Myrtacea)* that thrives in wet coastal rainforests or along lakes and rivers. Covered with smooth, almost luminescent cinnamon-red bark that peels off leaving strips of white, the arrayán typically develops multiple trunks, forming beautiful, dimpled and twisted branches. The tree has abundant white flowers and produces edible purple berries.

The evergreen arrayan grows very slowly, and its timber is used for ornaments and to make tool handles.

Avellano A member of the family of proteas *(Proteaceae)* which are found right across the southern hemisphere, the avellano *(Gevuina avellana)* is a medium-sized tree that grows in varying habitats in northern Patagonia. The tree can be identified by its shiny serrated leaves and ash-grey bark with white spots. Individual trees flower heavily between January and March, while the reddish breast-shaped fruits from the previous year still hang on the same stem.

Canelo A beautiful rainforest tree belonging to the magnolia family, the canelo *(Drimys winteri)* is sacred to the Mapuche and is found in particularly moist areas throughout the Patagonian Andes. Reaching a height of 30m and a diameter of one metre, the canelo has thick light-green elongated leaves that grow out radially around the branchlets. Between September and November the tips of the branchlets are covered with fragrant white flowers which develop into inedible red berries in March and April. The bark of the canelo (whose name means 'cinnamon' in Spanish) is especially rich in vitamin C, mineral salts, essential oils and natural antibacterial substances, and at one time it was exported from Chile.

Ciprés de la Cordillera The ciprés de la cordillera *(Austrocedrus chilensis)* is also known by its Mapuche name of lahuán, and belongs to the family of cypresses. This hardy but slow-growing conifer produces male and female flowers on separate, flattened scaly twigs, and when the trees are in bloom (in October) large puffs of pollen blow around the forests. Preferring a drier 'continental' climate, the ciprés de la cordillera is most widespread in the Araucanía and Lake District of Argentina, where it forms tall, pure-stand forests fringing the eastern foothills of the Andes. The tree is also present on the Chilean side of the Andes in dry highland areas such as Parque Nacional Laguna del Laja in the northern Araucanía.

Ciprés de las Guaitecas The world's most southerly conifer, the ciprés de las Guaitecas *(Pilgerodendron uviferum)* is another member of the cypress family. In stark contrast to the former species, however, it thrives in waterlogged ground in the intensely wet coastal areas of western Patagonia – most notably in the remote Archipielago de las Guaitecas. The tree looks similar to – though it is much

CLEM LINDENMAYER

The ciprés de la cordillera tree is also called the 'cedro', or cedar, and has the most northerly distribution of all Chile's conifers.

smaller than – the alerce, and it does not have the same reddish bark as the alerce. These two species of conifer are often found together, and – like the alerce – the ciprés de las Guaitecas is much prized for its fine timber.

Laurels Two almost identical species of the genus *Laurelia* grow throughout much of the southern rainforests. Known as tepa *(L. philippiana)* and laurel or trihue *(L. sempervirens)*, these tall, straight trees have thick sappy leaves with deep serrations. When crushed, the leaves of the tepa (and less so the trihue) give off a pleasant and intense aroma. These species are relatives of the similarly fragrant sassafras of southern Australia.

Mañíos Three species of mañío grow in the forests of the Lake District and Chiloé. Members of the genus *Podocarpus*, mañíos grow to be very large and attractive trees. They are recognisable by their distinctive waxy elongated leaves, and yield unpalatable red fruit. The trunks of older trees are reddish-brown and often deeply twisted, yet mañío produces timber of a high value.

In popular medicine the chilco is used to lower fevers. Common garden fuchsias, popular throughout the world, are domesticated varieties of this plant.

Tineo The tineo *(Weinmannia trichosperma)* is another Gondwanaland genus scattered across the South Pacific and is found in northern and central Patagonia. A very large tree, the tineo sometimes grows to a height of 50m and is easily recognisable by its distinctive scaly, serrated paired leaves which are arranged opposingly along the leaf branch in between triangular winglets. The tineo blooms in December when white flowers appear, growing into red capsules in summer to give the whole tree a reddish colour.

Shrubs & Bushes

Calafate The calafate *(Berberis buxifolia)* is a thorny bush found all over Patagonia, though it is much more commonly found in southern Patagonia and Tierra del Fuego. Growing from 1 to 3m high, the calafate has attractive bright yellow flowers in spring, and yields tasty round purple berries. Many other similar species of the widespread *Berberis* genus grow throughout the southern Andes, and these also produce edible (though usually less palatable) berries.

Chilco The chilco *(Fuchsia magellanica)* grows in cool humid areas, near waterfalls or by rivers. The flowers (which are a major source of nectar for hummingbirds) have a very distinctive fuchsia form, with bright red sepals and petals of a bluish-purple colour. Many cultivated varieties of the chilco are grown in gardens all over the world.

The colihue flowers from October to March, after which the plant dies. Charles Darwin commented on the dense, almost impenetrable stands of bamboo when he visited Patagonia in 1833.

Colihue *(Ch. couleu* with several subspecies) ranges farther south than quila. Colihue produces thicker and straighter erect yellow canes, with fewer lateral branches, which can grow up to eight metres high. The traditional Mapuche 'trumpet' (called a *trutruca)* is made by hollowing out a thick colihue cane. Colihue canes are also used for furniture or basket weaving.

Also see the aside titled 'The Quila Cycle' (page 153).

Nalca (or Pangue) The nalca *(Gunnera tinctoria)* is a vigorous perennial that thrives in wet places. Reaching up to three metres in height during a single growing season, the nalca produces enormous 'elephant ear' leaves. Because of the sourish taste of the nalca's succulent edible stems, which are sold at local markets in the Chilean Lake District, this remarkable plant has been likened to giant rhubarb. With the first frosts of autumn, the nalca dies back to survive winter under the thick insulating mulch of its own dead foliage.

Notro The notro or ciruelillo *(Embothrium coccineum)* is a distant relative of the spectacular South African proteas. Preferring sunny sites, the notro often colonises open terrain, where it may occasionally grow to be a small tree. Notro blooms early (around October) producing attractive red elongated flowers that develop into seed pods among its leathery, oval-shaped leaves.

Parrilla One of about 10 members of the genus *Ribes* present in the southern Andes, the parilla *(Ribes trilobum)* resembles the cultivated blackcurrant. The parrilla produces straggly clusters of yellow flowers that mature into deep-purple, seedy berries (which are edible though not particularly palatable). The plant was known as the mahul to the Mapuche, who prepared a medicinal infusion from its leaves.

Quila & Colihue These species of the native bamboo genus *Chusquea* grow in all areas covered by temperate rainforest, except for the far south. In tall mature forest, where the understorey is starved of light, quila *(Ch. quila)* is reduced to a few straggly canes, but as soon as the forest is disturbed – such as by tree fall – the pale-green canes of this vigorous opportunist spread out horizontally to colonise the opening. Quila regrowth is normally the first stage of regeneration after a forest fire or landslide, when it can form impenetrable thickets up to seven metres high.

Taique The Taique *(Desfontainia spinosa)* is a common underbrush shrub that trekkers can quickly learn to identify in order to avoid its scratchy, holly-like leaves (from which the Mapuche made a yellow dye). The taique's other, more pleasing distinction is its elongated goblet-shaped flowers, which are bright red with a touch of yellow on their outer tips.

Wild flowers

Casual observers might be surprised at the diversity of wild flowers found in the montane forests and alpine slopes of the Patagonian Andes. Below is a tiny selection of some particularly interesting and attractive native species.

Amancay Another Patagonian perennial widely cultivated in foreign parts is the amancay *(Alstroemeria aurea)*. The amancay is typically found growing in open stands of coigües in the Argentine Araucanía and Lake District, carpeting the lightly shaded forest floor with flamboyant orange flowers. Amancay means 'eternal love' in Mapuche, because according to indigenous folklore this beautiful flower is the reincarnation of a Mapuche girl who sacrificed herself in order to save her lover.

The taique grows in mixed stands with many other shrubs, but is commonly found growing with or near alerces. Related species grow as far north as Peru.

The botellita or 'little bottle' prefers shady forests and damp conditions, and its bark and flowers have traditionally been used as a tea.

With the reduction in range and numbers of pumas, guanacos have flourished in some areas. On Isla Navarino in Tierra del Fuego, they can be seen in large numbers and they are not as shy as those on the mainland.

Añañuca Añañuca is the common local name given to various members of the *Hippeastrum* genus found in the volcanic soils of the Araucanía. Growing from an onion-like bulb, these perennials produce large pink or red goblet-shaped flowers at the end of a long succulent stem. Añañuca cultivars of southern Andean origin are sold in florists all over the world.

Botellita A typical epiphyte species found in the moist temperate rainforests of the Araucanía and Lake District, botellitas *(Mitraria coccinea)* colonise fallen tree trunks, facilitating their decomposition as they rapidly cover the trunk in a deep-green mantle. The common Spanish name of this small vine-like creeper hints at the resemblance of its tiny crimson flowers to 'little bottles'.

Clavel del Campo Several members of the composite *Mutisia* genus found throughout northern Patagonia are referred to as clavel del campo ('carnation of the country-side'). These opportunistic stragglers are commonly seen along the roadsides in Parque Nacional Nahuel Huapi, where they cling to bushes by their leafy tendrils and produce pretty pinkish-white or orange daisy-like flowers.

Copihue The national flower of Chile, the copihue *(Lapageria rosea)* is a climbing plant often found growing on tree trunks in the rainforests of the Araucanía and Lake District. In late summer the copihue vine produces delicate pink flowers with yellow stamens.

Estrellita Similar to the botellita, the epiphyte estrellita *(Asteranthera ovata)* is a small climbing bush often seen on tree trunks in the moist rainforests of the Lake District (generally in association with alerce). It yields lovely scarlet flowers with four petals, hence its Spanish name meaning 'little star'.

Ourisia The hardy ourisia *(Ourisia)* thrives in permanently waterlogged sites beside streams or lakes. The ourisia forms delicate, striking red flowers that mature into small heavy seeds that sink back into the water.

Quellén or Frutilla Silvestre Often found in associa-tion with araucaria forest, the quellén *(Fragaria chiloenis)* is a subspecies of the native South American strawberry. In early summer this perennial bursts into life as a cluster of spotted green leaves and white flowers that quickly develop into small red round berries. The quellén was an important dietary supplement for the local Pehuenche people, who even made an alcoholic beverage from the sweet berries for festive occasions.

FAUNA

South America was once an isolated continent with a largely marsupial fauna, in some ways comparable to present-day Australia. However, with the creation of a natural land bridge at the Isthmus of Panama three million years ago, North American placental mammals migrated on a large scale. For this reason South American wildlife is generally more closely related to the fauna of regions further north. Many newly introduced animal species, such as pigs, horses, rabbits, beavers, exotic deer and even reindeer run wild and have altered local ecosystems.

Herbivores

Guanaco The guanaco *(Lama guanicoe)* is a cameloid relative of the vicuña (and its domesticated breeds of alpaca and llama). Guanacos are found mainly on the Patagonian steppes, but also inhabit mountain areas, where their tracks sometimes seem like well-graded hiking trails. The animals are sleek and powerful, with brownish-white bodies and long necks. The herds have been drastically reduced but guanaco still survive because of un-relenting human persecution of their chief predator, the puma.

Huemul The huemul *(Hippocamelus bisulcus)* was once abundant throughout the entire southern Andes. Ravaged by civilisation and forest fires, the numbers of this graceful native deer are now alarmingly low, and the huemul is seriously threatened with extinction. The huemul is brown with a black snout, has a shoulder height of about one metre and an approximate length of 1.5 metres. Male huemuls throw their two-branched antlers each year after mating. Agile with extremely acute hearing, herds of up to sixty normally inhabit the alpine areas above the tree line, descending into the protection of the forested zone in winter. Now strictly protected, the huemul is the subject of an extensive program (in Spanish, *Proyecto Huemul)* which aims to stabilise and restore its populations to sustainable levels.

Mara or Patagonian Hare Maras *(Dilochotis pata-gonum)* inhabit the dry steppes of eastern Patagonia, digging out their burrows in the shelter of bushes. Although often called the Patagonian hare *(liebre patagónica* in Spanish), the mara is actually a member of South America's large Caviidae family (which includes capybaras, guinea pigs and the tuco-tucos). Measuring around 70cm in length and weighing up to 12kg at maturity, the mara is actually much larger and heavier than the European hare – to which it does bear quite a strong resemblance. Tragically, the introduction of the far more prolific European hare in the late 19th century caused mara populations to collapse, and some biologists fear that the mara may soon disappear altogether from the Patagonian steppes.

Pudú The pudú *(Pudu pudu)* is the smallest of the world's deer species. Standing only 40 to 50cm from the ground, the pudú only weighs about 9kg at maturity. The male has pointed, branched horns. Found principally in the dense rainforests of the Araucanía and Lake District, this timid creature is occasionally spotted scurrying through the underbrush.

Tuco-Tuco Half a dozen or so species of tuco-tuco are endemic to Patagonia, where they are found from the northern Araucanía as far south as Tierra del Fuego. The tuco-tuco genus, *Ctenomys,* is one of the most differen-tiated and widespread in South America, with scores of

Deer reached tropical South America before the last ice age, and have diversified into many species. The huemul is now en-dangered and the subject of serious conservation efforts.

The pudú is the world's smallest deer and has simple, unbranched antlers that look like horns.

Because pumas have preyed on sheep, ranchers employed leoneros or lion hunters to keep numbers down. From the 1970s, many could no longer afford a lion hunter, so the puma's future seems assured.

members, mostly in lowland tropical regions. The Patagonian tuco-tucos are all burrowing species, with powerful incisors to cut into the earth as they dig. Their paws have brush-like rows of bristles with which they 'sweep' excavated debris out of the way. Their form is similar to that of a large rat, although they have a squarish face and small (deceptively underdeveloped) ears set far back on the head. Apart from the extremely rare and endangered tuco-tuco colonial (*C. socialbilis*), which is apparently found only in Parque Nacional Nahuel Huapi, they are not gregarious and don't often leave their burrows.

Predators

Gato Montés The gato montés (*Oncifelis geoffroyii*, whose Spanish name means simply 'mountain cat') is a more diminutive feline predator measuring a maximum of one metre from head to tail. A shy loner, the gato montés lives mainly in areas of dense closed forest, hunting birds, rodents and occasionally even pudú.

Huillín The huillín (*Lutra provocax*) is a species of otter that inhabits inland waterways and coastal areas of Patagonia. This amphibious carnivore grows to over a metre in length and weighs up to 10kg at maturity. The huillín's long tail and broad, short paws make it adept at swimming and diving, while its thick, impervious fur insulates the animal from the cold water. Digging its burrow close to the water along river banks or lake shores, the huillín only ventures out at dusk in search of crabs and mussels, which it locates using its extremely sensitive whiskers. Less often it preys on water birds, fish and rodents.

Huiña An even smaller native cat is the huiña (*Felis guigna*, which the Mapuche called codcod). Only slightly larger than your common domesticated cat, the huiña has reddish-yellow fur, which apart from the belly is completely covered with circular, dark-grey spots. Well camouflaged and cautious to avoid encounters with larger (especially humanoid) beasts, few trekkers ever see the huiña. It is nonetheless a common inhabitant of the northern Patagonian forests, where it preys largely on birds (and is particularly fond of the picaflor's sweet flesh).

Puma The puma (*Felis concolor*) is a large predator closely related to the cougar of North America, and is present everywhere on the Patagonian mainland where there is sufficient natural protection from its sole enemy, human beings. Both male and female pumas have a coat of a uniform sandy-brown colour, except for the dirty-white muzzle, and reach over two metres from head to tail. Although officially protected by law, the puma is still persecuted by farmers, whose livestock it sometimes preys upon. Pumas kill their prey, typically guanaco or huemul, by grasping the animal from behind and breaking its neck instantly with a powerful backward stroke of one front paw. The puma is considered virtually harmless to humans. Although you may occasionally hear stories of puma attacks on people, the truth is these are very rare. When such attacks occur they are invariably as an act of self defence by a cornered animal, or are the result of a puma mistaking

The zorro culpeo relies on smell and hearing to locate its prey, and has an adaptable digestive system that allows it to vary its diet to take advantage of seasonal abundance.

a person for its natural prey. In fact, pumas seem to have a fear or respect for humans that is rare among other large feline predators. Trekkers will be lucky to glimpse this principally nocturnal beast, although puma paw prints, about the size of a man's fist, are quite often seen in soft earth or snow.

Zorro Culpeo The second largest predator in Patagonia, the zorro culpeo (also called zorro colorado, *Dusicyon culpaeus*) is a native fox. Because of its prized reddish-brown fur coat, the animal has been hunted and trapped extensively. The zorro culpeo is nocturnal and lives primarily in lightly forested areas of the region.

Zorro Gris The zorro gris *(Dusicyon gymnocercus)* is a smaller fox that typically lives in open country of Patagonia. Eating a largely vegetarian diet supplemented by insects and the occasional small rodent, the zorro gris was introduced to Tierra del Fuego in the mistaken belief that it would help control the plagues of (also introduced) European rabbits. The zorro gris has few natural enemies, apparently because of its highly unpalatable flesh. Even when dead, condors and flies are reluctant to touch the carcass, which simply dries out and rots without ever becoming maggot-infested.

Rodents & Other Small Mammals

Coipo An aquatic rodent, the coipo *(Myocastor coypus)* is sometimes also called the nutria falsa, or 'false otter'. The animal looks more like an oversized hamster, with sharp and prominent front teeth. Feeding mainly on herbs and roots, the coipo lives in freshwater lakes and slow-flowing streams, where it builds its burrow under the banks (always below the water level to deter predators). The coipo is nocturnal, and most commonly seen at dusk. Exploited almost to extinction for its valuable pelt in the earlier part of this century, the animal is now protected by law. Ironically, coipos raised on fur farms in the US state of Louisiana have escaped into the wild, where they are now a major pest. This seems all the more ironic given that another aquatic rodent accidentally introduced by fur breeders – North American beavers – has reached plague proportions in Tierra del Fuego.

The coipo lives in freshwater lakes and streams, and its numbers are increasing after it was hunted for its fur earlier this century.

Chingue (or Zorrino) Closely related to the North American skunks, the chingue *(Conepatus humboldtii)* has a black coat with a single white stripe down its back between a bushy tail and a pointed snout. Like its cousins, it protects itself by ejecting an acidic liquid with a powerfully unpleasant odour. The chingue prefers to live in open areas, and feeds mainly on roots, fruits and insects, although birds' eggs and small rodents are its favourite food.

Llaca (or Monito del Monte) One of two surviving members of the marsupial order left in the southern Andes, the llaca *(Dromiciops australis)* is a very small creature with a browny-grey coat. The animal inhabits the rainforests of the Lake District, spending almost all of its time high up in the shelter of the trees. The llaca is often called *monito* ('little monkey') because its hands and feet have adapted to resemble those of monkeys, with four fingers

The llaca is the size of a small rat and feeds mainly on insect larvae and pupae. Some evidence points to an affinity with Australian marsupials, which would make it an important evolutionary link between marsupials of the two continents.

and an opposing thumb to facilitate climbing. As with all marsupials, the female nurtures her (typically three or four) young in a pouch on her belly. Adapted to the area's temperate environment, the llaca feeds on fruits and insects during the summer months, then goes into a seasonal torpor over the winter when it is nourished by fatty reserves in its tail.

Vizcacha (or Chinchillón) A wild Andean relative of the domesticated chinchilla, the vizcacha *(Lagidium vizcacha)* is a small burrowing animal (weighing no more than 1kg at maturity) with an appearance similar to a bearded squirrel. It has thick, soft fur ranging from yellow to a greyish colour with a dark, brush-like tail. The vizcacha prefers steep, rocky habitats offering natural protection from predators, where it forms large colonies. The older vizcachas keep a wary watch for approaching predators, letting out a shrill cry to alert other members of the colony at the slightest sign of danger. The diet of the vizcacha is strictly vegetarian – it eats grass shoots, moss and lichens.

Birds

With a wide variety of habitat zones – coastal, wetland, forest, alpine and steppe – concentrated within a relatively narrow band, the Patagonian Andes have a rich birdlife. Some of the most common and/or interesting species are listed below.

Aquatic Birds

Caiquén & Canquén Several closely related native geese of the genus *Chloephaga* are common in Patagonia. The caiquén *(Chloephaga picta)* or Magellanic goose, is common on the riverflats of southern Patagonia. Male caiquenes are white and grey while the female is coffee-black. Another common member of this genus is the canquén *(C. poliocephala,* called cauquén in Argentina), or ashy-headed goose, which is light brown and also prefers open damp areas. The canquén has a short beak with a sharp point that is ideal for cutting through grass.

Cisne de Cuello Negro The cisne de cuello negro, or black-necked swan *(Cygnus melanocoryphus)* is a large white swan with the characteristic elongated neck, which is black except for a striking red splash just behind the bird's bill. This adaptable swan inhabits both salt and freshwater areas and has extremely oily feathers, enabling it to remain in the water for several weeks at a time. The cygnets can occasionally be seen riding tucked between the wings and body on the back of adult birds.

Flamenco Rojo The flamenco rojo *(Phoenicopterus chilensis)*, or Chilean flamingo, is only plentiful in southern Patagonia, where it frequents shallows of (particularly saline) lakes and steppeland lagoons in the lee of the Cordillera. This elegant bird filters out tiny crustacea that live on the bottom of the lake, whose pigments give the bird's plumage its striking crimson-pink colour.

Huala Another highly adapted bird of the lakes (and less often rivers) is the huala *(Podiceps major)*, or great grebe, which is more commonly known in Argentina as the macá

The ashy-headed goose (canquén) is commonly found in open damp areas and is a bird of habit, returning to the same place year after year to mate, rear young and feed.

grande. This grey-black grebe is readily differentiated from other waterfowl by its conical beak and spiky crest; the front of the male's neck is yellowy-red. The huala is an excellent swimmer and diver, rarely even leaving the water (although it will sometimes fly from one lake to another). The bird builds a floating nest in the shelter of reeds or trees close to the shore, and within hours of hatching the chicks are able to swim (although at first they generally prefer to ride on the back of a parent). The huala's name is onomatapoeic and comes from its deep melancholic call.

Martín Pescador The martín pescador *(Ceryle torquata)* or ringed kingfisher, is a solitary bird found along streamways and lakes as well as coastal lagoons, where it is typically seen sitting on an overhanging branch patiently watching and waiting for an unsuspecting fish to swim by. Both the male and female have a grey head and neck separated by a white band, while the feathers of the underbelly are a brownish-red.

Pato de Torrentes The pato de torrentes *(Merganetta armata)*, or torrent duck, lives along the banks of mountain rivers. This remarkable water bird has a streamlined body, and feet that allow it to dive into even the most dangerous rapids in search of small fish and insects without being dragged along by the currents. The attractive plumage of the male and female is different.

Quetru Vapor Of the dozen or more species of native duck in Patagonia, one of particular interest is the quetru vapor *(Tachyeres pteneres)*, also called quetru no volador, or flightless steamer duck. It is so named because it is able to move with surprising speed across water by flapping its small underdeveloped wings in a circular 'paddling' motion. The quetru vapor is a large ground-dwelling bird, dark grey, and weighs up to 6kg. It mostly inhabits the southern islands or other coastal areas, where there are fewer predators.

Run Run The run run *(Hymenops perspicillata)* or spectacled tyrant, typically inhabits wetlands, lakeshores and riverbanks. The male and female show a marked difference in plumage. The male is all black except for a yellow beak and rings around the eyes, and a white primary feather on each wing. Solitary and territorial, the male signals his claim to territory by making a spectacular vertical take-off several metres into the air before dropping back to his previous position. The female, who is rarely seen with the male (which at one time led to the two being erroneously classified as separate species), has a dark brown upper body and wings, with coppery-red primary feathers, and creamy longitudinal stripes along her underbelly.

Tagua The tagua *(Fulica armillata)*, or red-gartered coot, builds a floating (though well-anchored) nest on lakes in regions distant from the Pacific coast, and is often found together with swans and flamingos. The tagua is slate-grey, with a black head and neck and a yellow beak.

Yeco (or Bigua) The yeco *(Phalacrocorax olivaceus)*, or olivaceous cormorant, usually called the bigua in Argentina, is a large black cormorant widely distributed throughout the Patagonian Andes. The diet of the yeco

The black necked swan has the unusual habit of carrying its chicks on its back, probably to protect them from the icy waters when they are very young.

The cachaña - also known as the austral conure - is a common parrot of Patagonian forests, where its favourite food is the seeds of Araucaria pines.

The carpintero negro, or black woodpecker, has strong claws for clinging to bark as it chisels away after insects and their larvae, which it then spears with its barbed tongue.

consists almost exclusively of fish – local anglers know that any place where yecos are found is sure to offer excellent fishing – which it catches by diving directly into the water (rather than swooping down to seize fish near the surface as does the martín pescador). The yeco builds its nest in trees or cliffs beside lakes and larger streams, both parents feeding the hatchlings with a regurgitated 'soup'. The yeco can sometimes be seen sitting on a rock or a log with its wings outstretched. It is often stated that this is to dry its wings, but there is no conclusive evidence that this is the case and cormorants can fly readily after diving.

Birds of the Forest

Aguilucho The rufous-tailed hawk, or aguilucho de cola rojiza *(Buteo ventralis)* and the common aguilucho, or red-backed buzzard *(B. polyosoma)* are native hawks that live in the forests throughout the southern Andes. These large birds prey on insects, small mammals and other birds.

Cachaña The flamboyant plumage and screeching call of the cachaña *(Enicognathus ferrugineus)*, also known as the austral conure, ensure that this delightful species is one of the most frequently sighted (and/or heard) bird in the forests of the Patagonian Andes. It is the most southerly member of the world's parrot family, and – incredibly, considering that most other species of parrot are found in tropical regions – it thrives even in areas which experience snowy winters and often frigid summer temperatures. The cachaña has dark green wings with lighter yellowy-green feathers on its head, breast and underbelly, and a long reddish tail. It feeds on the shoots, fruits and nuts of trees, typically congregating in noisy flocks of twenty or so among the branches.

Carpintero Negro The carpintero negro, or Magellanic woodpecker, also called the carpintero patagónico or carpintero gigante *(Campephilus magellanicus)*, can be found throughout the entire forested belt of the southern Andes. This energetic woodpecker – the largest in South America – can frequently be heard picking away at tree trunks and branches. The pitch-black birds are usually seen in pairs, the male being easy to distinguish from his mate by his striking red head.

Chucao The Mapuche name of the chucao *(Scelorchilus rubecula)* is onomatopoeic, and represents this tiny oran-gey-red breasted bird's distinctive call – a kind of two-syllable, chuckling warble – which the Mapuche regard as a salute to passing walkers. Feeding mainly on insects, the chucao is a type of tapaculo that typically inhabits quila or colihue thickets close to water courses in the understorey of temperate rainforests. Chucaos are ground-nesting birds, and in the spring the hen lays several dispropor-tionately large white eggs. While trekkers are moving through the forest the chucao remains timid and stays out of sight. If you stand still for a moment, however, the bird's natural curiosity quickly takes over and it will hop over to get a closer look at you.

Picaflores (Hummingbirds) The smallest of five species of hummingbirds native to the southern Andes, the tiny picaflor, or green-backed firecrown *(Sephanoides galeritus)* inhabits the moist rainforests of the Araucanía and northern Lake District. This green and bronze-coloured bird feeds largely on nectar, supplementing its diet with insects. Two species of hummingbirds also occasionally found in the Araucanía are the picaflor cordillerano, or white-sided hillstar *(Oreotrochilus leucopleurus)*, which lives at higher elevations, and the picaflor gigante, or giant hummingbird *(Patagona gigas)*, a larger forest dweller.

Pitío The pitío *(Colaptes pitius)*, or Chilean flicker, is a woodpecker with a brownish-grey crown, a creamy yellow face and upper neck, and white and coffee-coloured bands on the rest of its body. Often found in association with the carpintero negro (although the latter tends to dominate wherever present), the pitío is common on the slightly drier leeward side of the Cordillera, where its characteristic 'pee-tee-way' call (hence its common name) rings out through the montane forests.

Queltehue The queltehue *(Vanellus chilensis)*, or black-breasted lapwing, is one of the most commonly seen birds of the southern Andes, although on the whole it prefers lower-level areas outside the Cordillera. In southern and central Patagonia, a small (but otherwise almost identical) subspecies known as the queltehue austral *(V. chilensis fretensis)* is found. The plumage is black on the chest and tail tip, white on the underbelly and a metallic grey-green on the bird's upper body. In early spring the queltehue arrives from the north for the summer months to breed in Patagonia, building its nest in a hidden depression in the ground. It is an extremely defensive bird, confronting anyone who approaches the nest with a shrill warning cry before it begins a series of diving attacks. This 'over-reaction' to intruders has made the queltehue unpopular with local people (as well as hunters, as the bird's alarm call alerts their prey in advance).

Torcaza The torcaza *(Columba araucana)* or Chilean pigeon (known to the Mapuche people as the conu and to the Argentinians as the paloma araucana) is again found throughout the forests of the Araucanía and Lake District. This is a great relief to ornithologists and bird lovers, since the torcaza had an alarmingly close brush with extinction during the late 1950s and early 1960s when a disease of European origin reduced the bird's distribution to several small, isolated colonies. In the subsequent decades, however, the torcaza made a gradual comeback, and the bird is now virtually as plentiful and widespread as it was before the epidemic. The torcaza is typically seen in flocks of a dozen or so birds, picking over the ground in forest clearings.

Traro The traro *(Polyborus plancus)* or common caracara, is another bird of prey that trekkers are likely to spot (usually seen in pairs) on their hikes. This large southern member of the falcon family is represented in the mythology of all of Patagonia's indigenous people – from the Mapuche to the Ona of Tierra del Fuego – because of its audacity, craftiness and surprising aggressiveness. When hunting, the traro attacks other birds in flight or even wounded animals, and when males compete to pair off with a female – a mate for life – losers are regularly killed and

The specialised bill and long tongue of hummingbirds enable them to collect nectar from flowers. Hummingbirds have the fastest wing-beats of any bird, allowing them to hover and even fly backwards.

eaten by their rivals. The traro is widespread in Patagonia, particularly in forested areas, although it is most common in the far south.

Tucúquere The tucúquere *(Bubo virginianus)*, or great horned owl, has twin crests above its eyes that look like feathery horns. Its common (originally Mapuche) name is derived from its distinctive call. A nocturnal bird of prey, the tucúquere is found in forested areas throughout Patagonia, using its extraordinary eyesight and hearing to silently swoop down on rodents and other small mammals. Despite being highly beneficial to agriculture, the tucúquere is still persecuted by superstitious rural people who believe that the bird's presence brings bad luck.

Birds of the Grasslands & Steppes

Bandurria Found throughout Patagonia, the bandurria *(Theristicus caudatus)*, or buff-necked ibis, is a large omnivorous bird with a long curved beak and a reddish-yellow neck. Bandurrias are gregarious and are typically seen in flocks of 20 or more birds noisily picking over moist pastures for grass seeds, insects, worms, lizards or frogs. Bandurrias have a distinctive dull call like a car's horn.

Chincol Quite common throughout Patagonia and little bothered by humans, the chincol *(Zonotrichia capensis)* is a distinctive chirpy little bird hard to overlook or overhear, despite its modest size. This insectivorous red-collared sparrow typically lives in scrubland, where its call is audible throughout the day (and even well after sunset), but it migrates to milder coastal climes for the winter. The chincol has two black lateral bands running across the semi-erect feathers of its grey crown, while its wings are coffee-brown and its underbelly is off-white.

Chorlos Several species of chorlo (plovers) live mainly on the eastern side of the Cordillera. The chorlo de doble collar *(Charadrius falklandicus)*, or two-banded plover, is found around inland lakes; it has two black stripes around its white breast. The chorlo de campo *(Eudromias ruficollis)*, or tawny-throated dotterel, inhabits the drier steppes. Plovers belong to the large group of shorebirds known as 'waders', and several species make long-distance migrations.

Cometocino The cometocino *(Phyrgilus gayi)*, or greyhooded sierra finch, is a bluish-grey finch of the steppeland zone. It typically builds its nest among the protective thorny branches of the calafate bush.

Dormilona Rufa The dormilona rufa *(Muscisaxicola capistrata)*, or cinnamon-bellied ground-tyrant, lives in steppe and dry scrubland, nesting in eastern Patagonia and northern Tierra del Fuego but migrating north to over-winter in the central Andes. This small ground-dwelling bird feeds on insects it finds in the soil.

Loica The loica *(Sturnella loyca)*, or long-tailed meadowlark, is found in the semi-arid pastures and steppes on the

Loicas are part of a large family of birds called New World orioles. They build simple grass dome nests, and are best differentiated from closely related species by their call.

Andes' eastern fringe. Its joyful warbling calls can be heard ringing out from bushy thickets, where the loica nests in the shelter from the fierce Patagonian winds. The bird is raven-black, but the male has a fiery red patch stretching from its underbelly up to its beak, and two small red and white streaks above its eyes; only in flight does the loica reveals its white underwings.

Martineta Copetona The martineta copetona, or elegant crested-tinamou *(Eudromia elegans)*, belongs to a group of primitive ground-dwelling birds peculiar to Central and South America. Often hunted for its sweet flesh, this flightless bird has a black pointed crest and a plumage of fine black and ochre stripes that camouflage it well.

Ñandú (or Rhea) The flightless ñandú *(Pterocnemia pennata)* roams the dry steppes of eastern Patagonia, occasionally venturing into the Andean foothills. It is similar to, but smaller than the African ostrich (to which it is distantly related); an adult bird stands around 1.5m high. The ñandú can run very quickly, avoiding its enemies by constantly changing direction as it flees. After the eggs have been laid the male incubates and cares for the chicks.

Birds of the Mountains
Águila Mora The águila mora (or águila chilena, *Geranoaetus melanoleucus)* is known as the black-crested buzzard-eagle in English because of the black shield on the breast of the adult. The águila mora is one of the largest birds of prey in Patagonia, and when flying it is often mistaken for the condor. The águila mora prefers its meat well-dead, but when carrion is scarce the bird will hunt small mammals and sometimes even young lambs.

Carancho Another bird of prey is the carancho, or white-throated caracara *(Phalcoboenus albogularis)*, a species that lives only in the southern Cordillera. It's recognisable by its black head and back, white breast and underbelly, and yellow beak.

Condor The Andean condor *(Sarcorhamphus gryphus)* known to the Mapuche people as the mañque, is found throughout the Andes, building its nests on inaccessible rock ledges that afford easy take off and protection. This rather hideous member of the vulture family is superbly adapted for flight. It has a wingspan of over 2.5m, which apart from the wandering albatross, is the greatest of any flying bird. Often seen soaring around remote mountain peaks, condors are all black except for white feathers on the bird's collar and the tips of its wings. Condors are voracious eaters – a single bird weighing perhaps 8kg can reputedly eat an entire guanaco carcass in a week – and live on carrion or small rodents.

Yal Cordillerano The yal cordillerano *(Melanodera xanthogramma)*, known in English as the yellow-bridled finch, is common in the mountains of northern Patagonia; the male is grey and yellow. After the first falls of snow, the yal cordillerano retreats to the lowland valleys.

The male ñandú builds the nest and leads his hens (sometimes as many as 7 or 8) to it after he has courted and mated with them. Ñandú habitat has shrunk with the advance of agriculture, but ñandús can exist side by side with domestic grazing animals.

The Andean condor has a lengthy breeding cycle and rears young only every alternate year. It is found from sea level to the highest peaks of the Andes.

PEOPLE

The Argentinians

The Argentinians are a cultured and sophisticated people almost entirely of European stock. Since the last century, successive waves of immigrants have given Argentine society a cosmopolitan flavour unique among Latin American nations.

Of these migrants, Italians were easily the most numerous, and their influence is found throughout the country. There are also strong and recognisable elements of British, German and Yugoslav influence. The Argentinians are very outgoing and passionate, with a strong artistic flair. They tend to say what they think with little hesitation, and have a strong sense of identity and national pride that at times verges on outright arrogance and chauvinism.

The Chileans

Bordered by the Atacama Desert in the north and the mighty Cordillera to the east, Chile is geographically cut off from the rest of South America, and Chileans sometimes refer to their isolated country as *el último rincón del mundo*, or 'the last corner of the world'. The result of this isolation was that Chile's European and indigenous peoples mixed gradually to create an overwhelmingly *mestizo* population. The population has been modified relatively little by new arrivals, and the European immigration that shaped Argentina's growth did not occur on anything like the same scale in Chile. Politics notwithstanding, the Chileno is typically a cool-headed and modest person, not given to overly exuberant behaviour. This slightly reserved nature is sometimes considered a

The Mapuche

According to their mythology, the Mapuche – whose name in their own language means simply 'people of the land' – were born of a struggle between the ocean and the mountains. This is an unmistakable reference to the Mapuche heartland – southern Chile's longitudinal valley (which they called Lelfun-Mapu) – a region afflicted by repeated earthquakes, tidal waves, volcanic eruptions and floods.

Archaeological evidence suggests that by 500 BC the Mapuche already existed in southern Chile as a distinct ethnic group, and by the 16th century their population was probably approaching one million. In pre-Columbian times the Mapuche strongly resisted incorporation into the vast central Andean empire of the Incas (who called them Aukas, hence the term Araucarians), and later waged a relentless guerrilla war against the Spanish invaders. At the time of the arrival of the Spanish the Mapuche nation consisted of various loose tribal groupings, such as the Huilliche ('people of the south'), Pehuenche ('araucaria nut-eating people of the mountains') and Lafquenche ('people of the coast'). Their adoption of the horse in the mid 16th century, however, led to a major expansion of the Mapuche language and culture as they migrated eastwards into the northern Patagonian steppes. By the end of the 18th century the Mapuche had largely replaced other (ie non-Mapuche) indigenous peoples.

The Mapuche traditionally lived in small clustered settlements consisting of *rucas* – oval-shaped huts with a timber or bamboo frame and a thatched roof with smoke holes for simple ventilation. Small scale horticulture, fishing, hunting and the gathering of wild foods – most importantly the nuts of the araucaria tree (or pehuén) – kept them well fed and clothed; some Mapuche tribes also practised animal husbandry, herding small flocks of llamas for meat and wool.

The Mapuche were skilled artisans whose handicrafts included pottery, the weaving of plant and animal fibres into cloth, grinding of stone tools and weapons, wood carving and metallurgy – most particularly silverwork. They have long been renowned for their expertise in making silver jewellery. The Mapuche had an intimate knowledge of the native plants, a great many of which had ceremonial or medicinal significance.

In the decentralised Mapuche social structure there was no overall chief. Household heads *(lonkos)* made everyday decisions and in times of war were collectively responsible for electing military commanders. Originally the Mapuche were polytheistic, believing in a hierarchy of gods and goddesses. The Andes, which they called Pire Mapu ('land of snows'), were the abode of the Pillanes, the spiritual ancestors of all Mapuche tribes. Dreams were held to be the means of communicating with the supernatural, and sorcerers *(calcus)* and shamans *(machis)* – who could be male or female, but who must have suffered a prolonged serious illness – were responsible for the interpretation of dreams. They also diagnosed sicknesses, which they treated with herbal remedies or rituals. ■

common destiny among Patagonians than elsewhere within the two countries.

LANGUAGE

Both Argentinians and Chileans speak Spanish, or *castellano*, a term generally preferred in the Americas to *español*. In the cities quite a number of people know some English, but in the countryside this is rare. In certain parts of the south, small but influential communities of German, Italian, English, Croatian and even Welsh settlers continue to speak their languages. In some areas indigenous tongues still survive, the most notable being the Mapuche dialects of the Lake District. Most Mapuche Indians are now able to speak Spanish as well as or better than their traditional languages.

On the whole, Spanish is not difficult, and you should try to gain some knowledge of simple conversational Spanish before you travel. Being able to communicate even at a very basic level with locals will be helpful and satisfying. Because of the common Latin roots in many English and Spanish words, it can be surprisingly easy to understand written Spanish. Spelling follows simple phonetic rules, and pronunciation is not difficult. Despite the common Hispanic colonial past of Chile and Argentina, there are major differences between the forms of Spanish spoken in each country.

Argentine Spanish

Argentine Spanish has some interesting features. Pronunciation and accent have been heavily influenced by Italian immigration, which has given this dialect a pleasant, melodic sound. Vowels are often lengthened and pronunciation is more decisive. Many Italian words have also been absorbed into the national vocabulary. Another strong characteristic of Argentine Spanish is the continued universal usage of the archaic word *vos*, meaning 'you'. *Vos* (pronounced 'boss') completely replaces *tú* as the familiar singular form, and in the present tense requires special verb conjugations such as *vos pagás, vos tenéis, vos sos* ('you pay', 'you have', 'you are'). The Castillian sounds

Lake District farmer– farming has traditionally been the mainstay of Patagonians

sign of their introversion, yet the people of Chile are friendly and hospitable and they possess a sharp and ironic sense of humour.

The Patagonians

Patagonia is the meeting place of Chile and Argentina. The lower average height of the Cordillera in Patagonia has traditionally encouraged movement between the two countries, even in precolonial times. For more than a century, Chileans have migrated east to seek work on Argentine estancias or as labourers in the towns. A great number of the migrants were Chilotes, the mixed-race inhab-itants of the island of Chiloé, who also established settlements along the west Patagonian coast. Until quite recently many of these settlements were accessible only by boat, or via Argentine territory. Even today, a large percentage of the inhabitants of certain Argentine provinces are actually Chilean nationals or their children. Especially noticeable to the visitor is the high proportion of people in Patagonia with distinctly Indian features. Continual contact has left a greater homogeneity and sense of

represented by the letters 'll' and 'y' are either pronounced like a French 'j', as in Jean-Jacques, or more strongly like an English 'j', as in Jessie Jackson.

Chilean Spanish

Chilean Spanish is invariably spoken rapidly, and often has a high-pitched, lilting intonation that makes it immediately recognisable. Having been described as the 'Australians of the Spanish speaking world', many Chileans speak without appearing to move their mouths very much, and often mumble or swallow their words. The habit of some Spanish speakers to drop the letter 's' is almost universal in Chile, making it hard to tell whether nouns are in the singular or plural form. Chileans have developed a great amount of local idiom and slang. Particularly in the south of the country, some Chileans are inclined to pronounce the consonants 'll' and 'y' in a similar way to the Argentinians, though with less force. Don't be too surprised or worried if you have difficulty understanding the Chileans at first.

Patagonian Spanish

The different national forms of Spanish extend more or less right down into Patagonia. Nevertheless, there are certain words and phrases that make the speech of native Patagonians easily recognisable to their northern compatriots. For example the construction *puro ... no más*, instead of simply *puro*, produces phrases like *puro tábanos no más* ('nothing but horse-flies'). Another common tendency is to add *de* to expressions like *a caballo* and *a pié*, giving *de a caballo* and *de a pié* ('by horse', 'on foot').

Naturally, there are also many words of indigenous origin that describe things peculiar to Patagonia, such as *mogote*, referring to the native cushion plants and *puelche*, a warm wind that blows across the steppes from the north. Another example is the Tehuelche word *toldo*, meaning tent, which in modern-day Patagonian Spanish has been extended to produce *toldería*, meaning a camp.

Books

A phrase book and a small pocket dictionary are more or less essential. Avoid material that is based on European Spanish, however, because there is just too much variation (such as the difference between a Spaniard's and an Argentinian's use of the verb *coger*). Surprisingly, neither Chile nor Argentina seems to have a 'national dictionary' (such as the Webster, Macquarie and Oxford dictionaries used in English-speaking countries) to document the locally spoken Spanish. Two popular Spanish/English dictionaries that specifically cover Latin America are *The New World* and *University of Chicago* dictionaries, which are published in cheap paperback forms. Lonely Planet has produced a handy pocket-sized *Latin American Spanish phrasebook*.

Phrases

The following are some useful sentences in Spanish for typical situations in which trekkers may find themselves.

Trek Preparations

Where can we buy supplies?	*¿Dónde podemos comprar víveres?*
Can I leave some things here a while?	*¿Puedo dejar algunas cosas acá por un rato?*
Where can we hire a mountain guide?	*¿Dónde podemos alquilar un guía de montaña?*
I'd like to talk to someone who knows this area.	*Quisiera hablar con álguien que conozca este sector.*
How much do you charge?	*¿Cuánto cobra Usted?*
We are thinking of taking this route.	*Pensamos tomar esta ruta.*
Is the trek very difficult?	*¿Es muy difícil la caminata?*
Is the track (well) marked?	*¿Está (bien) marcado el sendero?*
Which is the shortest/easiest route?	*¿Cuál es la ruta más corta/más fácil?*

Is there much snow on the pass?	*¿Hay mucha nieve en el paso?*
We will return in one week.	*Volverémos (or vamos a volver) en una semana.*

Transport

When does the next bus leave for ...?	*¿Cuándo sale el próximo bus a ...?*
I'd like to charter a boat/taxi.	*Quisiera contratar un bote/remise.*
Come to pick us up in five days.	*Venga a buscarnos en cinco días.*
Can you take me to ...?	*¿Puede llevarme a ...?*
I'd like get off at the turn-off.	*Quisiera bajar en la bifurcación.*
I'll hitchhike.	*Viajo a dedo.*
We're leaving tomorrow.	*Partiremos (vamos a partir) mañana.*

Weather

What will the weather be like?	*¿Qué tiempo hará?*
Tomorrow it will be cold.	*Mañana hará frío.*
It's going to rain.	*Va a llover.*
It's windy/sunny.	*Hace viento/sol.*
It's raining/snowing.	*Está lloviendo/ nevando.*
It has clouded over.	*Se ha nublado.*
The rain slowed us down.	*Nos atrasó la lluvia.*
At what time does it get dark?	*¿A qué hora caye la noche?*

On the Trek

How many km to ...?	*¿Cuántos kilómetros son hasta ...?*
How many hours' walking?	*¿Cuántas horas son caminando?*
Does this track go to ...?	*¿Va este sendero a ...?*
How do you reach the summit?	*¿Cómo se llega a la cumbre?*
Where are you going to?	*¿A dónde va Usted?*
May I cross your property?	*¿Puedo cruzar su propiedad?*

Can you show me on the map where we are?	*¿Puede señalarme en el mapa dónde estamos?*
What is this place called?	*¿Cómo se llama este lugar?*
We're doing a hike from ... to ...	*Estamos haciendo una caminata desde ... a ...*

Camping

Where is the best place to camp?	*¿Dónde está el mejor lugar para acampar?*
Can we put up the tent here?	*¿Podemos armar la carpa acá?*
Is it permitted to make fire?	*¿Está permitido a hacer fuego?*
There is no fire-wood.	*No hay leña.*
I have a gas/petrol stove.	*Tengo una calent-ador (Arg)/anafe (Ch) agas/ bencina.*
I'm going to stay here two days.	*Voy a quedarme dos días aquí.*

Difficulties

Help!	*¡Soccoro!*
Careful!	*¡Cuidado!*
We've lost the way.	*Hemos perdido el camino.*
I'm looking for ...	*Estoy buscando ...*
Is it dangerous?	*¿Es peligroso?*
Can you help me?	*¿Puede ayudarme?*
I'm thirsty/hungry.	*Tengo sed/hambre.*
Can you repair this for me?	*¿Puede arreglarme ésto?*
I don't understand.	*No entiendo.*
Please speak more slowly.	*Por favor, hable más despacio.*

General Conversation

Good morning!	*¡Buenos días!*
Good afternoon!	*¡Buenas tardes!*
Hello!	*¡Hola!*
My name is ...	*Me llamo ...*
What's the time?	*¿Qué hora es?*
Where are you from?	*¿De dónde es Usted?*
Do you live here?	*¿Vive acá?*

Wait for me here.	*Espéreme aquí.*
It's a very beautiful spot.	*Es un lugar muy lindo.*
I'm sightseeing.	*Estoy paseando.*
We're getting to know the area.	*Estamos conociendo.*
See you later!	*¡Hasta luego!*
Goodbye!	*¡Adios!/¡Chau!*
Farewell!	*¡Que le vaya bien!*

Nationalities

The (a) forms are for women.

American	*Estadounidense/ Norte Americano/a*
Argentinian	*Argentino/a*
Australian	*Australiano/a*
Belgian	*Belgo/a*
British	*Britano/a*
Canadian	*Canadiense*
Chilean	*Chileno/a*
Dutch	*Holandés(a)*
English	*Inglés(a)*
French	*Francés(a)*
German	*Alemán(a)*
Irish	*Irlandés(a)*
Israeli	*Israelita*
New Zealander	*Neozelandés(a)*
Scot	*Escocés(a)*
Swede	*Sueco/a*
Swiss	*Suizo/a*
Welsh	*Galés(a)*

Ways of Transit

circuit	*circuito*
highway	*carretera*
path/trail	*sendero/picada/senda*
shortcut	*atajo*
road/vehicle track	*camino*
route (unmarked)	*huella/ruta*
sidewalk/footpath	*vereda*

Artificial Features

border post	*aduana*
bridge/footbridge	*puente/pasarela*
campground	*camping*
caravan park	*autocamping*
ditch	*zanja*
farm	*finca/(Arg) chacra/ (Ch) fundo*
fence	*cerco/alambrado*

firebreak	*cortefuego*
hut/mountain shelter	*refugio*
homestead	*caserío*
house/building	*casa*
jetty/landing pier	*muelle*
lighthouse	*faro*
park entrance	*(Arg) portada/ (Ch) portería*
ranch	*estancia*
ranger station	*guardería*
ski lift/ski tow	*aerosilla/andarrivel*
ski field	*cancha de esquí*
stockyard/corral	*galpón*
town/village	*pueblo/aldea*

Trail Terms

accommodation/ lodgings	*alojamiento*
to arrive	*llegar*
bivouac	*vivac*
to camp	*acampar*
campfire/fireplace	*fogata/fogón*
camping area	*campamento/campismo*
camp site	*sitio/area (de acampar)*
to carry	*llevar*
climb/to climb	*escalada/escalar*
firewood	*leña*
to fish	*pescar*
to follow	*seguir*
ford/wade	*vado*
hike	*caminata/andanza*
mountaineering	*andinismo/alpinismo*
horse ride/by horse	*cabalgata/a caballo*
rubbish	*basura*
signpost	*cartel indicador*
traverse	*traversía*
to walk/go on foot	*caminar/ir a pie*

Clothing & Equipment

altimeter	*altímetro*
anorak/rainjacket	*campera/chaqueta impermeable*
backpack/rucksack	*mochila*
batteries	*pilas/baterías*
billy/cooking pot	*olla*
bootlace	*cordón de bota*
boots	*botas*

camp stove	*cocinilla/(Arg) calentador/ (Ch) anafe*
candles	*velas*
canteen/water bottle	*cantimplora*
cap/beanie	*gorro*
carabiner	*mosquetón*
compass	*brújula*
crampons	*grampones/trepadores*
gaiters	*polainas*
gas cartridge	*cartucha de gas*
gloves	*guantes*
ice axe	*piolet/(Arg) piqueta*
pocketknife	*cortaplumas*
provisions/food supplies	*víveres/abastecimien tos*
runners/tennis shoes	*zapatillas*
rope	*cuerda*
sleeping bag	*saco de dormir*
sleeping mat	*colchoneta aislante*
sunglasses	*gafas de sol*
tent	*carpa*
torch/flashlight	*linterna*
walking stick	*bastón*
white gasoline	*(Arg) nafta blanca/ (Ch) bencina blanca*

Climate & Weather

clear/fine	*despejado*
cloud	*nube*
fog/mist	*neblina/niebla*
frost	*helada*
high/low tide	*altamar/bajamar*
ice	*hielo*
overcast/cloudy	*nublado*
rain/to rain	*lluvia/llover*
snow/to snow	*nieve/nevar*
spring melt/thaw	*deshielo*
storm	*tormenta/tempestad*
summer	*verano*
good/bad weather	*buen/mal tiempo*
whiteout/clag	*borrina/encainada*
wind	*viento*
winter	*invierno*

People

backpacker	*mochilero/a*
foreigner	*extranjero/a (or) gringo/a*
hut warden	*refugiero*
indigenous person/ Indian	*indigena/indio/a*
mountain guide	*guía de montaña/ baquiano*
mountaineer	*andinista*
park ranger	*guardaparque*
police	*(Arg) gendarmería/ (Ch) carabineros*
rancher	*estancionero*
traveller	*viajero*
cowboy	*(Arg) gaucho/ (Ch) huaso*

Vegetation

branch	*rama*
bush/shrub	*arbusto*
flower	*flor*
grass	*pasto*
leaf	*hoja*
lichen	*liquen*
moss	*musgo*
root	*raíz*
tree	*árbol*

Wildlife

beaver	*castor*
cat	*gato*
cow/cattle	*vaca/ganado bovino*
deer	*ciervo*
dog	*perro*
duck	*pato*
eagle	*águila*
fish	*pez*
flea	*pulga*
fly	*mosca*
fox	*zorro*
frog	*sapo/rana*
hare/rabbit	*liebre/conejo*
hawk	*halcón*
horse	*caballo*
horsefly	*tábano*
sheep	*oveja*
swan	*cisne*
seagull	*gaviota*
trout	*trucha*
vulture	*buitre*
wild pig	*jabalí*
woodpecker	*carpintero*

Directions

ahead/behind	*mas adelante/atrás*
adjacent	*al frente/contiguo*
ascent/descent	*subida/bajada*
before/after	*antes/después (de)*
below/above	*debajo/encima de*
beside	*al lado de*
between	*entre*
early/late	*temprano/tarde*
east/west	*este/oeste*
flat/steep	*llano/empinado*
here/there	*aquí/acá/allá*
height/depth	*altura/profundidad*
high/low	*alto/bajo*
(to the) left/right	*(a la) derecha/izquierda*
near/distant	*cerca/lejos*
north/south	*norte/sur*
on the other side of	*al otro lado de*
southern	*austral/meridional*
towards/away from	*hacia/desde*
up/down	*arriba/abajo*

Map Reading

altitude difference	*desnivel*
contour lines	*curvas de nivel*
frontier mark	*hito*
map	*mapa/carta*
metres above sea level	*metros sobre elivel del mar, or 'msnm'*
spot height	*cota*
tree line (timber line)	*nivel del bosque*

Landforms

Andean meadow	*alpage/coironal*
avalanche	*alud/avalancha*
bay/cove	*bahía/caleta*
beach	*playa*
bog/swamp	*pantano/mallín*
branch of a lake/river	*brazo*
brook	*riachuelo*
cairn	*mojón/pirca*
cave	*cueva/caverna*
chasm	*abismo*
cliff	*acantilado/ barranco/farellón*
coast, shoreline	*costa*
(snow) cornice	*cornisa (de nieve)*
crag	*peña/peñón*
crater (of a volcano)	*caldera*
creek/small river	*estero/arroyo*
crevasse	*grieta*
drainage basin	*hoya/cuenca*
face of a mountain	*muralla/vertiente*
fjord/sound	*fiordo/seno*
forest	*bosque*
frontier/border	*frontera/límite*
gap/narrow pass	*portillo/pasada*
glacier	*ventisquero/glaciar*
gorge/canyon	*cajón/barranco/ garganta*
hill	*morro/colina/loma*
hillside/mountain-side	*faldeo/ladera*
iceberg	*témpano*
island	*isla*
lake	*lago/laguna*
landslide	*derrumbe*
location/spot	*lugar/paraje*
lookout	*mirador*
moor	*turbal/mallín*
moraine	*morrena*
mountain chain	*cordillera/cordón*
mountain	*cerro/montaña/monte*
national park	*parque nacional*
outlet stream	*desagüe*
névé/permanent snowfield	*neviza/campo de nieve*
pass	*paso/portezuelo/abra*
pinnacle	*pináculo/ aguja/ diente*
plain/flat terrain	*llanura/planicie*
plateau/tableland	*meseta*
range/massif	*sierra/mazico*
rapid	*catarata*
reserve	*reserva*
riverbank/shoreline	*ribera/orilla*
ridge/spur	*filo/espolón/cresta*
river	*río/quebrada*
river bed	*cauce/lecho*
scoria	*escoria*
scrub/underbrush	*matorral/sotobosque*
slope/rise	*cuesta/pendiente*
source of a stream	*nacimiento*
spring	*fuente/manantial*
steppe/plain	*estepa/pampa*
stone/rock	*piedra*
strait	*estrecho*

stream junction	*horqueta/confluencia*
summit/peak	*cumbre/cima/pico*
thermal springs	*termas/aguas calientes*
torrent/gushing stream	*chorro*
valley	*valle*
volcano	*volcán*
waterfall	*salto (de agua)/ cascada*

Essential Mapuche & Tehuelche

Although there's absolutely no need to learn any Mapuche or Tehuelche, the significance of certain place names (particularly in the Araucanía and Lake District) will be clearer if you can decipher a few words of indigenous origin. Two good locally available dictionaries are the *Diccionario Mapuche Español* (Siringa Libros, Neuquén), a reprint of a 1944 work compiled by P Ernesto Wilhelm de Moesbach, and the *Diccionario Lingüístico-Ethnográfico de la Lengua Mapuche* (Editorial Andrés Bello, Santiago de Chile), a very recent Mapuche-Spanish-English title by the prominent Chilean linguist Maria Catrileo.

Most spellings given below are as used in local place names (which reflect Spanish phonetics), and some spellings differ both in orthography and pronunciation to the original Mapuche.

antü	sun/day
buta	large/great
cacique	Indian chief
calfu	blue
cautín	a native duck
che	people
co	water
coli/colu	brown

copa	green
cuel	hill
cura	rock/stone
cuy cuy	log bridge
filu	snake
futa	big
gol	stake/stick/pole
huapi	island
hue	place/location
hueico	tiny lake/puddle
huille	south
huiqui	thrush
iñim	bird
lafquén	sea/lake/plain
leufú	river
lemu	forest
llanca	a semi-precious blue stone
lonco	head
mapu	land
mahuida/mavida	mountain
mallín	moor
mañque	condor
mapu	land/earth
milla	gold
nahuel	tiger/jaguarete
ñamcu	eagle
ñiri	fox
pangi	puma
poco	frog
pile/pilén	frost/ice
pire	snow
pillán	volcano
puelche	warm northerly wind in Patagonia
púlli	mountainside
quilla	moon
repú	path/track
traful	confluence/river junction
tromén	cloud
tue	ground/soil

Facts for the Trekker

General Information

PLANNING

Before you depart, work out a rough but realistic itinerary including the areas that interest you most. If you're planning an extended trekking trip to southern Chile and Argentina, crossing a number of times between the two countries is likely to be the most time-efficient and interesting way to go.

Travel Maps

Travel maps for Patagonia are sold at newspaper kiosks or bookshops in Chile and/or Argentina, but it can sometimes be hard to get good up-to-date travel or road maps that properly cover both Chilean and Argentine Patagonia. One locally available map that features the road links between the two countries is the *Rutas Entre Chile y Argentina*, published by Inupal and available for around US$11.

In Chile, a good general road map covering all of the country is the *Gran Mapa Caminero de Chile* published by Inupal (US$11). Another good source of excellent motoring maps is the *Turistel Sur* (see Travel Guidebooks under the Books heading below) which contains excellent maps.

The best overview of Argentine Patagonia is the 1:1,000,000 road map *Patagonia y Tierra del Fuego*, which includes plans of nine major regional cities. Published by Automapa, it costs around US$12. For US$8 you could also buy the map *Patagonia Sur – Tierra del Fuego*, published by Juan Luis Matissi A Producciones, which shows the area of Southern Patagonia and Tierra del Fuego at a scale of 1:1,250,000. Argentina's national car club, the ACA, sells road maps of each province at various scales. Automapa publishes a good general travel map for Argentina scaled at 1:2,500,000.

For a description of topographical sheets suitable for mountain navigation, see Trekking Maps following.

When to Go

Although it can be shortened considerably at the whim of the elements, the trekking season in the Patagonian Andes lasts a maximum of six months. It begins in mid November and can continue until mid May, by which time the southern winter is really beginning to bite. Although each month has its own particular charms and drawbacks, for a balance of convenience and weather, February and March are overall the best two months for a trekking trip to the Patagonian Andes.

Following is a brief outline of each season.

Spring Spring in Patagonia begins in early September and continues to about late November, coming first to the Araucanía and Lake District because of those regions' more northerly latitudes. Lower-level routes are usually passable as early as late October, when the first wild flowers are coming out, but there is usually too much snow on the higher ranges to undertake more adventurous treks at this time. Snow-fed streams may also still be impassable and weather tends to be unpredictable.

Summer The Patagonian summer lasts from early December to late February. As the sun's intensity increases the weather becomes more settled, bringing often quite hot weather in northern and central Patagonia. At this time temperatures in the mountains occasionally even rise above 30°C, though farther south days tend to be milder.

During the busy local holiday season (January and February), transport and accommodation is often heavily booked, which may interfere with your travel plans. On the other hand, tourist services and public transport in some areas start to wind down after about the end of February. Another seasonal problem is the tábanos, swarms of blood-sucking horseflies that harass trekkers on low-level routes in the Araucanía and Lake District; they are generally at their worst during January.

Autumn The early autumn period (March to mid-April) typically brings cooler but slightly more stable weather. The red-gold colours of deciduous native tree species make this an especially pleasant time to trek. Towards the middle of May the days become short and temperatures fall steadily, yet conditions are often still suitable for trekking in the Araucanía and Lake District. Parties undertaking treks at this time should be equipped for possible heavy snowfalls.

Winter Heavy winter snow covers the Patagonian Andes from about early June at least until late September, when excursions into the mountains are strictly reserved for the very experienced (or the supremely foolhardy). Snowshoe treks up to the volcanic plateaus of the Araucanía and Lake District, which offer marvellous cross-country skiing, are an exciting possibility. However such activities require special skills and equipment, and are well outside the scope of this book.

Weather Information Weather in the Patagonian Andes is so fickle and localised that official forecasts should only be considered as a general indication of what to expect on your trek. The Santiago daily *El Mercurio* is available throughout Chile and contains (in the newspaper's 'C' section) a national four-day weather report covering all of the country's 12 regions. The information is presented in enough graphic detail to make the overall weather outlook fairly clear even to people with little knowledge of Spanish. Of course local newspapers also include local forecasts, although they rarely give longer than a two-day outlook.

TOURIST OFFICES
National airlines and the embassies/consulates of Chile and Argentina represent the tourist offices abroad. In both countries well organised tourist offices *(oficinas de turismo)* exist, and during the summer months (December to February) often operate in even quite small towns. Staff are generally helpful and sometimes have a smattering of English. Local tourist offices can supply lists covering accommodation in all price ranges; tourist maps and pamphlets are generally available free of charge.

DOCUMENTS
Your vital documents should be treated as valuables and kept in a safe place. Carry them with you on the trek – *don't* leave them with your other stored luggage. Ensure that your documents are kept completely dry (and out of sight) by storing them in a watertight bag or container – most backpacks have a 'hidden' compartment under the top flap for such uses.

Passports
Ensure that your passport has a *minimum* of six months validity before you travel. Consulates and embassies will otherwise not issue visas, and you may even be refused entry at borders. Carry your passport with you on all treks; you may need it as identification (particularly in areas close to the international frontier); at times you may be required to deposit your passport with the national park authorities.

Visas
Entry requirements may change over time and you should check on the current situation before departing. Multiple entry visas are the most convenient for travel in Patagonia, as you will probably want to cross between Chile and Argentina a number of times. Visas are not issued at borders, but must be obtained beforehand from embassies or consulates.

Chile Tourist visas for Chile are not required by citizens of most countries. Holders of Australian, British, Canadian, Irish, Japanese, Singaporean, South African, US and all west European (now including French) passports *do not* need visas. New Zealanders, however, *do* require visas. Upon arrival in Chile you receive an entry stamp which allows you to stay for 90 days. This can be renewed for a further 90 days. To stay in Chile longer than six months, it is usually easiest to travel to Argentina and then re-enter Chile.

Argentina Visas for Argentina are *not* required by British, Canadian, Irish, Japanese, US and citizens of most west European (and some Latin American) countries. Australians, New Zealanders, Singaporeans and South Africans *do* need visas. Argentine tourist visas are generally valid for 90 days from the first date of entry and can be renewed for an additional 90 days. To stay in Argentina longer than six months, travel to Chile (or any other neighbouring country) and get a new visa issued before re-entering.

Travel Insurance

All travellers should take out basic health and travel insurance before they leave. Ensure that adequate cover is given for all the activities you intend doing on your trip. Standard travel insurance policies usually cover trekking, but often exclude the more dangerous mountain sports such as roped climbing or river rafting.

Other Documents

Always carry photocopies of your passport and air ticket (separate from the actual documents), as your embassy or airline will be able to replace these documents if they get lost or damaged. Carrying a few additional passport photos (for visa applications) or other identification is also a good idea. Consider taking out an international driving licence – even if you have no intention of driving a car during your trip. Don't forget your list of essential addresses and telephone numbers.

CUSTOMS

Non-resident foreigners arriving in Chile and Argentina are generally waved through at Customs posts, but occasionally rigorous spot checks are made. The key to easy customs clearance is *never* to carry firearms

(or other dangerous weapons), illegal drugs or more than the maximum allowance of any merchandise subject to import duty. *Never* carry flammable substances (such as fuel for backpacking stoves) on aircraft or buses.

South America is the main source of world cocaine production, and international drug couriers have been known to board flights out of Buenos Aires (or less often Santiago) to Europe, North America or Australasia. For this reason trekkers may well find their baggage subject to special customs scrutiny upon arrival in their home countries.

MONEY

In Latin America the US dollar is the universal shadow currency, and even strong major European currencies (such as sterling and Deutschmark) are difficult to change outside Buenos Aires and Santiago. All prices in this guidebook are quoted in US$.

Currencies
Currency Exchange

Current approximate exchange rates follow:

Australia	A$1	=	Ch$300	Arg$0.72
Canada	C$1	=	Ch$300	Arg$0.72
France	FF1	=	Ch$68.2	Arg$0.16
Germany	DM1	=	Ch$229	Arg$0.55
New Zealand	NZ$1	=	Ch$263	Arg$0.63
UK	UK£1	=	Ch$656	Arg$1.58
USA	US$1	=	Ch$414	Arg$1.00

Chile The Chilean unit of currency is the peso (Ch$). Notes come in denominations of 500, 1000, 5000 and 10,000 pesos. Coins are in one, five, 10 and 100 peso denominations. Chile has historically very low inflation of around 6% per annum, and the Chilean peso is now regarded as one of Latin America's most secure currencies. At the time of writing the peso had a conversion rate of approximately US$1 = Ch$400.

Argentina After experiencing ruinous hyperinflation (approaching an annual rate of 8000%) in the late 1980s, Argentina abandoned the worthless austral and reintroduced the traditional Latin American peso as part of a comprehensive currency reform. Since then the annual inflation rate has averaged little more than 2%, and the national treasury's strict monetary policy has kept the Argentine peso pegged to the US$ at a rate of 1:1. In Argentina it is usually acceptable to pay directly with US$ notes (but not with coins).

Organising Your Money

The only really secure way of carrying your money is in the form of US$ travellers' cheques. Unfortunately, in remote areas of southern Chile and Argentina exchanging travellers' cheques for a reasonable rate is not always easy. Exchange rates are worse for travellers' cheques and (additional) heavy commissions are often charged, particularly in Argentina.

To avoid this expense and inconvenience, some travellers carry a sizeable cash reserve of US$ and/or pesos to cover their travel expenses between the bigger cities. Large amounts of cash should always be kept in a discrete money belt, perhaps with a portion kept separately in another inconspicuous place.

One way to avoid carrying too much cash is to use a credit card. In both Chile and Argentina, MasterCard is the most widely accepted credit card, followed by Visa. American Express and Diners' Club are also valid in many places. Note that there is sometimes a surcharge for paying by credit card; stores in Argentina often give a discount for cash payments instead.

The risk of being robbed while trekking in the Patagonian Andes is very low, so unless you're absolutely certain your hotel's storage room is even safer it's probably better to carry all valuables with you on the trek. Particularly in the parks of Torres del Paine and Nahuel Huapi, trekkers will find low-denomination notes in pesos handy for paying hut fees etc.

Costs & Budgeting

Since the 1991 currency reform Argentina has become the most expensive country in Latin America. With its booming economy and rapidly rising standard of living, Chile is no longer the travel bargain it once was either, so keeping to your budget may be as much of a challenge as the treks you do.

Prices for most things in Chile are now considerably lower than in Argentina (though in both countries prices tend to increase the farther south you go). In southern Chile a bed in a cheap pensión would typically cost around US$10 (including breakfast) while a simple meal in a restaurant might cost as little as US$6. In Argentina you'll generally pay at least US$15 for comparable accommodation, and a single cup of (espresso) coffee costs US$3.

Travellers can keep costs down by staying only at budget places and preparing their own meals wherever possible. *Hospedajes* and *casas de familia* (see Accommodation) often have cooking facilities for guests. Camping grounds are cheap, especially in Argentina where you'll pay only a few dollars per person. Stock up at supermarkets in the major regional centres rather than at more expensive shops near the start of the trek. People crossing from Chile into Argentina will save money by bringing plenty of food with them (but avoid carrying fresh fruit or vegetables). Remember that in southern Argentina flying is often cheaper than taking a bus.

At times it's worth bargaining for your hotel room, charter boat or taxi, but don't expect to beat the starting price down by more than about 20%. For obvious reasons, the more time you spend in the wilds the cheaper your trekking holiday will be, but the *minimum* you can realistically budget for per month is around US$350 in Chile and US$500 in Argentina.

POST & COMMUNICATIONS
Postal Services

Although the postal services in Chile and Argentina are decidedly better than in most other Latin American countries, they are inefficient by the standards of Western Europe and North America. To the dismay of philatelists, post offices in both countries often use franking machines instead of stamps. Bulky or heavy items not needed en route can be sent ahead to a post restante address and collected later, and bus companies will also transport unaccompanied baggage *(encomiendas)* for a reasonable fee, though usually not across international borders.

Chile Although delivery is slow, Chile's postal service is fairly dependable. Postage rates for letters and parcels are reasonable. The post restante *(lista de correos)* service is quite well organised, but mail is normally only kept for 30 days and there is a small charge for each article of mail collected.

Argentina The Argentine postal service is expensive and unreliable. Mail sometimes gets 'lost' in transit, so anything of value is best dispatched from Chile. The same goes for the post restante system.

Telephone
In both countries – particularly Chile – the telephone systems have been the subject of enormous restructuring during the last decade or so.

Chile Chile's privatised and intensely competitive telecommunications market is now one of the fastest-growing in the world, with a completely digitised telephone system that is by far the best in Latin America. There are eight major telecom companies – the five biggest being CTC, ENTEL, TelexChile, VTR and Bell South – who wage periodic price wars for market share. Long-distance callers are free to choose whichever telephone company they want by dialling its special access code before making the call.

At times the lowest discount rate to the United States may be as little as US$0.35 per minute; the lowest rates to Europe and Australasia are substantially higher, though still quite cheap by international standards. In order to take full advantage of the discount rates, however, callers have to dial from a private phone as well as know when, and through which company, to call. Rates at company telephone centres, which can be found in even the smallest towns, are more

expensive. Public telephones in Chile accept coins, phonecards and/or credit cards.

ENTEL is the only telephone company that does not charge an up-front fee for international collect/reverse-charge calls *(cobro revertido* in Spanish); collect/reverse-charge calls can be made (from any public or private phone) through ENTEL's toll-free number ☎ 800-800-123.

Argentina Despite the break-up and privatisation of the state telecommunications monopoly, ENTEL, in the early 1990s – into two separate companies, Telefónica and Telecom – Argentina's telephone system remains antiquated, overloaded and expensive. With major new investments in telecommunications technology there should be a dramatic improvement in the coming years. Most public telephones use tokens (called *fichas* or *cospeles)*, available from newspaper kiosks; some also accept phonecards and (in theory) credit cards.

Long-distance calls are best made from a telephone centre. In Argentina, where there is little difference between the peak and off-peak rates, you will pay around US$3 per minute to call the United States – up to ten times the discount rate in neighbouring Chile! Telefónica, which operates in southern Argentina, will not allow the reverse-charge/collect calls to certain countries (eg Switzerland).

BOOKS
Locally printed books tend to have small print runs, and are therefore expensive and quickly go out of print. A wide-ranging list of interesting and useful titles in English and Spanish follows.

Travel Guidebooks in English
Lonely Planet publishes *Argentina Uruguay & Paraguay* by Wayne Bernhardson, which covers the whole of Argentina and is a useful adjunct to this guidebook.

Another of Lonely Planet's titles is *Chile & Easter Island,* again by Wayne Bernhardson. It is a practical and detailed guidebook to travelling in Chile.

Lonely Planet's *South America on a shoe-*

string by Wayne Bernhardson et al gives a good overall coverage of the region. It contains a number of comprehensive and useful maps to all of the main cities and many of the regional towns in South America.

Chile and Easter Island by Gerry Leitner is also a detailed guidebook to Chile.

Travel Guidebooks in Spanish

Guía Ilustrada – Sur by Federico Kirbus (El Ateneo, Buenos Aires). This is a good locally produced handbook covering Argentina's Patagonian provinces, and it is available in Argentine bookshops, retailing for around US$20.

Turistel Sur, Turismo y Comunicaciones S.A., Santiago is an excellent tourist guide to southern Chile, and costs around US$10. *Turistel Sur* is revised annually and is published in both Spanish and English editions (although the English-language edition is somewhat more difficult to find). Although this book caters first and foremost to motor tourists, it does include several good suggestions for trekking excursions and is otherwise well worth buying just for its excellent colour maps.

Adventure Travel

Baja to Patagonia by Larry Rice (Fulcrum Publishing, Colorado, 1993). This is an adventure travel narrative at its best, with descriptions of climbing, kayaking and trekking trips in Latin America, and the book gives Patagonia more than its fair share of coverage.

An Englishman in Patagonia by John Pilkington (Century, 1991). A highly informative narrative by this well-known trekker-traveller who makes a point of getting off the beaten track.

In Patagonia by Bruce Chatwin (Jonathan Cape). A fascinating and engaging introduction to the people who inhabit the vast Patagonian steppes. Already a Patagonian classic.

The Longest Walk by George Meegan. An account of the author's exhaustive trek from Alaska to the southern tip of South America.

The Totorore Voyage by Gerry Clark (Century, 1988). The story of a circumnavigation of Antarctica by yacht. The voyagers spent considerable time exploring the remote fjords and channels of the west Patagonian coast.

Back to Cape Horn by Rosie Swale (Collins, 1986). The story of the author's journey through Chile on horseback. Rosie Swale spent over a year riding from Antofagasta to Cape Horn. Many treks, including some described in this guidebook, can be undertaken on horseback and her book makes a blueprint for novice riders as well as being a good read.

Exploration & History

Voyage of the Beagle by Charles Darwin (London, first published 1839). Essential reading for all travellers to South America, this fascinating story tells of the journey during which Darwin began to develop the theory of natural selection. The author's insight is remarkable for his time.

Idle Days in Patagonia by William Henry Hudson (Dutton & Co, first published 1917). In his classic book this famous British ornithologist recounts his travels in Patagonia in the first decades of the 20th century. Hudson – that's as in Volcán Hudson – also wrote half a dozen other books about his bouts of birding in (southern) South America.

Attending Marvels, A Patagonian Journal by George Gaylord Simpson (American Museum of Natural History, first published 1930). Another title by a well-known US scientist who spent considerable time reconnoitring the Patagonian Andes.

Through the Heart of Patagonia by H Hesketh (Pritchard, first published in 1902). This book deals with the author's explorations in Argentine Patagonia in the late 19th century.

The Uttermost Part of the Earth by E Lucas Bridges. This is the fascinating story of the pioneering Bridges family, who established Estancia Harberton, the first farm in southern Tierra del Fuego.

Land of the Tempest by Eric Shipton. An account of this famous explorer's expeditions in the southern Andes in the 1960s.

Tierra del Fuego by Natalie Prosser Goodall. A general but thorough history of the Isla Grande from pre-European times to the present. The book has a bilingual text in Spanish and English and is available from bookshops in Buenos Aires and southern Argentina.

From The Falklands To Patagonia by Michael Mainwaring (Allison & Bushby, 1983). The story of the Halliday family, who resettled from the Malvinas/Falkland Islands to the Patagonian pampa earlier in the century. Especially interesting are chapters dealing with the Tehuelche Indian tribes and Patagonian fauna.

Mountaineering

Andes Patagónicos by Alberto de Agostini (Buenos Aires, 1941, Italian edition, Milan, 1946). This classic work by one of Patagonia's great Andean expeditioners, Father Alberto de Agostini (see aside), is an atlas of the central and southern Patagonian Andes.

The Springs of Enchantment by John Earle (Hodder & Stoughton, 1981). The story of two climbing expeditions to the mountains of Chilean Tierra del Fuego in 1963 and 1979. They achieved a number of first ascents of major peaks in the savage Darwin Range.

The Cockleshell Journey by John Ridgeway (Hodder & Stoughton, 1974). This book is an excellent account of an expedition by inflatable raft through the channels and fjords of southern Patagonia and Tierra del Fuego. It culminated in the first crossing of the small icecap Gran Campo Nevado.

Patagonia: Dreamland for Climbers and Trekkers by Gino Buscaini & Silvia Metzeltin (Bruckman, Munich, 1990). An excellent introduction to the southern Patagonian Andes with many colour photos and maps. The book is primarily concerned with mountaineering and the history of Patagonian exploration. Editions in German and Italian only.

General Natural History

The Whispering Land by Gerald Durrell (Penguin, 1971). A narrative which introduces the fauna and marine life of eastern Patagonia as well as other areas of Argentina.

Flight of the Condor by Michael Andrews (Collins/BBC, 1982). Arguably the best layperson's introduction to wildlife of the Andean Cordillera. The first five chapters cover the continent's southernmost regions.

Patagonia Wilderness by Marcelo Beccaceci and Bonnie Hayskar (Pangea, 1991). This book is an excellent photographic collection that introduces the wildlife and landscapes of Argentine Patagonia. The accompanying English-language text is informative, if rather scant.

Chile's Native Forests: A Conservation Legacy by Ken Wilcox, (North Atlantic Books/NW Wild Books, 1996). A book that deals in depth with the ecosystems of southern Chile and the conservation issues facing its forests.

Bosques de Chile/Chile's Woodlands by Jürgen Rottmann (IGES, Santiago de Chile). The first volume of the excellent Naturaleza de Chile/Chilean Wildlife series, this book with dual Spanish/English text outlines the plants and animals typically found in the forests of the southern Andes. It has numerous outstanding colour photos, but at around US$55 it's a bit expensive for a work of only 100 pages.

La Patagonia Chilena/Chilean Patagonia by Jürgen Rottmann and Thomas Daskam (IGES, Santiago de Chile). At least as good (and expensive) as the above work, this is the second volume of the Naturaleza/Chilean Wildlife series. It features Patagonian landscapes, but also outlines many endemic species.

Aguas Interiores de Chile/Chile's Inland Water Realms by Jürgen Rottmann and Nicolas Piwonka (IGES, Santiago de Chile). This is the third volume of the Naturaleza de Chile/Chilean Wildlife series. Its bilingual text covers flora and fauna found near Chile's freshwater bodies.

Los Andes Chilenos/The Chilean Andes by Jürgen Rottmann and Nicolas Piwonka (IGES, Santiago de Chile). This is the seventh volume of the Naturaleza/Chilean Wildlife series.

Flora & Fauna Field Guides

The following field guides were available at the time of research and most should remain in print for some time.

Apuntes sobre la Fauna Argentina by Raul Leonardo Carman (Vásquez Mazzini Editores, Buenos Aires). Written by a notable Argentine naturalist, this work focuses on Argentina's fauna, ranging from the condor to the puma. It contains good colour photos.

Moluscos Australes by Sandra Gordillo (Zagier y Urrutia, Buenos Aires). Although suited more to Patagonian beachcombers than to Andean trekkers, this guidebook in Spanish covers shellfish (plus the odd kelp or crab species) found along Argentina's Atlantic coast.

Hongos de los Bosques Andino-Patagónicos by Irma Gamundi and Egon Horak (Vazquez Mazzini Editores, Buenos Aires). A recommended Spanish-language guide to native fungi of the (Argentine) Patagonian Andes; it includes edible species of mushroom.

Cien Aves Argentinas by Pablo Canevari and Tito Narosky (Editorial Albatros, Buenos Aires). A good Spanish-language field guide for amateur ornithologists that includes colour photos of 100 native birds of Argentina.

Field Guide to the Birds of Chile by Braulio Araya M and Guillermo Millie H (Editorial Universitaria, Santiago de Chile). This field guide contains accurate illustrations and some good colour photographs of the 339 species of birds found in Chile. It costs around US$25 and can be hard to find. The original Spanish-language edition is much more widely available.

Aves de Magallanes by Claudio Venegas (Ediciones de la Universidad de Magallanes, Punta Arenas). Although it only covers birds found in Chile's XII Region (Magallanes), this field guide is useful for the Patagonian Andes in general. The colour illustrations are of a high standard, and this book is good value at around US$30.

Árboles Nativos de Chile by Claudio Donoso Zegers (Marisa Cúneo Ediciones, Santiago de Chile). A handy little field guide (published under the auspices of the Chilean CONAF) to the native trees of Chile with text in Spanish and English.

Arbustos Nativos de Chile by Claudio Donoso Zegers (Marisa Cúneo Ediciones, Santiago de Chile). A companion to the above work, this booklet deals with the species of bushes commonly found throughout Chile.

Flora Silvestre de Chile – zona araucana, by Adriana E Hoffmann J (Ediciones Fundación Claudio Gay, Santiago de Chile). Written (in Spanish) by one of Chile's most eminent botanists and leading conservationists, this is a comprehensive field guide to the flora of the Araucanía and Lake District. The book has excellent colour illustrations of 250 different species of trees, bushes and wild flowers, but (inevitably) it omits many important plants. It is available in better Chilean bookshops for around US$25, and is highly recommended to anyone with an interest in the flora of the Patagonian Andes.

Flora Silvestre de Chile – zona central, by Adriana E Hoffmann J (Ediciones Fundación Claudio Gay, Santiago de Chile). Identical to the above publication in format and price, this is another excellent Spanish-language field guide to Chile's central zone. Although the book's coverage – the area extending several hundred kilometres north and south of Santiago – theoretically excludes Patagonia, this work includes many species of plants that range southwards into the Araucanía, Lake District or farther still.

Flora Patagonica by R Kiesling (Edición del Autor, Buenos Aires). An excellent Spanish-language field guide covering the flora of Argentine Patagonia. This work is hard to find in local bookstores.

National Park Guides

Chile, sus Parques Nacionales y otras areas naturales (Incafo SA, Madrid). A now incomplete but very worthwhile catalogue of Chilean national parks and nature reserves. This large format book contains many excellent colour photographs.

The National Parks of Argentina and other natural areas (Incafo SA, Madrid). An

English-language version of Incafo's Argentina guide (a series which covers the national parks of a number of Latin American countries), although it's not quite as good as its Chilean counterpart. It is available from bookshops in Buenos Aires – though at US$130 you'll surely want to put it straight back onto the bookshelf once you've had a good look at it.

South America's National Parks by William Leitch (The Mountaineers, Seattle). Although it covers national parks all over South America, this book covers those in southern Chile and Argentina well.

A View of Torres del Paine by G Nancul & O Nenen. A bilingual guidebook (English and Spanish) covering Chile's Parque Nacional Torres del Paine; emphasis is on wildlife.

Lago Argentino y Glaciar Perito Moreno by Miguel Angel Alonso (Zagier y Urruty, Buenos Aires). A translated version of the original Spanish-language edition, this informative book on Argentina's Los Glaciares area in southern Patagonia covers everything from glacier formation, geology, local history, and flora and fauna in just 120 pages.

Trekking Guides in English

Backpacking in Chile & Argentina by Hilary Bradt et al (Bradt Publications, UK, 1994). The only other trekking guidebook available in English that includes treks in Patagonia.

Adventure Handbook of Southern South America by Emilio Urruty (Zagier & Urruty, PO Box 526806 Miami, FL 33152-6806, USA). Although often decidedly vague on specifics, this is a worthwhile guidebook offering numerous suggestions for outdoor trips in the wilds of Patagonia (and elsewhere). A translated Spanish-language version of this title is widely available in bookshops in Argentina for around US$28.

Trekking Guides in Spanish

Patagonia – Guía de Trekkings y Excursiones by Clem Lindenmayer (SUA Edizoak, Bilbao, Spain, 1994). This is a translated Spanish-language version of the 1st edition of this very guidebook. Surprisingly few – if any – bookshops in Chile and Argentina seem to stock it.

Las Montañas de Bariloche by Toncek Arko (San Carlos de Bariloche, renewed periodically). A guidebook in Spanish on treks in the mountains of Parque Nacional Nahuel Huapi.

Miscellaneous

Andes Patagónicos – Imágines de un Sueño by Lucas Chiappe. A photographer's look at the alternative lifestyle scene in the valleys of the Patagonian Andes in Argentina.

Mapuche Silver by Raúl Morris von Bennewitz (Editorial Kaktus, Santiago de Chile). An English-language 'coffee table' book on the unique jewellery and other traditional items that the Mapuche people made (and continue to make) from silver.

Los Ríos Más Australes de la Tierra by Werner Schad (Marymar, Buenos Aires, 1983). The author has written other titles on canoeing and rafting the numerous wild rivers of Patagonia. In this book Schad has produced an informal guidebook to 23 river trips on both sides of the Cordillera. (The publisher, Editorial Marymar, has also published other titles which concentrate on Patagonian exploration).

MAGAZINES

The *South American Explorer* is an English-language quarterly published by the South American Explorers Club . The *South American Explorer* has articles dealing with a wide range of topics such as scientific research, local culture, history, adventure travel or book reviews. Although most issues focus on the continent's northern and central regions (particularly Peru, Bolivia and Ecuador), from time to time the magazine also includes interesting material on Patagonia.

Argentina's monthly *Aire y Sol* is a general outdoors magazine. It features articles (in Spanish) on anything from sport fishing and hunting to ski-touring and canoeing, but it also regularly includes tips on trekking and climbing in the Andes. It's available all over Argentina and costs $US4.50 per issue. Another worthwhile Argentine magazine is *Alta Montaña*, a bimonthly mainly for andinists and other mountain-goers that costs US$6 per issue. The biannual magazine *Patagonia* has reasonably interesting articles (in Spanish and English) on travel in southern Argentina. It's available for US$9 per issue from local newspaper kiosks or bookstores throughout the region.

TIME

Chilean time is four hours behind UTC/GMT while Argentine time is three hours behind UTC/GMT. (Incidentally, it may surprise readers to learn that Santiago, although situated on the *west* coast of South America, is actually one hour ahead of New York on the *east* coast of North America. The reason for this is that the South American continent's relative position on the globe is a long way east of North America).

In both Chile and Argentina daylight saving operates approximately from mid-October to early March, making Summer Time one additional hour later in each country. The problems are that Chile and Argentina don't make the seasonal changeover to summer time simultaneously and that the changeover varies from year to year.

ELECTRICITY

Chile and Argentina use the same round, twin-pronged power plug, and run a 220-volt current. This means you can use devices that need mains electricity in either country. Today, even the smallest and most isolated townships have a reliable electricity supply.

LAUNDRY

All larger towns in Chile and Argentina have modern and affordable laundry services where trekkers can get their sweaty dirties washed properly by machine for around US$8 per three kg load. You can often just drop your clothes off and pick them up half a day later fresh and neatly folded. In Argen-

tina, the *Laverap* launderette chain is the largest, but there are independent laundries.

WOMEN TREKKERS

With the exception of the larger urban centres, Patagonia is at least as safe for women travellers as Europe, North America and Australasia. Although attitudes to women are still not as progressive as those in most western countries, Chilean and especially Argentine women are relatively independent and self-assertive by Latin American standards. Even on longer routes it's not uncommon for local women (generally in pairs or small groups) to trek unaccompanied by men.

TREKKING WITH CHILDREN

Because of the lack of huts and other en route infrastructure, most overnight treks in the Patagonian Andes require packing a full range of camping gear. This makes it impractical and at times unsafe for parents to carry the additional weight of a tired, bored child on their backs. Overnight trekking with young children should therefore be limited to shorter-distance routes and day walks.

Children walk more slowly and need more frequent rest stops than adults. A simple rule-of-thumb for gauging what kids can comfortably handle is to use their age to get the distance (in kilometres) and to halve it to get the load (in kg); eg a 10-year-old should be happy to trek for about 10km per day in moderate terrain carrying a pack of 5kg. Children like to carry their own packs, and cheap children's packs are widely available (including locally), but an adjustable day pack would probably be suitable as well. Half-length sleeping bags used by mountaineers are of better quality than most kids' sleeping bags.

Remember that children are very sensitive to environmental extremes. This makes them more prone to hypothermia, heat stroke, heat exhaustion and sunburn. Children do not acclimatise to high altitudes as easily as adults, so they are more susceptible to altitude sickness (see the Health chapter).

Lonely Planet's *Travel with Children* contains tips for parents travelling with kids.

GENERAL SECURITY

Although you should never get too complacent about security, Chile and Argentina are unquestionably safer places for foreigners than certain countries immediately to their north. Serious incidents such as assaults are rare outside large cities, and almost unheard of in the countryside. The risk of robbery can be minimised by wearing an inconspicuous money belt under your clothes. In busy places such as bus and train stations, keep cameras and other valuable items out of sight and avoid putting your bag down. Don't pack valuables in the top of your rucksack and use small padlocks to deter petty theft. On the whole trekkers are an honest and upright bunch, so you're least likely to be a victim of theft or other crime while hiking up in the mountains.

DANGERS & ANNOYANCES
Emergencies

Before setting out, read through the route description carefully to decide whether you are sufficiently fit, well enough equipped and have the necessary experience to do the trek safely. Leave the details of the persons in your party, intended trekking routes and your expected date and time of return with national park authorities or police. Where possible stick to your previously specified route.

You should also avoid trekking alone. Two is the minimum number for a safe walking party, and at least one additional person in the group will enable someone to stay with an injured trekker while another goes to seek help. When in remote areas, special care should be taken to avoid accidents.

Be prepared to turn back or wait if you encounter weather-related or physical difficulties. Exercise caution when using potentially dangerous devices like petrol stoves, sharp knives and machetes. All trekkers should have a basic knowledge of current first aid practices and carry adequate medical supplies for treating injuries.

Remember that in an emergency help may be several days' trek away. Border posts, ranger stations, police or military installations and larger estancias generally have two-way radios. If absolutely necessary they will probably be able to organise the evacuation of an injured walker. Depending on how this is done, you may be asked to contribute all or a large part of the cost of the rescue.

River Crossings

Only a few of the treks described in this guidebook involve a serious river crossing, as most large streams have bridges. Trekking parties should nevertheless be well practised in river crossing techniques. Where possible, wade at the bottom of a long pool to avoid being swept off your feet by the current. If necessary link arms with other party members and use a heavy tree branch to stabilise the group, crossing the stream with the branch in line with the flow of water. Ropes are sometimes useful for crossing narrow streams, but the rope itself may entangle and endanger a wading trekker.

Fast-flowing glacial streams call for the greatest caution as fine sediment often clouds the water, making it difficult to gauge the depth. Streams of glacial origin usually reach their highest level in late afternoon (after the sun's intensity has begun to wane), so a morning crossing will generally be easiest. River levels may still be high in November and early December because of melting winter snows. Heavy rain can quickly make rivers impassable, but remember that mountain streams tend to fall almost as rapidly as they rise. Be prepared to wait a day or two before crossing.

Bamboo

Bamboo grows in the understorey of all but the most southerly temperate rainforests. Where tracks have been slashed through clusters of bamboo, short cut-off canes are left sticking out of the ground. These make sharp and potentially dangerous obstacles.

Particularly where the slippery bamboo rods have not been cleared off the track, there is the risk of slipping and falling onto the spikes. Walk very carefully anywhere the track leads through bamboo, especially on steep muddy descents.

Dogs

On the whole, Patagonian pooches are a placid breed, but don't try to pat sheep dogs – they are workers, not pets, and don't like to be touched, especially by strangers. At times trekkers have to pass by farmhouses guarded by decidedly unfriendly dogs. If you are suddenly confronted by an aggressive dog, the rule is not to panic. Remember that you are encroaching on its territory, so avoid eye contact – which the animal would interpret as a territorial challenge. Retreat discreetly or make a wide circle around the farmyard. Picking up hard projectiles in front of a snarling canine should earn you instant respect. If this normally unambiguous signal fails to make the dog back off, however, the recommended course of action is to open fire!

Bites from farm dogs should be treated seriously, as the animals may carry parasites causing hydatid cysts (see the Health chapter).

Tábanos

A collective term for several species of blood-sucking horsefly – but particularly the large and voracious red-black ones – tábanos are the scourge of the Patagonian Andes. Tábanos generally appear for about six weeks, from Christmas until late January, in the forests of the Araucanía and Lake District, and later in central Patagonia. They are far less common in southern Patagonia. Spells of hot, dry weather typically bring out swarms of frenzied tábanos, when regular insect repellents don't work for long, if at all. Trekkers are likely to hear various home-grown methods for keeping the insects at bay. Some people say you should never wear dark (particularly blue) clothing, as this attracts the insects, while others claim that eating fresh cloves of garlic – until your sweat and blood taste noxious – acts as a natural repellent. When tábanos are out in

force, however, the only sure method of avoiding them is to trek well above the tree line.

Other Pests

The Patagonian Andes are completely free of ticks. Leeches are very common in the wet rainforests of archipelagic Chile, however, although they are not dangerous to your health. Leeches can easily be removed by applying salt, stove fuel, direct heat or even hot spices such as paprika (chilli); the skin often remains itchy around the bite for a few days afterwards. Small biting gnats, insects sometimes called *petros*, are found in central and southern Patagonia. There are also mosquitoes, but they are generally less bothersome than in other moist areas of the world. Distinct from mosquitoes in tropical areas, those in Patagonia are not carriers of malaria or any other known disease.

BUSINESS HOURS

In general, bank hours are from 10 am to 4 pm, and offices are normally open from 9 am until 12 noon, then from 2 to 7 pm. In the bigger cities supermarkets and larger shops often stay open throughout the day, but in more remote areas, even in the cool south, the siesta break can be as long as four hours.

SUGGESTED ITINERARIES

Since you'll probably only make it to the Patagonian Andes once during your lifetime, give some thought to your priorities as you put together your (flexible) travel itinerary. Although nothing beats trekking, don't forget Patagonia's other great natural attractions, such as the Glaciar San Rafael (the world's 'most equatorial' glacier), Península Valdés (famous for its marine and bird life) or its petrified forests and penguin colonies. While you're in southern South America you might also visit Iguazú (the continent's greatest waterfall) or even scale Cerro Aconcagua (the highest peak in the world outside the Himalayas).

The author suggests including the following treks/parks in a three-month trip. This itinerary should give you enough time to rest and travel between each trek: Villarrica Traverse/Parque Nacional Villarrica; Puyehue Traverse/Parque Nacional Puyehue; Nahuel Huapi Traverse/Parque Nacional Nahuel Huapi; Río Anay Trek/Parque Nacional Chiloé; Around Cerro Castillo/Reserva Nacional Cerro Castillo; Paine Circuit/Parque Nacional Torres del Paine; Fitz Roy Area/Los Glaciares.

ACCOMMODATION

Apart from the seasonal vacation rush, finding clean and cheap accommodation is usually not too difficult even in out-of-the-way places. In larger towns and tourist centres there is generally quite a range of accommodation. The local tourist office usually has the most up-to-date list of accommodation alternatives from the more humble casas de familia to the most expensive hotels.

Places to stay and camp close to the trail head are listed under the Accommodation & Camping headings within the Trekking Information sections of each trek.

Huts or Refugios

In certain areas, mountain huts exist for the benefit of trekkers. Called *refugios* (literally 'refuges') in Spanish, some huts are just draughty wooden shacks with a dirt floor. Other refugios, such as those in the mountains around Bariloche or in Parque Nacional Torres del Paine, are comparable in standard to mountain huts in New Zealand or Europe, with a fee payable to the resident hutkeeper. Mountain huts can quickly become overcrowded in wet weather or during the holiday season, and it is recommended that you carry a tent even in areas where there are good refugios.

Hostels

The Hostelling International (HI, formerly known as Youth Hostel Association) hostels (called *albergues* in Spanish) generally offer the cheapest form of accommodation. The HI network is rather limited in both countries, although it is better organised in

Argentina. Many hostels only operate during the busy summer holiday period (particularly January), and frequently use schools or other public buildings for dormitory accommodation. Charges are always minimal (usually under US$3 per night), but it's sometimes hard to find out whether a town has a hostel until you actually get there. Ask at the local tourist office.

For more information on Argentina's HI hostels contact: Hostelling International, Talcahuano 214 Piso 2, Oficina 6 (1013), Buenos Aires (☎ & fax 476 1001/2537).

Casas de Familia & Hospedajes

These are usually the cheapest form of accommodation available to travellers. A casa de familia is a private home where the family lets out one or two spare rooms to travellers, often only during busier holiday periods. Hospedajes are similar, but tend to be more permanent. Both are generally very good value for money and have hot water. Prices per person are roughly US$5 to US$8 in Chile and US$8 to US$12 in Argentina, often including a continental breakfast.

Residenciales & Pensiones

Although they are usually also family-run concerns, *residenciales* and *pensiones* are more up-market and (pensiones especially) generally offer better facilities and more privacy. Depending on price, rooms may even have their own bathroom. Prices per person range from around US$6 to US$10 in Chile and US$10 to US$15 in Argentina, which usually includes breakfast.

Hotels

The term hotel is usually used for more up-market accommodation, but sometimes quite cheap places also call themselves hotels. 'Real' hotels offer rooms with at least a bathroom with hot water, and probably a private telephone. In larger towns there are many mid-range hotels, but international style luxury accommodation is rarely found outside the main cities. Hotels typically charge upwards of US$12 per person in Chile or US$20 in Argentina.

CAMPING

Camping is very popular in Chile and Argentina, and is quite safe. Since all serious Patagonia trekkers will have a tent, it provides an economical and convenient alternative form of accommodation. The Accommodation & Camping section of each trek gives details of camping options close to the trail head.

'Wild' Camping

The term 'wild' camping means pitching your tent outside established camping areas or camping grounds. Many national park authorities have now banned wild camping and only allow camping at designated sites. Provided you don't light a fire and are otherwise respectful of the environment, however, this restriction is usually not strictly enforced. During the busy summer holiday period, when cheap accommodation is scarce, wild camping close to roads and towns is common among local backpackers, though it calls for some discretion; where possible ask for the owner's permission before camping on private land.

Camping Grounds

In Argentina especially, organised camping grounds (with flush toilets, hot showers and sometimes other facilities) are widespread and generally offer good value. Camping grounds fill up quickly in the busy summer holiday season, however, and can get very noisy, with groups of young backpackers playing music and singing around a campfire until dawn. Camping grounds in Argentina tend to charge per-person rates (around US$4), while Chilean camping grounds charge a per-site fee (of up to US$12).

FOOD

Surprisingly, there are quite a few vegetarians in Argentina and Chile, particularly among the alternative-lifestyle communities of the southern Lake District. Restaurants usually have at least one or two main-course dishes without meat.

See also Backpacking Food under Trekking Information.

National Cuisines

Chile Fish and seafood are the great speciality of Chilean cuisine. Shellfish were first eaten by the Indians of the west Patagonian coast, and today oysters, mussels and clams form the bases of various traditional soups and casseroles. *Curanto*, originally a dish from Chiloé, is a rich potpourri of various kinds of seafood, beef or chicken cooked with vegetables such as pumpkin and potato. On the coasts of Chiloé and Magallanes pink salmon are farmed both for export and domestic consumption, and salmon is served as a speciality in the south.

In the Fuegian islands, king crabs, known as *centollas,* are harvested. A cheap and universal Chilean take away food is the *empanada*, a pastry filled with anything from sweetened maize *choclo* or vegetables to minced meat.

Argentina Argentine food is typified by meat dishes, especially roast lamb and beef. Argentina's famous gaucho-style roasts are called *asados*, where a whole sheep or calf is grilled on a vertical spit around a large open charcoal fire. Italian food is generally excellent in Argentina because of the profound cultural influence of Italian immigration. Pasta and real pizza – Chileans think pizza is a sort of lightly toasted cheesy bread sandwich – are served in restaurants throughout the country.

DRINKS

Bottles of carbonated mineral water and durable one-litre cardboard cartons of fruit juice are cheap liquid refreshments, but are too heavy to be carried for long in your backpack. Bottled beer has a fuller flavour than the local draft beer (known as *chopp*) sold cheaply in restaurants. Chile is world-renowned for its outstanding wines, particularly the smooth mellow reds. Argentine wines are not bad either, but more expensive than their trans-Andean counterparts.

Trekking Information

TYPES OF TREK

Trekking in the Patagonian Andes is generally more demanding than walking in the Swiss Alps or the Scottish Highlands. Often the path itself is the only form of waymarking, and above the tree line there may be nothing more than a vague line of cairns or indistinct walking pads to follow. Most of the routes described in this guidebook are therefore best suited to self-reliant trekkers. Although in some areas there are refugios, it is always advisable – and usually essential – to carry a tent and full trekking gear.

Most routes go through national parks or reserves. Unlike the Himalaya, the Alps or the Peruvian Andes, where the highland valleys have been settled for thousands of years, treks in the Patagonian Andes take you through wilderness (or semi-wilderness) areas where there are no mountain villages and only the occasional remote alpine farmlet. Using porters to carry gear and supplies is unnecessary and virtually unheard of in Patagonia, although in the more popular trekking and climbing areas you can hire local mountain guides.

The selection of treks in this guidebook comes nowhere near all the possibilities in Patagonia, and trekking parties are limited only by their experience in back country travel. Trekkers planning off-track exploration are advised that dense vegetation often makes the going difficult, particularly in the Chilean Lake District. Above the tree line movement is generally easier. Concise descriptions of other recommended trekking areas are listed in Other Treks sections at the end of each section or chapter. These should help you plan your own treks.

Trekking Times

A trek's overall length should always be calculated in terms of the required number of trekking hours, rather than its distance. To help you to better assess the trekking standard, however, the length of each stage is also given in kilometres (km). The varying trekking times indicate the different pace at which the fastest and the slowest trekkers (carrying between 15 and 25kg on their backs) will progress. The quoted trekking times *do not* include any extra time taken for rests, lunch stops or optional side trips.

The average length of the treks is three or four days, though taking optional side trips may considerably lengthen the trek. The route description divides each trek into separate stages. These are intended only as suggestions. I have checked the trekking times given in each route description/trekking stage during the 'ground research' for this book. All quoted trekking times – unless the text says otherwise – are measured from the place where the last trekking time was given. The sum of these trekking times should therefore (more or less) equal the number of hours quoted for the whole of that route description/trekking stage.

Trekking Standards

The trekking standards used in this guidebook rate the overall 'seriousness' of a trek, and are based on a combination of factors such as difficulty, path condition, overall length and en route shelter options. Remember that both trekking times and standards can vary considerably according to weather and snow conditions. Before you begin the trek always read through the route description carefully to get an idea of what to expect.

Treks in this book are graded as *easy*, *medium* or *hard*. Where conditions vary, the intermediate gradings of *easy to medium*, and *medium to hard* are also used. On the whole, the more demanding treks pass through less disturbed areas, but the grading in no way indicates a trek's overall attractiveness.

A description of the gradings follows:

- *Easy* treks follow generally well-marked trails, require little navigational skill and only an average standard of physical fitness.
- *Medium* treks require more experience and better physical condition, and are therefore best attempted after you have completed a number of

easy treks. More strenuous trails and well-marked, but exposed, routes may be encountered. At times you may have to do your own route finding and/or navigation.

• *Hard* treks are exclusively for parties led by experienced hikers. They generally follow largely unmarked routes through rugged, exposed or remote country. You will require a high level of navigational skill, self reliance and fitness.

Trans-Andean Treks

The Southern Andes (though not always the continental divide itself) form most of the common border between Chile and Argentina. On the whole the two nations have cordial relations, but the frontier remains a sensitive area. As the topographical maps of either country often show, there is not always complete agreement about the exact location of the border. Border police patrol key sectors on either side of the frontier. In Argentina a special paramilitary force of the Gendarmería Nacional is responsible for controlling the border, while in Chile this is done by the Carabineros.

The Chilean authorities are chiefly concerned about preventing the spread of plant and animal diseases. The concern has eased now that foot and mouth disease (*fiebre aftosa*) has been virtually eradicated in Argentina, but in Chile livestock is still not permitted within 5km of the border. It is still prohibited to take most unprocessed foodstuffs and dairy products across the frontier from Argentina. Smuggling of animals and other saleable commodities still occurs, however, but because of the high Argentine peso contraband traffic now tends to go west to east.

Unless you pass through an official *aduana* (or border post) en route, immigration authorities in both Chile and Argentina will not be enthusiastic about you crossing the frontier on foot. Theoretically, trekkers must obtain permission from the local consul or embassy before entering the country concerned (which may turn out to be a time-consuming and/or impossible business). Upon arrival, trans-Andean trekkers may find that they receive only a non-extendable short-term entry visa that obliges them to leave the country within a week or so. According to some travellers' accounts the whole thing is likely to be less problematic if you cross the border from Argentina into Chile rather than vice versa.

As there is some superb territory for trekking close to the frontier, restrictions like this are frustrating. Bear in mind, however, that the border's very existence has most likely kept many frontier areas wild and intact by hindering their development. In the remoteness of the mountains, of course, if you walk a short way across the frontier, it is generally not a problem whatsoever as long as you return to the same country from which you set out.

Some officially sanctioned paths do indeed cross into the neighboring country, though only for short distances where the local topography makes it the only convenient route. In the (unlikely) event of meeting a border patrol on a trans-Andean trek, you will be expected to produce identification papers and your gear may be searched.

Guided Trekking Tours

An increasingly large number of adventure travel companies organise guided treks and/or climbing expeditions in the Patagonian Andes. These include:

Australia
> Peregrine Adventures, 2nd Floor, 258 Lonsdale St, Melbourne, Vic 3000 (☎ 03-9663 8611; fax 03-9663 8618)
> Willis' Walkabouts, 12 Carrington St, Millner NT 0810 (☎ 08-8985 2134; fax 08-8985 2355). Highly recommended.
> World Expeditions, 3rd Floor, 441 Kent St, Sydney, NSW 2000 (☎ 02-9264 3366; fax 02-9261 1974)

France
> Explorator Expeditions, 16 rue de la Banque, 75002 Paris (☎ 53 45 8585; fax 42 66 5389)

Switzerland
> Horizons Nouveaux, Rue de la Poste/Case Postale 196, CH-1936 Verbier (☎ 027-771 6267; fax 027-771 7175)

UK

Exodus Worldwide Adventure Holidays, 9 Weir Road, London SW12 OLT
(☎ 181-675 5550; fax 181-673 0779)
Explore Worldwide, 1 Fredrick St, Aldershot, Hants GU11 1LQ
(☎ 01252-319448; fax 01252-343170)

USA

Aventuras Patagonicas, PO Box 2071, Valdez, AK 99686 (☎ 907-835 4976; fax 907-835 5264). Recommended.
Ibex Expeditions, 2657 West 28th Ave, Eugene, OR 97405-1461 (☎ 541-345 1289 or 800-842 8139; fax 541-343 9002)
Mountain Travel Sobek, 6420 Fairmount Ave, El Cerrito, CA 94530-3606
(☎ 510-527 8105; fax 510-525 7710)
Southwind Adventures, PO Box 621057-G, Littleton, CO 80162
(☎ 303-972 0701, or 800-377 WIND)

NATIONAL PARKS & RESERVES

Both Chile and Argentina have a well-organised system of national parks *(parques nacionales)* and national reserves *(reservas nacionales)*. The parks are run by dedicated rangers *(guardaparques)* who work with very limited resources and generally do an excellent job.

Even if you do not speak enough Spanish to converse with staff, it is generally well worth visiting the national parks offices or information centres before you set out on your trek. Ranger stations *(guarderías)* are frequently located at the start and/or end of each trek.

Most Argentine and many Chilean national parks have restricted areas *(reservas naturales estrictas)* where public access is strictly controlled, and generally allowed only under the supervision of national park personnel.

Officially, trekkers are required to obtain a permit to hike in all Argentine national parks and in many of those in Chile. In general, the more heavily visited national parks take trekking permits most seriously. In most Argentine national parks, a fee of US$5 is charged each time you enter.

In Chile the fee varies from nothing to as much as US$12.50 (in Parque Nacional Torres del Paine, which is also the only national park where foreigners must pay a different – ie higher – price than residents of Chile). Refer to the Permits & Regulations headings at the beginning of each walk description for an outline of the situation in each national park or trekking area.

Chilean National Parks & Reserves

In Chile, national parks, national reserves and national forests are all administered by the Corporación Nacional Forestal, or CONAF. At most national parks and (larger) reserves there is at least one guardería. CONAF's information office (☎ 696 6749) is in its main building at Avenida Bulnes 285 in Santiago. CONAF also has offices in regional centres throughout the country, which are given in the Trekking Bases sections at the beginning of each chapter.

Argentine National Parks & Reserves

In Argentina, the responsible authority is the Administración de Parques Nacionales (APN), whose head office is at Avenida Santa Fe 690, 1059 Capital Federal (☎ 312 0257/311 0303) in Buenos Aires. The APN has fewer regional offices throughout Argentina than CONAF has in Chile, but those of relevance to trekkers are also listed under Trekking Bases.

OTHER INFORMATION SOURCES
Mountain Clubs

Provincial centres, particularly in Argentina, often have some kind of mountain club. Usually calling themselves *club andino* or *club de montaña*, these local mountain clubs tend to be small and have informal arrangements. In some cases they are centred around just a few enthusiasts. Many have no permanent office address (and even fewer will answer mail), but regional mountain clubs that can give advice to trekkers are listed under Trekking Bases.

The two most relevant organisations for trekkers visiting southern Chile and Argentina are the Federación de Andinismo de Chile and the Club Andino Bariloche (CAB).

Both publish periodical journals (in Spanish) on recent club activities and exploits.

Federación de Andinismo de Chile The Federación de Andinismo de Chile (☎ 222 0888), at Almirante Simpson 77, Santiago, represents most regional Chilean mountain clubs and has a good library of mountaineering literature.

Club Andino Bariloche The CAB (☎ 0944-24531; fax 0944 24579, at 20 de Febrero 30, in San Carlos de Bariloche, is one of the largest mountain clubs in Latin America. The club, which built most of the refugios in the nearby Parque Nacional Nahuel Huapi, has an excellent information service and library.

Codeff Codeff's head office (☎ 251 0262; fax 251 0287) is at Bilbao 691, Providencia, Santiago. Codeff, an acronym of Comité Nacional por Defensa de la Fauna y Flora, is a conservation organisation affiliated with the Friends of the Earth (or Amigos de la Tierra) based in Santiago de Chile. The organisation produces various periodicals in Spanish on conservation issues affecting Chile.

South American Explorers Club The South American Explorers Club (SAEC) is a non-profit organisation that anyone with a general interest in South and Central America should consider joining. The club's services include giving advice, use of its well-stocked libraries, discounts on books and even helping members out with travel problems and during emergencies. The SAEC collects 'trip reports' on places recently visited by members, which can be of value to trekkers. The SAEC publishes the *South American Explorer* (see Magazines), a quarterly magazine available only to club members – in itself a good enough reason to join up.

SAEC membership is open to everyone for the annual fee of US$40 (or US$47 for residents of countries other than the USA, Canada and Mexico), which includes delivery of the *South American Explorer*. The

SAEC's head office is at 126 Indian Creek Road, Ithaca, NY 14850, USA (☎ (607) 277 0488), and the club has two South American offices, in Lima and Quito.

MAPS
Where possible, try to obtain maps for all treks which in this guidebook are graded moderate or difficult. Even where navigation is straightforward, a map of the surrounding area will increase your appreciation and enjoyment of the landscape.

As in many Latin American countries mapping is carried out by the military, and Chile and Argentina both have a central mapping authority called the Instituto Geográfico Militar. You can only get IGM topographical maps in the national capitals, so if you are passing through Buenos Aires or Santiago be sure to buy all sheets there. It is possible to mail-order maps, but delivery time within the respective country may take up to two weeks. The Chilean IGM produces a brochure-catalogue of available maps.

Unfortunately maps of large sectors of the southern Cordillera at any useful scale are still not available. Maps of a scale greater than 1:100,000 – the next size upwards is usually 1:250,000 – are generally unsuitable for accurate ground navigation. In Argentina topographical maps are sometimes only updated every few generations, so some key sheets are now woefully out of date.

Maps start to disintegrate once they become damp or torn. To prevent this it's a good idea to use a transparent map-holder (available from trekking stores) that allows you to look at the relevant section of the route without having to continually unfold the map. More laborious methods of protecting trekking maps are covering them with a transparent adhesive laminate or applying a liquid map sealant (such as Aquaseal).

Chilean IGM Maps
The Chilean IGM has two sales offices, both in Santiago. Their main office (☎ 696 8221/8228, extension 263; fax 698 7278) is at Dieciocho 369 in Santiago. (This is almost opposite the historical mansion and museum

of the Braun-Menendez family, near metro station Toesca). It's open Monday to Friday from 9 am to 5.30 pm. The Chilean IGM also has a smaller and less well stocked sales office at Alameda O'Higgins 240.

The Chilean IGM has divided the country into 12 sections *(secciones)*, or mapping zones, given a letter from A to L. All Chilean treks in this book are within the (southern) mapping zones G to L. Individual sheets are numbered and have a name. At the Chilean IGM sales offices folders containing all sheets of a particular section will be given to you on request. Always quote the sheet's name, number and mapping zone letter when ordering (eg *Volcán Puyehue*, Sección H, No 27).

The standard series covering the south is scaled at 1:50,000. Generally these are topographically quite accurate, though trekking routes are often not properly indicated. The IGM has raised its prices considerably in the last few years. Sheets in the 1:50,000 series now sell for about US$11. Out-of-print maps *(hojas agotadas)* can be bought as single-sheet photocopies for US$7. An old and very rough 'preliminary' series of 1:250,000 scale sheets is also still available, but the quality is insufficient for trekking. More detailed colour maps of the Chilean Lake District and Araucanía have been prepared at the same scale.

The main library in Santiago has a complete collection of IGM maps, and if you leave your passport as a guarantee of return these can generally be borrowed for photocopying. It is sometimes possible to borrow forestry maps from CONAF offices for photocopying. CONAF maps are usually traced black and white sheets based on the IGM originals with other special features drawn in. CONAF also produces sketch maps for some of the more popular Chilean national parks. Sketch maps show features not included on IGM maps (such as tracks and huts), but are usually unsuitable for serious navigation. Confusingly, even on quite recent CONAF maps the altitudes given for the contour lines are often in feet, while the spot elevations on the same maps are shown in metres.

Argentine IGM Maps

The Argentina IGM (☎ 771-3032/3039, ext 127/118; fax 698 7278) sales office is at Avenida Cabildo 381 in Buenos Aires, and is open from 8 am to 1 pm. Take the subway *(subte)* to the termination of line D and walk four blocks north.

All maps are identified by national grid reference numbers, but are catalogued under their provinces. The sales office staff won't let you look at more than a few sheets at a time, so if unsure about which sheets to buy you should go to the IGM library next door. The standard scale for maps of southern Argentina is 1:100,000. Especially in Río Negro and Neuquén provinces, many sheets are hopelessly out of date and show topographical information poorly, but many of these are being revised and the new sheets should become available during the life of this guidebook. The 1:100,000 sheets cost US$10 per sheet. There is usually a one-day waiting time if you order photocopies of out-of-print sheets, and the cost per sheet is US$15 for colour photocopies, or $US5 for black and white.

Excellent colour maps scaled at 1:250,000 are also available for most of the southern Argentine Cordillera. In areas very close to the border (eg Volcán Lanín), Chilean IGM maps overlapping into Argentine territory are sometimes more useful.

Trekking Maps

Quality maps produced specifically for trekkers (by independent cartographic publishers, rather than the national IGMs) are sometimes available, but remain the exception rather than the rule. Where good contoured trekking maps exist, such as for Nahuel Huapi, Los Glaciares, Torres del Paine and the Comarca Andina, they are the recommended maps to use.

Navigation & Routefinding

Navigation means using a map and compass (or GPS receiver) to determine your position, while routefinding refers to a trekker's skill in picking up and following a route. Of course, the two terms overlap quite a bit, but in practice trekkers only rarely need to seriously navigate their way in the Patagonian Andes. Routefinding, on the other hand, is a particularly useful skill since Patagonian trails are notorious for being overgrown or confused by diverging cattle pads; at times just using your intuition may be the most effective routefinding aid. Trekkers who are sure they're on the right route could help maintain waymarkings by rebuilding cairns, re-erecting marker stakes and removing overgrowing branches – but don't overdo it!

Compasses Especially on treks rated moderate and difficult, all parties should carry a compass to aid in navigation. The entire area of Patagonia is within the so-called South Magnetic Equator (SME) zone, and only compasses balanced for South American countries or southern Africa are suitable. Compasses set for magnetic conditions in Australasia, Europe or North America tend to give inaccurate readings. If buying a compass in South America, check whether the needle dips down at one end when held horizontally, as this indicates improper balancing. Magnetic deviation in the Southern Andes is minimal, and ranges from close to 8°E in parts of the northern Araucanía to about 14°E in the islands around Cape Horn.

GPS Receivers Originally developed by the US Department of Defense for military purposes, the Global Positioning System (GPS) is a network of over 20 earth-orbiting satellites that continually beam coded signals back to earth. Small computer-driven devices, so-called GPS receivers, can decode these signals to give users an extremely accurate reading of their location – to within 10m, anywhere on the planet, at any time of day, in any weather. The cheapest hand-held GPS receivers now cost under US$500 – which puts them well within the price range of serious trekkers – but only more expensive devices are likely to have a built-in averaging system that minimises signal errors and gives readings of acceptable accuracy. Other important factors to consider when buying a GPS receiver are its weight (preferably

under 500g) and battery life. New GPS receivers come onto the market each year, so there is little point in recommending specific brands or models here.

It should be understood that a GPS receiver is of little use to trekkers unless used with an accurate topographical map – the GPS receiver simply gives your precise position, which you must then locate on the local map. GPS receivers will only work (properly) in the open. Directly under high cliffs, for example, the signals from a crucial satellite may be blocked (or even bounce off the rock) and give inaccurate readings. GPS receivers are more vulnerable to breakdowns (including flat batteries) than the humble magnetic compass – a low-tech device that has served navigators faithfully for centuries – so don't rely on it entirely.

Place Names
Much of the Spanish nomenclature in Patagonia is monotonous. The southern Cordillera seems to have an endless number of lakes with names like 'Laguna Verde' or 'Lago Escondido', and rivers called 'Río Blanco' or 'Río Turbio'. Many land features bear the names of battles or heroes from the wars of independence, such as Cordón Chacabuco, Lago O'Higgins and Cerro San Martín.

Naturally all places which were significant to indigenous people already had names. These were often disregarded by the new settlers, or were swept away with the extermination of the Indians. In the Araucanía, however, the nomenclature often still shows indigenous origins, having been taken mostly from local Mapuche languages. Like other inhabitants of the New World, Chileans and Argentinians are slowly rediscovering their nations' indigenous past, and some native Indian place names are coming back into use. A complicating factor is the different dialects that were spoken by tribes on either side of the border. For example, a key Mapuche pass in the southern Lake District is called *vuriloche* in Chile and *bariloche* in Argentina, both meaning 'the people on the other side'.

In order to make route descriptions less confusing and more interesting, I have given (hopefully appropriate!) Spanish titles to land features that still don't have official place names. In such cases the particular lake, mountain pass or stream etc appears in the text in inverted commas (eg 'Pasada Peñón') to emphasise that the name is not official. Where there are several place names, the more popular or simpler word has been taken.

Some of the more common Spanish and Mapuche words found in place names are listed in the Language section. See also the Glossary near the back of this book for an explanation of various common terms used in the route descriptions.

BACKPACKING FOOD

Although food (especially farm produce) can often be bought on the trekking route, it is very unwise and often unfair to depend too much on locals for supplies – carry enough to last the whole trek. Most practical are lightweight foods that can be quickly prepared. With the exception of certain specialised freeze-dried products, supermarkets in Chile and Argentina stock a similar range of food to those in Australasia, Europe and North America.

The longer the trek, the greater should be the proportion of dehydrated foods, but taking along some fresh fruit and/or vegetables will make your meals more enjoyable and nutritious. Always carry two days' extra rations for unplanned side trips, emergencies or miscalculations. It is prohibited to take most unprocessed dairy and agricultural products across the border from Argentina into Chile – remember this if you intend doing a trek immediately after crossing into Chile. Like everything else, food is considerably cheaper in Chile, although the quality tends to be better in Argentina.

Ready-made lunch and snack foods are quick and easy to prepare, although they tend to be heavier and bulkier. Most trekkers will cook their evening meal on a gasoline stove, so choosing foods that cook quickly will save fuel. Naturally everyone has their own tastes and preferences in camp food. The following local specialities are particularly recommended and should be obtainable from most centres:

Instant cereals containing dextrine *(cereales dextrinados instantáneos)* – these are nutritious, lightweight, easy to prepare and taste surprisingly good. One local brand is *Blevit*.

Muesli – another nourishing mixture of grains that requires no cooking

Harina tostada – toasted wheat flour, mixed with milk to form a kind of instant porridge

Cheese *(queso)* – excellent in Argentina; try *pepato* and *roquefort*

Wholemeal bread *(pan integral)* – available in larger supermarkets and occasionally health food stores in most larger centres of Chile and Argentina

Dulce de leche or *manjar* – caramelised condensed milk eaten as a spread for bread and cakes

Callampas – dehydrated mushrooms available in small packets

Packet soups – try exotic flavours like *choclo*, *marisco* and *lenteja*

Mussels *(cholgas)* – available dried at markets in Chile

Pasta and spaghetti *(fideos)* – a wide range is available in Argentina

Dried fruits *(frutas secas)*

Walnuts *(nueces)* – especially good in Chile

Dulce de batata, dulce de membrillo – a semi-solid dessert made from sweet potato and quince, respectively

Home made chocolates – especially good in San Carlos de Bariloche, San Martín de los Andes, Calafate and other towns in southern Argentina

Fruit cake *(pastel de pascua)* – full of calories and if packed carefully won't crumble too much – just the thing for a sunny southern Christmas day

Wild Foods

Wild foods can usually only provide a small supplement to your diet, and should not be depended on for survival.

Berries The most common treats are the abundant native berry species. February and March are the best 'berry producing months'. None of the edible-looking fruits that grow in Patagonia are poisonous (although many are unpalatable).

Chauras – These are red to white berries growing on heath-like bushes, usually at their best when found just above the tree line. There are a great many species growing throughout the southern Andes.

Calafates – The calafate is a seedy, smaller version of the blueberry. At least five calafate species (genus *Berberis*) grow all over southern Patagonia. Sharp thorns protect the deep purple-coloured berries from excessive exploitation. A popular Patagonian folk song claims 'whoever eats the calafate comes back for more'.

Frutilla de Magallanes – This is a bright red berry usually found growing in moist, rich locations such as along streams. The frutilla has a flavour not unlike a raspberry.

Moras – Moras are introduced European blackberries, and are found growing beside country roads, particularly in the Araucanía and Lake District. The fruit ripens in mid to late March.

Murtas – Murtas are mildly sweet, somewhat bland red berries with a scaly skin produced by a large bush (*Ugni candollei*) that grows in forest clearings in the Chilean Lake District. Murtas ripen in early autumn and are sometimes sold in local markets.

Quellenes Quellenes, more often simply called *frutillas silvestres* ('wild strawberry') by Chileans and Argentinians, are related to cultivated strawberries, but are smaller and less abundant.

Chauras produce edible berries, and are usually at their best above the tree line

Other Wild Foods

Piñones – These are the nut-like fruit of the araucaria pine found growing in the Araucanía and northern Lake District. Giant cluster-cones of piñones fall from the trees in late summer, scattering across the ground. The pinkish kernels look a bit like elongated cloves of garlic. After roasting or boiling they can be easily squeeze peeled to reveal a starchy flesh that has a flavour something like chestnut, but with an interesting, slightly resinous aftertaste. Be sure not to collect germinating nuts, and always leave enough to allow proper regeneration.

Pan del indio – This is the local term for the parasitic, round edible growths (of the genus *Cyttaria*) that form on the trunks and branches of southern beech (*Nothofagus*). The 'fruit' have the form of immature champignons, with a rubbery texture and a musty fungal taste. Although no great delicacy, pan del indio is an abundant source of carbohydrate and was a staple food for some indigenous tribes of the south.

Nalca – When eaten uncooked, the thick succulent stems of the nalca (or *pangue*) are vaguely reminiscent of celery – as much for their fibrous texture as for their a bland, slightly sour flavour. Sucking on the fresh stems is considered a good thirst-quencher. When stewed with sugar, nalca stems have a taste comparable to rhubarb (and the plant is sometimes actually called 'Chilean rhubarb'). To prepare nalca stems, the harder skin of soft thorns must be stripped off.

Mushrooms – Eating wild mushrooms is not recommended unless you have sufficient knowledge of edible native species. A recommended field guide that includes edible mushroom species is *Hongos de los Bosques Andino-Patagónicos* by Irma Gamundi and Egon Horak.

BACKPACKING DRINKS

Packets of sweet, flavoured drink powders (such as *Tang*) are available in local supermarkets and make a refreshing source of glucose on the trek. Herbal teas, including the native *boldo* and *manzano*, are available in tea bag form and are ideal for an after-dinner brew. Trekkers are likely to be offered *yerba mate*, a high-caffeine beverage that is a national obsession in Argentina and quite popular in southern Chile.

WATER

Water is often a problem in the far southern Andes, usually because there is just *too much of it*. For this reason it is usually unnecessary to carry more than a small canteen of water with you. Camp sites are invariably close to a good source of water. The exceptions to this are the volcanic ranges of the Araucanía and Lake District and areas of arid land that fringe the Patagonian Andes. In volcanic areas heavy deposits of lava or pumice ash often make the ground so porous that surface water quickly seeps away into subterranean streams, making it difficult to find water. Walking over lava fields in sunny weather can be surprisingly hot work, and when trekking in such areas be sure to carry water to last the whole day.

Refer also to the Water Purification section in the Health chapter.

EQUIPMENT

Specialist trekking/outdoors stores can be found in Santiago and Buenos Aires as well as certain regional centres close to main trekking centres (most notably Bariloche, Calafate and Puerto Natales), but it's difficult to buy most quality trekking equipment at a reasonable price in both Chile and Argentina. This applies particularly to tents, though less to quality (*Goretex*) rainwear and *fibrepile* garments, which are more widely available. It's therefore advisable to bring all necessary gear with you. Fishing/hunting suppliers normally have a small range of general outdoor gear which may serve as emergency replacements.

For the Spanish names of items, see the Language section in the Facts about the Region chapter. A comprehensive list of the trekking gear that you may need for trekking in the Patagonian Andes follows.

General Clothing

Warm Weather Wear Especially above the tree line in volcanic areas of the Araucanía and Lake District, summer can get very hot and you should wear lighter clothing such as shorts and cotton shirts. Wear a hat with a broad visor to keep the sun off your face and ears. Regardless of what the weather conditions are when you set out, warm clothing should always be carried in case the weather suddenly deteriorates.

Cold Weather Wear It is essential that you carry at least one very warm fibrepile or woollen sweater. This will retain much of its insulating ability even if it gets wet. Trekkers who are very sensitive to cold might consider buying a lightweight down jacket (but keep it dry!) Also carry a pair of warm trousers. Thermal underwear can be worn in the sleeping bag or in cold conditions. Silk garments are exceptionally warm for their weight, and are very pleasant to wear. A woollen cap or balaclava should be carried. Gloves or mittens are also highly recommended.

Rainwear

An essential piece of clothing that must be carried by all trekkers is a waterproof and windproof rain jacket. This should have a hood which properly covers your head. Experienced trekkers often prefer totally impervious rubberised rainwear to the newer 'breathable' garments, as the latter tend to leak after a few hours in extremely wet conditions. Waterproof ponchos, usually large enough to slip over the pack, are popular with local walkers. Ponchos don't offer the same protection from the elements as tailored rainwear, however, and tend to catch on branches as you pass. A pair of waterproof overpants is also highly recommended.

Footwear

Robust trekking boots with good ankle support are best. A pair of lightweight running shoes should also be carried as alternative footwear and for wading across streams. Reasonably well made leather trekking boots can be bought locally in Buenos Aires or the Argentine Lake District, especially in San Carlos de Bariloche. In the boggy terrain of the west Patagonian Archipelago and Tierra del Fuego, local trekkers often prefer walking in rubber boots, though it's probably not worth bringing rubber boots with you unless you intend doing a lot of trekking in those areas. It's advisable to impregnate boots with a waterproofing agent to protect the leather and keep your feet dry. You should wear gaiters *(polainas)* to protect your lower legs, especially if you wear shorts.

Tent

Good tents are difficult to buy in this part of the world, and (even in the few areas where reliable huts exist) it's always advisable to carry a tent. Trekkers should therefore *bring a tent* with them. More than any other piece of equipment it is well worth paying extra for a high quality tent. Remember that your tent may provide the only available shelter in an emergency, so make sure it is absolutely waterproof and able to withstand the windy conditions you will surely encounter. Of course a tent also serves as alternative accommodation, making travel more flexible, and even between treks camping out is a cheaper and often more pleasant option than staying in hotels or pensiones. An inconspicuous colour – a dull fawn or olive blend is best – will allow you to camp more discreetly.

Backpack

Your pack should transfer as much weight as possible – theoretically all of it – off your back and onto your hips. Distributing the load to the middle of the body not only improves a trekker's balance, but also greatly reduces long-term strain and injury on the back. In order to do this the pack must have a robust and well-padded belt that comfortably holds it onto your waist without swaying around as you move. The two shoulder straps serve only to steady the pack, and should be loosened to carry a minimal load. 'Convertible' packs that can be zipped up to look like hand luggage should be avoided, since they compromise severely on trekking comfort. Carry a spare 'quick-clip' pack belt buckle in case the others break; good quality pack buckles are hard to find in this part of the world.

Remember that you will be travelling between treks, so be sure your pack also has enough carrying capacity for the gear you take (or may accumulate). Internal-frame packs with at least 70l of volume are best. Removable daypacks that attach to the top of the pack are a convenient innovation, but side pockets – which tend to get caught on bushes, bus racks etc – are not recommended. Locally made (particularly Argentine) backpacks are generally good only as replacements for a lost or damaged pack. Despite the manufacturers' claims, packs are never completely waterproof, and you should keep the contents dry either by packing everything inside a large, robust internal plastic bag like a garbage bag and/or by using a well-fitting pack cover.

Sleeping Bag

Sleeping bags should have a rating of at least minus 10°C. For treks in the far south or anywhere early or late in the season, bags with an even lower rating are preferable. Some trekkers keep pack weight down by wearing their warm clothing in bed. If you're absolutely sure you can keep it dry, a sleeping bag with a filling of super down is recommended. If your down bag gets wet two days into a six day trek then you're in for some uncomfortable nights.

Although continual technological improvements are gradually closing the gap, sleeping bags that use a special artificial-fibre filling (such as *Dacron*) are still bulkier and heavier for their warmth than down-filled bags. Artificial-fibre bags do, however, have the significant (safety) advantage of being able to effectively insulate your body even after they have become wet. Good Argentine down sleeping bags (and down jackets) are available in Bariloche.

Portable Cooker

In all trekking areas, fire is neither a reliable nor an environmentally sound means of cooking, and some national parks have now banned the lighting of campfires altogether. For this reason all trekking parties must carry a camp stove. The most practical cookers are those that can burn a range of fuels like standard kerosene, petroleum or white gasoline (*Shellite*). Two types of portable cooker that offer such fuel versatility are the MSR and the similarly designed SIGG stove (which is at least as good, but much cheaper).

Petrol (gasoline) is known as *bencina* in Chile and *nafta* in Argentina, while kerosene is called *parafina* or *kerosene*. Locally sold petrol is often full of impurities, so it's best to filter it before use. *Bencina blanca* or *nafta blanca* are the local terms for white gasoline. In Chile, white gasoline is available at every second pharmacy or hardware store, and prices vary enormously, from as little as US$1 up to US$2.50 per litre. White gasoline can be hard to find in Argentina, however, where it is usually sold as industrial solvent *(solvente industrial)*. Users of MSR-style cookers will find the high performance gasoline 'Ultra 2000' (sold at ACA service stations in Argentina) a reasonable substitute for white gasoline.

For trekkers with 'Trangia'-style alcohol-burning stoves, methylated spirits is fairly widely and cheaply available in larger supermarkets or hardware stores. 'Camping Gaz' type stoves are popular among local backpackers. They are safe and virtually foolproof to use, and make a good alternative to the somewhat more hazardous liquid fuel stoves. However, gas stoves won't operate effectively in low temperatures, so the apparatus must always be kept warm. Remember that it is prohibited to take gas canisters on all aircraft. Canisters are now often available even in quite small towns, where they are usually sold in hardware stores and cost around $3 each. Cheap Brazilian-made versions of the cookers are available locally – if you buy one, check it carefully first.

Cooking Ware

Depending on the size of the party, a number of cooking pots should be carried. Suitable aluminium utensils of quite good quality are manufactured in both Chile and Argentina. Fans of stainless steel should bring their own. A pot-grip is a very handy device that helps prevent burnt fingers.

Thermal Mattress

For sleeping comfort and insulation, some kind of lightweight mattress is essential. Closed foam cell mats weigh no more than a few hundred grams, but are bulky and awkward to pack. Reasonably priced Taiwanese-made versions are locally available. 'Thermarest' or integrated 'Stephenson's' type inflatable mattresses are heavier and much more expensive, but offer greater sleeping comfort and take up less room in the pack. To avoid punctures clear the ground of any sharp matter (such as araucaria needles and calafate thorns) before setting up the tent.

Optional Extras

Some of the additional items that you may consider taking along include:

Ice Axe – may be necessary if you intend climbing the higher summits (such as Volcán Lanín or Monte Tronador) early in the season. For general summer and autumn trekking the considerable weight of an ice axe and crampons cannot be justified.

Machete – will come in handy where tracks are overgrown, and should be carried on all off-track expeditions. A leather glove will prevent blistering.

Pocket Knife – a very practical instrument. 'Swiss army' type pocket knives are the best.

Barometer/Altimeter – measures air pressure to show your approximate altitude and gives an indication of the approaching weather. New integrated wristwatch models with sophisticated functions – such as an automatic chime when your reach a set altitude, or average altitude gain/loss over a set period – are now available (but probably not in Chile and Argentina) for as little as US$150.

Watch/Alarm Clock – this instrument ensures an early start to make the most of your day. Should be completely shockproof and waterproof.

Camera – lightweight compact cameras (but that allow you to attach a polarising and/or UV filter) are the best. (See also Photography in the Activities on the Trek section.)

Walkman/Shortwave Radio – a good form of alternative entertainment.

Binoculars – a must for bird and animal watchers, and they will also help you to scout out the route ahead. Excellent compact and lightweight models are available.

Sunglasses – should be carried on all higher treks, particularly early in the season when snow fields may have to be crossed. For maximum eye protection, only UV-Polaroid lenses should be worn.

Solar Battery Recharger – Especially if you carry more than one electrical item, using rechargeable batteries with a small portable solar-powered recharger *(encargador solar de pilas)* for AA size batteries is convenient and environmentally friendly.

ON THE TREK

Take a leisurely attitude to trekking – limit your walking time to no more than six hours per day and don't carry unnecessary weight. On most treks camp chores will take up several hours each day. Typically your early morning routine will begin with preparing breakfast, then packing up and finally breaking camp – a procedure that seems to take forever, with few trekkers actually managing to get away in much less than 1½ hours from the time they wake. Setting up camp in the evening and cooking dinner takes a bit less time.

En Route Activities

Taking time out for various en route activities – from making side trips and identifying wildlife species to picking wild berries – will enhance your trek. You should set aside time to rest so your trek is not a mad rush from camping ground to refugio. If you stop to take photographs and simply enjoy the views, it will make your trekking far more pleasurable.

Bird & Animal Watching With over 5% of the world's bird species, Patagonia is a birdwatcher's paradise. The region's rich feathered fauna includes numerous native species of cormorants, ducks, eagles, gulls, hawks, hummingbirds, parrots, pigeons, woodpeckers and a swan – a good many of which are endemic to Patagonia. A powerful pair of binoculars and a good field guide are essential items for the amateur ornithologist.

Because of their shyness, nocturnal habits and increasing rarity, Patagonia's native animals are relatively seldom seen. Sightings tend to be unexpected and fleeting – sometimes you'll have to be content with finding the odd dropping or hoof print. Trekkers are almost assured of seeing guanacos and foxes, however, and have a fair chance of spotting a chingue, coipo, huillín, pudu, tuco-tuco or vizcacha. If you managed to sight a puma or a rare huemul in the wild it would be the highlight of your trip.

Some of the more common bird and animal species found in southern Chile and

Equipment checklist

This list is a general guide to trekking in Patagonia. As you gain experience, you might want to add or take away from it.

- [ ] tent with pegs, poles, guy ropes and fly
- [ ] groundsheet
- [ ] spare nylon cord
- [ ] pack with waterproof liner and spare buckle
- [ ] sleeping bag with inner sheet
- [ ] insulation mat (foam or air filled)
- [ ] waterproof jacket and overpants
- [ ] gaiters
- [ ] warm hat and gloves
- [ ] sun hat or visor
- [ ] long-sleeved shirt
- [ ] thermal underwear
- [ ] pullover and warm jacket
- [ ] waterproof poncho
- [ ] warm pants
- [ ] spare underwear and socks
- [ ] runners and boots
- [ ] stove and fuel
- [ ] metal can for boiling water
- [ ] pot scourer
- [ ] eating utensils
- [ ] pocket knife
- [ ] pot grip
- [ ] water containers
- [ ] toilet paper, trowel for digging hole
- [ ] torch with spare batteries and globe
- [ ] candles and matches
- [ ] first aid kit and toiletries
- [ ] sun block cream
- [ ] sunglasses
- [ ] map, guides and compass
- [ ] notebook and pencil
- [ ] whistle
- [ ] camera and film
- [ ] barometer/altimeter
- [ ] watch/alarm clock
- [ ] walkman/shortwave radio
- [ ] binoculars
- [ ] solar battery recharger

Argentina are outlined in the Facts about the Region chapter; also see the Books section in this chapter for relevant literature.

Fishing Sport fishing has become very popular among locals in both Chile and Argentina. In particular, the Lake District and the Aisén region of Chile are attracting increasing numbers of fly anglers from all over the world. This has led to the establishment of scores of new fishing lodges in these areas.

The southern lakes and rivers of Chile and Argentina are well stocked with introduced North American river trout, European brown trout and rainbow trout. Also present, though now far less abundant because of predation and competition from introduced species, are native Patagonian fish such as perch, pejerrey *(Basilichthys microlepidotus)*, puyen *(Galaxia* species) and peladilla *(Haplochiton* species).

In Chile and Argentina anglers must have a fishing permit *(Licencia de Pesca Deportiva)*. The closed season *(temporada de veda)* in either country varies depending on the province or region and the fish species, as do the rules regarding tackle, quotas and other restrictions. In some rivers (particularly in Argentina), catch-and-release is compulsory. Anglers should pay careful attention to other local regulations.

In Chile, recreational fishing permits are valid for one year throughout the entire country (including national parks). Chilean fishing permits can be purchased for US$2 at all regional offices of the Servicio Nacional de Pesca (SERNAP) and sometimes (but usually not) at national park offices.

In Argentina, sport fishing is an altogether more expensive and tightly controlled affair. Fishing permits can be bought at national park administration (APN) offices or the provincial offices of the Recursos Naturales department as well as some specialist anglers' stores. For non-residents of Argentina, a

---

Responsible Trekking

Since more and more trekkers are visiting the Patagonian Andes each year, it is increasingly important that they understand the minimum-impact code. For those who need reminding, here are the fundamentals:

- *All* non-biodegradable rubbish, including soup packets, tin cans, cigarette butts and tampons, should be carried out in your pack – not dumped, buried, or hidden under some rock.
- Don't pick wild flowers or deliberately damage plants when trekking or putting up your tent.
- Keep to the graded trails where possible. Don't short-cut corners, as this causes severe erosion – particularly on steep ascents and descents.
- Particularly in the busier national parks, camping may be restricted to specified sites – don't camp anywhere outside these park-authorised areas.
- Use en route toilets where they are provided. Otherwise defecate at least 20m from streams and lakes on the downhill/downstream side of camp sites or houses. Bury your bodily wastes as well as your soiled toilet paper in a hole roughly 20cm deep – thoughtful trekkers carry a small garden trowel for this purpose. These simple precautions may prevent walkers who later visit the spot from getting a nasty bout of diarrhoea.
- Don't dump food scraps around camp sites, as this will attract rodents or other wild animals. Bury any food waste or throw it – but nothing else – in the bin provided.
- Keep the rivers and lakes pure by not washing with soaps or detergents – using sand or a pot scourer will be just as good.
- Take special precautions if you light a campfire – read the aside titled 'Fire' on the next page to understand the consequences of not doing so. Use only established fireplaces and burn dead, fallen wood. Never burn plastics or food packet liners (which often leave aluminium fragments in the ashes).
- Respect private property and local customs – where possible ask permission before crossing farmland and refrain from nude bathing at places frequented by others. ■

Fire

It would be difficult to overstate the devastation that forest fires can cause in the Patagonian Andes. Particularly in the colonisation of southern Chile, fire was frequently used as a means of clearing land for farming and grazing. Often strong winds would whip the flames out of control, resulting in enormous fires that soon became impossible to contain. It was not uncommon for such fires to remain burning throughout the whole summer, laying waste to vast tracts of valuable forest as they spread.

During the worst periods of the 1930s and 1940s smoke and ash from huge forest fires in Chile's Aisén Region was deposited as far away as Argentina's Atlantic coast. Several million hectares of virgin forest in the southern Andes were destroyed in this way. Even today forests of dead trees are the enduring landmarks of many regions, and scar entire mountain ranges.

Slow regeneration after forest fires makes soil erosion a severe problem in Patagonia. The destruction of the forest along the middle course of the Río Aisén in Chile caused the river to silt up so badly that the city of Puerto Aisén became useless as a port. Fire is also partly responsible for the alarming decline in numbers of some animal species, most particularly the *huemul* and *pudú*.

If you must light a campfire, please exercise special care. Only light your fire in an established fireplace and *never* leave it unattended. When you leave make sure it is properly extinguished. Never light a campfire in areas with peat soils. Peat largely consists of organic matter that is often quite dry and porous, making it difficult to extinguish once ignited. ■

single fishing permit that is valid for all of Argentina's Patagonian provinces as well as Argentine Tierra del Fuego costs US$30 for 10 days, US$60 for one month or US$100 per year. It comes with a booklet (in Spanish) explaining the rules that apply in the various regions.

Recommended reading for all Patagonia anglers would be *Argentine Trout Fishing: A Fly Fisherman's Guide* by Bill Leitch (Frank Amato Publications, Portland Oregon, 1991), and *Fisherman's Winter*, by Roderick Haig-Brown.

Photography Few trekkers will want to go without a camera. If possible try to limit your overall photographic equipment to about one kg. SLR camera owners are advised to settle for a 28-110mm zoom lens rather than taking three or more separate lenses. Compact cameras are reasonably priced and weigh only a few hundred grams. Compact cameras that have a mini zoom lens with variable angle (usually 35-70mm) are ideal for trekkers, but make sure the lens has provision for attaching a filter.

The fine gritty dust found particularly in volcanic highlands and on the dry windy steppes east of the Cordillera is a constant problem for photographers. A lens cap and a plain glass or UV filter are standard items for lens protection. You should regularly use lens tissues and a 'puff brush' to clean the camera. When changing film be especially careful to prevent dust entering the camera chamber.

A padded camera case with a shoulder strap will lengthen the life of your camera appreciably, and it is a convenient way of carrying it on short trips. When trekking in wet areas be sure to adequately protect your camera from water damage. This can be done by keeping it in a waterproof container, but watch out for condensation! A polarising filter is more or less essential for successful results where there is intense solar reflection, such as midday shots of scenes with glaciers, snow fields or shimmering lakes.

Film is relatively expensive throughout Chile and Argentina, but is available duty-free at the *zona franca* in Punta Arenas and – for only slightly less than the normal retail price – in the free port of Ushuaia. Having film developed in Argentina is expensive, so it may be best to get it developed in Chile or in your home country. All types of camera batteries can be bought locally.

Most serious outdoor photographers prefer to use slide film. Agfa, Fuji (pronounced 'foo-he' in Spanish) and Kodak slide film is available in larger regional centres, but it can be hard to find it in 200 ISO or 400 ISO. As neither Chile nor Argentina have laboratories for developing Kodachrome, it is not sold locally, so if you want to use Kodachrome you'll have to bring enough to last the whole trip. Fuji Professional or Ektachrome Elite are reasonable locally available alternatives, and cost around US$12 for a roll of 36 exposures (excluding developing).

Swimming In hot sunny weather Patagonia's countless unpolluted lakes and rivers entice many a trekker to stop for a refreshing dip and splash. In the Araucanía and Lake District the water is generally bearably cool below the forest line, but the higher up or farther south you go the chillier it gets. On a few treks described in this guidebook you can even relax in steamy thermal springs. In both Chile and Argentina, skinny dipping and topless bathing – at least by women – is *not acceptable* at public bathing areas. Out in the watery wilds, however, what you (don't) wear is your own business.

NATIONAL CAPITALS
Although the Chilean and Argentine national capitals are not without their charms, trekkers impatient for the Patagonian wilds will be loath to lose too much time in these large metropolises. Refer also to Trekking Bases (at the beginning of each chapter) for convenient regional centres in the Patagonian Andes.

Buenos Aires
Home to 12 million people, the Argentine capital, Buenos Aires, is one of the world's major cities. Situated on the broad bay known as the Río de la Plata, or River Plate, the city has a moist subtropical climate that often produces unpleasant, sticky weather. Mass immigration has given Buenos Aires an ethnic diversity and cosmopolitan flavour not found in other Latin American capitals, and as Argentina's undisputed cultural, political, and economic hub it completely dominates the nation. Understandably, the city's rather self-indulgent atmosphere often annoys Argentinians from 'lesser' parts of

the country (such as Patagonia), as does the sometimes arrogant manner of its inhabitants.

With many parks, squares, cafes, pedestrian walkways and interesting architecture, central Buenos Aires is an attractive place, and there is a lot to see and do here. A good tip for those with the time is a day trip to the nearby provincial capital of La Plata to see the natural history museum founded by Francisco 'Perito' Moreno.

Buenos Aires' main tourist office (☎ 371 7054) is at Callao 235. The main sales office of the Argentine IGM is at Avenida Cabildo 381, which is best reached by taking the subway to the termination of D line then walking four blocks north. The Argentine national parks authority, the Administración de Parques Nacionales (APN) office (☎ 311 0303, ext 165) is at Santa Fe 680 (around the corner from where the Florida mall ends). The Centro Andino Buenos Aires (☎ 381 1566), at Oficina 201, Rivadavia 1255 is the capital's main mountaineering organisation.

Santiago
Dominating Chile at least as much as its trans-Andean counterpart dominates Argentina, Santiago lies at only around 600m above sea level yet is very much an 'Andean capital'. This city of over six million people looks out (through an increasingly thick layer of exhaust smog) onto the adjacent central Cordillera, whose towering snow-capped peaks reach over 6000m. Santiago has a pleasantly dry and warm climate, with maximum summer temperatures rarely going above 35°C. Summer nights in Santiago are relievingly cool, as chilled air from the Andes regularly descends on the city after sunset.

The city has a modern metro whose network is currently being expanded. Santiago has good art galleries, museums, restaurants, cafes and parks, and there is plenty to keep you occupied for quite a few days.

The headquarters of the forests and national parks authority, the Corporación Nacional Forestal, or CONAF, (☎ 696 6749), is at Avenida

Bulnes 285. Also well worth visiting is the Federación de Andinismo de Chile (☎ 222 0888), at Almirante Simpson 77 (see Mountain Clubs), which can give information on trekking and climbing in the central Cordillera just outside Santiago. Another good reason for staying a little longer in Santiago is to buy topographical maps at the Instituto Geográfico Militar (IGM) (☎ 696 8221/ 8228, extension 263; fax 698 7278) at Dieciocho 369, as the IGM has no sales office in southern Chile.

Health & Safety

Fortunately this is a short chapter, since there are few real heath hazards in southern Chile and Argentina and standards of hygiene are high. There are no poisonous reptiles or insects, nor dangerous animals of prey in the entire Patagonian Andes. In the vast South American tropical zone to the north, however, conditions are very different; travellers intending to go on to those regions should acquire a good basic knowledge of tropical diseases and conditions.

PREDEPARTURE PREPARATION

For travel in Patagonia only common sense health precautions need to be taken. Of course you'll need to be physically fit to trek in the Patagonian Andes, and it's wise to have a thorough medical checkup before you begin your journey; having a dental checkup is also a good idea.

Vaccination

Vaccinations are not required for entry to either Chile or Argentina, though it is a sensible travel precaution to be vaccinated against hepatitis and typhoid (see following sections).

Medical Kit

A small medical kit containing the basics for simple first aid should be carried by all trekking parties. For the treatment of minor complaints you can often simply consult a pharmacist. A wider range of medications can be bought without a prescription than is the case in Australasia, the USA or Western Europe. The items in the medical checklist are recommended.

HYGIENE ON THE TREK

So that others don't get a nasty bout of 'your' runs, use en route toilets or otherwise properly dispose of your bodily wastes (see Responsible Trekking in Facts for the Trekker). Don't dump food scraps around camp sites, as this will attract rodents.

Medical Kit Checklist

- [ ] **Antibiotics** – often only available by prescription from a doctor. Some people are allergic to certain antibiotics such as penicillin or sulpha drugs
- [ ] **Antihistamine** – such as Benadryl, useful as a decongestant for colds, for allergies, to ease itching caused by insect bites and to help motion sickness
- [ ] **Antiseptic** – such as Betadine, which comes as impregnated swabs or ointment, and an antibiotic powder or similar 'dry' spray, for cuts and grazes
- [ ] **Bandages and sticking plaster**
- [ ] **Burn cream**
- [ ] **Calamine lotion** – to ease irritation from bites or stings
- [ ] **Insect repellent** – it might stop the *tábanos* for a while!
- [ ] **Lomotil, Imodium or Kaolin preparation** – for the treatment of diarrhoea and intestinal troubles
- [ ] **Painkillers** – aspirin or panadol for pain or fever
- [ ] **Scissors and tweezers**
- [ ] **Thermometer** – note that mercury thermometers are prohibited on aircraft)
- [ ] **Sunscreen and lip chap stick** – the latter will save your lips from the dry, incessant winds encountered east of the Cordillera
- [ ] **Water sterilisation tablets**

Water Purification

Even in the towns and cities of Chile and Argentina, water is rarely a health problem. As anywhere, trekkers sensible enough to avoid drinking from suspicious water sources are quite unlikely to suffer stomach troubles. Provided there is no other source of water contamination (such as a farm or major camping area upstream), the water in remoter trekking areas is likely to be far purer than your tap water at home and should not need sterilisation. But if there is any doubt, boil it (see also notes on Liver Fluke Cysts later in this section).

Water can be made drinkable by a variety of methods, described here.

Boiling Boiling water for around five minutes is sufficient to kill all potentially harmful organisms, even at high altitude.

Chemical Sterilisation Iodine, in the form of tetraglycine hydro-periodide, lugol's solution or iodine crystals, has long been used to decontaminate water. Most convenient are iodine tablets, as they are measured to a given quantity of water. Unfortunately, water treated with iodine tastes terrible, but adding flavouring (such as *Tang*) makes it easier to drink.

Chemical (usually chlorine-based) agents can also be used to make contaminated water drinkable, but – although higher dosages accelerate the sterilisation process – they need more time to work than iodine. One good product is *Drinkwell*, a Swiss-made solution whose active ingredient is sodium hypochlorite; several droplets will sterilise a litre of water within 30 minutes. *Drinkwell* also makes a dechlorinating solution that removes the slightly unpleasant taste once sterilisation has occurred. *Puritabs* is another widely available water sterilising agent; one tablet will decontaminate a litre of water in a similar time.

Water Filters Water filters have become popular among backpackers in the last decade or so, but at around US$130 they are not cheap. Filtering murky, stagnant water will certainly make it look and taste more drinkable, but there is some disagreement as to whether a water filter can effectively remove viruses that cause diarrhoea or hepatitis (which are so small they could easily pass through the smallest holes in the filter). You probably won't have to treat water very often in the Patagonian Andes, so the extra bulk, weight and expense of a water filter is hard to justify.

MEDICAL PROBLEMS AND TREATMENT
Altitude Sickness (AMS)

For trekkers, the generally lower elevation of the Andes in Patagonia virtually eliminates the danger of altitude sickness, which is called *soroche* or *puna* in South America. (The threat of acute mountain sickness (AMS) is significantly greater to Patagonian climbers, however, as they are more likely to ascend to higher altitudes quickly and stay there for longer periods.) In the treks featured in this book, altitude sickness is extremely unlikely except perhaps for the ascent of Volcán Lanín (altitude 3776m). There is some disagreement regarding the lowest elevation at which cases of AMS can occur, but the condition is rare below 2500m above sea level.

AMS is basically caused by the body's failure to acclimatise to the lower atmospheric pressure of high altitudes. Because mountain air has a lower oxygen concentration, the alveoli in the lungs cannot pass on enough oxygen into the blood. The lungs begin to work harder and breathing is quickened. Fluid accumulates in between the cells in the body and eventually collects in the lungs and brain. As it builds up in the lungs, the fluid starts to cause breathlessness and a progressively worsening cough. If they do not descend, sufferers are ultimately drowned by this fluid. This syndrome is called high altitude pulmonary edema (HAPE).

When the fluid build up occurs in the brain, the first symptoms are headache, loss of appetite and nausea. As the condition progresses the patient feels constantly tired and lethargic. If allowed to progress, balance and coordination become distorted (ataxia), and eventually the patient lies down and slips into a coma. Unless immediately brought to lower ground, the patient will die. This dangerous syndrome is referred to as high altitude cerebral edema (HACE). HAPE and HACE can occur by themselves or in combination.

Similar symptoms to HACE can occur as a consequence of dehydration, too much sun, or other unrelated illnesses. Sleeplessness and loss of appetite are a common reaction to rapid ascent, and do not necessarily indicate altitude sickness. If such symptoms seem to be getting worse, the only sensible thing to do is descend. Failure to do so could result in death.

Hypothermia

Hypothermia, also known as exposure, is the ultimately fatal excessive cooling of the body and is an ever present danger in all alpine areas. The Patagonian Andes are renowned for the unpredictability of their weather, and hypothermia is a constant danger. Even in summer, severe storms can roll in suddenly from the Pacific, bringing heavy rain or snowfall. Trekkers should always be alert to signs of an impending breakdown in the weather. Familiarity with the typical symptoms of a developing hypothermic condition and methods of treating exposure is essential.

Key signs of hypothermia include slurred speech, dizziness, lethargy, difficulty with coordination, numbness of the skin, lack of feeling in the extremities and irrational behaviour. Always carry enough warm clothing, including a completely windproof and waterproof garment that covers at least your upper body and your head. Avoid crossing (or camping in) high and exposed areas in poor weather. Even in areas where there are refugios, carrying a tent will ensure you always have shelter in an emergency.

To treat hypothermia, first get the affected person out of the wind and rain. Have them remove all wet garments and put on dry clothing. Give the patient hot drinks (not alcohol) and simple sugary foods. If they still do not show signs of recovery, their condition is more serious. Put the patient into a well-insulated sleeping bag with another person to give additional body warmth. If possible place the patient in a warm bath.

Never treat a hypothermic person in the following ways.

- Do not rub the patient.
- Do not place the patient near a fire.
- Do not remove the patient's wet clothing unless they are sheltered from the weather.
- Do not give alcohol.

Diarrhoea

Diarrhoea is perhaps the most common affliction suffered by travellers in Patagonia, although it is far less of a problem than in other parts of South America. While a change of water, food or climate can also cause the runs, diarrhoea caused by contaminated food or water is more serious. In some parts of northern Chile, sewage water is still commonly used to irrigate and fertilise crops, and fruits or vegetables that grow on or close to the ground (eg strawberries, lettuce and carrots) should not be eaten before they have been cooked or otherwise sterilised (with a chemical sterilising agent – see Water Purification).

Despite all your precautions, you may still have a bout of mild travellers' diarrhoea, but a few rushed toilet trips with no other symptoms is not indicative of a serious problem. Moderate diarrhoea, involving half a dozen loose movements in a day, is more of a nuisance. Dehydration is the main danger with any diarrhoea, particularly for children, in whom dehydration can occur quite quickly.

Treatment of Diarrhoea Fluid replacement remains the mainstay of management. Soda water, weak black tea with a little sugar, or soft drinks allowed to go flat and diluted 50% with water are all good. With severe diarrhoea a rehydrating solution is necessary to replace minerals and salts. Commercially available ORS (oral rehydration salts) are very useful; add the contents of one sachet to a litre of boiled or bottled water. In an emergency you can make up a solution of eight teaspoons of sugar to a litre of boiled water and provide salted cracker biscuits at the same time. You should stick to a bland diet as you recover.

Lomotil or Imodium can be used to bring relief from the symptoms, although they do not actually cure the problem. Only use these drugs if absolutely necessary – eg if you *must* travel. Imodium is preferable for children, but under all circumstances fluid replacement is the main message. Do not use these drugs if the person has a high fever or is severely dehydrated.

In some situations, such as the following, antibiotics should be taken:

- Watery diarrhoea with blood and mucous. (Gut-paralysing drugs like Imodium or Lomotil should be avoided in this situation.)
- Watery diarrhoea with fever and lethargy.
- Persistent diarrhoea for more than five days.
- Severe diarrhoea, if it is logistically difficult to stay in one place.

The recommended drugs (adults only) would be either norfloxacin 400mg twice daily for three days, or ciprofloxacin 500mg twice daily for three days. The drug bismuth subsalicylate has also been used successfully. It is not available in Australia.

The dosage for adults is two tablets or 30ml and for children it is one tablet or 10ml. This dose can be repeated every 30 minutes to one hour, with no more than eight doses in a 24-hour period. The drug of choice in children would be co-trimoxazole (Bactrim, Septrin, Resprim) with the dosage dependent on the child's weight. A three-day course is also available. Ampicillin has been recommended in the past and may still be an alternative.

Giardiasis

Although not endemic to Patagonia, the parasite *Giardia lambilia* has been introduced to the region from other infected areas. Trekkers generally ingest Giardia by drinking contaminated water; the parasite produces muscle cramping and diarrhoea known as giardiasis, normally beginning at least one week after ingestion. Giardia can only spread where people practise poor sanitation close to waterways, so the parasite is most likely to exist in lakes and streams around heavily used camping areas (such as in popular national parks like Torres del Paine and Nahuel Huapi).

Boiling water that is even only possibly suspect is the best means of prevention. Giardiasis is treated with the drug metronidazole (Flagyl), taken in 250mg doses three times a day, but antibiotics are useless against the parasite.

Hepatitis

The term hepatitis groups several different diseases that attack the liver.

Hepatitis A Hepatitis A is associated with poor sanitation and is therefore not especially common in southern Chile and Argentina. With good water and adequate sewage disposal in most industrialised countries since the 1940s, very few young adults now have any natural immunity and must be protected. Havrix, a new vaccine against Hepatitis A, is now widely available and is believed to give immunity for at least 10 years. Havrix is administered in two shots, the first intramuscular (deltoid), the second, a booster, six months later. The other (older) form of protection against Hepatitis A is the antibody gamma globulin, which provides immunity for a maximum of six months.

Hepatitis A is spread by contaminated food or water. The symptoms are fever, chills, headache, fatigue, feelings of weakness and aches and pains, followed by loss of appetite, nausea, vomiting, abdominal pain, dark urine, light coloured faeces and jaundiced skin; the whites of the eyes may turn yellow. In some cases you may feel unwell, tired, have no appetite, experience aches and pains and be jaundiced. You should seek medical advice, but in general there is not much you can do apart from rest, drink lots of fluids, eat lightly and avoid fatty foods. People who have had hepatitis must forego alcohol for six months after the illness, as hepatitis attacks the liver and it needs that amount of time to recover.

Hepatitis B Hepatitis B, which used to be called serum hepatitis, is spread through contact with infected blood, blood products or bodily fluids, such as through sexual contact, unsterilised needles and blood transfusions. Other risk situations include having a shave or tattoo in a local shop, or having your ears pierced. The symptoms of type B are much the same as type A, except that they are more severe and may lead to irreparable liver damage or even liver cancer.

Although there is currently no treatment

for hepatitis B, an effective prophylactic vaccine is readily available in most countries. The immunisation schedule requires two injections at least a month apart followed by a third dose five months after the second. People who should receive a hepatitis B vaccination include anyone who anticipates contact with blood or other bodily secretions, either as a health care worker or through sexual contact with the local population, or anyone who intends to stay in the country for a long period of time.

Typhoid

The typhoid germ, *Salmonella typhosa*, can cause stomach pains, a rash, high fever and tiredness. In the worst cases it causes intestinal bleeding and can rupture the bowel. It may lie dormant in the body for years causing no symptoms, but can still infect others. The organism is most commonly found where sanitation is not good, and can be passed on through water, food and even ice. It is treatable by antibiotics, but it is, of course, better not to contract it in the first place.

Thphim Vi is a new typhoid vaccine, requires one less needle than the old one and has fewer side effects.

Typh Vax Oral is an oral typhoid vaccine, which is great if you're squeamish about needles. You should avoid some anti-malarial tablets and antibiotics for seven days before, during, and for seven days after taking the capsules. There is a live culture in the capsules, and antibiotics will kill it and render the treatment ineffective.

Hydatid Cysts

The only organism in Patagonia that has the potential to cause you real harm is the liver fluke. The liver fluke *(Tenia equinococco)* is a worm-like parasite that usually lives in the digestive tract of sheep, but may also infect cattle or pigs. This parasite's eggs are generally passed on to humans through contact with dogs that have fed on the entrails of infected animals. So-called hydatid cysts occur where the parasite establishes itself in organs of the body – especially the liver, kidneys or lungs – and develops gradually over a number of years. This condition (in Spanish, *hidatidosis*) is extremely serious, requiring surgery to remove the cysts.

To control liver fluke, an extensive government program is now under way to educate farmers not to allow their dogs into areas used for slaughtering animals. The parasite is found all over the world, and this simple precaution has largely eradicated it from countries such as Iceland and New Zealand. It is advisable not to pet suspect dogs – such as those on more remote farms – or other canines that may be infected with liver fluke, and to boil all water when passing through grazing country. In wilder mountain areas, however, the risk of contracting liver fluke is virtually nil.

Hanta Virus

The hanta virus is carried by rodents, and causes a rare but potentially fatal disease. There was a breakout of hanta virus around the Argentine town of El Bolsón in 1995. Avoid camping near rodent colonies and keep food out of their reach. Boil water from even possibly contaminated sources, and avoid areas where there are rodent faeces.

Rabies

Rabies is completely absent from Patagonia, but there have been outbreaks in northern regions of both Chile and Argentina in recent years.

Rabies is caused by a bite or scratch by an infected animal, especially dogs and cats. Any bite, scratch or even lick from a warm-blooded, furry animal should be cleaned immediately and thoroughly. Scrub with soap and running water, and then clean with an alcohol solution. If there is any possibility that the animal is infected medical help should be sought immediately. Even if the animal is not rabid, all bites should be treated seriously as they can become infected or can result in tetanus. A rabies vaccination is now available and should be considered if you are in a high-risk category – eg if you intend to explore caves (bat bites could be dangerous) or work with animals.

Minor Medical Problems

Blisters Blisters are an almost inevitable part of trekking, but it's worth doing all you can to avoid getting them anyway. Be sure to wear in new boots properly before you undertake a long trek, and protect susceptible parts of your feet as soon as – if not before – the skin starts to get tender. Various brands of 'second skin' adhesive bandages and sticking plasters are available that both prevent blisters and allow you to walk comfortably even after they occur.

Fungal Infections Warm summer weather in the Araucanía and Lake District provides ideal conditions for the spread of fungal infections of the skin. These most commonly effect trekkers between the toes (a condition known as athlete's foot). Another common complaint is 'crotch rot', a painful rash in the groin-to-buttocks area caused by the combination of rubbing and sweating as you walk; simple solutions include wearing comfortable, non-abrasive clothing and keeping clean. Ringworm (which is a fungal infection, not a worm) is picked up from infected animals or by walking on damp areas like shower floors.

If you do get a fungal infection, wash the infected area daily with a disinfectant or medicated soap and water, and rinse and dry well. Apply an antifungal powder like the widely available Tinaderm. Try to expose the infected area to air or sunlight as much as possible and wash all towels and underwear in hot water as well as changing them often.

Heat Exhaustion Although Patagonia has a cool-climate, heat exhaustion may occasionally become a real concern, especially in exposed volcanic country above the tree line. Dehydration or salt deficiency can cause heat exhaustion, so ensure that your body gets sufficient liquids. Salt deficiency is characterised by fatigue, lethargy, headaches,

The 'Ozone Hole'

Although it occurs in extremely low concentrations, the gas known as ozone plays a vital role in keeping the planet habitable for animals and plants by filtering out harmful ultra-violet (UV) rays high up in the atmosphere before they can reach the earth's surface. The discovery that this protective layer of atmospheric ozone is gradually being destroyed – chiefly by certain artificial chemical compounds called chlorinated fluoro-hydrocarbons (or CFCs) – is therefore deeply worrying.

Because of complex chemical processes, the frigid conditions that prevail in the polar regions during winter allow CFCs to break down atmospheric ozone more effectively there than in the earth's temperate and tropical zones. For this reason ozone depletion is progressively more severe closer to the polar regions. Antarctica experiences a much colder winter than the North Pole, and ozone depletion is therefore most severe in the southern hemisphere.

In Patagonia, the most critical period is in the (southern) spring months of October and November, when the area of ozone-depleted atmosphere – the so-called 'ozone hole' – expands northwards, reaching roughly 42° (the latitude of the cities of Puerto Montt and El Bolsón). By early December the ozone hole has contracted back towards Antarctica. There has, however, been some outrageously irresponsible reporting of the ozone hole in recent years, particularly in the foreign news media. Some of the most alarmist reports have described whole flocks of sheep blinded by cataracts in Patagonia, and street cats in Cape Town with ears frizzled away by apparently laser-like UV rays. It's therefore important to put into perspective the real danger that the ozone hole presents to trekkers in the Patagonian Andes.

One of the most important considerations is that the *natural* level of UV radiation in the earth's higher latitudes is relatively low compared to the tropical regions, and that UV radiation rises progressively with increasing altitude. The Patagonian Andes lie far outside the tropics, and treks are generally at fairly low elevations anyway (rising above 1500m only occasionally). Indeed anyone who treks in elevated (sub) tropical regions – such the Himalaya, the Peruvian Andes or the mountains of Papua New Guinea – will be exposed to higher levels of UV radiation than in the Patagonian Andes. Another mitigating factor is that the ozone hole has largely receded towards Antarctica by the time the Patagonian trekking season gets under way (in early December).

When trekking anywhere, of course, you must give proper attention to UV protection – by wearing a broad-brimmed hat and applying sunblock liberally and regularly to all exposed parts of your body. ■

giddiness and muscle cramps, and in this case salt tablets may help. One way trekkers can avoid the heat is by getting an early start, then taking it easy during the hottest part of the day.

Sunburn Particularly in November/December, when the sun is high but there is still plenty of snow about, routes above the tree line expose trekkers to relatively high levels of UV radiation. Since most trekkers dress lightly in such conditions, often wearing only a T-shirt and shorts, sunburn is often a problem. Remember the danger of sunburn is especially high when large snow drifts have to be crossed.

Protect your skin by wearing a broad-rimmed hat and keeping your limbs and face either covered up or well smeared with a good UV sunscreen (available locally). A good strong pair of polarising sunglasses is highly recommended, if not essential.

Getting There & Away

AIR

South America is really only directly accessible by air, and getting to Chile or Argentina is relatively expensive, especially from Australia or New Zealand. Discount fares from 'bucket shops' are available in most countries. These are usually substantially cheaper than the normal airfare. Check on the maximum period you are allowed to stay. Some return airfares allow a maximum stay of only four months, so check before you book.

Note that in most of the following examples, the return fare quoted is a special excursion fare and is therefore subject to certain conditions. Ask the relevant airline for further details.

Peru

Aero Perú has daily flights from Lima to Tacna for about US$90 one way. The other possibility is a flight from Lima to Santiago. Aero Perú flies from Lima to Santiago four days a week for around US$280 one way. Together LanChile or Ladeco have flights between Santiago and other major cities in Latin America.

Peru and Argentina don't have a common border, so all route possibilities are by air. From Lima, Aerolíneas Argentinas and Aero Perú fly regularly to Buenos Aires. The one-way airfare is around US$320.

Bolivia

There are normally several flights per week from La Paz to Arica (US$115) and Santiago (US$240).

Brazil

There are many daily flights between Santiago and Rio de Janeiro/São Paulo with airlines such as Varig, LanChile and Ladeco, and the one-way airfare from Rio de Janeiro to Santiago starts at around US$480.

From Río and São Paulo, Aerolíneas Argentinas and Varig have daily flights to Buenos Aires. There are also many daily buses to Buenos Aires and the more luxurious have sleeping compartments.

Australia & New Zealand

Flights from Australasia to South America are expensive. For travellers going on to Europe or Asia, round-the-world (RTW) tickets will probably work out to be much better value for money. If you are coming from Australia or New Zealand and intend travelling overland from the USA to Latin America, the cheapest option is to fly to San Francisco or Los Angeles and journey south through Mexico. Those intending to fly direct to South America from North America should refer to the following section.

A number of agents offer discounted airfares for flights out of Australia. Two of the main competitors are The Flight Shop and STA Travel. Customers of STA don't have to be students. There are also Flight Shops in the larger New Zealand cities. Look in the travel sections of newspapers for the most suitable and competitive airfares.

From Sydney, Qantas and UTA fly to Tahiti. From Tahiti LanChile has trans-Pacific flights via Easter Island to Santiago for around A$2200 return. Check whether the quoted price includes transfers and accommodation in Tahiti, and whether you can make a stopover on fascinating Easter Island – which for many travellers is the main reason for choosing to fly this more expensive and longer route – without additional cost. Various RTW ticket combinations with one-year validity include this route as the first stage. Other itineraries, including stopovers on many different islands of the South Pacific, can be built into such tickets.

From Australia and New Zealand, the cheapest and most direct way to South America is with Aerolíneas Argentinas from Sydney via Auckland to Buenos Aires; the return fare is around A$2000 and there are three flights per week during the (southern) summer months. It usually costs little or nothing more if you buy a connecting flight to Santiago (or any other South American capital serviced by Aerolíneas Argentinas). This route is the first stage of various RTW ticket combinations from Australasia. The cheapest flights from Australia to Argentina are with Malaysian Airlines via Kuala Lumpur to Johannesburg and Cape Town, then on direct to Buenos Aires; this return ticket costs around A$1600.

North America

Most flights from the USA to southern South America leave from Los Angeles, Miami or New York, and the major carriers are Aerolíneas Argentinas, Aero Perú, American Airlines, Eastern Airlines, Korean Airlines, Ladeco, LanChile, Lloyd Aéro Boliviano, United Airlines and Varig. You should be able to pick up a return air ticket (with at least four months validity) from the USA to Santiago or Buenos Aires for around US$1300.

In Canada, non-students can also book tickets with the national student travel agency, Travel CUTS, whose central office (☎ 416-977 3703) is at 171 College St, Toronto M5T 1P7. Travel CUTS also has offices in Ottawa, Montreal, Halifax, Saskatoon, Edmonton, Vancouver and Victoria. In the United States the Student Travel Network (STN) and the American Council Travel (CIEE) offer various route combinations to many places in Latin America. Both STN and CIEE have discount prices and you don't have to be a student to buy a ticket from them. STN has offices in Boston, Chicago, Los Angeles, Philadelphia, San Francisco, Seattle and Washington. CIEE has offices in Berkeley, Boston, New York, San Diego, Seattle and Los Angeles. The independent Odyssey Travel (☎ 1-800-395-5955) in Colorado specialises in Latin American travel.

South Africa

Malaysian Airlines and South African Airways (SAA) each have two flights per week from Johannesburg/Cape Town to Buenos Aires; SAA flies via Rio de Janeiro or São Paulo. Varig flies on Friday from Johannesburg via Cape Town.

UK & Europe

London and certain other capitals in Europe are excellent places to buy cheap air tickets. In Britain, magazines and newspapers like *Time Out* and the *Independent* have very good information about cheap air tickets. STA Travel and Trailfinders (0171-938 3939), 194 Kensington High St, London W8, are two recommended travel agents. Journey Latin America (☎ 0181-747 3108; fax (☎ 0181-742 1312), 14-16 Devonshire Road, Chiswick, London W4 2HD, a well-known specialist on South American travel, sells discounted airfares and runs tours all over Latin America. Direct flights from continental Europe are a bit more expensive. It might work out cheaper going to the USA or Canada and flying to South America from there. In Amsterdam (probably the most competitive prices in Europe after London), contact Malibu Travel (☎ 020-623 6814), at Damrack 30.

The Russian airline, Aeroflot, has two direct flights per week to Santiago from Shannon (Ireland), Stockholm and Moscow for US$1275 return (which includes connecting Aeroflot flights between Moscow and most western European capitals). British Airways flies to Santiago for £363 one way/£589 return. Other important airlines that fly from Europe to Santiago are LanChile, Iberia, Air France, Lufthansa, Alitalia, Sabena, SAS and Swissair.

British Airways flies direct from London to Buenos Aires (around £300 one way/£495 return). Aerolíneas Argentinas has direct flights to Buenos Aires from Amsterdam, Madrid, Rome, Paris, Frankfurt and Zurich. A great range of other carriers have flights from European cites to Argentina.

OVERLAND
Peru

Peru's southern border with Chile is the point of entry for many travellers. There are two ways of entering Chile from Peru. The only overland route is from the southern Peruvian town of Tacna to Arica in the far north of Chile. Tacna can be reached daily by either bus, train or taxi *(colectivo)*.

Bolivia

From Bolivia there are a number of routes into Chile. Bolivia has a long border with Chile, but most of the land traffic is between La Paz and Arica in Chile's far north. From La Paz there are train, *ferrobus* (a kind of bus mounted onto a rail carriage base) and regular bus services to Arica.

The main road link between Bolivia and Argentina goes via La Quiaca/Villazón on the northern border in Jujuy Province. From Villazón there are daily buses to the Argentine provincial capitals of Salta and Jujuy.

Brazil

Travellers coming from the north usually make the crossing from Brazil into Argentina at the spectacular Iguazú Falls. Regular buses leave from the Brazilian side of the falls at Foz do Iguaçu to Puerto Iguazú in Argentina.

Getting Around

Chile and Argentina have modern, efficient and reasonably cheap long-distance public transport. In most cases, getting to and from the start or finish of a trek is easy by local public transport.

AIR

In southern Argentina, flying often works out cheaper than a combination of buses, but flights are heavily booked during busy holiday periods. Air links between cities of Argentine Patagonia are less extensive, and it's often necessary to fly via a third city (such as Río Gallegos). The main national airlines, Austral and Aerolíneas Argentinas, have the most extensive network of flights in Argentine Patagonia. Small regional carriers like TAN, LAP, LAPA and Kaikén tend to be somewhat cheaper and often fly routes more convenient to trekkers in Patagonia. Although its services have been reduced because of heavy competition and cuts in government subsidies, the no-frills, military-run airline Líneas Aéreas de Estado (LADE) is still the cheapest way to get around Patagonia.

In Chile, the two main national airlines, LanChile and Ladeco (which have recently merged but will continue to operate as separate carriers), fly between the main cities. A new national airline, ALTA, has about 80 domestic flights per week, including the long Santiago-Valparaíso-Temuco-Puerto Montt-Coyhaique-Puerto Natales-Punta Arenas 'kangaroo route' – which offers the only *direct* transport between Coyhaique and Puerto Natales. There are also small regional airlines which service remote areas of the far south. Most notable is DAP, which flies from Punta Arenas on the Chilean mainland to the Fuegian destinations of Porvenir, Puerto Williams and Ushuaia (in Argentine Tierra del Fuego).

Air Passes

Air passes are tailored to travellers who want to jet around a country or region in a short time, and are therefore less suited to trekkers.

However, one special circle fare offered by Aerolíneas Argentinas in combination with LanChile that may be suitable for users of this guidebook is the 'Southern Lake Crossing' fare. This special Buenos Aires-Bariloche-Puerto Montt-Santiago-Buenos Aires air ticket is very good value at US$318 (considering that a one-way Bariloche-Buenos Aires fare, for example, would cost US$248).

Both Chile and Argentina have special air passes for foreign tourists. The 30-day 'Visit Argentina Fare' is valid on the entire domestic network of both Aerolíneas Argentinas and Austral. It allows only one stopover at any one destination, but transit stops are allowed. The price depends on the number of flights: four flights cost US$450, eight flights cost US$930 and 12 flights cost US$1410. Both LanChile and Ladeco offer a southern version of its 21-day 'Visit Chile Fare' for US$300. This air pass covers the domestic network of *either* airline southwards from Santiago. The Visit Chile Fare allows unlimited stops, but you may not fly into the same city more than twice (including for transit stops) nor fly any route in the same direction more than once.

BUS

Except in parts of southern Argentina and Tierra del Fuego (where flying often works out cheaper) bus travel is likely to be the main form of inter-city transport for budget travellers. Buses are usually the most reliable form of land transport and are both comfortable and fast. There are bus stations in all the large provincial cities, and these serve as departure and arrival terminals for virtually all local and long-distance services. On well-travelled routes there is a considerable difference in ticket prices between bus companies, so it usually pays to compare prices. On international routes, always remember that a bus service across the border will usually be much more expensive for the distance travelled than a combination of regular buses.

At times trekkers may find it convenient to send on inessential gear by bus (as a so-called *encomienda*). This service is especially cheap in Chile (where 10kg of goods transported 100km typically costs under US$2), but bus companies in both countries are reluctant to transport unaccompanied goods across international borders. Goods can be claimed at the bus company's office or terminus at the destination; there's usually no extra fee even if you don't pick it up for a week or more – so it is also a good way of storing gear.

TRAIN

Although in both countries privatisation of the badly run-down national railway systems should eventually bring an improvement to passenger train services – at least on major lines – train travel will remain slower and less reliable than bus travel for the foreseeable future. Trains, however, are a much more pleasant way of travelling and often follow more scenic routes than the road.

In Chile, the railway goes from Santiago to Puerto Montt in the Lake District, but there are no railways farther south. These trains are slower and less popular with the public than buses, and in busy holiday periods may be the only transport available. The Chilean government is considering a proposal by a consortium of local and overseas companies to provide a new high-speed rail link between Santiago and Puerto Montt. Apart from an isolated 300km stretch of rail from Río Turbio to Río Gallegos, the Argentine national network goes only as far south as Esquel (the terminus of the narrow-gauge 'Old Patagonian Express' steam train). If travelling inland from Buenos Aires, the rail services from the capital to Córdoba and Mendoza are relatively rapid, comfortable and well priced. Other trains are very slow and only recommended for rail enthusiasts with plenty of time.

TAXI

Sometimes chartered taxis (called *remises* in Argentina) are the best way of getting to the start of the trek. Out of season it may be necessary to hire a taxi if tourist buses are no longer running. Depending on your travel budget, a long trip by taxi may only be economical for trekking parties of more than three or four.

CAR & MOTORCYCLE

Particularly for trekkers who intend to visit out-of-the-way areas (such as Parque Nacional Perito Moreno), the advantages of having your own means of transport are considerable. All non-resident drivers must have a valid International Driver's Licence issued by your own national/state automobile association. In Argentina, non-residents are generally not permitted to take a private vehicle out of the country. Apart from the main highways, roads in the south are usually unsurfaced.

Petrol (gasoline) prices average around US$0.90 per litre in Chile. It is heavily subsided in Argentina's Patagonian provinces (Neuquén, Río Negro, Chubut, Santa Cruz and Tierra del Fuego), where it only costs around half as much (about US$.50 per litre) as in other parts of Argentina.

Car Rental

Chile has reasonably cheap and hassle-free car rental by South American standards, but some companies won't hire out vehicles to people under 25. A 4WD pickup *(camioneta)* such as a Chevrolet Luv D/C costs around US$250 per week (with unlimited km), but rates are typically much higher in Argentina. There's no problem taking rented vehicles across the border, but it will always cost you a hefty surcharge unless you return the car to the original point of rental.

BICYCLE

Particularly since the advent of the mountain bike, increasing numbers of travellers seem to be pedalling their way around southern Chile and Argentina. Other kinds of bike are probably not robust enough for the mainly unsurfaced roads. Locally produced mountain bikes are reportedly of inferior quality and cope poorly on the area's trying roads. When planning your route through Argentine

Patagonia pay special attention to prevailing wind directions, which in summer tend to blow from the east to north-east. The frustration of pedalling against eastern Patagonia's strong and incessant head winds causes some cyclists to give up. There are bicycle shops in all the larger cities, but in out-of-the-way places spare parts can be hard to find.

HITCHING

The Spanish term for hitching is *viajar a dedo,* literally 'to travel by finger'. Hitchhiking in Chile and Argentina is reasonably reliable along the main routes during the busy summer holiday period, but remember that for many local backpackers hitchhiking is the only affordable way to see their country, so try not to compete with them for rides unless there is no other viable means of transport.

On lonelier stretches of road you may have to wait a long time – even days – for a ride. One of the slowest hitching routes in Patagonia is the 900km stretch of the Ruta 40 between Esquel and Calafate. The Ruta 40 is a very long and dusty dirt highway which follows the Andean foothills in the Argentine provinces of Chubut and Santa Cruz. This area is thinly settled, and lengthy stretches along the Ruta 40 are best avoided as there is usually little traffic. The good coastal highway between Comodoro Rivadavia and Río Gallegos (Ruta 3) is much busier and carries most of the long-distance traffic bound for inland destinations.

Considering the low vehicle density, Chile's Carretera Austral has surprisingly good hitching. As the only possible north-south route, the Carretera channels all long-distance traffic onto a single road. The drivers in this remote region are also more inclined to stop. The Carretera Austral is popular with locals and the hitchhiking routes often reach saturation point. The hitching tends to be slightly better if you're going north to south rather than vice versa.

The less densely populated south of both countries is relatively safe for travellers and assaults are rare. Even so, an unaccompanied female hitchhiker is more likely to get into

dangerous situations than a lone male. Women who hitchhike are advised to travel with male company or in pairs.

BOAT

In southern Chile, sea-based transport is very important, and boats are still the only means of access for some isolated settlements. Long-distance ferries *(transbordadores)* run by the company NAVIMAG ply the beautiful fjord-studded coast south from Puerto Montt. NAVIMAG's *Puerto Eden* runs between Puerto Montt and Puerto Natales three or four times per month in either direction, while the *Evangelistas* runs between Puerto Montt and Puerto Chacabuco. In summer the *Evangelistas* continues to Laguna San Rafael.

In addition to maritime traffic, regular ferry services on many of the large lakes of southern Chile and Argentina are an important means of transport for travellers. In some cases, such as on Lago Nahuel Huapi in the Argentine Lake District, these are mainly tourist boats. In lakes such as Lago Pirehueico in the Chilean Lake District and Lago General Carrera in central Patagonia, ferry services are simply the most practical form of transport. Particularly along Chile's Carretera Austral, numerous rivers must be crossed by simple car ferries.

In a few cases (the access to the Termas de Calláo for example) the best way to get to a walk is by chartered boat. You will have to negotiate payment and transport yourself here.

CROSSING THE BORDER

The best way to see Patagonia's national parks is probably to start in the north and work your way southwards, crossing between Chile and Argentina a number of times. In the Araucanía and Lake District there is a good number of international routes with public or tourist transport available. In remote parts of southern and central Patagonia, however, most of the border crossings are in fairly remote and inaccessible areas. People with their own transport will have fewer worries on the remoter passes. Hitchhikers who are in a hurry are better off keeping to the better travelled roads.

Following are the principal Chile-Argentina routes:

Pucón to Junín de los Andes

This is an attractive but largely unsurfaced road across Paso Mamuil Malal (called Paso Tromén in Argentina) and is the point of access for treks in Parque Nacional Villarrica and for the ascent of Volcán Lanín. There are only eight buses each week in either direction along this road and there is not much other traffic. Buses generally run between Temuco and San Martín de los Andes via Pucón and Junín de los Andes.

Puerto Fuy to San Martín de los Andes

This is a very scenic boat and bus route of roughly 70km. Puerto Fuy is situated on the remote north-western end of Lago Pirehueico and is accessible by daily bus from Panguipulli. From Puerto Fuy a ferry can be taken to the lake's south-eastern shore, from where passengers can meet a synchronised bus service to San Martín. The route gives direct access to the Queñi Circuit trek just on the Argentine side of Paso Hua Hum.

Osorno to San Carlos de Bariloche

This is the most important international route in the Lake usually the quickest way across the border. A good surfaced road goes via Entrelagos across the Paso (or Portezuelo) Puyehue and around Lago Nahuel Huapí. In District and summer, there are many buses between Bariloche and Osorno, Puerto Montt, Valdivia and even Santiago. The route provides access to walks in both Puyehue and Nahuel Huapí national parks and it features beautiful scenery.

Petrohué to San Carlos de Bariloche

This is essentially a route designed for tourists, and is slower and more expensive than the main Osorno-Bariloche road.

From Petrohué boats go across Chile's Lago Todos los Santos to Peulla, where a short section of international road leads to Laguna Frías in Argentina. From Puerto

Frías another boat goes to Puerto Alegre on Lago Nahuel Huapí, from where you can board a third ferry either to Llao-Llao or to Bariloche. This route offers superb Lake District scenery and I highly recommend it. The whole trip can take up to two days, and can be done as a complete package (sold as the 'Cruce de los Lagos') from around US$90 including meals and overnight accommodation.

Futaleufú to Esquel

This very scenic 75km road route which starts from the remote village of Futaleufú links the Carretera Austral with the Argentine city of Esquel, which is the gateway to the large Parque Nacional Los Alerces. Minibuses run between Esquel and Futaleufú four or five times per week. There is moderate traffic along the road during the summer period, but the route is popular with local hitchhikers.

Coyhaique to Río Mayo & Comodoro Rivadavia

The unsurfaced road over the low Paso Coyhaique passes the small reserve of Dos Lagunas. Río Mayo is a remote settlement of roughly 400 people on Argentina's Ruta 40. There are several international buses per week in either direction between Coyhaique and Comodoro Rivadavia on the Atlantic coast.

Chile Chico to Los Antiguos & Perito Moreno

This is a more popular route with travellers heading to the Argentine town of Perito Moreno. The trip involves first taking the ferry across Lago General Carrera from Puerto Ingeniero Ibáñez on the lake's northern shore to the pleasant village of Chile Chico. From Chile Chico a short road goes via the southern shore of Lago General Carrera (whose name changes to Lago Buenos Aires at the Argentine border) to Los Antiguos.

Cochrane to Bajo Caracoles

The is the most isolated of all the international pass routes and leads through the Valle

Chacabuco across Paso Roballos. There is no public transport and traffic is extremely thin, so the route is only suitable for those with their own transport or plenty of supplies, time and patience.

Puerto Natales to Calafate

This route is of key interest to trekkers because it connects these two 'gateway' towns to Torres del Paine and Los Glaciares national parks.

Buses run between Puerto Natales and Calafate almost daily from November/December until March/April via the scenic Paso Baguales. The fare is about US$20 – which is cheaper than it used to be, but still overpriced for a distance of less than 200km. The route passes the 50km turnoff road that leads into the Parque Nacional Torres del Paine about halfway.

Puerto Natales to Río Turbio & Río Gallegos

This is an uninteresting route but may be your fastest way of getting to Río Gallegos. Workers' buses run roughly hourly across the border to the border town of Río Turbio. The road has little traffic during the tourist season from December to February, and virtually none outside that time, so hitchhiking carries the risk of a very long wait.

Punta Arenas to Río Gallegos

Punta Arenas is connected to Río Gallegos by a 260km surfaced road. The route follows the coast of the Straits of Magellan before heading inland at the border, and passes the road turnoffs to the Laguna Azul and Pali Aike reserves. There are frequent buses between the two cities.

Puerto Williams to Ushuaia

This roughly 70km route across the Beagle Channel is the most southerly border crossing possible. A tourist boat operates weekly between Puerto Williams on Navarino Island and Ushuaia on the mainland of Tierra del Fuego (although the service is subject to frequent interruptions because of the tense border situation); the return fare is around US$60. Puerto Williams can also be reached by plane or boat from Punta Arenas. Yachts sailing down to Cape Horn and Antarctica are often required to register with authorities at Puerto Williams on the way, and it is often possible to get a ride with one of these many sailing vessels.

The Araucanía

The Araucanía extends southwards from the Río Biobío to the snows of Volcán Villarrica. Like the Lake District, which shares many of its typical features, the Araucanía is extremely active volcanically, and offers a fascinating variety of natural phenomena such as many thermal springs, volcanoes and mountain lakes. The area is the heartland of the Araucarian (or Mapuche) Indians, who relied heavily on the edible nuts of the araucaria 'pine' for food. These glorious trees still grow throughout the Araucanía, where they are protected by the region's many national parks and reserves.

TREKKING BASES
Los Angeles (Chile)

A regional capital a short distance north of the Río Biobío, Los Angeles is just outside Chile's Araucanía region. Los Angeles is a transit point for the Laguna del Laja and

Araucanía

TREKS IN THE ARAUCANÍA

Tolhuaca national parks as well as many other potential trips into the nearby Cordillera. The city is just west of the Panamerican Highway, and is easily reached from the north or south. The tourist office is in the post office on the Plaza de Armas. Accommodation is rather expensive in Los Angeles, so try to avoid staying here. A cheaper place is the *Hotel Winser* (☎ 31 38 45), near the main bus station at Casa Matríz Rengo 138, which has tiny and very basic rooms from US$12.

You should note that Los Angeles has two bus stations. In the centre of town is the regional bus station (Terminal Santa Rita), from where buses depart to local destinations (such as to El Abanico near the entrance to Parque Nacional Laguna del Laja), whereas the new long-distance bus station is east of town. Los Angeles' area code is ☎ 43.

Temuco (Chile)

With a population of about 220,000, Temuco is the largest city in the Araucanía. Temuco is the gateway for trips to the national parks of Villarrica, Huerquehue, Conguillío, Nahuel Buta and Laguna del Malleco. A pleasant local place for a short urban hike is Cerro Ñielol, a small CONAF-administered nature reserve bordering the town (access via Calle Prat).

Temuco is the capital of Chile's IX Región and the main centre of Mapuche culture. Over half of the population of Temuco is of Mapuche origin. The most interesting things to see relate to the Araucanía's Mapuche past and present. The Museo Regional de la Araucanía, at Avenida Alemania 84, has a collection devoted to Mapuche history.

Temuco also has an interesting fruit and vegetable market, and a handicrafts market, where Mapuche silver jewellery, belts, ponchos and other woollens are sold. The Casa de Arte Mapuche, near the regional bus station just before the corner of Matta and Avenida Balmaceda, is a Mapuche cultural centre that also sells books and artwork.

Temuco's tourist office (☎ 21 1969; fax 21 5509) is opposite the Plaza de Armas at Bulnes 586. CONAF has its regional headquarters in Temuco at Bilbao 931 on the 2nd floor; (☎ 21 1912), and there's another CONAF office at Montt 1151, 2nd floor; (☎ 21 2784). Anglers can buy a Chilean fishing license at the regional SERNAP office (☎ 23 8390), General Mackenna 215. There are numerous budget places to stay in Temuco. Situated right on the Panamerican Highway, the city has excellent transport connections to all locations in the Chilean Araucanía. Long-distance buses generally depart from the office or terminal of each company, but buses to regional destinations all leave from Temuco's rural bus station (Terminal de Buses Rurales). Temuco's area code is ☎ 45.

Aluminé (Argentina)

The small town of Aluminé lies in the Andean foothills of central Neuquén province on the Ruta 23, and is the best trekking base for the northern sectors of Parque Nacional Lanín. The Fiesta del Pehuén, a thematic festival that centres around the araucaria tree, is held here every April. Aluminé's tourist office is at the Plazoleta on the road into town, and the town's area code is ☎ 0942.

Pucón (Chile)

The gateway to the national parks of Huerquehue and Villarrica, the tourist resort of Pucón lies on the eastern shore of Lago Villarrica directly below the superb perfect cone of Volcán Villarrica. The town has a laid-back atmosphere that attracts well-to-do Chilean holiday makers and humble backpackers alike. Quality native wood products (such as salad bowls carved out of raulí) are on sale. Pucón's tourist office (☎ 44 1238; fax 44 1079) is at the eastern end of Avenida O'Higgins. The CONAF office (☎ 44 1261) is at Camino Internacional 1450, at the eastern edge of town (on the road to Puesco).

Recommended lower budget places to stay are the *Hospedaje Lincoyán* (☎ 44 1043) at Lincoyán 630 or the *Residencial Lincoyán* (☎ 44 1144) at Lincoyán 323. JAC runs buses every half hour in both directions between Temuco and Pucón (via Villarrica). Pucón's area code is ☎ 45.

Parque Nacional Laguna del Laja

Parque Nacional Laguna del Laja is east of the Chilean provincial city of Los Angeles, just north of the Río Biobío. Although it covers an area of little more than 100 sq km, the park includes several unique features: the perfect cone of Volcán Antuco, the classic many-armed highland lake of Laguna de la Laja, and – just outside the park boundary – the impressive glaciated range of the Sierra Velluda. With altitudes ranging from 1000 to almost 3000m above sea level, this park is a varied and surprisingly compact Andean wilderness.

GENERAL INFORMATION
Geographical Features
At the centre of the park is the near-perfect 2979m cone of Volcán Antuco, just one of the region's many dormant volcanoes. The tiny summit caldera still steams and puffs out sulphuric gases, but – for the moment – is otherwise fairly quiet. Immediately to the south-west is the Sierra Velluda, a spectacular range that rises to 3585m. Choked by numerous hanging glaciers and icefalls, these non-volcanic peaks contrast sharply with the smoother contours of Volcán Antuco.

At the eastern foot of Volcán Antuco lies the Laguna de la Laja. This large highland lake is the source of the Río Laja, the major river of Chile's Chillán region, whose famous Salto del Laja is passed far downstream on the Panamerican Highway. The lake's interesting form of several narrow arms was created during the volcano's 1873 eruption, when thick streams of molten lava blocked the Río Laja, impounding its waters and drowning the valleys upstream. Unfortunately, hydroelectric development has disturbed the laguna's natural shoreline (which is around 1400m above sea level), but the lake's setting among lofty peaks still presents a dramatic scene.

Natural History
Because of its climate, height and recent volcanic activity, the park is relatively sparsely vegetated, but one feature of its flora is the ciprés de la cordillera *(Austrocedrus chilensis)*. Known to the Mapuche as the lahuán, this small coniferous tree thrives in the drier alpine conditions, and can be seen on the surrounding mountainsides on the approach road to the park. There are also small areas of evergreen coigüe forest and, higher up, deciduous ñirre scrub.

Another major feature of the Laguna del Laja area's botany is its hardy wild flowers, which in spring and early summer grow sporadically in the loose volcanic earth. Some of the most attractive are the alpine violets *(Viola* species), whose delicate blooms often produce a 'desert garden' landscape. There are also specialised species of succulents, including the unique maihuén *(Maihuenia poeppigii)*, a rather atypical member of the cactus family.

The maihuén grows in large spiny mounds that look a bit like closely mown lawns (though you wouldn't want to sit on them), from which clustered bright yellow flowers emerge in early summer. The pink-petalled mutisia volcanica *(Mutisia oligodon)*, and the white, vaguely carnation-like estrella de la cordillera *(Perezia carthamoides)*, and several bulbous *Rhodophilias*, are some of the rarer local plant species.

It's interesting to observe the regeneration patterns following Volcán Antuco's last catastrophic eruption. This has proceeded only gradually, although in places islands of vegetation have been left untouched within the desolate fields of lava. The native fauna is far less abundant and seldom seen, although pumas, foxes and vizcachas exist in and around the park.

Climate
Parque Nacional Laguna del Laja (which represents the most northerly area covered in this book) has a climate more like the mountain areas farther to the north. Here the seasons show a marked annual contrast, with hot dry summers and cold winters. Most of

the year's precipitation falls in winter as snow. The average midwinter (July) snow cover at the administration centre (approximately 1200m above sea level) is 2m, but this increases with elevation. Skiing is possible, and a small ski village has been built at around 1400m on the north-western slopes of Volcán Antuco.

The warmer weather of spring (October–November) quickly melts away the snow cover, however, and by late January the largest patches of snow remain only above approximately 2000m. Volcán Antuco and the Sierra Velluda cause a rain shadow on the eastern edge of the volcano, blocking precipitation producing drier conditions in that sector of the national park.

Place Names

For many visitors, the name Parque Nacional Laguna *del* Laja is confusing, since the lake itself is called Laguna *de la* Laja. The reason for this is that the park's Spanish name actually refers as much to the Río Laja as to the lake itself. It might therefore be translated as the 'Lake of the River Laja' national park. The Spanish word *laja* means 'smooth rock', and was first given to the section of the Río Laja far downstream – you won't see too much smooth rock in Parque Nacional Laguna del Laja!

Antuco, the name of the park's magnificent volcano, is made up of two Mapuche words. The word *antu* means 'sun', while *co* is Mapuche for 'water'. The origins of Velluda, the nearby mountain range, come from a Spanish surname.

Other geographic features of the area, including the individual peaks of the Sierra Velluda and the pass crossed on the Around Volcán Antuco trek described later, have apparently still not been given (official) names.

PRACTICAL INFORMATION
Information Sources

The best source of information in the park itself is the CONAF information centre (Centro de Informes) at the administration centre (700m uphill from the Guardería

Chacay). This small museum has recently been renovated and outlines the park's local flora and fauna. The knowledgeable manager of the Centro Turístico Lagunillas (see Accommodation) is a trekking guide for ascents of Volcán Antuco and in the Sierra Velluda.

Permits & Regulations

An entry fee of US$2 per person is payable at the park entrance gate (Portería El Álamo), although this may be waived (or simply overlooked) if you don't arrive with your own vehicle. No special permit is required for this trek, but the standard rules apply regarding signing in before you leave. Visitors can sign in at the Guardería Chacay, or (better) at the administration centre 700m farther uphill.

There are few restrictions on camping in the park, but trekkers who decide to pitch their tent on the shore of Laguna de la Laja are asked to give special consideration to sanitation and to make sure all garbage is carried out.

Park authorities may insist that trekkers ascending Volcán Antuco (see Other Treks in Parque Nacional Laguna del Laja) are accompanied by a local guide, but this is not really enforced.

When to Trek

The best months to trek in Parque Nacional Laguna del Laja are December (when the interesting wild flowers are at their best) or April (when there is little snow on the pass and conditions are not so hot). Before mid-November much of the park (including the Around Volcán Antuco route) is still snowbound. From mid-December until late January, *tábanos* (see Dangers & Annoyances in the Facts for the Trekker chapter) can be bothersome at lower elevations. On the other hand, trekkers will find the going hot and dusty in January and February. Depending on the seasonal variation, cooler yet snow-free conditions can generally be expected from late March until early May.

Around Volcán Antuco

Duration 3 days
Distance 47km
Standard Easy-Medium
Start/Finish Guardería Chacay
Entry US$2, no permit needed
Season December or April
Summary A highly scenic circuit around the snowcapped cone of Volcán Antuco, a dormant volcano whose lava flows dammed the nearby Río Laja to create the Laguna de la Laja.

The circumnavigation of Volcán Antuco is the only longer trekking possibility in Parque Nacional Laguna del Laja, and takes you up into the wildest parts of the park.

MAPS

The entire park is covered by one Chilean IGM 1:50,000 sheet, *Laguna de la Laja* (Section G, No 21). Although this map indicates topographical detail very well, some higher areas are left uncontoured and the trekking routes themselves are not indicated. Don't confuse the high-altitude traverse through the Sierra Velluda – which this sheet does show – with the Around Volcán Antuco route described here.

DAYS REQUIRED

The trek can be done in two very long days, but parties should plan to take three days. An ascent of Volcán Antuco (from either the northern or south-eastern side of the mountain) would take an additional day.

TREKKING STANDARD

The trek completely circumnavigates Volcán Antuco, and crosses bare and exposed lava flows and loose volcanic earth for virtually the entire distance. It involves a climb from the Guardería Chacay (115m) to a 2054m pass, and the route is fairly straightforward, but largely unmarked. In this central section of the route there is no real path and deep snow may lie well into January. The long final section is along an easily navigable dirt road. Fine summer weather can quickly make the going hot and unpleasant, particularly lower down.

The circuit can be walked in either direction, but the recommended way to go is anticlockwise. The trek has been given a *medium* grading. The total walking distance is 47km.

ACCOMMODATION & CAMPING

Just before the turn-off to the park, near the village of El Abanico, are two places to stay: the friendly *Hospedería del Bosque* offers dormitory accommodation for around US$7 and rooms for around US$12 with breakfast; adjacent is the more up-market *Hotel Malalcura* (☎ 43-31 3183 or 43-32 3163), which has a dormitory as well as better rooms for around US$25.

Within the park itself is the *Centro Turístico Lagunillas* (for information and reservations call the Hostería Manantiales, at the Salto del Laja on the Panamerican Highway ☎ 31 4275), on the banks of the Río Laja about 1km up the road from the Portería El Alamo on the banks of the Río Laja. This privately run camping ground offers excellent self-contained six-person cabins for US$90 per night and camp sites for US$12 per site. There are hot showers and a kitchen for guests as well as a restaurant/bar.

Higher up at the small ski village of Volcán Antuco is the *Casino Club de Esquí/ Refugio Antuco*, which offers dormitory accommodation for around US$10 per person. Although much busier in winter, the refugio is open all year round and serves meals and drinks. As there are no huts along the route, this trek cannot be done safely without a tent. CONAF has plans to construct a basic emergency shelter below the pass on the south-western slopes of Volcán Antuco at some time in the future, but this would not alter the need for trekkers to carry a tent.

The camping conditions along the route are mostly reasonable considering the often difficult terrain. Firewood is fairly scarce in most places, so carry a stove and sufficient fuel.

SUPPLIES

Trekking supplies cannot be purchased within the park. The nearest stores are in El Abanico and Antuco, but Los Angeles is by far the best option for stocking up.

GETTING TO/FROM THE TREK

Parque Nacional Laguna del Laja is 90km by road east of Los Angeles (see Trekking Bases at the start of this chapter). There is no public transport the whole way out to the park, but there are half a dozen or so daily buses from Los Angeles via Antuco to El Abanico, a village at the turn-off to the park. Buses leave from Los Angeles central bus station (Terminal Santa Rita). The last bus leaves at about 7 pm, but the last return bus from El Abanico departs earlier, at around 5.30 pm, and the trip takes roughly two hours each way. After Antuco the road becomes unsurfaced and gets a bit rough in places, but it is gradually being improved.

From the El Abanico turn-off the road leads 11km up beside the rapids of the Río Laja to the guardería and administrative centre at Chacay. This stretch can be walked in three or four hours, but there is enough friendly traffic during the busy tourist season to make successful hitchhiking reasonably certain. The Around Volcán Antuco trek described here begins at the Guardería Chacay, a minor ranger station 700m before the park administration centre.

THE TREK

Stage 1: Guardería Chacay to Estero Los Pangues Camp
4.5km, 2¾ to 3¾ hours

Follow the path (signposted 'Sendero M. Los Zorros/Sierra Velluda') from just above the Guardería Chacay due south up the slope past the clusters of mountain cypresses. Head up a steep eroding ridge to reach a signposted junction at the edge of a tiny plateau overlooking the Río Laja after 30 to 45 minutes.

The right branch goes to the **Meseta de los Zorros** (shown on IGM maps as Los Pangues). To get there follow the track down through light forest to a lovely grassy meadow set among ciprés and coigüe trees. There are good views across the valley towards the adjacent rocky range. Just below the spectacular torrent, Estero Los Pangues washes black volcanic scoria out from the mountains. This easy return side trip takes from 45 minutes to one hour.

Take the left branch (marked 'Sierra de Velluda') up over the low and sparsely vegetated ridges until you come to a lava flow. The path first skirts rightwards along the edge of the lava, passing interesting tiny islands of quila scrub left undisturbed in the mass of solidified slag, then crosses through the broken rock to reach the small but fast-flowing **Estero Los Pangues** after 60 to 80 minutes. Here you meet another foot track coming up the east bank of the stream.

Follow the path through the remains of an old cattle pen, and continue upstream for a further 30 to 40 minutes past a wide green curve of the Estero Los Pangues fringed by the lava on one side and the abrupt northern side of the Sierra Velluda on the other. This attractive grassy plain lies directly below waterfalls crashing down from hanging glaciers, and is grazed by horses and native animals.

Camp Sites The only recommended places to camp are the Meseta de los Zorros or the grassy river flats at the end of this section. Although at the latter sites there is little firewood and the ground closer to the stream is soggy in places, the views directly up to Sierra Velluda are spectacular.

Stage 2: Estero Los Pangues Camp to Los Barros
13km, 4½ to 6 hours

Head south-east across the scoria towards the obvious low point between the Sierra Velluda to your right and the majestic cone of Volcán Antuco. Marked only by occasional cairns, the track stays within earshot of the Estero Los Pangues, avoiding the vast expanse of broken volcanic rock. After you pass a steep ridge descending from the Sierra Velluda, the tiny upper valley widens to reveal more glaciers up to the right.

Head up across a rusty-red alluvial wash,

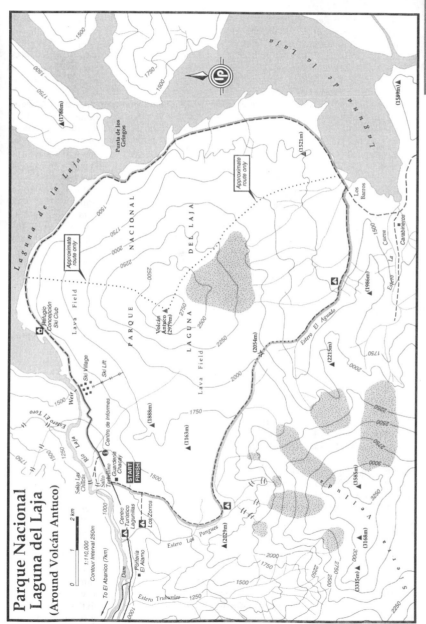

Parque Nacional
Laguna del Laja
(Around Volcán Antuco)

0   1   2 km
1:110,000
Contour Interval 250m

then cross over to the southern side of the now tiny stream. From here on, winter avalanches have mostly erased any markings leading up to the pass, but the best ascent option is probably the loose-rock ridge that goes up steeply leftwards between two eroded gullies. Where this peters out, sidle rightwards around the slope to arrive at the pass, 2¼ to three hours from the Estero Los Pangues Camp.

The pass lies at 2054m, and gives wonderful views ahead down the valley to the southern arm of the Laguna de la Laja and the ranges along the Chile-Argentina frontier. Immediately adjacent is the impressive glacier-clad eastern face of the Sierra Velluda's 3585m main summit.

The pass is likely to be snowed over and corniced well into January, so it be may be necessary to traverse leftwards along the ridge top for 500m or so before dropping down into the small basin below the pass. Snowdrifts here in early summer provide good glissading before you directly descend the steep, loose-earth slopes to meet a faint trail on the banks of the milky **Estero El Aguado** after one to 1¼ hours. If coming from the other direction, look out for a large cairn opposite a chasm with a waterfall before you reach the head of the valley. This points directly to the pass.

Proceed downstream through the sparsely vegetated Valle El Aguado. Away from the moister ground near the Estero, the vegetation consists only of low shrubs and small vegetated mounds. The dusty path follows the northern bank, passing small waterfalls and crossing several clear streams emanating from the snows on Volcán Antuco's southern slopes. As you approach a lone araucaria, stay close to the stream to avoid a boggy area over to the left, then continue a short way on to reach a small wooden bridge at **Los Barros** after 1¼ to 1¾ hours. Here the flat shoreline of Laguna de la Laja is periodically inundated when the lake rises.

Camp Sites There is no sheltered camping along this section until you cross the pass. In the upper Valle El Aguado occasional grassy patches among ñirre thickets on the true right (south) bank of the stream (which is easily waded) make nice camp sites. Lower down there are also good sites on the true left bank, although the ground is uneven or soggy in places.

Stage 3: Los Barros to Guardería Chacay
23km, 5 to 8 hours
There are no permanently running streams along this hot and sandy section, so it's advisable to carry water from the Estero El Aguado. (The lake itself is not always easily accessible, though its water is generally safe to drink.) There is modest traffic along the rough and narrow road – mostly of sport fishers or the odd truck from the summer-only *estancia* at the southern end of the lake – so it may be possible to hitch a ride with some of this traffic.

Head off northwards around the western side of Laguna de la Laja, through a volcanic desert caused by the eroding sand and rain shadow of Volcán Antuco and the Sierra Velluda. In the heat of the late afternoon occasional meltwater streams flow down from the volcano's upper slopes. Across the turquoise waters of Laguna de la Laja impressive bare eroding crags drop straight down to the shore, while mountains farther to the north and south are heavily forested. The road dips and rises constantly, passing the curiously named narrow of **Punta de los Gringos** after two to three hours.

Make your way around south-eastwards into an enormous lava flow (responsible for damming the Río Laja to create the lake) and on past the **Refugio Concepción Ski Club** (a run-down ski lodge, closed in summer). The road continues through this raw landscape, soon bringing the peaks of the Sierra Velluda back into view, and passes a weir built over the lake outlet just before reaching the **Volcán Antuco ski village** (see Accommodation & Camping earlier in this section) two to three hours on. This small winter sports centre consists of 20 chalets scattered around the base of a ski lift.

Follow the (now much improved) road as it winds steadily down into the upper Valle

Laja past the large cascading streams of the **Estero El Toro** pouring down from the range on the opposite side of the valley. Just after crossing a small brook the road passes a (signposted) turn-off leading a few minutes left through the coigües to the park **Centro de Informes** (administration building) and visitors' information centre to arrive back at the **Guardería Chacay** after a final 1½ to 2 hours.

Camp Sites There is reasonably good camping around the shore of Laguna de la Laja, although the ground is quite muddy in some places.

Other Treks in Parque Nacional Laguna del Laja

SALTO LAS CHILCAS & SALTO EL TORBELLINO

The Río Laja is famous for the waterfall known as the Salto del Laja, far downstream near the Panamerican Highway bridge. The Salto Las Chilcas and Salto El Torbellino are two of the river's uppermost waterfalls, where at various points the subterranean flow of water from Laguna de la Laja and Volcán Antuco emerges from the porous ground. The waterfalls offer a spectacular one-hour return walk from the park administration centre, and you can easily visit them before or after the Around Volcán Antuco trek described above.

Take the signposted track from opposite the park administration turn-off and follow this to a fork. The right-hand path goes five minutes on to the Salto Las Chilcas. A perched basalt platform provides a natural lookout to a large cascade of the Río Laja, but heed the sign warning you not to venture too far beyond a conspicuous crack in the rock as this section is likely to break away at any time. The left-hand path leads 10 minutes on to a ridge lookout between the

Río Laja and the Salto Torbellino, a noisier spouting waterfall of a large side stream. There are some superb specimens of ciprés de la cordillera near the river as well as many wild flowers, including the crimson-coloured ourisia, which thrives close to the plunging waters.

ASCENT OF VOLCÁN ANTUCO

The regularly tapering 2979m cone of Volcán Antuco ends in a tiny crater just 40m in diameter, which at times emits gases and steam. This summit grants a superb panorama that takes in the upper Valle Laja to the west and the adjacent Sierra Velluda to the south. Across Laguna de la Laja you will see Volcán Chillán (3122m) to the north, and the ranges extending into Argentina to the east. Volcán Antuco can be climbed by several routes, but the ascent should not be attempted by inexperienced parties.

One route to the summit starts 4km up from the ski village on Volcán Antuco's north-eastern slopes beyond the lava flow. From there it is a steep and direct climb and descent that takes around eight hours return, but a less steep and somewhat faster route goes up from Los Barros via the volcano's south-eastern slopes. There is no trail to follow along this route.

You need to be particularly careful around the summit, because there is a dangerously crevassed glacier near it on the volcano's upper southern slopes. Depending on annual seasonal snow conditions, ice climbing equipment such as crampons and ice axe are generally advisable (sometimes essential) before about mid-January. (Note, however, that such equipment cannot be hired at the national park.)

The ascent is actually more strenuous when there is no snow covering the loose and steep volcanic earth. Inexperienced trekkers and trekking groups are advised to enquire at the park administration centre or the Centro Turístico Lagunillas (see Accommodation & Camping in the Around Volcán Antuco section earlier in this chapter) for a local person to act as a guide.

Parque Nacional Conguillío

Parque Nacional Conguillío is east of the Chilean provincial city of Temuco in one of the most volcanically active parts of the southern Andes. Established in 1950, the park takes in slightly more than 600 sq km. Conguillío is a volcanic highland with elevations ranging from just 900m at its lowest point to the twin summits of Volcán Llaima, which reach 2920m and 3125m. Volcán Llaima's western side lies within the park's Los Paraguas sector.

GENERAL INFORMATION
Geographical Features
Volcán Llaima, a periodically active volcano, lies at the heart of the park. Even when seen from the Panamerican Highway some 80km to the west, Llaima's distinctive form stands out as a key landmark of the region.

Eruptions over the years have left an extensive volcanic wasteland surrounding the impressive double cone. In some places, there are interesting islands of vegetation that were left untouched by the lava as it flowed around them.

Volcán Llaima's repeated intense volcanic activity has obstructed the nearby Río Traful-Traful and formed three lakes around its northern and eastern sides. The youngest of these lakes is Laguna Captrén, which was created in 1957 by a lava flow.

The largest lake, Laguna Conguillío, is set in a dramatic landscape bordered on the south by a barren expanse of broken volcanic rock. Broad fields of lava descend from the slopes of Volcán Llaima almost to the shoreline. The waters of Laguna Conguillío escape underground through the porous volcanic subsoil.

The Sierra Nevada range rises up immediately north of Laguna Conguillío, enclosing the lake on three sides. The lower slopes of the Sierra Nevada are covered by beautiful pristine forests, while its higher summits remain snowcapped throughout the summer period.

Natural History
More than any other species found in Parque Nacional Conguillío, the araucaria most typifies the local vegetation. This superb tree grows in almost pure stands that stretch along the southern shores of Laguna Conguillío, and higher up in the surrounding ranges it is the dominant tree in the forest. In the past the local Pehuenche people visited these highland forests in autumn to collect the rich supply of *piñones*, or araucaria nuts, from which they prepared a starchy meal.

Also well represented among the forest trees are a number of *Nothofagus* species, including the common coigüe, coigüe de Magallanes, lenga and raulí. The ciprés de la cordillera (or lahuán), a conifer adapted to dry montane conditions, thrives on the park's southern edge which lies in the rain shadow caused by Volcán Llaima. Other tree species found in Conguillío's forests are canelo *(Drimys winteri)*, lingue *(Persea lingue)*, boldo *(Peumus boldus)* and quillay *(Quillaja saponaria)*. As hinted at by its botanical name, the bark of the quillay contains a strong natural detergent, which in the past was exported to Europe and North America.

Growing in the sandy volcanic soil among the araucarias you'll find the quellén, or llahuén, *(Fragaria chiloensis)*, a native wild strawberry that produces typical yellow-white flowers in December that ripen into edible berries by March. The striking, deep red flowers of the notro bush *(Embothrium coccineum)*, which grows on sunny sites, stand out in early summer.

Some of Conguillío's common mountain wild flowers are the añañuca, which produces several pink flowers in an elongated goblet form growing from a single succulent stem; the violeta del monte *(Viola reichii)*, a yellow subalpine violet species; and capachitos *(Calceolaria* species), herb-like plants with attractive yellow, white or pink flowers. Tough snow grasses endure in less exposed places above the tree line.

The local fauna includes the elusive puma and its much smaller feline cousin, the huiña, as well as the pudú and the tree-dwelling llaca (or monito del monte). At times trekkers may sight falcons circling the ridge tops, and native ducks like the pato cuchara *(Anas platalea)* and the pato real *(Anas sibilatrix)* around the lakes and rivers. A black woodpecker species, the carpintero negro, inhabits the forests.

Climate
The park's elevated position and inland location produce a mild temperate climate. Annual precipitation levels are about average for the mountains of the Araucanía, ranging from 2000mm in the valleys to almost 3000mm in the higher ranges. Normal midwinter (July) snow cover is around 2m in the valleys, when the low temperatures cause Laguna Conguillío to freeze over. Winter access to the park administration centre is often cut off, though the two resident rangers remain there throughout the colder months. Precipitation in the southern part of the park is lower, because Volcán Llaima partially shields this area from the moist westerlies, creating a slight rain shadow.

Place Names
The name Conguillío (usually pronounced 'con-GEE-yo') comes from a Pehuenche (or Mapuche) word meaning 'water with pine nuts', and hints at the local indigenous people's reliance on the fruit produced by the extensive araucaria forests found in this area. The Spanish word *paragua* refers to the araucaria tree's unusual 'umbrella' form. The Pehuenche word *llaima* roughly translates as 'the revived one', an apparent reference to the volcano's repeated eruptions, while *traful* means 'junction of rivers'. The Sierra Nevada, whose name means simply 'snowy mountain range' in Spanish, is so called because its upper slopes retain their white winter topping well into summer.

PRACTICAL INFORMATION
Information Sources
The park administration centre at Lago Conguillío has an excellent visitor's centre with displays on local flora and fauna. A resident ranger is available to advise you on present conditions. In summer CONAF staff give lectures with slide shows on local ecology and organise guided walks as well as boat excursions on Laguna Conguillío. There are also minor ranger stations at the park's northern and southern entrance gates.

For the CONAF regional head offices in Temuco, see Trekking Bases at the start of this chapter.

Permits & Regulations
A per-person entry charge of US$3.50 is payable at either of the park's northern and southern gates; there is no additional charge for vehicles. No special permit is required to hike in the park, but all trekkers should sign in at the administration centre before setting out. In order to avoid backtracking, you can advise staff of your safe return at the CONAF office in Temuco (see Regional Centres).

Camping is no longer permitted in Conguillío outside the organised camping grounds near the administration centre. In practice, this rule is not enforced (nor enforceable) in remoter areas of the park, but 'wild' campers must not light a fire and should otherwise pay maximum attention to looking after the environment.

When to Trek
Because of their relatively low altitude, several easy day walks can be done from the park administration centre at Lago Conguillío from early October until about mid-May. Hot weather between mid-December and late January usually brings out horseflies, or tábanos, which can be a particular nuisance below the tree line.

More serious treks or climbs in the park's mountains are limited to the period from early summer (November/December) to autumn (March/April). Above 1750m winter snows often linger until mid-December. Sturdy snow bridges cover the streams encountered on the Sierra Nevada trek until early to mid-January, but after this time the streams may be harder to cross.

Sierra Nevada

Duration 3 days
Distance 34km
Standard Medium-Hard
Start Laguna Conguillío
Finish Lower Río Blanco or Curacautín-Lonquimay road
Entry US$3.50, no permit needed
Season October-May
Summary An exhilarating trek through araucaria-clad ranges giving dramatic views of the adjacent Volcán Llaima and the beautiful Laguna Conguillío.

The Sierra Nevada forms a roughly T-shaped range to the north of Laguna Conguillío. Although incomparably less grandiose than those of the range's mighty namesake in North America, these heavily glaciated basalt peaks reach over 2500m, offering superb views of the surrounding volcanic lakeland and the adjacent Volcán Llaima.

MAPS

The IGM 1:50,000 sheet *Volcán Llaima* (Section G, No 75) covers all but the western periphery of the walk. This map does not show hiking routes, but is otherwise accurate and very useful. The adjoining sheet, *Laguna Quepe* (Section G, No 74) takes in the lower Río Blanco and the western slopes of Volcán Llaima.

DAYS REQUIRED

Stage 1 can be done as a long return day trek from the park administration centre on Laguna Conguillío.

For experienced parties the trek can be extended by an additional two (perhaps three) days by continuing through the Sierra Nevada then out via the lower Río Blanco.

TREKKING STANDARD

Stage 1 easily follows the shore of Laguna Conguillío, climbs on via a well-maintained path along a forested spur, then makes a final ascent up a long rocky ridge to a lookout saddle on the Sierra Nevada range. The first part of Stage 1 is fairly straightforward and presents no real difficulties, but the trek on up to the Sierra Nevada lookout calls for more route-finding ability. Less experienced trekkers are advised to hike only as far as the lookout, but if you do Stage 1 as a day hike be sure to get a reasonably early start.

Stage 2 traces a rough route above the tree line, rising and dipping between 1600m and 1800m through the difficult untracked country on the western side of the Sierra Nevada. Here the terrain is dissected by deep stream gullies where snow may lie well into the summer. Snow bridges can normally be safely crossed until early to mid-January, but after this time the streams may be dangerous to cross until the snow thaw ceases. The occasional route markings (which consist of cairns and/or red and white paint splashes on rocks) cannot be relied on, so Stage 2 should only be attempted in fine weather by strong parties – not individual trekkers – with good navigational abilities.

Stage 1 is rated *medium*. The untracked section onward to the upper Río Blanco is rated *hard*. From the start of the trek to the upper Río Blanco the distance is 14km. Whether you hike out via the lower Río Blanco (as recommended) or finish the trek at the Curacautín-Lonquimay road, the final stage is around 20km.

ACCOMMODATION & CAMPING

There are several separate camping grounds near the park administration. These cost US$15 per site (up to two tents), which includes a supply of firewood and use of the hot showers. Behind the administration centre is a cheaper camping area for more humble backpackers, where the charge is US$4 per person. There are also nine cabins (built around the trunks of araucaria trees) that sleep six people and cost US$80 per night.

The park has no huts for trekkers and it is essential to carry a tent. 'Wild' camping (ie pitching your tent anywhere other than the organised camping grounds) is not officially permitted in the park. Up in the Sierra

Nevada, however, it is tolerated providing trekkers *don't light a fire* and otherwise respect the environment.

SUPPLIES
In the main tourist season (January/February) the store/cafeteria near the administration centre on the shore of Laguna Conguillío sells only a few simple supplies. Any important provisions should be bought before you arrive there, and the best places are Temuco and Curacautín.

GETTING TO/FROM THE TREK
There are two route possibilities from Temuco (see Trekking Bases at the start of this chapter) to the park administration centre at Laguna Conguillío. The park can be approached from the north via the town of Curacautín, or from the south via the village of Melipeuco.

Although the overall distance is longer, the best roads and the only public transport out to Laguna Conguillío run via Curacautín. Erbuc runs around 10 daily buses from Temuco to Curacautín; the trip takes about two hours via Lautaro, or 2½ hours via Victoria. From Curacautín there is a twice-weekly bus service to the park's northern entrance gate; these leave from Curacautín's tiny bus station (opposite the Plaza de Armas) every Monday and Friday at approximately 5 am, and return from the park entrance at around 7.30 am the same morning. Although unsurfaced, the 42km road between Curacautín and the park administration centre is in reasonable condition, and carries enough traffic to make hitchhiking a reasonably reliable prospect.

Melipeuco can be reached by half a dozen daily (IGI Llaima or Puma) buses from the rural bus station in Temuco. The trip runs via Cunco (after which the road becomes much rougher), and takes about three hours. From Melipeuco the distance to the park administration centre is only 27km, but there is no public transport and the less-transited road makes a hot and dusty (though reasonably interesting) walk. In Melipeuco it might be possible to find someone prepared to drive you out to the park, but expect to pay around US$30 (ask at the police station).

In the tourist season (January/February), various companies in Temuco run bus tours to Laguna Conguillío (enquire at the city tourist office). A tour may be the most convenient way of getting to the park, but you'll probably have to pay the full rate even if you remain at Laguna Conguillío.

If you do the Sierra Nevada trek as far as the upper Río Blanco, there are two alternative exits. The less recommended option is to follow the road 19km out to the main Curacautín-Lonquimay road, where you can flag down passing buses back to Curacautín. The other alternative is to head 21km down the lower Río Blanco to the Curacautín-Conguillío road 4km north of the park's northern entrance gate, from where you can hitch or catch the very infrequent bus to Curacautín.

THE TREK
Stage 1: Administration Centre to Sierra Nevada Lookout
11km, 4¾ to 6½ hours; 7 to 10 hours return
From the park administration centre, take the road down to the cafeteria on Laguna Conguillío. Head east, either along the volcanic sand beach itself or via the road running past the camping grounds, then pick up a trail leading on around the lightly forested lakeshore to reach **Playa Linda** after 60 to 80 minutes. (A quicker but less scenic alternative is to walk 2.5km east along the road through the araucaria forest to a small car park, where a short signposted path goes down to Playa Linda.)

Just behind Playa Linda (on the path up to the car park), a well-graded track branches off left (south-east). It soon swings roughly north-east and begins a steady climb through the forest, passing massive old coigües as it winds up onto a prominent spur to reach a viewing point with a log bench high above the lake after 45 minutes to one hour. This spot overlooking some small forested islands in a bay of Laguna Conguillío is among a beautiful mixed araucaria and lenga forest with scattered bushes of notro.

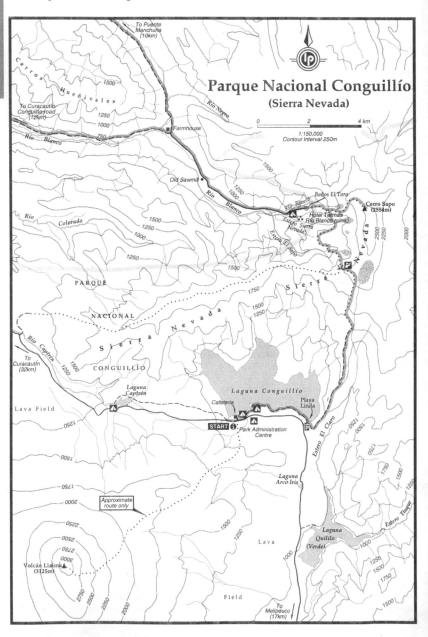

Parque Nacional Conguillío
(Sierra Nevada)

0   2   4 km

1:150,000
Contour Interval 250m

As the path continues up more gently along (or just to the right of) the progressively narrowing ridge top, the vegetation becomes more stunted with increasing altitude and exposure. Meltwater cascades from snowfields on the Sierra Nevada provide the source of the Estero El Claro, which flows on through a deep gully down to your right. Near where the spur terminates at the base of the Sierra Nevada, move over leftwards into the scrub and head up in a few short switchback curves to where the path finally peters out completely, 60 to 80 minutes on.

With the craggy range up to the right, sidle north-west along slopes of native grasses and wild flowers. After crossing a stream (where *Pinguicula antarctica*, a carnivorous flytrap plant that produces a single white flower, thrives in the boggy ground), cut left across the bottom of a glacial basin to reach an obvious rocky rib.

This long band of rock leads up above the deep snowy trough on your right, and although there are cliffs on either side and the upper section is interrupted by a small gully, it can be followed without real danger or difficulty.

Just before you get to a large rock knob, traverse several hundred metres leftwards across the open stony slope (or snowdrifts) to gain the main ridge connecting the western branch of the range to the higher Sierra Nevada proper. Make your way down (ie westwards) 300m along the ridge top to reach the first saddle (marked by a cairn), two to three hours from the termination of the spur and the graded path.

This lookout point gives tremendous views south-westwards across the tranquil blue waters of Laguna Conguillío to the great rumped form of Volcán Llaima immediately adjacent, and beyond as far as the distant yet unmistakable snowy cone of Volcán Villarrica as well as the less distinctive outline of Volcán Quetrupillán (just to its left). Directly to the north you can see the 2806m Volcán Tolguaca (on the left) and Volcán Lonquimay, at 2865m one of the region's most active volcanoes. Nearer to where you stand, small glaciers cling to the sides of the Sierra Nevada.

Camp Sites Apart from at the organised facilities around the park administration centre, camping anywhere on this stage is not officially permitted. Despite this, trekkers have been known to pitch tents near the tiny stream a short way on from where the path peters out, where semi-sheltered sites can be found in the scrub. Campers should not light fires, and must carry out all rubbish.

Stage 2: Sierra Nevada Lookout to Upper Río Blanco
5km, 6½ to 9 hours

This more difficult section should be attempted by experienced parties in fine weather only.

Drop down northwards into the deep stream gully below the saddle, first carefully negotiating the loose semi-vegetated rocky slopes or snowdrifts, then easing slightly rightwards to pick up steep grassy spurs that bring you down to the **Estero El Sapo** after 45 minutes to one hour. In early summer this deep gully is filled with a thick layer of snow, which generally allows a straightforward and safe crossing of the stream. Later in the season there is the danger of these snow bridges collapsing under your weight, but by early autumn (March) the stream can generally be crossed quite easily. Proceed cautiously.

Cross the Estero El Sapo a short way up from where it enters a gorge, then head 100m up into a side gully (snowbound early in the season). After climbing around rightwards above a tiny cascade fed by a snowy basin, sidle back to the left to a stand of young araucarias at the tree line. The route continues just above the weather-battered scrub over steep snow grass slopes overlooking (and overhearing) the Río Blanco to a group of old, slowly dying araucarias.

At this point look out for marker cairns leading up right to the edge of the next deep stream basin. Avoiding the temptation to descend too early, contour several hundred metres into the canyon before dropping down over steep rocky-grassy slopes to reach the **'Estero Sierra Nevada'** (unnamed on IGM maps), 1½ to two hours from the Estero El Sapo. Lying under the towering icy crags of the Sierra Nevada, winter avalanches from the range often choke this gully until late summer.

Cross the stream (taking the same precautions as with the Estero El Sapo), then climb away via loose-earth chutes in the adjacent embankment. After cutting up through an open area in the stunted lenga brush, make a steep and direct ascent northwards over the ridge and descend easily into a small grassy hollow 50 minutes to 1¼ hours on. Here you meet an indistinct route (marked only by sporadic cairns) that goes up to **Cerro Sapo**, at 2554m the highest peak in the Sierra Nevada. (The way up to Cerro Sapo first follows the ridge you just climbed over, swinging around north-eastwards before doubling back to the right (ie south-east) to gain the summit after two to three hours).

Pick up the cairn markings leading westwards down a spur (recognisable by an old araucaria tree at its upper end), initially avoiding small diverging ridges on the left. A rough foot track gradually develops, and with careful route-finding this can be followed as it becomes increasingly steep down through the forest. The last section descends via a narrow chute of a tiny stream to reach the **Baños El Toro** after 45 minutes to one hour. As your nose will have told you for much of the descent, fumaroles in this eroding slope of reddish-white earth emit a steady stream of suphurous volcanic gases. At one time thermal waters were piped 1km to the former hotel site, but today the Baños' several trickling mineral springs are slightly tepid at best.

Take the old graded pipeline track westwards well above the gushing Río Blanco, negotiating occasional minor landslips and fallen trunks blocking the way. The path winds its way on down through lovely forests of raulí and coigüe to reach the burnt-out ruins of the **Hotel Termas Río Blanco** after a final 20 to 30 minutes. The head of the enclosed valley is dominated by the snow tops of the Sierra Nevada, rising 1500m above the Río Blanco.

Camp Sites Little sheltered camping is available on the entire traverse route through the Sierra Nevada. There are poor camp sites on rocky and uneven ground around the two larger streams passed on this section. There is also only very poor camping around the Baños El Toro, but there are better sites at the end of this stage near the Río Blanco.

Stage 3A: Upper Río Blanco to Curacautín-Lonquimay Road
19km, 4 to 5½ hours
The end of this route has better public transport, but it is a less interesting alternative to Stage 3B.

Wade the glacial waters of the small Río Blanco, and follow the initially rough road down through forest of tepa, raulí and coigüe separated by grassy pastures dotted with clumps of rose bushes and quila. Just where it makes a sharp curve around to the north, after 1½ to two hours (or 7km), the road crosses a small clear stream on a bridge. (Trekkers intending to hike on down the Río Blanco should now refer to Stage 3B.)

Carry some water from here, as there are few streams along the way from here on. The road soon crosses the small **Río Negro** on a wooden bridge and continues north-westwards through rolling pastures and occasional crop fields for 2½ to 3½ hours to reach the main road between Curacautín and Lonquimay (see Getting to/from the Trek) at the **Puente Manchuria** bridge.

Camp Sites There is little good camping once you leave the upper Río Blanco, since finding running water can be a problem.

Stage 3B: Upper Río Blanco to Curacautín-Conguillío Road (via Río Blanco)
21km, 4½ to 6 hours
This slightly longer alternative takes you down the Río Blanco on a route that provides basic access to farms along the river's lower course.

About 100m before the bridge (described in Stage 3A), turn off left through a wooden gate. Head past a neat farmhouse on your right to the Río Negro, and after fording this small clear stream pick up a horse trail leading down past its confluence with the much larger Río Blanco. The route continues up over open slopes, which offer fleeting views back towards the Sierra Nevada, then on down the valley through alternating areas of forest, pastures and isolated clusters of cherry trees to meet a dirt road at a wooden farmhouse after 1¼ to 1¾ hours.

The road gradually improves and takes you on down past more typical Chilean rural dwellings and sheep paddocks bordered by makeshift wooden fences. In its central section the Río Blanco flows within a broad coarse-gravel bed, where occasional fly fishers may be seen wading the icy river. Farther downstream the road climbs high to avoid a gorge, before breaking away north-west to reveal Volcán Llaima from a different angle and (eventually) intersecting with the Curacautín-Conguillío road after 3¼ to 4½ hours. There is a small bus shelter here, and enough traffic to make hitchhiking a reasonable proposition.

Camp Sites Good sites can be found in places along the Río Blanco for much of its course, but camp a discrete distance away from farmhouses.

Other Treks in Parque Nacional Conguillío

LAGUNA CAPTRÉN
Laguna Captrén is a lovely lake in the forest. Like Laguna Conguillío, several kilometres to the east, this tiny lake was formed when lava spilling down from Volcán Llaima created a natural dam wall. Unlike its much larger neighbor, Laguna Captrén was created more recently, as indicated by the remains of drowned trees in its waters.

Laguna Captrén can be visited from the park administration centre in an easy but rewarding walk taking around 3½ hours return. The path leaves the road at a signpost not far west of the administration centre, leading for 5km roughly north-west through

beautiful forest to the lake, where a short circuit trail runs around the shore. An alternative way back is simply to follow the road.

ASCENT OF VOLCÁN LLAIMA
The main 3125m peak of Volcán Llaima's distinctive double-cone summit always excites the attention of foreign and local 'volcandinists' (volcano-bagging andinists). Volcán Llaima can be climbed from the Laguna Conguillío (ie north-eastern) side, but the volcano is more often tackled from the much higher ski lodge on its southwestern slopes. This is because the gradient and terrain are somewhat gentler there, and the climb begins from several hundred metres higher.

Ice axe and crampons are generally necessary at least until the end of January, but it is currently not possible to hire such equipment in either sector of the park. Due to recent mountaineering mishaps, the park authority may introduce the requirement that all climbers be accompanied by a professional guide (similar to Volcán Villarrica ascents). The western side of Volcán Llaima (the park's Los Paraguas sector) is accessible only by private vehicle from the village of Cherquenco, which can be reached by four daily Erbuc buses from Temuco. From Cherquenco the road climbs 21km up to the ski lodge, which has only sporadic traffic in summer.

AROUND LAGUNA CONGUILLÍO VIA SIERRA NEVADA
This excellent panoramic high-level route leads around Laguna Conguillío along the crest of the Sierra Nevada's western range. The trek begins at a small bridge over the Río Captrén, 12km north-west of the park administration centre on the road to Curacautín. After following an old logging track up through the forest to point 1760m on the top of the range, the route rises and dips eastwards at an average height of 1900m to reach the large cairn on the lookout saddle (at the end of Stage 1 in the Sierra Nevada trek described previously). Follow Stage 1 of the Sierra Nevada trek in reverse to return to the Park Administration Centre.

This is a very long day (or overnight) trek, with few or no route markings. The most difficult part of the trek is finding your way up from the small bridge, so the best way to do the trek is from west to east. The top of the range is very exposed to the elements, and from midsummer finding water may be a problem. The trek is suited only to experienced hikers with very good route-finding ability.

Parque Nacional Huerquehue

The small national park of Huerquehue lies to the east of Lago Caburgua, 35km northeast of the popular resort town of Pucón. This is a gentle landscape of little lakes nestled among moderately high ranges clothed in a thick mantle of rainforest. Apart from some wonderful hikes, swimming and fishing in the lakes are popular activities. The surface water in Lago Tinquilco reaches around 20°C in summer, and although the higher lakes in the central part of Huerquehue are generally a few degrees cooler they are fine for a quick dip.

GENERAL INFORMATION
Geographical Features

The core area of the 125 sq km Parque Nacional Huerquehue consists of a tiny subalpine plateau lying at around 1300m above sea level. Due to the dense cover of temperate rainforest, only this central sector of the park is easily accessible. However, this is also the most beautiful part of Huerquehue; numerous lovely lakes of varying size nestle into the plateau, enclosed by steep and often craggy ranges that almost touch 2000m and somewhat sheltering the park from extremes of weather.

The lowest point in the park is the eastern shore of Lago Tinquilco, which fills a small but deep glacial trough at just above 700m. This 3km-long lake has tiny beaches fringed by forests, and is enjoyed by swimmers and anglers.

The area immediately surrounding Parque Nacional Huerquehue is extremely active volcanically. This is not much in evidence within the park itself, but past eruptions have left a thick layer of volcanic ash covering the ground over much of the Huerquehue area. There is a surprising number of thermal springs nearby, including the undeveloped Termas de Río Blanco (visited on the Central Huerquehue walk featured here) and several developed hot springs along the Río Liucura on the southern side of the park. In the isolated valleys on the park's periphery, small farms struggle to make a modest living in the few areas of level ground.

Natural History

The park's name (see Place Names) refers to the zorzal patagónico (*Turdus falklandii*), a native thrush which inhabits this densely forested area. Among other bird life in the park is the ubiquitous chucao, whose chuckling calls resound throughout the undergrowth of the forest floor. The area is also home to two woodpecker species, the carpintero negro and the carpintero chico (*Dendrocopus lignrius*). The tiny native deer, or pudú, is occasionally spotted scurrying through the underbrush.

As in much of the Araucanía, the araucaria tree, or pehuén, dominates the more elevated areas, often forming pure stands. These beautiful conifers fringe the shores of the higher lakes, and their distinct umbrella-like form stands out on the ridge tops. Here, the southern beech (*Nothofagus*) species lenga (*N. pumilio*), a beautiful deciduous tree, and evergreen coigües (*N. betuloides* and *N. dombeii* are also present. Lower down, the forests are dominated by tepa (*Laureliopsis philipiana*), identifiable by their serrated, deliciously fragrant leaves, and mañíos. Lower elevations also favour the boldo (*Peumus boldus*), a tree with oval-shaped leathery leaves which are used to make an aromatic infusion containing a variety of medicinal compounds. A parasitic plant called the quintral *(Notanthera heterophylla)* lives on the boldo, and unsuspecting observers might erroneously consider its more flamboyant white, red-tipped blooms to be those of the boldo, whose flowers are pale yellow.

Wherever the forest is fully mature, the understorey is quite open and surprisingly sparse, with epiphyte species such as the botellita and the estrellita. Typically seen growing on tree trunks, these two climbing vines produce fine red flowers that brighten up the shady forest floor.

Quila grows in small clusters anywhere that receives even a few stray rays of direct sunlight. Around the shores of Lago Tinquilco you will also see the graceful arrayan *(Myrceugenella apiculata)*, a water-loving myrtle species with smooth, almost luminescent orange bark.

Climate

Huerquehue is in a climatic transition zone between the warm temperate lowlands and the cooler Andes. The Lago Tinquilco area has a moderate climate with a mean annual temperature of 11.5°C. Precipitation is concentrated between the winter months of May and September – when the upland area above 1300m receives heavy snowfalls – and annual levels reach a relatively moderate 2000mm in the ranges of central Huerquehue.

The warmer weather of spring (October-November) quickly melts away the snow cover, however, and by late January only the open tops of the Nevados de Caburgua and a few of the higher summits have any snow. Summer weather can be pleasantly hot, but rain showers mean long periods of dry weather are fairly uncommon.

Place Names

There seems to be some doubt regarding the origin of the name *huerquehue* (pronounced 'where-KAY-way'). According to some sources it is a corruption of the original Mapuche word *huilquehue*, meaning 'place of the thrushes', a reference to the zorzal patagónico (see Natural History). In its present form, however, it translates as 'place of the message'. The Mapuche word *caburgua*, which means 'scraper', may indicate that this simple tool was often fashioned from materials found in the area. Similarly, the name Renahue, a small valley bordering the park, means 'digging place'.

PRACTICAL INFORMATION
Information Sources

The only ranger station at Parque Nacional Huerquehue is the Guardería Tinquilco, just inside the park boundary about halfway along the eastern side of Lago Tinquilco. About 300m on is the information centre, which has exhibits on local flora and fauna. The staff are helpful and friendly.

Various adventure companies in Pucón, including Sol y Nieve (☎ 45-44 1070) on Avenida O'Higgins, organise guided walks in the Huerquehue area. For details of the CONAF offices and other information sources in Pucón, see Trekking Bases at the start of this chapter.

Permits & Regulations

The entrance fee to Parque Nacional Huerquehue is US$2/0.50 per adult/child, and is payable at the Guardería Tinquilco. No special permit is necessary to trek in the park, but anglers should note that they require a fishing permit (see Activities on the Trek in the Facts for the Visitor section). Trekkers can sign in at the Guardería Tinquilco before setting out, but if you do not backtrack via Tinquilco you should report your safe return to the CONAF office in Pucón.

Officially, camping is no longer permitted anywhere within Parque Nacional Huerquehue other than at the park's own camping ground on Lago Tinquilco (all other nearby camping grounds lie outside the national park boundaries). Since to cross (and exit) the park requires a very long day's walk, the attending ranger at the Guardería Tinquilco may insist that trekkers who arrive in the afternoon deposit their backpacks there to ensure that they don't make a 'wild' camp. In practice, though, the park authorities have been known to turn a blind eye to illicit campers, providing they show an exemplary respect for the local environment and do not light a fire.

When to Trek

Treks can normally be undertaken in Parque Nacional Huerquehue from mid-November until late April. Note, however, that horseflies (tábanos in Spanish) can be bothersome between mid to late December and early February.

Central Huerquehue

> **Duration** 3 or 4 days
> **Distance** 36km return (from Lago Tinquilco to the Termas de Río Blanco)
> **Standard** Easy-Medium
> **Start/Finish** Lago Tinquilco
> **Entry** US$2, no permit needed
> **Season** November-April
> **Summary** A gentle return trek to the Termas Río Blanco via a subalpine plateau where small lakes lie hidden in the temperate rainforest.

This trek explores the charming central part of Parque Nacional Huerquehue, a tiny lakeland plateau.

MAPS

Almost the entire Huerquehue area is covered by the Chilean IGM 1:50,000 series sheet *Nevados de Caburgua* (Section G, No 96). For general orientation an adjoining sheet, *Lago Caburgua* (Section G, No 95), may also be of value. Although topographically very accurate, these maps do not show the trekking routes.

After paying the entrance fee, walkers receive a much simpler 1:50,000 contoured map of Huerquehue. This map indicates the main paths with a fair degree of accuracy,

and most trekkers will find it good enough to do the trek.

DAYS REQUIRED

There are a few different ways of doing the trek, so various walking times are given. The lakes in the central part of the park can be visited fairly easily as a day trek from Lago Tinquilco. If you intend continuing as far as the Termas de Río Blanco, then backtracking to Lago Tinquilco, allow at least two (but preferably three) days. The trip from the other direction, starting at Playa Negra (Norte) on Lago Caburgua, is best done in three or four days. Playa Negra (Norte) should not be confused with the other, better known Playa Negra, which is near the holiday resort of Caburgua at the southern end of the lake.

TREKKING STANDARD

The route mostly follows well-trodden trails, with signposts at a few important junctions. The section between the north-western corner of Lago El Toro and the upper Estero Renahue is, however, less travelled, and in places some minor route-finding may be required. Note also that some of the unbridged streams, including the inlet to Lago Tinquilco at the beginning of Stage 1, may be difficult to cross after rain.

If you begin the walk from the other direction at Playa Negra (Norte), on Lago Caburgua's northern shore, you must trek up the Río Blanco. Doing the walk this way does not involve backtracking, and would actually be preferable if Playa Negra (Norte) were not such a remote spot. The route from Playa Negra (Norte), described in Stage 3, follows a good dirt road the whole way up the valley to the Termas de Río Blanco.

There is a small cluster of houses in the vicinity of the Termas de Río Blanco, but no accommodation for walkers. Unless you visit the area as a return day hike from Lago Tinquilco, the Central Huerquehue trek cannot be done safely without a tent.

The section from Lago Tinquilco to Lago Huerquehue is graded *easy*. The rest of the trek is *easy to medium*. The total distance from Lago Tinquilco to the Termas de Río Blanco is 18km, or another 14km (making a total of 32km) if you walk to/from Playa Negra (Norte).

ACCOMMODATION & CAMPING

There are two hospedajes just off the road to Lago Tinquilco before it crosses the Río Quinchol bridge. Most recommended is Tante Hilda, run by a German-speaking local.

There are two private camping grounds near the southern end of Lago Tinquilco. The better equipped and more expensive is *Lago Tinquilco* (☎ 45-24 2087 or 63-21989), which charges US$12.50 per site including toilets, hot showers and firewood. Recommended is the national park's own camping ground at Guardería Tinquilco, where very attractive tent sites along the shore fringed by arrayán trees cost around US$7.50 per site (which includes firewood and cold showers). At the north-eastern end of the lake is another private camping ground, the *El Rincón Tinquilco*, with sites for US$7.50. It also runs a small hospedaje offering rooms.

The 'camping ground' at the Termas de Río Blanco is on private property, and the owners now charge a fee of US$6.50 per tent site. There are no facilities here except for a makeshift picnic table and fireplace. At Playa Negra (Norte), near the isolated northern end of Lago Caburgua, is the camping ground *Llanqui Llanqui*, which charges US$13.50 per site (up to three tents) including use of hot showers. Provisions can be bought at a small store here.

There is an official ban on camping anywhere within Parque Nacional Huerquehue other than at the CONAF camping ground at Lago Tinquilco. Many visitors disregard the ban, however, and – provided trekkers do not light a fire and are otherwise mindful of the minimum-impact code – the national park rangers tend to turn a blind eye to such minor infringements.

SUPPLIES

The most convenient town to base the trek from is Pucón, where there is accommodation in all price ranges.

There is no local store, so the best places to stock up in are Pucón and Villarrica. The private hospedaje/camping ground Rincón Tinquilco at the north-eastern end of Lago Tinquilco sells a few basic supplies on request like bread, meat and sugar. The hospedajes along the Lago Tinquilco road sell home-made jam and German-style cakes as well as other simple refreshments.

GETTING TO/FROM THE TREK

The trek starts 35km from Pucón at the Guardería Tinquilco. The closest you can get to the park by public transport is Paillaco, 7km from the park entrance.

Throughout the summer there are three daily buses from Pucón to Paillaco, which leave around 7 am, 12 and 4 pm from the Buses Lit & Jac terminal on the corner of Palguín and O'Higgins. The trip takes about one hour (including a detour to Caburgua, a lakeside holiday resort on the southern shore of Lago Caburgua), and from Paillaco it's 1½ to two hours walk (mostly uphill) to the Guardería Tinquilco.

During the main holiday season (January/February), there are irregular organised tours to the nearby Termas de Huife, which often include a visit to Huerquehue. The park is also a popular day excursion for motorists, which makes hitchhiking out to the park a reasonable proposition in summer. Campers can park cars for free near the Guardería Tinquilco, but vehicles must otherwise be left at the private car park at the north-eastern end of the lake (day fee US$1.25).

The trek can be done in reverse from Playa Negra (Norte), at the northern end of Lago Caburgua, by walking up the road through the Río Blanco valley to the Termas de Río Blanco. Playa Negra (Norte) has an organised camping ground and is only accessible by private vehicle via Cunco or Villarrica (then around the scenic northern side of Lago Colico), or by private boat from Caburgua, at the lake's southern end. In summer the prospects of hitching to Playa Negra (Norte) – perhaps even by boat – are reasonable, especially if you're not in a hurry.

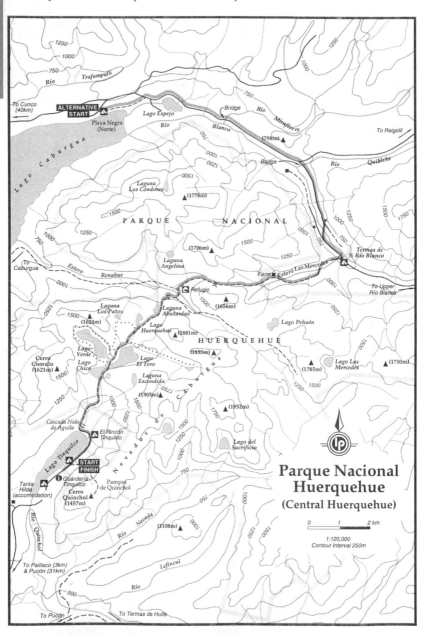

Río Trafampulli

1250

1000

750

To Cunco
(40km)

ALTERNATIVE
START

Playa Negra
(Norte)

Lago Espejo

Río

Bridge

Río

Blanco

Miraflores

(798m) ▲

To Reigolil

Lago Caburgua

Laguna
Los Cóndores

▲ (1778m)

1500

1250

1000

Bridge

Río

Quilliche

P A R Q U E   N A C I O N A L

1500

1250

1000

750

(1706m) ▲

Laguna
Angelina

1500

1250

Termas de
® Río Blanco

(To
Caburgua)

Estero
Renahue

1000

Farm ■ Estero Las Mercedes

To Upper
Río Blanco

▲ Refugio

1500

(1656m) ▲

Laguna
Los Patos

1500

▲
(1624m)

Laguna
Abutardas

Lago
Huerquehue

▲(1881m)

H U E R Q U E H U E

Lago Pehuén

Lago
Verde

Cerro
Cómulo
(1621m) ▲

Lago
Chico

Lago
El Toro

(1835m) ▲ ▲

Laguna
Escondida

1500

(1905m)▲

1750

(1952m) ▲

1750

(1785m) ▲

Lago Las
Mercedes

▲ (1730m)

1500

Cascada Nido
de Águila

El Rincón
Tinquilco

1500

1250

1250

Lago del
Sacrificio

Lago Tinquilco

▲ START
FINISH

Tanta
Hilda
(accomodation)

ⓘ Guardería
Tinquilco

Pampas
de Quinchol

Cerro
Quinchol ▲
(1457m)

750

**Parque Nacional
Huerquehue**

(Central Huerquehue)

Río
Quinchol

Río   Nevada

(1108m) ▲

1000

0   1   2 km

1:120,000
Contour Interval 250m

To Paillaco (3km)
& Pucón (31km)

Lefincul

500

Río

To Pucón

To Termas de Huife

THE TREK
Stage 1: Guardería Tinquilco to Upper Estero Renahue
11km, 3½ to 5 hours

From the guardería, follow the dirt road past the information centre, then on to the hospedaje/camping ground **El Rincón Tinquilco** on freehold land at the north-eastern corner of the lake. A rougher vehicle track continues on to cross a large clear inlet stream at a gravel wash – this normally easy crossing becomes difficult after rain – to reach a signpost at the trail head proper, 25 to 35 minutes from the Guardería Tinquilco.

Head up gently north-eastwards past the **Cascada Nido de Águila**, a mossy-ferny waterfall within the lovely forest of mañío and laurel. Here the tree trunks are often smothered by estrellitas and botellitas, two native climbing vines with delicate crimson flowers. The path first rises at a leisurely gradient, re-entering the national park through a stile just before it begins a steeper winding ascent (giving nice views back down to Lago Tinquilco) to reach **Lago Chico**.

The trail immediately crosses the outlet of Lago Chico on a small footbridge, then leads smoothly around the eastern shore through stands of coigües and araucarias to an intersection just after crossing the lake's first inlet (flowing down from Lago El Toro), 1¼ to 1¾ hours on.

From this point trekkers can make a quick detour to Lago Verde, or opt for the longer alternative route via Laguna Los Patos to Lago Huerquehue (see Side Trips following). Otherwise, take the right branch a few minutes on to where **Lago El Toro** comes into sight. The path rises and dips gently along the western side of Lago El Toro to reach a picturesque little inlet at the lake's north-western corner after 20 to 30 minutes. Here, a rough route runs off to the right around the northern shore of Lago El Toro.

The main route heads up north-eastwards through the forest. After 500m it passes a fork, where a foot track up to **Lago Huerquehue**, one of the most attractive lakes in the park, departs off to the left. This fork is unmarked and not very obvious, but worth looking for as Lago Huerquehue is not visible from the main route. Climb on more steeply until the you come to a small open plateau (at an altitude of approximately 1320m), with a pure stand of graceful old araucarias among deciduous lengas, 40 minutes to one hour from Lago El Toro.

Pick up the trail 50m ahead to the right, and continue slightly downhill below a craggy tree-clad ridge. After 20 to 25 minutes the path passes the small shallow lake of **Laguna Abutardas** a short way up from its marshy eastern shore. Continue slightly east of north out onto fire-cleared slopes high above a small steep valley at whose termination you can see the blue waters of Lago Caburgua. The route makes a steep, winding descent through regenerating brush, before easing rightwards into the forest to meet a small brook. Follow the true left bank a short way upstream, then cross and head down (leaving another path that proceeds up along the stream) to where the small brook merges with another stream to form the **Estero Renahue**, 30 to 40 minutes from Laguna Abutardas.

A rudimentary refugio stands here (at roughly 1040m) below high ridges on a grassy lawn between the two small branches of the upper Estero Renahue. This hut (which is generally kept locked) is constructed in the traditional split-log style so common in southern Chile. From here it is possible to trek down the Estero Renahue and along the shores of Lago Caburgua to the holiday resort of Caburgua at the lake's southern end, a trip taking at least two days.

Side Trips From the path fork near Lago Chico's first inlet stream, trekkers can explore the delightful lakes of the central Huerquehue area. This takes at least two hours.

The left-hand path leads north-west across another inlet stream, whose true right (west) bank you follow to the southern end of **Lago Verde**. This tranquil lake is surrounded by high forested hills crowned by the umbrella-like outlines of araucaria trees. A rough anglers' path rises and dips around Lago Verde's elongated shoreline, returning to the lake's southern end in around one hour.

From the south-eastern side of Lago Verde (about 300m after crossing the lake outlet), a less distinct trail heads northwards, crossing a low ridge to reach the hidden tarn of **Laguna Los Patos**. A final section of this route continues south-east over another forested ridge to **Lago Huerquehue**.

The walk (back) from Lago Huerquehue to Lago Chico is the same as that given in the main description, but in reverse order.

Camp Sites Details of the organised camping grounds at Lago Tinquilco are included under the Accommodation & Camping heading earlier in this section. Wild camping within the national park itself is officially prohibited.

The lakes of central Huerquehue offer some of the most idyllic camp sites imaginable, however, and this tempts many a trekker to disregard the ban. If you do make an unauthorised camp in this area, please pay special heed to some fundamentals of ecology: *don't* damage or disturb the vegetation and wildlife, *don't* light a fire, *do* carry out all your garbage.

The grassy lawn surrounding the hut in the upper Estero Renahue (at the end of Stage 1) is ideal for tents. This spot also lies inside the national park boundaries, but is seldom visited by rangers.

Stage 2: Upper Estero Renahue to Termas de Río Blanco
7km, 2½ to 3 hours

Linking **Lago Caburgua** with the Río Blanco, a pronounced trail comes up the valley past the hut. This eroded and often muddy horse track rises steadily north-eastwards through alternating fire-damaged and intact forest to cross an indistinct watershed (at roughly 1300m) after 30 to 40 minutes. Contour on gently downwards, passing slopes of mature araucarias, before a steeper descent (where in places the path has eroded into a deep trench) takes you across a side stream to reach the uppermost farmhouse at the head of this tiny valley after a further one to 1¼ hours.

Follow the now broader track down across

a wooden bridge over the small **Estero Las Mercedes**. Continue above the stream's southern side past pastures and tiny orchards, after which the valley narrows and the horse trail turns into a rough road. This leads down through a forest full of mañío and fragrant laurel, crossing and recrossing the small stream before intersecting with the main road along the **Río Blanco** after 50 minutes to one hour.

The **Termas de Río Blanco** are five or 10 minutes upstream on the northern bank of the river opposite the private camping ground. The Río Blanco is crossed on a rustic wooden footbridge. Although the locals bathe here regularly, the thermal springs are quite undeveloped. They consist of a few open pools of varying warmth dug out of the rocky river bed several metres from the icy waters of the Río Blanco.

Camp Sites Between the upper Estero Renahue and the Río Blanco there are no especially suitable sites. Camping is therefore only recommended at the Termas de Río Blanco, but the owners of the land charge a fee (see Accommodation & Camping).

Playa Negra (Norte) to Termas de Río Blanco
13km, 4¼ to 5¾ hours

This extra walking stage is for trekkers doing the walk in the opposite direction to that described previously (ie from Lago Caburgua via Termas de Río Blanco to Guardería Tinquilco). Almost the entire stretch follows unsurfaced roads, although traffic is infrequent.

Playa Negra (Norte) is about 1km southwest of the most northerly tip of Lago Caburgua. If you arrive by vehicle, follow a road down 700m to the lakeside. In summer the camping ground has a modest number of holiday-makers. As is often the case in the lakes of the Chilean Araucanía, the beach is composed of black volcanic sand.

Pick up a short cut track heading eastwards above the lake to the road. The road leads around the northern side of **Lago Espejo**, a tranquil lake with a picturesque homestead on its adjacent shore, where the Río Blanco comes into view. Follow the road on as it rises and dips through pockets of forest on the northern side of the river to cross the **Río Miraflores**, the largest tributary of the Río Blanco, at a road bridge just above the confluence after 1¾ to 2¼ hours.

Continue upvalley another 1¼ to 1¾ hours past a rougher turn-off going left (ie north-eastwards) towards Reigolil, a remote village near the Argentine frontier. A short way on, the road crosses the **Río Quililche**, another large side stream. Climb on past occasional small farms, where in places fire-clearing has produced impenetrable thickets of quila and other quick-growing regeneration species and cross over the bridge to the true left (south-west) bank of the Río Blanco. From here proceed across the **Estero Los Mercedes** to the camping ground at the Termas de Río Blanco after a final 1¼ to 1¾ hours.

Camp Sites Playa Negra (Norte) offers basic organised camping. Acceptable spots can also be found sporadically by the river along the lower section of the Río Blanco road, particularly at the Reigolil turn-off. Dense vegetation often blocks access to the stream. Once past Río Quililche the valley closes considerably and places to camp are more difficult to find. See Stage 2 for information on camping at the Termas de Río Blanco.

Other Treks in Parque Nacional Huerquehue

CERRO QUINCHOL

The 1457m Cerro Quinchol is a minor summit at the southern end of the Nevados de Caburgua. The Nevados stand on the eastern side of Lago Tinquilco and form the highest range in the Parque Nacional Huerquehue. Despite its relatively low height, Cerro Quinchol makes an excellent natural lookout, giving a splendid panorama of the surrounding countryside and of nearby Volcán Villarrica to the south-west. The *easy to medium* hike up to Cerro Quinchol takes 3½ to 4½ hours return. From the road 100m north of the visitor's information centre at Lago Tinquilco, the signposted path climbs steeply onto a broad saddle known as the Pampas de Quinchol, then follows the ridge line south-west to the summit.

Parque Nacional Villarrica

Parque Nacional Villarrica lies 30km north-east of Pucón, a popular Chilean tourist centre on the shores of Lago Villarrica. Created in 1925 (from a forest reserve originally set aside in 1912), it is the oldest and one of the most accessible national parks in Chile.

GENERAL INFORMATION
Geographical Features

At roughly 39°S, the 610 sq km Parque Nacional Villarrica stretches along a volcanic range running south-east from Volcán Villarrica. The lowest point in the park is around 900m above sea level, while the 3776m summit of Volcán Lanín on the Chile-Argentina border is its highest point.

The park's major attraction and most obvious feature, however, is the much lower Volcán Villarrica, a classic 2847m volcanic cone that towers over the surrounding countryside. Despite its continuing activity, Villarrica is probably the most climbed peak in Chile. Volcán Villarrica has erupted repeatedly during the last century. The most recent major eruptions were in 1971 and 1984. The first of these two eruptions destroyed the small township of Coñaripe and only just spared Pucón. The volcano puts out a trail of smoke visible from all over the northern Lake District and, at night, the summit has an eerie glowing orange halo.

The slopes of Villarrica are covered by numerous recent and older lava flows. These show the fascinating battle of natural forces, as the local vegetation struggles to survive against recurring intense volcanic activity. The upper slopes of Volcán Villarrica are permanently snowcapped or covered by glaciers and the mountain has been developed for winter skiing.

To the south-east in the centre of the park around the extinct Volcán Quetrupillán lies a volcanic plateau rising above the tree line. Volcán Quetrupillán exploded to create its now wide and open form. A number of attractive alpine lakes lie within this stark lunar landscape of lava flows, scoria and pumice.

Climate

Parque Nacional Villarrica's elevated topography ensures it higher average precipitation levels and lower temperatures than the surrounding Araucarian lowlands. Reaching nearly 5000mm annually (concentrated between May and early September), precipitation are highest on the western slopes of Volcán Villarrica, which lie directly in the path of the moist Pacific airstream. The winter period brings frequent and heavy snowfalls above 1000m, producing an average snow cover of 2m (that is ideal for downhill and cross-country skiing). Even higher up in these ranges the weather can be surprisingly hot in January and February, however, because the extensive fields of black lava rock heat up under the intense midsummer sun.

Natural History

The lower slopes of Parque Nacional Villarrica are clothed by rich virgin forests, where montane southern beech species such as raulí, roble and the evergreen coigüe predominate up to an elevation of approximately 1000m. Above this altitude lenga and ñirre, alpine species of southern beech, coexist with superb forests of araucaria (or pehuén) trees.

The araucaria is often found in pure stands that form the tree line (at around 1600m above sea level). Typical southern Andean wild flowers, such as the añañuca, a species recognisable by its pink goblet-like flowers, and the orquídea del campo, an orchid of the Chloraea genus, are well represented. Hardy shrubs, including the michai, a thorny member of the Berberis genus (similar to the calafate) with yellow flowers, and chauras (Pernettya species) thrive on the upper slopes of these volcanic mountains. Usually present in alpine herb fields of the Araucanía is the senecio gris (Senecio chionophilus), a native yellow daisy. The volcanic soils also favour the brecillo (Empetrum rubrum), a small shrub that produces edible purple berries (often seen in the scats of native foxes).

The shy native fauna is more seldom seen in Parque Nacional Villarrica, though it is much easier to spot birds. A bird once again common in the park is the torcaza (Columba araucana), a large grey pigeon which the Mapuche call the conu. Although this species seemed dangerously close to extinction in the early 1960s, populations of the torcaza have recovered dramatically in recent decades. Another local bird is the cachaña (Microsittace ferruginea), an alpine parakeet that feeds largely on araucaria nuts, which it splits open with its sharp beak. The luxuriant forests also provide an ideal habitat for the black woodpecker, the carpintero negro, which can often be seen tapping about the tree trunks.

Place Names

The language of the indigenous Mapuche people is still very much alive in the local nomenclature. The Mapuches knew Volcán Villarrica by the name of Rucapillán ('house of the spirits') and considered the mountain to be the abode of their ancestors. The name Quetrupillán, a volcano just to the east, refers to the native quetru ducks frequently seen in the area. Puesco, a river that rises near the frontier with Argentina, means simply 'water of the east', while Coñaripe, the name of a small town at the southern foot of the national park, means 'the path of the warriors', a reference to a pass in the Villarrica range that was used as a crossing by local tribes. Llancahue, the name of a small river passed on the Villarrica Traverse trek, can be translated from the Mapuche as 'place where the llanca is found'. Llancas, small copper-coloured pebbles highly valued as ornaments by Mapuche women, were once widely used as a means of payment.

PRACTICAL INFORMATION
Information Sources
CONAF has a new office (☎ 45-44 1261) in Pucón at Camino Internacional 1450, at the eastern edge of town on the road to Puesco. There are resident *guardaparques* (park rangers) at the Guardería Chinay (near the end of the Around Volcán Villarrica trek) and near the customs post of Puesco (at the end of the Villarrica Traverse).

Other sources of information are the dozen or so outdoor adventure companies in Pucón (most with offices on Avenida O'Higgins), which organise guided rafting, trekking and climbing trips.

Permits & Regulations
The entry charge to Parque Nacional Villarrica is US$1.50/0.50 for adults/children. Apart from several CONAF-organised camping grounds, camping is only permitted in the park at places one day's walk or more from the nearest road.

Unless they can show some official mountaineering qualification (the definition of which is not always clear), trekkers are not permitted to climb Volcán Villarrica without a guide. (For more details see Ascent of Volcán Villarrica under the Other Treks in Parque Nacional Villarrica.)

When to Trek
Unless you take skis, little of Parque Nacional Villarrica is accessible to trekkers outside the summer season, whose maximum extension is from early November until late April. Early in the season snow may still cover large areas of the route along the treks described below. In early summer some of the larger streams may require careful wading. Summer weather (December to

February) can be surprisingly hot. From about late December until early February bothersome tábanos (see Dangers & Annoyances in the Facts for the Trekker chapter) are out in force in the forests, but above the tree line they're much less of a problem.

Around Volcán Villarrica

Duration 3 to 4 days
Distance 43km
Standard Medium-Hard
Start Pucón/Refugio Villarrica
Finish Palguín-Coñaripe (where trek joins Villarrica Traverse) or the Termas de Palguín
Entry US$1.50, no permit needed
Season November-April
Summary A high-level trek (mostly above the tree line) around the near-perfect cone of Volcán Villarrica

This round-the-mountain trek passes the western and southern sides of the conical Volcán Villarrica, giving a constantly changing panorama. The guided ascent of Volcán Villarrica itself is an unforgettable experience, and can be done on the first day of the trek.

MAPS
One Chilean IGM sheet scaled at 1:50,000 covers the entire walk: *Pucón* (Section G, No 104). Unfortunately the summit of Volcán Villarrica is shown uncontoured, and the map does not indicate the track or other important features, such as ski lifts and refugios. Certain areas covered by lava flows are inaccurately depicted. Two neighbouring sheets, *Villarrica* (Section G, No 103) and *Liquiñe* (Section G, No 113), may be useful for additional orientation.

DAYS REQUIRED
Allow three or four days to complete this trek, plus an additional day if you make an ascent of Volcán Villarrica (see Other Treks in Parque Nacional Villarrica). The trek can

be combined with the Villarrica Traverse, increasing the walking time by a further three or four days.

TREKKING STANDARD

The route follows a rough foot track through difficult volcanic terrain just above the tree line. Recent lava flows and fields of broken scoria often make the going strenuous. Particularly in the central section of the route, the trail is often quite vague, with only occasional cairns and/or paint markings. Except for the final stage, the entire walk is very exposed to the elements.

The ground is always porous and well drained, and finding water can be difficult as many streams flow underground lower down. Remember that many of the smaller meltwater streams stop running overnight. If you camp by small streams be sure to collect water for the next day before retiring. Keep your water bottles full for the long and thirsty sections between streams.

The recommended way to do the trek is anticlockwise. In this direction route-finding is easier and there is less climbing. It also allows trekkers the option of ascending Volcán Villarrica before setting out.

The trek is rated *medium to hard*, and has a total distance of 43km.

ACCOMMODATION & CAMPING

The *Refugio Villarrica* (☎ 45-44 1176 in Pucón) is a large ski lodge at an altitude of 1420m on the volcano's lower slopes. It caters essentially for winter skiers, and doesn't normally take guests in summer. Near the end of the trek is the *Hostería Termas de Palguín* (☎ 45-44 1968 in Pucón), where there is mid-range accommodation for around US$40 per night (including an evening meal).

There are CONAF camping grounds at the park entrance on the road up to the Refugio Villarrica, and at Chinay in an attractive meadow surrounded by coigües. The cost per night is US$7.50 per site. Facilities at both are very basic (little more than fireplaces with picnic tables).

There are no huts at all along the route, so

the trek cannot be done without a tent. Much of the route is very exposed, although trekkers will find relatively sheltered camp sites along the way. Firewood is often scarce.

SUPPLIES

Most trekkers visiting Parque Nacional Villarrica will base themselves in Pucón (see Regional Bases) or the town of Villarrica. All necessary supplies can be bought there.

GETTING TO/FROM THE TREK

The trek begins from the road up to the Refugio Villarrica, some 12km from Pucón. No public transport exists, but taxis can be hired out to the park for around US$15 one way. You can walk to the start of the trek in around four hours. Hitchhiking some way past the park entrance gate is a reasonable prospect, but thereafter there is much less traffic.

A dozen or so local outdoor adventure companies organise guided ascents of Volcán Villarrica. In fine weather in the main tourist season (January and February) several guided parties are likely to make the climb each day. These trips include transport by their own minibus to and from the upper end of the road at the Refugio Villarrica, and if there is extra space in the minibus they will take you up to the start of the trek for around US$7.50 (one way).

The trek finishes at the Palguín-Coñaripe road (which higher up is little better than the standard of a 4WD track). As no public transport exists from this point, you will probably have to walk at least as far as the Termas de Palguín. For this reason the long final section to Palguín Bajo (on the road to Puesco) is also included in the track notes. There is some tourist traffic to the Termas de Palguín from Pucón, and you may be able to get a ride.

THE TREK
Stage 1: Refugio Villarrica to Estero Ñilfe
10km, 4 to 5½ hours

Especially early in the day it may be difficult to find running water along the first part of this stage.

Near a large tin shed at the upper end of a winter ski tow, the route leaves the access road to the Refugio Villarrica (visible about 500m up to your left) and initially traces a 4WD track south-west below another ski lift. Cut over a (usually dry) rocky stream bed and make your way over open slopes of hardy Andean heath and wild flowers just above the tree line of lengas. The foot track continues through lava fields and alluvial washes, before beginning a steeper climb leftwards via a small rocky spur that eventually brings you out onto a snow grass ridge after about 1½ hours.

The route rises and dips along the uppermost edge of the forest as it negotiates more (probably dry) stream gullies, lava fields and occasional snowdrifts. Up to the left is the snowy crown of Volcán Villarrica, while the shining blue waters of Lago Calafquén gradually move into view down to the south-west.

A gentle descent leads through a beautiful forest of mature araucarias, whose thick grey trunks and proportionately small tufts of branches at the crown give them an almost palm-like appearance, to reach a path junction at the edge of a deeply eroded stream bed, the **Zanjón Pino Huacho**, 60 to 80 minutes on.

Here a 33km path (signposted 'Salida Villarrica') diverges down north-westwards via the Río Voipir to the town of Villarrica. (This is a useful exit route in bad weather, but it's not otherwise recommended.) Down in the base of this small canyon, a wooden pipe ducts water from a tiny spring trickling out of the sandy embankment. Cross and climb out of the Zanjón Pino Huacho and continue walking around the mountainside through the mixed lenga and araucaria forest. The path crosses two more dry gullies and another area of lava, then leads gently on past a tiny pond to reach a trail intersection (marked only by an unusually large old araucaria) after 60 to 80 minutes. The left-hand branch goes between two larger pools within the forest up to a glacier coming down from the volcano's south-western flank.

The main route follows the right-hand path, which takes you across yet another two dry stream beds before coming to the **Estero Challupen**. Jump the small rocky stream and once again continue up through the lenga forest before meeting the **Estero Ñilfe**, a permanently flowing glacial stream, after 45 minutes to one hour. Here you come out onto open slopes, which give you a clear view south towards the snowcapped summit of Volcán Choshuenco, rising behind forested ranges.

Camp Sites There is a camping ground with minimal facilities at the park entrance gate on the road up to the Refugio Villarrica.

Many smaller streams on the first part of Stage 1 are fed by melting snow, and therefore generally only flow – if they flow at all – from (late) afternoon until an hour or two after sunset. You can camp beside the pools in the forest passed after the Zanjón Pino Huacho, but the stagnant water should be boiled. Scenic but more exposed camp sites can also be found nearby by following the left-hand route branch from near the pools for 15 minutes up to a murky stream on the open rocky slopes below the glaciers of Volcán Villarrica.

There is little even ground beside the Estero Challupen, but trekkers should be able to improvise a camp spot. This is a small stream, and it may stop running at the end of a dry summer. The best place to camp is the Estero Ñilfe, where you'll find suitably sheltered tent sites among the low lenga forest on the stream's northern bank.

Stage 2: Estero Ñilfe to Río Pichillaneahue
12km, 5 to 7½ hours

Follow cairns across the open slopes scattered with occasional senecio gris, a yellow daisy-like wild flower. The path ahead is vague in places, but the route is relatively straightforward. It leads to the left of a rounded hillock through an old lava flow, continuing over sparsely vegetated ridges and sporadically flowing streams. Head between two extinct volcano cones (point 2006m and point 1616m) to reach a gap, 1½ to two hours from the Estero Ñilfe. From

THE ARAUCANÍA

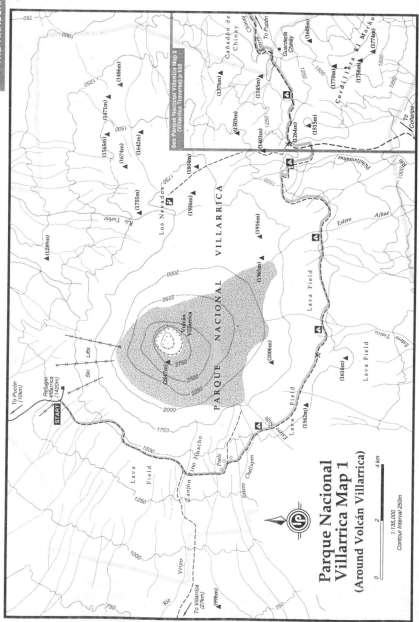

Parque Nacional
Villarrica Map 1
(Around Volcán Villarrica)

1:135,000
Contour Interval 250m

0 2 4 km

See Parque Nacional Villarrica Map 2
(Villarrica Traverse) p 132

START

Refugio Villarrica (1420m)
To Pucón (10km)

Ski Lifts

Volcán Villarrica
(2847m)

PARQUE NACIONAL VILLARRICA

Los Nevados

Río Turbio

Lava Field

Lava Field

Lava Field

Lava Field

Estero Aihue

Estero Traico

Estero Challupen

Estero Pino Huacho

Zanjón Pino Huacho

Pools

Río Voipir

To Villarrica (27km)

To Pucón

Cordillera El Mocho

Cañadón de Chinay

Estero Chinay

Guardería Chinay

Pichillanquihue

To Coñaripe

CLEM LINDENMAYER

CLEM LINDENMAYER

CLEM LINDENMAYER

Trekking in the Araucanía takes you to the edge of scores of volcanoes and over volcanic terrain. The Sierra Velluda (top) is in the vicinity of Volcán Antuco. From the slopes of Volcán Villarrica, the snow-covered peak of Volcán Choshuenco is visible on the horizon (middle). The Sierra Nevada affords views of the surrounding volcanoes and mountains (bottom).

WAYNE BERNHARDSON

CLEM LINDENMAYER

CLEM LINDENMAYER

CLEM LINDENMAYER

Volcán Llaima (top left) and the Sierra Velluda (right) are among the highlights of the Araucanía, which offers stunning scenery and curios from the early days of European settlement (middle left). The peaceful Lago Verde (bottom) is surrounded by high forested hills in the highlands of Parque Nacional Huerquehue.

here you get the first clear views south-east towards the exploded crater of Volcán Quetrupillán and the majestic 3776m ice-encrusted cone of Volcán Lanín behind it.

Descend via a ridge leading around to the right to cross a trickling stream, then climb over a steep grassy ridge to meet the **Estero Traico** after 30 to 45 minutes. This is a permanent glacier-fed stream that flows through a deep trench. The foot track again peters out here, and after you wade or jump across a steep climb up the adjacent embankment brings you to the edge of a broad lava flow. On the far side of this roughly 1km-wide band of rugged volcanic rock stands a row of mushroom-like araucarias, silhouetted against the classic outline of Volcán Lanín. Cross by continuing ahead through a narrow open area, then bear slightly right to reach a tiny stream where the lava borders an obvious eroding reddish-brown ridge, after a further 45 minutes to one hour.

Climb directly to the bare ridge top and follow it north-eastwards in view of heavily crevassed icefalls that spill well down the southern sides of Volcán Villarrica. Go just past a low cliff, then drop away right via a rock rib into a tiny upper valley fringed by a beautiful araucaria forest. Cross the normally dry stream near the forest line and climb ahead past some young araucarias re-colonising the grassy slope.

This soon brings you across another small stream bed, where a gently sloping plain begins. Head eastwards (ie towards an imaginary point about halfway between Volcán Lanín on the right and the much lower Volcán Quetrupillán) over low vegetation to reach the **Estero Aihue**, one to 1½ hours on.

Cross the stream easily and climb the loose sandy embankment. Make your way on across the open slopes for 15 to 20 minutes, easily crossing a few minor gullies to pick up the path again at a cluster of araucarias standing just above the normal tree line. Sidle around left past more araucarias to a tiny dry stream bed, where cairns and/or paint markings show the way up onto grassy slopes covered in wild flowers. (Be

sure to take the higher route here, not a lower one that peters out near the forest line.)

Head north along this old graded foot track, crossing numerous streams as you contour around the open mountainsides scattered with pink añañucas. After 30 to 45 minutes descend right into lenga scrub (affected by past fires), then follow blazings on down through taller trees. The path makes a final, steeply spiralling descent through coigües and quila to meet the **Río Pichillaneahue** after a further 30 to 45 minutes. There is no bridge here, but there are suitable places to ford this large, clear stream.

Camp Sites The upper slopes are exposed to the elements and firewood is scarce, so there are few ideal camp sites along most of this stage. You can camp on grassy sites at the stream just before you reach the Estero Traico, but the mostly steep banks of the Estero Traico are less suitable for tents. At the Estero Aihue grassy areas beside the stream make attractive camp sites but are unsheltered. The Río Pichillaneahue is the recommended place to camp. Particularly along the true left (east) bank of the river, many good sites can be found in the coigüe forest.

Stage 3: Río Pichillaneahue to Palguín Bajo
21km, 5½ to 7½ hours

The path leads 600m downstream along the east bank, then climbs left over a low ridge to come out at the **Palguín-Coñaripe road** after 15 to 20 minutes. (At the time of research there was no signpost.) Turn left along this often rough – almost 4WD standard – road running up through the araucaria forest to a pass at 1264m on the top of the main Villarrica range after 30 to 40 minutes. From here a 5km trail (signposted 'A Los Nevados') on the left climbs northwards to a lookout on a broad snowy plateau on the north-eastern slopes of Volcán Villarrica.

Follow the winding road down for 30 to 40 minutes past the (very basic) CONAF camping ground in the upper **Cañadón de Chinay**. The road descends through rich forests of mixed southern beech species, crossing and recrossing the rushing **Estero Chinay** to reach the **Guardería Chinay** after a further 35 to 45 minutes.

The road crosses the park boundary and continues for 3km downvalley to reach a Y junction, 40 to 50 minutes on, where you bear left down the valley of the Río Palguín. (If you undertake this trek from the other direction – ie from the north – there is a signpost 'Al Parque 3 Km' at this junction to direct you.)

Below this junction the road is noticeably more well travelled and in a better condition (although it can be quite dusty after dry weather). It leads down past the **Termas de Palguín** (see Accommodation & Camping), then on through raulí and roble forest and open fields past the signposted turn-off to the **Salto El León**, a waterfall that can be visited in 20 minutes return. The road comes out at **Palguín Bajo** after a final three to four hours. There are local buses from here to Pucón roughly every hour.

Camp Sites There is organised camping along the upper Estero Chinay. Some people also pitch their tent near the Salto El León.

Villarrica Traverse

Duration 3 or 4 days
Distance 41km
Standard Medium
Start Termas de Palguín
Finish Puesco
Entry US$1.50, no permit needed
Season November-April
Summary A marvellously scenic trek along the top of a wild volcanic range that connects Volcán Villarrica with Volcán Lanín on the Chile/Argentina border.

This very scenic high-level route follows the broad range extending south-east from Volcán Villarrica towards Volcán Lanín. The central part of this range forms a broad volcanic plateau intersected by small calderas and lava flows. The altitude of the plateau varies from about 1700 to 2000m, and its rocky treeless landscape is fringed by rainforests enriched by beautiful stands of araucarias.

MAPS
Three 1:50,000 Chilean IGM sheets cover the area of the park: *Pucón* (Section G, No 104), *Curarrehue* (Section G, No 105), *Liquiñe* (Section G, No 113) and *Paimun* (Section G, No 114). These maps do not show the track or Laguna Blanca, but are otherwise topographically accurate.

DAYS REQUIRED
The walk can be done in three or four days, but an additional day for side trips or rests is time well spent. It is possible to combine the Villarrica Traverse with the Around Volcán Villarrica trek, increasing the walking time by a further three or four days.

TREKKING STANDARD
The trek follows a relatively good path for almost the entire distance. In the central section high and very exposed terrain well above the tree line must be crossed. Here deep winter snow remains well into November, and bad weather or low cloud can quickly move in to make navigation difficult.

The range's aspect tends to catch passing storms, so good rainwear is absolutely essential. The route is marked by paint on rocks and trees, and on the higher slopes with wooden or bamboo stakes. Strong winds and deep snow tend to push over the marker stakes – please re-erect them wherever necessary. The recommended way to do the trek is from west to east, as the route is generally easier to follow in this direction.

The Villarrica Traverse is graded *medium* and covers a total distance of 41km.

ACCOMMODATION & CAMPING
There are no refugios along this route, so all trekkers must carry a sturdy mountain tent. At the start of the trek is the *Termas de*

Palguín hostería, where there is mid-range accommodation with all meals (from around US$40 per night).

There is a CONAF-run camping ground at Puesco, at the end of the trek, where tent sites cost US$7.50 per night; facilities are basic.

Recommended is the *Hospedaje Agricultor* at Piedra Mala, 2km north of Puesco along the road towards Pucón immediately below the peak known as La Peineta. The hospedaje offers dormitory accommodation for US$3 per night as well as cabins with gas stove and cold shower by the river from as little as US$6.50 per person.

SUPPLIES

Most trekkers visiting Parque Nacional Villarrica will base themselves in Pucón or the town of Villarrica. All necessary supplies can be bought there. There is a small cafeteria just north across the bridge from Puesco, but no store as such.

GETTING TO/FROM THE TREK

The trek begins at the Termas de Palguín, 12km from Palguín Bajo on the road to Coñaripe. In January and February there are irregular organised tours to the Termas de Palguín from Pucón. The taxi fare from Pucón to the Termas de Palguín is around US$15 (or about US$20 if you wanted to be dropped off higher up, at the turn-off into the Estero Mocho valley). Regular local buses to Curarrehue and Puesco go past the turn-off at Palguín Bajo, from where the pleasant walk up to the Termas can be made in three to four hours. The final section of road into this sector of the national park crosses private property along the Estero Mocho. The owners seem happy to allow trekkers access via their land, but be on your best behaviour here!

It is also possible to do the trek after crossing from Argentina. There are up to a dozen buses per week from San Martín de los Andes and Junín de los Andes, usually passing the Termas de Palguín turn-off in mid-afternoon. Tell the driver where you want to get off.

The trek ends at the tiny village of Puesco on the international road across Paso Mamuil Malal (also called Paso Tromen). For reasons of courtesy, present your papers at the customs office here, but make sure the staff realise that you have not just crossed from Argentina. From Puesco there are local buses to Pucón at around 8 am and in the early afternoon on most days. Boarding a bus coming from Argentina is usually no problem, as long as there's space. It's unlikely, however, that you'll be allowed to get on a bus heading across the frontier unless you've already booked and are on the neatly typed list of passengers – but if one of the Argentine cities of Junín and San Martín de los Andes is your preferred destination you should certainly have a try.

THE TREK
Stage 1: Termas de Palguin to Laguna Azul
18km, 5¼ to 7 hours

From the termas, walk one to 1⅓ hours uphill to the road fork (recognisable by the signpost 'Al Parque 3 Km'). Here take the left branch, which comes almost immediately to a large gate and cottage where you enter private property.

Follow the often dusty road across the **Río Palguín** just above its confluence with the Estero Mocho, then through newly cleared fields and past a group of farmhouses. Where the road fords the stream near a wooden-shingled shack, continue ahead through the burnt out clearing. The track makes a gentle climb into the forest past a makeshift log gate (the national park boundary), then a few hundred metres on pick up a path diverging right (marked by red-painted blazings on trees), 1¾ to 2¼ hours after leaving the Palguín-Coñaripe road.

Ascend steeply through the coigües to a broad ridge, then follow this a short way up leftwards to cross a stream. The path climbs on via a forested spur, first in an easterly direction past old lichen-covered araucaria trees, then south-eastwards to reach two trickling streams near the upper limit of the lenga scrub (at around 1550m) after 1¼ to 1¾ hours. This spot gives the first clear view of the magnificent puffing summit of Volcán

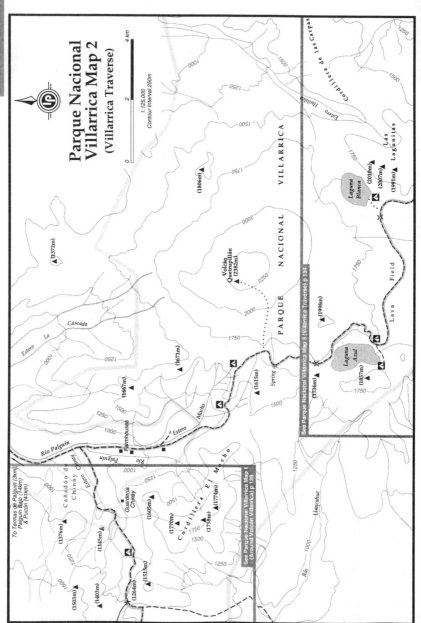

Parque Nacional Villarrica Map 2 (Villarrica Traverse)

1:125,000
Contour Interval 250m

0   2   4 km

Villarrica, which dominates the skyline to the north-west.

Head out over the open plateau to the left of a rounded rock bluff (which is an old volcanic plug). Make your way on south-eastwards over alpine grassland and raw volcanic scoria through a stream gully (snow-filled early in the season, but dry later in the summer) to meet the upper **Río Llancahue**, after 30 to 40 minutes. From here a vague route goes up eastwards to the exploded crater of **Volcán Quetrupillán**, a side trip taking around three hours return.

Follow a rough path for 10 minutes downstream to a large spring gushing directly out of a small ridge, then cross the stream. Cairns and old paint markings on rocks guide you left at first, up snow grass ridges with sporadic clusters of wild orchids, then rightwards up more sparsely vegetated slopes into a rocky gap after a further 40 to 50 minutes. From here there are more fine volcanic vistas towards the north.

Sidle south-west to get your first glimpse of the dark blue lake directly below to your right. The route soon swings back south-eastwards, bringing the giant of the region, Volcán Lanín, as well as Volcán Choshuenco, the lower double cone off to the south, into view. Maintain a high route over the coarse slopes and snowdrifts that persist well into summer, then drop down to the right in zigzags along a loose-earth ridge to reach the eastern shore of **Laguna Azul** after 50 minutes to 1¼ hours. This very impressive lake lies in a deep trough whose outlet stream was dammed by the large lava flow nearby.

The path can be followed another 15 to 20 minutes around the lakeshore to cross the outlet stream on stepping stones, before climbing over the grassy slopes to the ruins of the Refugio Azul. (This hut may be reconstructed at some time in the future.) From here a rough walking route continues down north-westwards along the Río Llancahue to the Palguín-Coñaripe road.

Camp Sites The access road to the trail head goes through private property, so trekkers should refrain from camping until they enter the national park. A few quite reasonable camp sites can be found among the araucarias just a minute or two above the stream passed 25 to 35 minutes up from the Estero Mocho. Better camp sites are higher up, where the path reaches the upper edge of the lenga scrub. It's also possible to camp near the upper Río Llancahue, but sites are more exposed and there is little firewood.

A suitable place to camp at Laguna Azul is on a flat open area at the south-eastern shore of the lake. More scenic but less sheltered spots exist across the outlet stream on the grassy saddle several minutes down from the ruins of the refugio.

Stage 2: Laguna Azul to Laguna Abutardas
14km, 4½ to 6 hours
From the south-eastern shore of Laguna Azul, head east between the broad band of lava and the ridge you descended on the previous stage. Occasional paint markings and small tree branches propped up with cairns lead easily through the broken rock. Climb on over a minor crest, then cut through another regenerating lava field and continue north-east along a broad, barely vegetated ridge to a barren rocky area. Edge down to the right of this to meet a silt-filled stream bed, before making your way left 500m. At this point head up north-eastwards immediately left of a tiny stream to reach a narrow sandy gap after 1½ to two hours. From here you get a view across the desolate moonscape to **Laguna Blanca**, a small lake lying at just above 1600m.

Drop down the eroding slopes into the barren basin. (You can easily reach the lakeshore in five minutes by leaving the foot track and crossing the raw plain to your left.) Head on around to the right into a dry gully, following this until it turns eastwards, then climb away around the eastern rim of a small extinct crater. Continue on southwards towards the distant twin peaks of Volcán Choshuenco, before crossing leftwards over a small spur marking the Chile-Argentina frontier. The route sidles around slopes over-

THE ARAUCANÍA

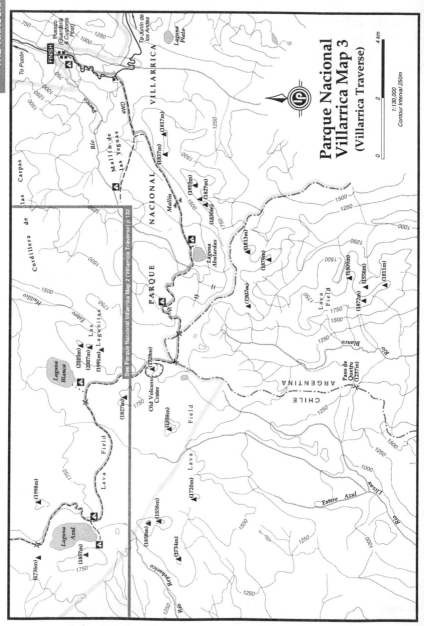

Parque Nacional
Villarrica Map 3
(Villarrica Traverse)

1:130,000
Contour Interval 250m

0   2   4 km

See Parque Nacional Villarrica Map 2 (Villarrica Traverse) p 132

looking the wild forested valley of the Río Blanco in Argentina, dips into a bare bowl-like basin, then ascends north-east to reach a ridge top back on the international border, 1½ to two hours from Laguna Blanca.

The often windy gap on this ridge looks out north-east (into Chile) across a small valley, whose grassy upper section holds several tarns. Behind are the jagged peaks of the Cordillera de las Carpas and beyond the valley of the Río Puesco, farther over to your right, stands an impressive saw-shaped range, which locals call La Peineta (dress comb'). You can also enjoy the last clear views of Volcán Lanín over to your right.

Drop to the right, then ease down leftwards beside the stream over hardy grasses and herbs in the waterlogged soil. One wild flower that thrives here is the hardy madeco (*Ranunculus chilensis*), a yellow buttercup common in the southern Andes. Pick up the path 300m over to the left (ie north) from where the stream tumbles over a low escarpment, before descending in a few quick switchbacks (often snowbound until mid-summer). The route doubles back rightwards below the cliff face above another area of saturated alpine moorland to cross the stream below the waterfall after 40 to 50 minutes.

Jump across the stream and continue ahead gently up through marshy areas and lenga scrub to an open ridge top separating two branches of the upper Río Puesco. Up to your right more small cascades tumble over the escarpment, while there are enticing glimpses of a welcoming lake down in the valley below you. Follow the ridge to just before a rock knob, then watch out for markings on the right that indicate where the trail starts its steep descent south-east through the forest. When you come to a tiny boggy clearing, head down rightwards immediately across a stream then through another small clearing until you come out onto an open grassy area at the western corner of **Laguna Abutardas**, 30 to 40 minutes on.

Make your way directly east across the marshy plain grazed by noisy flocks of bandurrias, bounding across babbling brooks to pick up the trail again at the edge

of the trees. This sometimes indistinct track sidles through the forest above the lake's mostly steep north side, before dropping down right onto open grassy areas at the eastern end of Laguna Abutardas after a final 20 to 30 minutes.

A short cut through a band of lenga scrub gives access to the narrow sandy beach, from where you can best appreciate this charming lake. Laguna Abutardas lies at around 1450m, and is enclosed on three sides by steep forested ranges. In hot weather the water is just the right temperature for a leisurely dip (and also gives some respite from the voracious swarms of tábanos that infest this area in late December and January).

Camp Sites Along much of Stage 2 camping is not advisable because of high, exposed terrain and a lack of running water. Before Laguna Blanca there are no suitable camp sites. The camping at the lake is fairly exposed and there is no firewood – please don't burn marker stakes. There is a space for one or two tents by the stream just below where it cascades over the low escarpment. The best camp sites are on the open grassy area at the eastern shore of Laguna Abutardas.

Stage 3: Laguna Abutardas to Puesco
9km, 3¾ to 5 hours

Rejoin the trail back where you left it in the forest, and head north-east gently down through the tall lenga forest and quila, crossing a small stream to reach a *mallín* (swamp) clearing after 30 to 40 minutes. Make your way 350m through this boggy strip, then look for markings on the right where the route re-enters the trees. Continue north-east, rising and dipping over low ridges, before you drop down through the coigüe forest scattered with quellenes (wild strawberries) and long-abandoned farm clearings to meet an old road after a further 1½ to two hours.

Turn right and follow this often very rough track (which is now impassable except to foot traffic) through ñirre and notro scrub. The road sides gently down in an almost easterly direction above the raging Río Puesco, crossing through a remnant cherry orchard to pass a small house just before it intersects with the Pucón-Junín de los Andes international road, one to 1½ hours on. Go left here and descend northwards through the forest of raulí and roble, watching out for unmarked short-cut trails that lead down more directly between the road's numerous switchback curves to arrive at **Puesco** after a final 40 to 50 minutes.

Puesco (see Accommodation & Camping and Getting to/from the Trek) is little more than a cluster of houses (at around 700m) serving the nearby border post and ranger station. Go to the *aduana* (customs office) and explain that you are not coming from Argentina. The immigration staff may want to inspect your gear anyway.

Camp Sites There is mediocre camping near the stream 30 to 40 minutes from Laguna Abutardas, but few other good options exist along Stage 3. Nice riverside sites among araucarias can be reached by walking west (ie left) along the road for 30 to 40 minutes. CONAF has a basic though pleasant camping ground by the river at Puesco.

Other Treks in Parque Nacional Villarrica

ASCENT OF VOLCÁN VILLARRICA

Volcán Villarrica is the most climbed higher summit in Chile. From the crater rim at the summit there are superb views of virtually every major peak in the southern Araucanía and northern Lake District. The volcano is still extremely active, with glowing molten magma deep down in the core. During occasional periods of increased activity, red-hot lava may even spurt up to near the rim.

Although technically very straightforward, the climb requires a good level of fitness, and takes six to nine hours return from the Refugio Villarrica (see the Around Volcán Villarrica trek). Crampons, ice axe and well-insulated boots are essential. As the volcano continuously emits sulphur dioxide and other noxious gases, climbers should approach the rim cautiously to avoid being overcome by the acrid sulphurous fumes; you should also watch out for sudden wind changes.

The park authorities now require everyone – apart from properly trained mountaineers and guides, who must present adequate proof of their qualifications – to make the ascent with an approved guide. Almost a dozen outdoor adventure companies in Pucón organise guided ascents of Volcán Villarrica. These companies charge around US$50 for the climb, which includes all gear, the special fee for climbers of US$4.50 and even life insurance! One company which has been particularly recommended by trekkers is Apumanque (☎ 45-44 1085; fax 44 1361), whose office is at Avenida O'Higgins 412; this company's guides split participants into 'slow' and 'fast' groups before making the ascent.

Other Treks in the Araucanía

VOLCÁN DOMUYO – ARGENTINA

Although Monte San Valentín (4058m) in the Hielo Norte (northern continental icecap) of Chile is a more 'genuinely Patagonian' peak, by strict definition the 4709m summit of Volcán Domuyo is the highest point in the Patagonian Andes, simply because it is in the Patagonian province of Neuquén. Standing in Neuquén's remote northernmost corner at the northern end of the Cordillera del Viento, a high range well to the east of the main Andean divide, the summit of this enormous volcano is exposed to the moist Pacific winds and is covered by extensive névés and glaciers. Volcán Domuyo is one of the few volcanoes entirely within Argentina that still has significant geothermal activity, such as fumaroles, geysers and thermal springs.

Volcán Domuyo can be climbed in a minimum seven-day mini-expedition from the south via the Río Curileuvú. Although technically fairly straightforward, this is a serious high-alpine ascent (with the associated dangers of altitude sickness – see the Health & Safety chapter) in a remote area, and therefore requires proper experience, equipment (including ice axe and crampons) and planning. Access is by private 4WD vehicle only. Volcán Domuyo stretches across four still unpublished sheets on Argentina's 1:100,000 series national grid. It could take the national IGM decades to publish useful topographical maps of the area, but some of the local mountain clubs in Neuquén may have prepared their own trekking/climbing maps of Volcán Domuyo.

VOLCÁN COPAHUE – ARGENTINA

The 2925m Volcán Copahue is still active and lies in the remote north-west of Neuquén province on the Argentina-Chile frontier. The lower slopes of the volcano are covered by beautiful araucaria forests, and part of the area is protected within a nature reserve known as the Parque Provincial Copahue. In summer itinerant graziers and their families herd flocks of sheep up here to graze in the surrounding highland pastures.

The summit crater of Volcán Copahue (which means 'sulphur' in the language of the indigenous Mapuche people) is filled by a lake. The temperature of the lake water oscillates – depending on the season and the level of volcanic activity – between 20° and 40°C. Since pre-European times the Mapuche have journeyed up to Volcán Copahue to collect the lake's mineral water, which they believe to have special health and healing properties, and bottles of Copahue water are even sold at regional markets (such as in the Chilean city of Los Angeles).

A two to three-day trekking route leads southwards up from Copahue, a tiny mountain resort (with mineral and thermal springs as well as modest winter skiing facilities) to the summit of Volcán Copahue, from where there are good views west into the headwaters of the Río Biobío. The descent is made south-eastwards to the spa village of Caviahue, at an altitude of 1650m above the

picturesque Lago Caviahue (also called Lago Agrio).

The only topographical maps of any real use are two Chilean IGM sheets: 1:50,000 *Volcán Copahue* (Section G, No 44), whose current edition is basic, and the 1:250,000 sheet *Laguna de la Laja*, a good colour sheet whose scale is nevertheless too large to show detail accurately. Caviahue's small mountain club, the Club Andino de Caviahue (☎ 0948-95064) may be able to offer more information and advice on local trekking.

Copahue is on the Ruta Provincial 26 (which continues over the 1890m Paso Los Copahues into Chile). You can get to/from Caviahue by one daily bus via Loncopue, a town 50km by road to the south-east, which in turn is served by several daily buses to/from the small city of Zapala, 120km to the south.

PASO ANCHO – ARGENTINA

Paso Ancho is a tiny winter ski centre in the Andes of central Neuquén on the road (Ruta 22) over the Paso de Pino Hachado (marking the frontier with Chile), 50km west of the town of Las Lajas. The surrounding ranges are covered with araucaria forests and open highland meadows, and make excellent trekking country. One easy day walk in the area goes to the Arenas Zumbadoras, a steep sand slope that – according to local legend – Mapuche warriors had to run up in order to prove they were ready for battle. Those who came last would have to stay back and guard the women of the tribe.

An ancient 1;100,000 Argentine IGM sheet, *Pino Hachado* (Neuquén, No 3772-12) covers the area. The Chilean IGM's 1:50,000 *Río Pino Hachado* (Section G, No 74-88) might also be useful, but the sale of this sheet is restricted.

There is no public transport to Paso Ancho, but, given the modest flow of traffic going across the Paso de Pino Hachado into Chile throughout the summer months, it should be possible to hitch there then. There is a simple ski lodge (fax 0942-99178 in Las Lajas) at Paso Ancho, which *may* offer summer accommodation (and could possibly even help you arrange transport).

PARQUE NACIONAL NAHUEL BUTA – CHILE

Parque Nacional Nahuel Buta is located in the Coast Range (Cordillera de la Costa) 35km west of Angol. This 683 sq km park was established to protect one of the last great araucaria forests of the Chilean Araucanía. Nahuel Buta is the only place on the mainland where the zorro chilote *(Pseudolopex rufipes)*, a species of fox otherwise endemic to the island of Chiloé, is known to exist. You can make short day treks from the administration centre to the lookouts of Piedra El Aguila and Cerro Anay.

The Chilean IGM 1:50,000 sheets *Elicura*, (Section G, No 36) and *Los Sauces* (Section G, No 37) cover most of the park. Access is from Angol by daily bus.

PARQUE NACIONAL TOLHUACA – CHILE

The 637 sq km Parque Nacional Tolhuaca is 49km by road north of Curacautín in the northern Araucanía. The park comprises a volcanic range whose highest point is the 2806m Volcán Tolhuaca. The Tolhuaca park administration centre is at Laguna Malleco. Overnight treks within the park are not allowed, but day walks can be undertaken to the Salto de Malleco (waterfall), Laguna Verde, the Prados de Mesacura, and the tarns of Lagunillas. Camping is permitted only at the camping area near the guardería.

The Chilean IGM sheet *Laguna Malleco* (Section G, No 52) covers all of the park, but trails are not shown. Curacautín can be reached by daily buses from Temuco, but there is no regular transport out to the park (although patient trekkers have a fair chance of hitching there during the summer holiday months).

LAGO QUILLÉN TO LAGO MOQUEHUE – ARGENTINA

This four to six day trek leads through relatively remote country in the northernmost sector of Parque Nacional Lanín. A foot track leads north from the eastern end of Lago Quillén following a track around the eastern side of the Cordón de Rucachoroi before dropping down to meet a road on the south shore of Lago Rucachoroi. From here the route heads north-west up the Arroyo Calfiquitra and across a watershed at Mallín Chufquén before again descending to Lago Ñorquinco via the Arroyo Coloco.

At Lago Ñorquinco a road continues north-west around the lake shore into the Arroyo Remeco valley and up to a pass, then heads north-east down a wide valley to Lago Moquehue. This trek requires good route-finding ability as the trail is overgrown in places.

Two old Argentine IGM 1:100,000 sheets, *Lago Ñorquinco* (Neuquén, No 3972-23) and *Quillén* (Neuquén, No 3972-29), cover the area (but not the track) of this walk. From Junín de los Andes there are daily buses to Rahué, from where it is 30km to Lago Quillén.

Lake District

The luxuriant rainforests of the Lake District contain the greatest diversity of plants and animals found anywhere in Patagonia. The Lake District's outstanding scenery includes large glacial lakes, volcanic plateaus, fresh, clear streams and wild mountain passes, making this area a real delight to explore. Of particular interest are ancient forests of the alerce tree, a conifer that reaches gigantic proportions, and the pudú, a native midget deer species. The area's obvious appeal and easy accessibility have helped it become the premier trekking region of Chile and Argentina, and this is reflected in the number of Lake District treks in this book.

TREKKING BASES
Junín de los Andes (Argentina)
Located just west of where the dry steppes begin in the central Argentine Lake District, Junín de los Andes is neither a particularly interesting nor attractive place. One worthwhile feature is the Museo Mapuche at Ponte 540, which deals with the history of the local Pehuenche tribes. This small town of 7400 inhabitants does make a good base for trips to Volcán Lanín or Lago Huechulafquén, the largest lake in Parque Nacional Lanín. Junín's tourist office (☎ 91160; fax 91296) is at Padre Milanesio 590. The Club Andino Junín de los Andes, or CAJA, is at O'Higgins 369 and can give information on climbing and trekking in the region. There is little real budget accommodation, but the *Residencial Marisa* (☎ 91175) at Rosas 360 is relatively affordable. Buses run regularly between Junín and San Martín de los Andes, 41km south by road, and Aluminé, roughly 100km to the north; daily buses en route to/from Pucón and Temuco in Chile also call in at Junín. Junín's area code is ☎ 0944.

Valdivia (Chile)
The only major coastal city between Concepción and Puerto Montt, Valdivia is a neat and attractive place. Valdivia is the starting or terminating point for treks between the Río Bueno and Corral on the coastal strip to the city's south (see the Other Treks section). SERNATUR (☎ 21 3596) is at Avenida Prat 555, and the regional office of CONAF (☎ 21 2001) is at Ismael Valdés 431. Codeff (☎ 62 3904), a national conservation organisation, has its local office at Carampangue 432. Valdivia is off the Panamerican Highway, although many buses en route between Puerto Montt and Santiago call in to the city. Valdivia's area code is ☎ 63.

San Martín de los Andes (Argentina)
San Martín de los Andes is at the eastern end of Lago Lácar. This expanding regional centre (with a current population of 17,000) is the gateway to Argentina's large and lovely Parque Nacional Lanín. San Martín is also a winter sports centre, with skiing at Cerro Chapelco. Fronting the Centro Cívico (town square) at the corner of Rosas and San Martín, you will find the tourist office (☎ 27347). Also on the Centro Cívico at Emilio Frey 749, is the APN Intendencia (☎ 27233), the main administrative centre for Parque Nacional Lanín. The local Club Andino San Martín (☎ 7640 1060, or 664 6758), is at José C Paz 800 (on the corner of Alvear). Cerro Torre, at San Martín 950, is a local outdoor adventure company that organises trips into the surrounding mountains and hires out climbing gear. A lower-budget place to stay is the *Residencial Los Pinos* (☎ 27207), at Almirante Brown 420.

There are many daily buses south along the scenic Ruta 234 highway to Bariloche as well as north (via Junín and Pucón) to Osorno in Chile. A longer and more interesting way into Chile is to take a bus to Puerto Fuy, from where a ferry crosses Lago Pirehueico. Austral, LADE and TAN have flights most days to Buenos Aires, Esquel, Neuquén and nearby Bariloche. San Martín's area code is ☎ 0972.

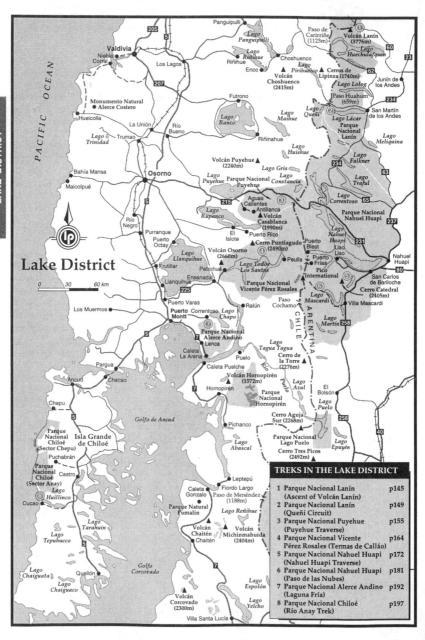

LAKE DISTRICT

Lake District

PACIFIC OCEAN

ARGENTINA / CHILE

0   30   60 km

TREKS IN THE LAKE DISTRICT

Osorno (Chile)

The city of Osorno has a population of around 110,000 (with one of the strongest German-speaking communities in Chile). It is an ideally located trekking base for trips to the national parks of Puyehue and Vicente Pérez Rosales in the central Chilean Lake District. SERNATUR (☎ 23 4104) has a tourist office in the Edificio Gobernación Provincial on the Plaza de Armas. The local CONAF office (☎ 23 4393; fax 23 4393) is at Martínez de Rozas 430. A good budget place to stay in Osorno is the *Residencial Ortega* at Colón 602. Osorno is on the Panamerican Highway and a major regional transport centre. Osorno's area code is ☎ 064.

San Carlos de Bariloche (Argentina)

Apart from being the largest Argentine city in the Patagonian Andes, San Carlos de Bariloche is also easily the most touristy. The city is nevertheless very attractive, although it can be expensive. On the south-eastern shores of Lago Nahuel Huapi in the southern Lake District, Bariloche is the gateway to Argentina's superb Parque Nacional Nahuel Huapi. The Museo de la Patagonia at the Centro Cívico has interesting displays on the indigenous Mapuche people, European settlement and local natural history.

All trekkers should pay a visit to the Club Andino Bariloche (☎ 24531; fax 24579), at 20 de Febrero 30, which has an excellent information service and library. The APN administration centre (☎ 23111; fax 22989) for Parque Nacional Nahuel Huapi, is at San Martín 24 opposite the Centro Cívico. Its opening hours are from Monday to Friday between 9 am and 2 pm. A convenient and central place to stay for budget-conscious trekkers is the *Albergue Patagonia Andina* (☎ 22783) at Morales 564 (just three blocks uphill from the Club Andino Bariloche), which charges US$12 including an excellent breakfast. The *Hotel Argentino* (☎ & fax 25201) at Avenida Costanera 12 de Octubre 655, offers bed and breakfast in double/triple/quad rooms for US$20/$18/$15.

Numerous daily buses run south along Ruta 258 to El Bolsón and Esquel as well as north to San Martín. There are also two or more daily buses via the Paso Puyehue to Osorno in Chile. A more scenic route into Chile goes across the lakes of Nahuel Huapi, Frías and Todos los Santos, involving a combination of several launches and buses to reach Puerto Montt. Bariloche is the Patagonian Andes' best connected city for air services, with several daily flights to/from Buenos Aires and many other flights to most larger cities throughout Patagonia. The main local carriers operating are Aerolíneas Argentinas (☎ 23091), LADE (☎ 23562), Sapse (☎ 28257) and TAN (☎ 27889). Bariloche's area code is ☎ 0944.

Puerto Montt (Chile)

Sprawling along the sheltered northern shore of the wide bay known as Seno Reloncaví, Puerto Montt is the gateway to the national parks of the southern Chilean Lake District and the Great Island of Chiloé. This booming port city with over 100,000 inhabitants still has many fine examples of southern Chilean wooden and corrugated iron architecture, although these are rapidly giving way to less characteristic modern buildings.

Puerto Montt's tourist office (☎ & fax 25 4580) is in the Plaza de Armas. CONAF (☎ 25 4488; fax 25 4882) has its main regional office on Ochagavía 464, but the local CONAF office at Calle Ejército 512 is generally more helpful. Anglers can pick up a fishing license at the regional office of SERNAP (☎ 25 7244) at Urmeneta 433. The Argentine Consulate is at Cauquenes 94 (on the 2nd floor) near the junction with Varas. The *Residencial Embassy* (☎ 25 3533), Valdivia 130, has lower-budget rooms, and the *Hotel Gamboa* (☎ 25 2741), at Pedro Montt 157 in the heart of town, has middle-range accommodation.

Puerto Montt is the transport hub of the southern Chilean Lake District, and all buses depart from the large bus terminal on the city's central foreshore. There are well over a dozen daily buses north along the Panamerican Highway to Santiago. There are also around eight daily flights (ALTA, LanChile, Ladeco and National) to Santiago, as well as several daily flights to Coyhaique and Punta Arenas. Puerto Montt is the arrival and departure point for ships plying the west Patagonian canals. The *Puerto Eden* makes the scenic three-day voyage south to Puerto Natales several times a month, and the *Evangelistas* runs between Puerto Montt and Puerto Chacabuco in the Aisén region (continuing on to Laguna San Rafael in January and February) once or twice a week. Puerto Montt's area code is ☎ 65.

Castro (Chile)

With a population of about 20,000, Castro is the biggest town on Chiloé. Castro is an attractive place to stay and the best base for trips into Parque Nacional Chiloé. The town has interesting examples of corrugated iron buildings (most notably the remarkable cathedral) as well as wooden architecture more typical of Chiloé. The local CONAF

(☎ 2289) and SERNAP (☎ 63 2105) offices are in the provincial government building (Edificio Gobernal Provincial) at O'Higgins 549, opposite the Plaza de Armas. The main office of SERNATUR (☎ 5699) is at O'Higgins 549, 1½ blocks north of the Plaza de Armas (main square), but the small tourist booth in the plaza is more helpful. A lower-budget place to stay is the *Residencial Mirasol* at San Martín 851.

From Puerto Montt there are almost hourly buses to Castro which, like almost all traffic to and from the island, cross on the regular car ferries running between Pargua on the mainland to Chacao on Chiloé's northern tip. The large bus company Cruz del Sur has its own terminal on San Martín, one block north of the Plaza de Armas in Castro, and the municipal terminal (Terminal Municipal) is three blocks farther north along San Martín. Castro's area code is ☎ 65.

Parque Nacional Lanín

Parque Nacional Lanín is a long thin strip of land stretching south through the Andes of Neuquén Province. Until the late 19th century the vast area of the park was inhabited by the Pehuenche people. The lifestyle of this large Mapuche tribe was integrally linked with the annual harvest of *ñülli* (pine nuts – known as *piñones* in Spanish) from the region's extensive montane forests of coniferous araucaria trees. Two Pehuenche Indian reserves within the park, at Rucachoroi and Curruhuinca, are all that remain of the former Pehuenche lands.

GENERAL INFORMATION
Geographical Features

Extending 180km along the frontier with Chile from roughly 39°S to 41.5°S, the 3790 sq km Parque Nacional Lanín is the most northerly of the five vast national parks in Argentine Patagonia (the others being Nahuel Huapi, Los Alerces, Perito Moreno and Los Glaciares). Parque Nacional Lanín

includes areas denominated as reserves and as park proper, the latter experiencing full protection while some development and controlled harvesting of timber is allowed in areas with reserve status. The two tiny Mapuche reservations of Curruhuinca and Rucachoroi – fragments of the vast territory formerly held by the indigenous people – are located within the park, and are fittingly called *reducciones*.

Volcán Lanín's ice-crowned 3776m summit is unquestionably the park's most dominant topographical feature. Volcán Lanín lies directly on the border, and its north-western side, about one-sixth of the volcano's bulk, is actually in Chile. Unlike its near neighbour Volcán Villarrica, whose smouldering summit is clearly visible from its higher slopes, the perfect cone of Volcán Lanín is no longer active. Volcán Lanín divides the park into northern and southern zones.

The northern zone – which theoretically belongs to the Araucanía region – covers about one third of the park's area, and is centred around the elongated, fjord-like Lago Quillén.

The much larger and broader zone to the south of the great volcano forms a band of more rugged mountains from which three other major glacial lakes, Lago Huechulafquén, Lago Lolog and Lago Lácar (along with several other very sizeable water bodies of glacial origin) splay out up to 100km eastwards, almost as far as the Patagonian steppes. None of the lakes in Parque Nacional Lanín even approaches the great size of Lago Nahuel Huapi to the south, although at around 900m above sea level they are considerably more elevated. The lowest point in the park is 630m.

Natural History

Argentina's richest forests of southern beech (*Nothofagus*) grow in Parque Nacional Lanín. The evergreen coigüe (spelt coihue in Argentina, *N. dombeyi*) is present mainly at the lowest elevations. The most dominant subalpine beeches are generally raulí (*N. alpina*) and roble (or pellín, *N. obliqua*), two deciduous species absent in the Andean-Patagonian forests farther south. Raulí has long leathery, almost oval-shaped leaves, while its close relative the roble has distinctive 'oak-like' leaves with deep serrations.

In the alpine zone (roughly above 1000m), two other deciduous southern beech species, ñirre (*N. antarctica*, spelt ñire in Argentina) and lenga (*N. pumilio*) are found. The two trees are easily distinguishable: lenga leaves have rounded double notches, while ñirre has leaves with irregularly crinkled edges. Lenga grows right up to the tree line in low, weather-beaten scrub (known in local Spanish as *bosque achaparrado*). In autumn the mountainsides are aflame with colour as these mixed deciduous beech forests turn a beautiful golden red.

Various parasitic plants attack the southern beeches, embedding their roots in the branches or trunk of a host tree and drawing off its sap. Common parasites are the liga, or injerto, *(Misodendrum* species), native mistletoes, the quintral *(Tristerix tetrandus)*,

whose red flowers full of nectar attract many species of hummingbirds, and the llao-llao *(Cyttaria* species), a fungus that deforms the wood into a large, knotted growth on which round spongy balls form.

Clothing the northern zone of Parque Nacional Lanín are extensive forests of umbrella-like araucaria, or pehuén, a unique tree with long branches covered in sharp scales. In autumn the araucaria yields head-size cones containing starchy nuts, which were the staple food of the local Pehuenche tribes (who called them *ñülli*). Particularly in the park's southern zone, forests of ciprés de la cordillera, or lahuán, with occasional stands of maitén *(Maytenus boaria)*, a native willow-like species, spread across the less well-watered Andean foothills.

Found in drier places, or where the forest cover has been removed by past fires, are the pingo-pingo *(Ephedra chilensis)* and the retama *(Diostea juncea)*, two different native shrubs that produce a profusion of lateral branchlets forming impenetrable thickets. Typical steppeland plants such as tussock grasses mark the beginning of the dry Patagonian plains.

As always in the Patagonian Andes, numerous native wild flower species can be identified. The bright spots of yellow scattered around the floor of the montane forests could be the delicate violeta amarilla *(Viola reichii)*, a yellow species of violet, whose unusual colour belies the name of this large world-wide genus of flowers, or perhaps the yellow topa topa *(Calceolaria crenatiflora)*, which resembles a large pea flower. Two pretty white species are the centella *(Anemone decapetala)*, a native anemone, and the cuye eldorado *(Oxalis adenophylla)*, which grows low to the ground on well-drained and exposed mountainsides above the tree line – typically in otherwise bare volcanic soils – and has pale blooms with pinkish edges. The cuye eldorado has long been a favourite of gardeners in the British Isles.

Parque Nacional Lanín is one of the last habitats of the tunduco *(Aconaemys fuscus)*, an extremely rare species of native rat. A member of an ancient rodent family (the

LAKE DISTRICT

so-called octodontids), the tunduco typically inhabits quila and colihue thickets, feeding on the roots and shoots of these bamboo species. Other mammals found in the park include the llaca (or monito del monte), pudú, coipo, vizcacha and the rare Andean deer known as the huemul, and these animals are variously preyed upon by the puma, zorro culpeo, huillín and huiña.

Well represented are small ground-dwelling birds called tapaculos, such as the chucao, the huet-huet *(Pteroptochos tarnii)* and the churrín *(Scytalopus magellanicus)*, or Andean tapaculo, which find shelter in bamboo thickets, forest underbrush or alpine heathland. Unmistakable because of its absurdly long tail – which is about double the length of the bird's body – is the colilarga *(Sylviorthorhynchus desmursii)*, or Des Murs' wiretail.

Climate

Parque Nacional Lanín has a continental climate ranging from subalpine to alpine, with a relatively low proportion of rainfall outside the spring-to-autumn period. Summers are warm to hot, particularly in the park's northern (Araucanía) sector, while winters are crisp and white, particularly on the higher ranges. The areas immediately east and north of Volcán Lanín lie in a marked rain shadow created by the volcanic range extending east from Volcán Villarrica. From an annual maximum of 4500mm on the snowy upper slopes of Volcán Lanín, precipitation levels drop away sharply to well under 1000mm near the dry plains bordering the eastern fringes of the park. Towards the south, in the moist temperate forests of the park's mountainous western sectors, annual precipitation is around 2500mm.

Place Names

Lanín, the volcano from which the park gets its name, comes from a Mapuche word whose literal rendering is 'died of over-eating', an allusion to the past eruption which finally extinguished Volcán Lanín. Nonthué, the name of a lake, means 'place of the raft', while the adjoining Lago Lácar

means 'inspiring fear', although it's not quite clear what the Mapuche found so foreboding about this lovely lake.

Queñi, another nearby lake, means 'bales' or 'bundles', perhaps a vague reference to the way native bamboo collected in the area is bunched together and tied. Tromen ('cloud'), a low Andean pass frequently crossed by local tribes, has the alternative Mapuche name of Mamuil Malal, which means 'wooden corral'.

PRACTICAL INFORMATION
Information Sources

The administration centre (Intendencia, ☎ 0972-27233) for Parque Nacional Lanín administration centre is on the Centro Cívico in San Martín de los Andes. There are two small local mountain clubs which may be able to advise on trekking and climbing in the park. These are the Club Andino Junín de los Andes, or CAJA, (☎ 0944-91207), at O'Higgins 369 (CC 104), 8371 in Junín de los Andes, and the Club Andino San Martín (☎ 7640 1060 or 664 6758), at José C Paz 800, Esquina Alvear, 1650 in San Martín de los Andes.

Permits & Regulations

Treks in Parque Nacional Lanín generally involve little red tape, but there is an entry fee of US$5 (only payable when you enter via an APN *portada*, or entrance gate). Before setting out, you should always sign in at the local *guardería*, leaving details of your party and intended route, and advise staff upon your safe return. Camping is not permitted outside organised camping grounds and established en route camping areas.

When to Trek

Lower-level routes, including the Queñi Circuit trek featured here, can generally be undertaken from early November until early May. In the higher ranges, where winter snow remains longer, the trekking season doesn't really start until mid-December and (depending on autumn snowfalls) may end by early April.

Ascent of Volcán Lanín

Duration 3 days
Distance 14 km return
Standard Medium-Hard
Start/Finish Guardería Tromen
Entry US$5, no permit needed
Season December-April
Summary An energetic but straightforward ascent of an extinct 3776m volcano giving a stunning panorama of the northern Lake District and southern Araucanía.

Towering over the northern Lake District, Volcán Lanín rises from a base plain of around 1100m to a height officially given as 3776m. The mountain is the last of three cones that form an interesting volcanic range extending east from Volcán Villarrica in Chile. Viewed from any other direction than the east, Volcán Lanín appears almost impossible to climb, as its upper third is covered by a thick cap of heavily crevassed glacial ice. When tackled from its eastern side, Lanín is a strenuous yet relatively straightforward climb, and this is probably the highest summit in Patagonia attainable without ropes.

MAPS
The best map is the Chilean IGM 1:50,000 sheet, *Paimún*, (Section G, No 114). This map provides good topographical information on Volcán Lanín, but does not show huts, ascent route or the correct position of glaciers. This sheet is also useful for the Villarrica Traverse trek in Chile. The Club Andino de Junín de los Andes has reasonable sketch maps covering Lanín's usual ascent routes.

Two ancient Argentine IGM 1:100,000 sheets, *Volcán Lanín* (Neuquén, No 3972-28) and *Quillén* (Neuquén, No 3972-29) also cover Volcán Lanín. The detail on these sheets is very poor so their use is not recommended.

DAYS REQUIRED
The recommended walking time is three days return. This allows for a late start on the first stage of the trek, spending the night in one of the two refugios on the mountain. The summit can be climbed on the second day, and the return to Guardería Tromen made the day after that. Very fit trekking parties may prefer to do the climb in two days by making a complete descent from the summit on the second day.

TREKKING STANDARD
The trek involves an ascent from around 1100m above sea level to the 3776m summit of Volcán Lanín. Because of its height, the route is very exposed to the elements. This includes the penetrating summer sun as much as the chill winds likely to be encountered near the summit. There is also a possibility of altitude sickness (see the Health chapter).

Although the climb is technically very straightforward, before early March the upper slopes of Volcán Lanín are still covered by old winter snow. A good snow cover stabilises the slopes and makes the ascent easier, but for such conditions you should carry (and know how to use) an ice axe and crampons. Remember that after midday snow becomes soft and slushy, making the going tiring uphill and hazardous on the descent. Later in the season, crampons and ice axe will probably not be needed for the ascent, although the park authorities may insist that climbers carry them anyway. Climbing gear is available for hire in Junín and San Martín de los Andes (see Trekking Bases). The steep and loose earth makes a frustratingly unstable walking surface, and you need to step very carefully to avoid slipping. To protect your shins and prevent small rock fragments filling your boots, wear a pair of gaiters. In addition all parties must carry a sleeping bag, gloves, a waterproof jacket, sunglasses, sunscreen and a hat. A climbing rope is of little use and is not required.

Trekkers should be physically fit and have some experience in mountainous terrain. The route described here follows the Espina del Pescado, a narrow ridge providing the most direct access. Although often strenuous, a well-worn path can be easily followed until you reach the higher slopes. Here there are sporadic cairn markings, bamboo stakes and occasional splotches of paint on rocks, but for much of this section it is necessary to find your own way. It is important that you sign in at Guardería Tromen before you set out and that you also inform the ranger on your return. The resident ranger at Guardería Tromen, who makes regular ascents of the mountain and is up-to-date on current conditions, checks that you have the required climbing equipment when you sign in.

The route is rated *medium to hard*, and covers a distance of about 14km return.

ACCOMMODATION & CAMPING
No accommodation is available near the start of the climb. The nearby tourist cities of San Martín or Junín (see Trekking Bases) are the best regional centres from which to climb Lanín. There is a free camping area near the Guardería Tromen, but except for a few poor sites near the Refugio RIM, a hut built by the Argentine army's Regimiento de Infantería de Montaña (RIM), the volcano's very exposed and mostly steep slopes are definitely no place for tents.

There are two free, unstaffed refugios on Lanín, both roughly halfway up the mountain. The refugios provide good shelter, but are otherwise extremely basic. It is essential to carry your own means of cooking and a warm sleeping bag. Refugio RIM, with sleeping capacity for up to 10 people, is at 2450m and is an option if the other hut is overcrowded. About 30 to 45 minutes away, at 2600m, is the Refugio CAJA. Built and owned by the Club Andino de Junín de los Andes, this smaller refugio has space for about six people. The ascent of Volcán Lanín is a popular excursion among Argentinians, and in the peak holiday season the number of climbers on the mountain may exceed the huts' comfortable capacity.

SUPPLIES
It is not possible to buy any provisions at Tromen, so you must bring whatever you need from San Martín or Junín. If coming from Chile, buy your provisions in Pucón or Villarrica.

GETTING TO/FROM THE TREK
This trek begins at the Guardería Tromen, 4km from the frontier with Chile on the international route across Paso Tromen (which the Chileans call Paso Mamuil Malal). The Argentine border post is opposite.

In summer there is at least one bus daily in either direction along this road; buses generally run between Temuco and San Martín de los Andes via Pucón and Junín de los Andes. Buses heading in both directions leave early in the morning and normally arrive at the first border post at around 11.30 am. The climb is conveniently located for people crossing into Argentina from Chile, who can disembark at Tromen. The ascent of Volcán Lanín can also be done as a return excursion from San Martín de los Andes. If you do this, it might be worthwhile reserving a seat with the bus company for the trip back out, even if you have to pay a bit extra.

For trekkers intending to cross into Chile after the climb, the situation is more problematic, as boarding a bus to Chile in Tromen is not usually permitted unless you are on the official passenger list. In either San Martín or Junín you may be able to make arrangements to join a bus on its way across the border a few days later. The road is remote and carries little traffic, so hitchhiking is not recommended.

THE TREK
Stage 1: Guardería Tromen to Refugio Caja (via Espina de Pescado)
7km, 4½ to 5½ hours
As there is unlikely to be any running water for most of today's sweaty climb, fill up your canteen at the camping area when you sign in at Guardería Tromen. Pick up the trail behind the Gendarmería Nacional building, and follow this roughly south-west through attractive forest of lenga then across a plain of volcanic sand to reach the **Arroyo Turbio** after 30 to 45 minutes. (Early in the day this stream may carry little or no water here, but

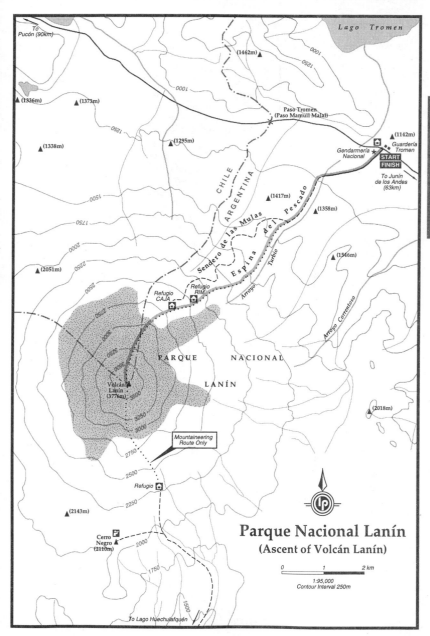

LAKE DISTRICT

Parque Nacional Lanín
(Ascent of Volcán Lanín)

0   1   2 km

1:95,000
Contour Interval 250m

Lanín's melting névés and glaciers normally produce a steady flow by late afternoon.)

You will notice the **Espina de Pescado**, a long lateral moraine ridge that snakes around to the right above the stream. Climb this 'spine', following the narrow ridge top as it steepens and curves slightly rightwards past an old secondary crater on the left to reach a path intersection after one to 1½ hours. From the **Sendero de las Mulas**, a longer alternative route (which comes out at Refugio CAJA) departs to the right.

Keep to the craggy ridge line, where unstable rock calls for careful footwork and minor detours are necessary to negotiate small outcrops. The route climbs on up alongside a long, broken-up glacier down to your left to arrive at the red and orange painted **Refugio RIM**, two to 2½ hours on. Built on ground left almost level after the recession of the nearby glacier, the refugio sleeps up to 10 people. Afternoon meltwater can be collected from the glacier, but take care not to get too close to where the ice falls away abruptly. Tread cautiously on dirt-covered ice, and save enough water for the next day.

Just above the refugio, pick up a vague trail leading up beside the glacier, following this up to where the rock rib disappears. The route continues up for 100m, before leaving the ridge line and heading right through an area of broken-up rock rubble to reach **Refugio CAJA** after 25 to 35 minutes. The tin-roofed hut is built on a low flat ridge and has space for about six people. Collect water from a small névé just around to the west.

Camp Sites There is a free camping area near the Guardería Tromen, but camping is not permitted anywhere else around the base of Volcán Lanín. Near Refugio RIM there are a few camp sites on levelled-out rocks below the rock rib, but these are sheltered from westerly winds only. There are no other camping options anywhere else on Volcán Lanín.

Stage 2: Refugio Caja to Summit of Volcán Lanín
7 to 11 hours return

This section requires a climb of over 1100m on extremely unstable scoria slopes, with a return to either of the huts on the same day. Do not try for the summit unless the weather is good. Allow yourself plenty of time. *Carry enough water with you to last the whole day!*

From Refugio CAJA head up the initially gentle slope over large patches of snow, passing between two larger permanent snow fields (about 400m over from the glacier), where the gradient begins to steepen. As the ground becomes looser, often giving way as you step, keep an eye out for marker stakes and paint splashes on rocks. Layers of volcanic rock have weathered unevenly to produce very low ridges that lead up the slope. These are much more stable and if winds are not too strong they may make easier climbing.

Although strenuous, the route is now straightforward. In the last stages before you reach the summit, a scramble over rock ledges leads up past the impressive seracs of a glacier which descends westwards. Follow a few rock cairns left onto the small névé leading up to the summit of Volcán Lanín, which – atypically for a volcano – is not topped with a wide caldera. The relatively small summit is capped by glacial ice which falls away sharply on the south side. Sometimes small crevasses open up and, particularly in early summer, you should be extremely careful on the summit.

Llaima, Villarrica, Tronador and many other major peaks of the Lake District and Araucanía are visible from the summit of Lanín. Directly north and south are the large lakes Tromen and Huechulafquén, and a number of beautiful smaller lakes lie on the north-western slopes of the volcano. In clear conditions you might even be able to make out Chile's Pacific coast far to the west.

Most climbers return via the ascent route, but some parties take the more difficult alternative descent route leading first south then south-east to a refugio at 2400m (which also belongs to the CAJA); from here a path goes on southwards down to Puerto Canoa on Lago Huechulafquén (see Other Treks). Once down, be sure to report back at the Guardería Tromen or the Guardería Puerto Canoa.

Queñi Circuit

Duration 3 days
Distance 35km
Standard Easy-Medium
Start/Finish Gendarmería Hua Hum,
Entry US$5, no permit needed
Season November-May
Summary A circuit trek through beautiful Lake District forests that visits some secluded hot springs.

An undemanding trek starting at the western end of Lago Nonthué, the Queñi Circuit circumnavigates the 1855m Cerro Chachín, passing secluded farms in the Chachín Valley and on Lago Nonthué. The Queñi area is renowned for its beautiful forests of raulí, roble, lenga, ñirre and coigüe. Selective logging is carried out in the Queñi area, though this is scarcely visible on the trek itself. Bamboo is also harvested locally and, particularly in late summer and autumn, you can sometimes see bundles of scorched canes stacked up on the lake shores, left for later collection. A highlight of this trek is the Baños de Queñi, undeveloped thermal springs that gush out into a series of hot pools at varying temperatures in the forest.

MAPS

The entire walk is covered by Argentine IGM 1:100,000 sheet, *Hua Hum*, (Neuquén, No 4172-4). Dating from the 1940s, this old map does not show the route in the central part of the trek. The Chilean IGM produces a 1:50,000 sheet, *Baños de Chihio* (Section H, No 8), which overlaps to cover this central Queñi area. It shows topography far more clearly, and although the route is not indicated, this map may be of some use. The Guardería Queñi may also have pamphlet maps showing all or part of the route.

DAYS REQUIRED

The trek is a circuit that is best completed in three leisurely days.

TREKKING STANDARD

This gentle trek follows partly overgrown vehicular tracks through two valleys connected by a low watershed. This is a low elevation route that remains well below the tree line and is therefore quite sheltered. For this reason the trek can be done as early as October or as late as May, when other walks are not possible, but the ideal time is mid-autumn (April) when the deciduous beech forests are at their most colourful.

Only a basic level of physical fitness is required and even inexperienced trekkers should have little difficulty with route-finding. The small Río Chachín must be waded a few times, and early in spring it may be difficult to cross.

The Queñi Circuit is rated *easy to medium* and covers an overall distance of 35km.

ACCOMMODATION & CAMPING

There are no refugios for trekkers in the Queñi sector of Parque Nacional Lanín, so you must carry a tent. Convenient accommodation for travellers can be found in San Martín de los Andes (see Trekking Bases).

SUPPLIES

There is no store at the start of the trek in Hua Hum, so bring everything you need. San Martín has several well-stocked supermarkets, down-to-earth bakeries and angling shops. If coming from Chile via Lago Pirehueico, your last (if limited) opportunity to stock up is in the village of Choshuenco.

GETTING TO/FROM THE TREK

The Queñi Circuit starts and finishes at the Gendarmería Hua Hum, 47km west of San Martín de los Andes on the international road to Lago Pirehueico in Chile. The trek is ideally located for people on their way across the border, and at Hua Hum there is generally no problem boarding buses for Chile after you have finished the trek.

There are two ways of getting to the start of the trek. In the summer season, there is a daily bus to **Lago Pirehueico** at 7 am (except Sunday) from the San Martín bus terminal, arriving at Hua Hum around 9.30 am. On its return journey to San Martín the bus passes through Hua Hum at about 11:30 am.

Navegación Lago Lácar (☎ 27750) in San Martín operates daily launch trips across Lago Lácar and Lago Nonthué to Hua Hum (which generally call in at Puerto Elvira, several kilometres before Hua Hum). The boats leave from the San Martín wharf at 9 am and arrive at Hua Hum around noon. The return fare is around US$23 and it's possible to arrange to rejoin the tour at a later date.

THE TREK
Stage 1: Guardería Hua Hum to Lago Venados
15km, 4½ to 6 hours
If arriving by bus, get off at the gendarmería building in Hua Hum and head 50m further along the road to Chile, turning left across the bridge. The guardería is on the right above **Lago Nonthué**, 500m from the international road.

After signing in, continue along the road around the shore of the lake, passing many tiny pebble beaches to reach **Puerto Elvira** after 30 to 40 minutes. There is a jetty here for tourist launches from San Martín. A worthwhile short side trip from Puerto Elvira goes to the **Cascada Chachín**, where the river plummets 30m. Cross the **Río Chachín** and follow the road around the lakeside through a pretty meadow with scattered wild rose bushes. The road rises and falls slightly where steeper sides meet the lake, passing small farms on flats around the tiny stream deltas before coming to **Pucará**, a small village by the **Río Nonthué**, after a further 1¼ to 1¾ hours.

Turn off to the right onto a narrow vehicular track about 100m before you reach the schoolhouse. Follow the track gradually up for 30 minutes, first through light forest and then through an attractive clearing to ford a side stream of the Río Nonthué. Passing a makeshift shack on the right, continue into the forest. The track moves steadily away from the river, passing to the right of a low hill. Many old logging trails lead off the main track, but keep to the most travelled way, which is the correct route.

After climbing gradually for a further 50 minutes to 1¼ hours, the track rapidly descends to river flats covered by ñirre woodland. Cross the young Río Nonthué and head directly up the valley. There are views of the craggy ranges on either side. Where the track makes a sharp curve to the right and re-enters the forest, look for a path which continues straight ahead. This leads down to the sandy eastern shore of **Lago Venados**.

Camp Sites At the start of the trek there is good camping near the guardería (but boil the lake water). Once you leave Lago Nonthué there is only poor camping in the damp forest, but there are some nice spots at the eastern end of Lago Venados.

Stage 2: Lago Venados to Baños de Queñi
5.5km, 2½ to 3½ hours
Go back to the main track and follow it across the lake's outlet stream. A few paces on you pass a tiny thermal spring on the right. Usually too cool and muddy for bathing, the pool is detected by its luxuriant weed growth and sulphurous smell. The track now moves back into the forest and climbs above the steep-sided Lago Venados. There are very few views of the lake because of the dense forest, and in places bamboo leans over the track. The track imperceptibly crosses above a low watershed and after 1½ to two hours it drops down to the **Río Chachín**.

Ford the icy river, recrossing where necessary as you follow its gravelly banks downstream. The track now leaves the river and leads through dense bamboo thickets, reaching the **Baños de Queñi** after one to 1½ hours. A warm stream crossing the track indicates the presence of the thermal springs. In the forest above, a 'bath' with space for three or four people has been dug out and dammed with rocks. Do not wash with soap or detergents as they pollute the water.

Camp Sites After leaving Lago Venados there are no suitable camp sites until you reach the Río Chachín, where possibilities exist along the banks. There is reasonable

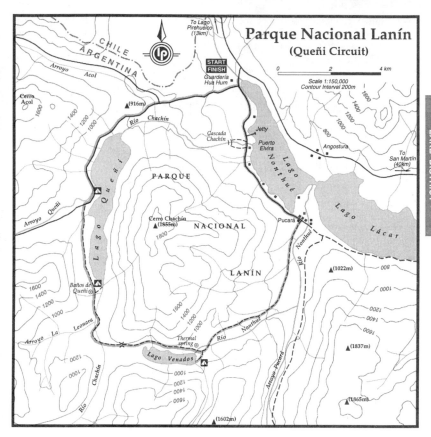

Parque Nacional Lanín
(Queñi Circuit)

camping by the river near the Baños de Queñi, or near the main track beside Lago Queñi. More sheltered and scenic spots can be found on the south-eastern shore of Lago Queñi. From the baños take the first track off to the right, and follow it for 10 minutes to the inlet stream.

Stage 3: Baños de Queñi to Guardería Hua Hum

14km, 4½ to 6 hours

Head on a short way to **Lago Queñi** and begin walking around the western side of the lake. The track dips and rises continually

through the evergreen coigüe forest, then begins descending a ridge into an area of pleasant clearings beside the lake. It continues past a tourist lodge and a sheltered inlet to cross a bridge over the **Arroyo Queñi** after 1½ to two hours. Continue north-eastwards around Lago Queñi, leaving the lake behind before crossing the **Arroyo Acol** to meet a larger road, a further 1½ to two hours on.

Follow the now more prominent road past pretty farms, rising gently into the forest and continuing past more farms to come out on the Lago Nonthué road near the Guardería Hua Hum after a final 1½ to two hours.

Camp Sites Nice camp sites can be found on lakeside clearings near the Arroyo Queñi. Farther on there is only poor camping in the forest beside the road.

Other Treks in Parque Nacional Lanín

LAGO HUECHULAFQUÉN TO VOLCÁN LANÍN

This alternative access to the top of Volcán Lanín begins from the APN Guardería at Puerto Canoa on Lago Huechulafquén. It leads northwards up the Arroyo Rucu Leufu (stream) to Cerro Negro, a lookout above the araucaria forest, then continues up to a refugio run by CAJA on the south-eastern slopes of Volcán Lanín. From here a more difficult mountaineering route leads first north-west then directly north to the summit. The descent can be made via the easier route

described above in the Ascent of Volcán Lanín trek. The ancient 1:100,000 Argentine IGM sheets *Volcán Lanín* (Neuquén, No 3972-28) and *Junín de los Andes* (Neuquén, No 3972-35) cover the trek.

CERRO MALO

Cerro Malo stands between Lago Nonthué and Lago Lácar immediately north-east of Hua Hum. Despite its negative Spanish name, meaning bad or evil, this 1941m peak makes a superb panoramic point and can be reached in a five-hour return day hike from Angostura, 4km before (ie east of) Hua Hum on the road from San Martín. The path climbs steeply northwards through the forest, crossing clear streams (some of thermal origin) to reach the summit of Cerro Malo, giving 360° views that include Volcán Lanín, Volcán Villarrica, Volcán Osorno and Monte Tronador, as well as the two large lakes on its northern and southern sides. For access and map details see the Queñi Circuit trek earlier in this section.

Parque Nacional Puyehue

Situated to the east of the Chilean provincial city of Osorno, Parque Nacional Puyehue consists of 1070 sq km of forested wilderness stretching from the eastern shores of Lago Puyehue and Lago Rupanco as far as the Chile-Argentina frontier. Volcán Puyehue and a fascinating broad volcanic plateau stretching out to its north-west are the central features of the park.

GENERAL INFORMATION
Geographical Features

Most of Parque Nacional Puyehue lies between Volcán Puyehue and Volcán Casablanca, within the basin of the Río Golgol, along whose course the international highway runs via the Paso de Puyehue to Bariloche. The park also includes the area around the north-eastern and eastern edge of Lago

Rupanco. The Río Golgol, from which the local Mapuche tribes extracted alluvial gold in past centuries, has its source in Lago Constancia, a remote highland lake near the frontier.

The 2236m Volcán Puyehue is the highest point in the park. The boundary actually runs across the volcano's summit, although some maps show Volcán Puyehue outside the park boundary. Volcán Puyehue experienced a major eruption in 1960, spewing great quantities of pumice and ash over its once forested upper slopes. Trunks buried by this and previous eruptions protrude from the eroding hillsides in places. Volcán Puyehue has remained dormant since then, and vulcanologists suspect that the area's centre of geothermal activity may be shifting north to the nearby Volcán Carrán, a much younger and lower volcano that erupted twice in the early 1990s.

The combination of intense volcanic activity and high precipitation levels gives rise to numerous hot springs. They include Chile's premier spa resort, Aguas Calientes/Termas de Puyehue at the park's western extremity, there are numerous other small, undeveloped thermal springs in the area.

Natural History

Luxuriant temperate rainforest – the most species-rich ecosystem found anywhere in the Lake District – blankets the slopes surrounding Volcán Puyehue and Volcán Casablanca. The chief botanical ingredients of these so-called Valdivian forests are several southern beech species, the three mañíos, ulmo *(Eucryphia cordifolia)*, and fragrant tepa and laurel, two closely related species belonging to the Monimiacea family. Paired tree species often encountered growing in close association are melí *(Amomyrtus meli)* and luma, *(A. luma)* members of the myrtle family. The tineo *(Weinmannia trichosperma)*, which has attractive 'fern-like' branchlets with serrated opposing leaves, is also common, and there are even examples of the coniferous alerce and ciprés de las Guaitecas.

The extremely moist conditions produce vigorous thickets of native bamboo or quila *(Chusquea* species); after flowering in 1993, much of the quila in the Anticura area has died, leaving a mesh of dry canes (see the aside on the quila cycle). The often very thick forest understorey nurtures species such as the chilco *(Fuchsia magallanica)*, whose nectar attracts the green-backed firecrown, a tiny hummingbird.

Half a dozen or so species of the genus *Baccharis* grow as small upright bushes that produce fluffy, pale yellow flowers. The pañil *(Buddleja globosa)*, a shrub that can grow in a variety of habitats, produces interesting blooms of tiny orange-yellow flowers arranged into balls on the end of opposing stems. Bushes of murta *(Ugni molinae)*, whose five-petalled, bell-shaped pinkish-white flowers develop into small, edible (if

The Quila Cycle

Numerous species of native bamboo of the *Chusquea* genus grow in the moist temperate 'Valdivian' rainforests of Patagonia. Even for botanists, these species are difficult to differentiate, although most members of the genus – but particularly the most abundant species, *Ch. quila* – are commonly known by the Mapuche name of quila. Quila is an extremely vigorous and aggressive plant, often smothering smaller trees as it spreads out to monopolise sunnier sites in the forest.

Like many other bamboo genera found throughout the world, quila flowers only at the end of its reproductive cycle. In a given area up to 90% of the quila may be on the same cycle – approximately 25 years for most species – which results in the quila blooming over wide areas simultaneously. Once the plants have produced fruit they die off, leaving a mass of dry canes which present a worrying fire hazard that lasts for many years afterwards. The flowering of the quila is also noted with apprehension by locals, because mice and rats multiply out of control as they gorge themselves on the nutritious fruit. Once this food source is exhausted, the rodents move out of the forest into the surrounding farms and villages.

Quila can barely survive in a mature, closed rainforest because too little sunlight reaches the ground, yet its regrowth is particularly vigorous after fires, which destroy the shade of the forest canopy and release nutrients. This has led some botanists to theorise that quila may actually have evolved its die-back cycle as a way of 'provoking' fires, in order to create new openings in the forest. ■

somewhat bland) berries that ripen in January, are found at the edge of forest clearings.

The flowering trees and shrubs support an abundance of insects. Two native beetles are the beautiful coleóptero del coigüe *(Cheloderus childreni)*, a multicoloured species, and the carnivorous peorro *(Ceroglossus* species), a large carabid whose black shell-like abdomen has a luminescent reddish-green sheen, and which crawls about tree trunks sniffing out ants and other tiny prey. Also remarkable is the neuroptera *(Mantispidae)* species, a very well camouflaged predatory insect with pale-green wings that resemble the leaves of the quila. One extraordinary butterfly is *Eroessa chilensis*, almost a 'living fossil' whose evolutionary development has remained static for millions of years; it is found in close association with the thorny tayu or palo blanco *(Dasyphyllum diacanthoides)*, an ancient tree species that has also changed little over this time.

Two species of wren known as chercán often seen in the park both have a yellow underbody and coffee-coloured black-striped wings and tail. Also quite common is the zorzal patagónico *(Turdus falklandii)*, a native thrush which migrates up from the Pacific coast to spend the summer foraging for insects, seeds and berries in the rainforests of Puyehue. The zorzal patagónico has brownish wings and head with a white breast, while the beak and legs are yellow. The tórtol cordillerana *(Metriopelia melanoptera)*, or black-winged ground dove, lives in the forests of the montane zone above 600m.

The less conspicuous mammalian wildlife includes the vizcacha, llaca (or monito del monte), pudu, puma and the zorro gris, a small grey fox.

Climate

The park's proximity to the higher mountains along the continental divide produces a very wet climate, even by southern Lake District standards. Precipitation levels start at around 4000mm annually in Anticura and Aguas Calientes on Puyehue's western edge, rising progressively towards the east. At elevations above 1000m winter snows begin to accumulate after May, when skiing is possible at the alpine resort of Antillanca on Volcán Casablanca, but by early summer (December) the snow cover is mostly confined to areas above about 2000m.

Place Names

Most of the nomenclature is of Mapuche origin. Puyehue's name (pronounced 'pooh-YAY-way') comes from a Mapuche word meaning 'place of the puye', a small native fish abundant in the freshwater lakes and rivers of the Lake District. Two important place names in the Puyehue area contain the Mapuche word *antü*, meaning 'sun': Anti-

cura ('rock of the sun'), and Antillanca ('jewel of the sun'). Llancas are semi-precious blue stones which were traded by the Mapuche. Antillanca is the Mapuche name for Volcán Casablanca. Golgol, the river which drains most of the park, means 'many cudgels' in Mapuche, apparently because the surrounding mountains were thought to have the appearance of warriors' clubs. According to local legend, the Salto del Indio ('waterfall of the Indian') near Anticura, gets its name from a Mapuche Indian who eluded the invading Spaniards by hiding behind the cascading curtain of water. The names of both Lago Ranco and Lago Rupanco are both Mapuche variants of 'flowing water'. Caulle, Puyehue's principle mountain range (and also a local farm), is a reference to a common seagull.

PRACTICAL INFORMATION
Information Sources

There are guarderías in each of the park's two administrative sectors. The Guardería Aguas Calientes, 4km along the road turn-off to Antillanca, has a visitors' information centre. The Guardería Anticura (☎ 23 4393), 94km from Osorno, is on the international highway (Ruta 215) leading to Bariloche in Argentina. Unfortunately, the visitor's information centre at Anticura had closed at the time of researching this book, but will hopefully reopen after a renovation.

Permits & Regulations

Trekkers are required leave their names and relevant details at the nearest ranger station (guardería) before setting out, and be sure to inform the park authorities after your safe return. The US$1.50 entrance fee to Parque Nacional Puyehue is only charged to those entering the park's Aguas Calientes sector.

The start of the Puyehue Traverse trek featured here leads through private property belonging to the farm of El Caulle. The owners of El Caulle now levy a US$2.50 'toll' for each trekker passing through their land. There is no alternative access, so you'll have to pay up. The only justifying factor is that the owners of El Caulle keep 'their' section of this path exceptionally well maintained and marked.

When to Trek

The best months for higher-level trekking are December to April, although this can vary depending on weather and snow conditions. The Puyehue plateau and the slopes of Volcán Casablanca (which has lifts) are ideal for cross-country skiing trips from the beginning of June to the end of October.

Puyehue Traverse

Duration 4 days
Distance 75km (including side trips)
Standard Easy-Medium
Start Anticura
Finish Riñinahue
Entry US$1.50, no permit needed
Season December-April
Summary A trek to the fascinating broad volcanic plateau with geothermal activity.

This marvellous trek takes you across the raw plateau formed by the repeated eruptions of Volcán Puyehue. Here among dune-like ridges of pumice and wide bands of solidified black lava, you can observe various volcanic phenomena in a wild and unspoiled setting. Steaming fumaroles (*azufreras*, or volcanic steam vents) break through the ground in places, depositing sulphurous crystals over the bare earth. Geysers gush out among pools of perpetually boiling water and bubbling mud pits, and thermal springs provide naturally heated bathing high above the tree line.

MAPS

Two Chilean IGM 1:50,000 sheets cover this trek: *Volcán Puyehue* (Section H, No 27) and *Riñinahue* (Section H, No 17). The hiking route and many roads as shown on the latter map are incorrect. There are also some other general topographical errors, and areas of local thermal activity (fumaroles etc) are not indicated. A rough 1:250,000 CONAF map of Parque Nacional Puyehue that shows the park's main trekking routes is available from the Guardería Anticura for US$0.50; but take note that the contours are in feet, not in metres.

DAYS REQUIRED

The recommended walk is from Anticura to Riñinahue, but the trek can easily be done as a return trip based at Refugio Volcán Puyehue.

As a return trek from Anticura, the Puyehue area can be visited in three relatively easy days. The extended Puyehue Traverse to Riñinahue is best done in about four days. For the more experienced and curious, at least one additional day might be added to explore some of the interesting but trackless expanse of volcanic country on the northwestern side of the Puyehue plateau.

TREKKING STANDARD

The route follows a relatively good and well-trodden foot track, although on steep sections, loose pumice (a very light volcanic rock) makes the going tiresome. The central part of the route crosses a very exposed and unvegetated plateau well above 1500m, where it is surprisingly easy to get disoriented in poor weather. Here the pumice is easily shifted by wind, rain and snow, making the trodden path more difficult to follow. Above the tree line, wooden stakes have been mounted to mark the way, but unfortunately these are often pushed over by the winter snows, or even removed by irresponsible trekkers for firewood. Trekkers are asked to re-erect any fallen marker stakes they encounter along the route.

South to north is definitely the best direction to walk, as starting out from Riñinahue makes route-finding more difficult. The trek is rated medium and has a distance of 75km (including the return side trip to Los Geisires).

ACCOMMODATION & CAMPING

There is only one refugio along the route, the Refugio Volcán Puyehue, at the end of the first stage of the trek. This four-bed refugio has become rather run-down, so all trekkers – even those who don't do the whole traverse as far as Riñinahue – should carry a tent.

At Anticura there is a CONAF camping ground across the road from the guardería. The charge per site (up to two tents) is US$6; the sites are attractively situated in the rainforest, but facilities are basic. The only places to stay at Anticura are several *casas de familia*, houses of locals who offer bed and breakfast accommodation; ask at the guardería.

At Riñinahue, where the trek ends, there are one or two simple hosterías and two organised camping grounds near where the Río Riñinahue runs into Lago Ranco.

SUPPLIES

You cannot buy supplies in Anticura so bring everything you need for the trek. The most convenient place to buy provisions is Osorno. If you plan to start the trek immediately after arriving from Argentina, remember that you can't import raw agricultural or dairy products.

GETTING TO/FROM THE TREK

The trek starts from the Guardería Anticura, 94km (roughly 1¼ hours) from Osorno on the international highway (Ruta 215) running to Bariloche in Argentina. From Monday to Friday Buses Puyehue runs an evening bus to Anticura, departing at 5.15 pm from the company's terminal at the eastern end of the Mercado Municipal. The fare is around US$1.80 but this service does not operate on weekends. Taxis *(colectivos)* also wait at the municipal market. Another way of reaching Anticura is to take one of the more frequent international buses running from Osorno to Bariloche in Argentina. Four companies run buses to Bariloche from Osorno's main bus terminal. Tas-Choapa is the most likely to take trekkers, but all of the companies will only carry you to Anticura if there are spare seats (or you pay the full US$22 fare); those travelling only as far as Anticura will have to buy their tickets on the bus once it has departed for Bariloche.

The Puyehue Traverse finishes at Riñinahue, on the eastern shore of Lago Ranco. This route is well serviced by several buses passing through Riñinahue village each day en route to Osorno and La Unión.

THE TREK
Stage 1: Guardería Anticura to Refugio Volcán Puyehue
11km, 3½ to 4½ hours

After signing in at the guardería, walk for 25 to 30 minutes north-west along the highway across the **Río Golgol** bridge to a rustic 'tollhouse' (see Permits & Regulations above) at the entrance gate to **El Caulle**. The farm road leads around to the right past the main homestead among the pastures to a left-hand turn-off a short way after crossing a tiny stream. This bulldozed track rises slightly through the trees and goes over into a foot track just before it cuts through an open field, 25 to 30 minutes from the highway.

Head right into low rainforest where woodpeckers tap about the tree trunks, and colihue, notro or chilco bushes form the understorey, following a good path marked with arrows mounted on wooden posts (your 'taxes' at work). The route first leads up gently north-eastwards to cross two trickling streams after about 1½ to two hours, then contours around over eroded gullies before continuing up in increasingly steep switchbacks over slopes of unstable volcanic earth. Make a final climb on through a pleasant open lenga forest to emerge onto grassy alpine slopes, and sidle a few hundred metres along to the right to arrive at the **Refugio Volcán Puyehue**, a further one to 1½ hours on.

The refugio stands at roughly 1650m, just on the tree line, in a very scenic spot right at the base of **Volcán Puyehue**. The hut has a stove and four bunks, but has become rather run-down in recent years. The tiny stream in the nearby gully tends to flow underground, but higher up along its course it's often running by mid-afternoon. Avoid collecting water from anywhere below the hut because of the chances of contamination (boil it if you do).

Side Trip to Salto del Indio This very pleasant one-hour circuit walk to this churning,

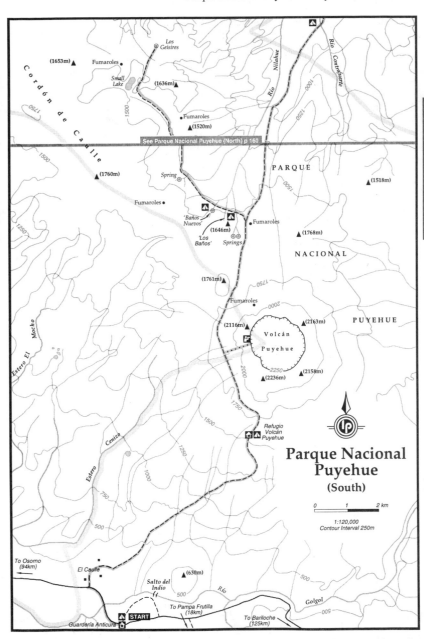

LAKE DISTRICT

See Parque Nacional Puyehue (North) p 160

**Parque Nacional
Puyehue
(South)**

0   1   2 km

1:120,000
Contour Interval 250m

6m high waterfall of the Río Golgol leaves from the CONAF camping ground at Anticura. Take the nature trail (signposted 'La Princesa') which leads through the fragrant tepa forest past a cataract and anglers' pool before climbing up to the waterfall. Rather than backtracking you can take a short cut (signposted 'Salida 215') that comes out on the highway about 1km above the guardería.

Camp Sites At Anticura fees are charged per tent site at the CONAF camping ground opposite the guardería, but there are no showers. Camping is not permitted within the private estate of El Caulle. There is a poor camp site by the first stream you come to, about halfway up, but thereafter no sites exist until you reach Refugio Volcán Puyehue. Good sites can be found around the refugio where the forest fringes the alpine meadows.

Stage 2: Refugio Volcán Puyehue to 'Baños Nuevos'

9km, 3½ to 4¼ hours

Head to the right of a stream gully over grassy meadows dotted with daisy bushes, following staked cairns up moderately north-north-east onto the bare upper slopes of Volcán Puyehue. From here you can enjoy an excellent panorama of the major volcanic peaks to the south: Osorno (the magnificent cone to the south-west), Puntiagudo, Casablanca and Tronador (the high, irregular ice-covered mountain to the south-east). Lago Puyehue is below to the west. The foot track sidles north-west upwards around the rocky mountainside across ravines (filled with snow until midsummer) and small ridges.

Volcán Puyehue is best climbed via a spur not far on from the second stream you come to, 45 minutes to one hour from the refugio. There is no path, but this straightforward route leads up easily to reach the ice-filled crater after 30 to 40 minutes. Deep snow usually covers the upper slopes well into January. Snow-corniced cliffs drop away into the crater, so be careful where you tread. From the rim there is a superb view of the surrounding countryside, with the double-

summit of Volcán Choshuenco now also visible towards the north-east, as well as Lago Rupanco to the south-west.

Contour slightly upward along the steep slope, gradually turning north onto the barren, rolling Puyehue plateau. The route leads you under puffing fumaroles on the volcano's raw north-western side, then dips into a basin of eroding pumice after 1¼ to 1½ hours. Apart from isolated wooden stakes and even more occasional cairns, the extremely faint trail itself is the only route marking in most places from here on.

Continue north-eastwards along a dry stream bed past a reddish, yellow-black rock ridge to your right, then cut left over a flat sandy plain. The route now leads roughly north-west along a low rounded ridge among desert-like dunes to where two cold springs emerge from the grey earth. Continue around to the right here, following the eastern side of the right-hand stream to a vague route junction before dropping left into the deep, green gully past some dying fumaroles, 1¼ to 1½ hours on. This is where the now dry hot spring known as **Los Baños** used to be.

Jump the Baños stream and follow the path 10 to 15 minutes north-westwards through the desolate terrain to the junction of a larger stream and a tiny side stream. Beside the larger stream is an extremely hot steaming pool, which unfortunately is no good for comfortable bathing because it mixes too abruptly with the cold running water. A few metres over to your left at a tiny thermal spring half concealed by giant nalca leaves, however, are the **'Baños Nuevos'**, where the water is a pleasant 28°C and low in acidity. The earth around the spring has been dug out to the size of a large bathtub (which tends to fill up with sandy sediment, so dig it out again after use).

Side Trip to Los Geisires This easy, 14km four-hour return walk to this small field of bubbling mud tubs, effervescent pools and geysers is a must. Head a short way on to cross the (larger) stream and continue northwards through a minor gully, then over a sparsely vegetated plain to wade the shallow main upper branch of the **Río Nilahue**. The path (which was evidently routed for the convenience of horse-riders) recrosses the small river a number of times as it leads upstream along the eroding banks past fumaroles on the slopes over to the right.

As you near the upper valley, climb away right (west-north-west) to the top of a minor ridge above an undrained depression, which normally resembles a shallow lake until late summer. Bits of wreckage from a small aeroplane that made a harmless crash-landing on this muddy plain in the mid 1970s can still be found here. Follow the ridge as it turns abruptly to the right and cut across to the far end of the boggy basin, then climb steeply up right onto a ridge. The rather indistinct final section leads north-eastwards across a deep stream gully to the fascinating area of **Los Geisires**. For your own safety and to preserve the delicate formations be careful where you tread. Return via the same route.

Camp Sites There are semi-sheltered camp sites around the dried-up thermal spring at Los Baños. Firewood is very scarce so make sure you bring your own stove and adequate fuel. Camp sites at 'Baños Nuevos' are also good, although somewhat more exposed. Camping is also possible near the upper branch of the Río Nilahue.

Stage 3: 'Baños Nuevos' to Lower Río Contrafuerte
15km, 6½ to 8 hours
Backtrack to the fumaroles above the Los Baños camp, then head north-north-east (the odd marker stake shows the way) along bare pumice ridges between the upper branches of the Río Nilahue. The vague trail descends from high above the cascading eastern branch via slopes of chaura heath overlooking the densely forested Nilahue valley. Watch carefully for where the route drops down steeply right to cross the stream before climbing the opposite bank to join a long-disused road after 30 to 45 minutes.

Continue through some semi-sheltered camp sites by the track, where alpine lenga forest is regenerating after fires. As you

begin to dip into the trees the going becomes slow because of fallen logs and overgrown sections of quila (bamboo). The often badly eroded route winds through beautiful lush rainforest via a broad ridge separating the Río Nilahue from the **Río Contrafuerte** to your right. After two to three hours edge right to cross the Río Contrafuerte, before returning to the left bank further on.

Climb back to the ridge top and make your way along the gradually more visible (although quite muddy) route through the forest to finally meet a broader 4WD track after three to four hours. Ignoring minor diverging logging roads, follow the main track past an old sawmill on your right. The now well-graded road turns left to pass a primitive shelter in an attractive meadow scattered with wild blackberry bushes beside the Río Nilahue, 60 to 80 minutes on.

Camp Sites Good camp sites can be found just before you drop below the tree line. There is more sheltered (though less scenic) camping where the track meets the Río Contrafuerte about halfway down. Camping in the forest is damp and there is usually no running water. At the end of the section, potential camp sites by the Río Nilahue road are excellent, but in places vigorous blackberry growth makes it hard to get to the river.

Stage 4: Lower Río Contrafuerte to Riñinahue
26km, 7 to 10 hours
Follow the road north to pass a first farm (which has bread and cheese for sale) just before the bridge over the Río Nilahue not far above its confluence with the Río Contrafuerte. The road, which is muddy in places because of heavy logging trucks, climbs away steeply through forest and patches of cleared grazing land. After three to four hours the road crosses the **Río Los Venados** bridge, just up from where the Contrafuerte enters the Río Nilahue. Continue past more small dairy farms and the picturesque Laguna Pocura on your right.

The lower valley is open and more populated and developed. The road leads through

LAKE DISTRICT

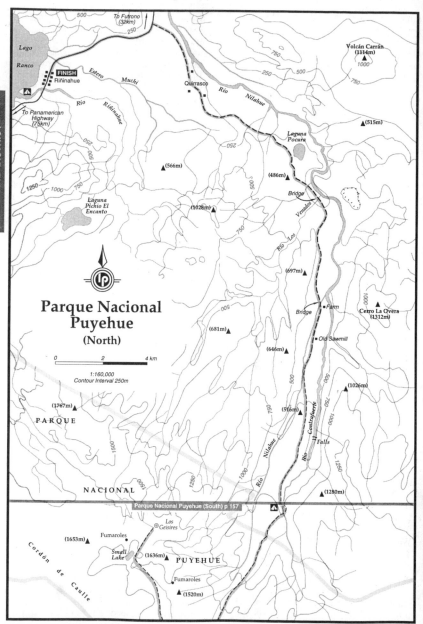

The Puyehue Plateau (top & middle) is intensely volcanic. The striking folded terrain of old lava flows lies along the Puyehue Traverse, where you pass steaming fumaroles, or volcanic vents. Lago Triángulo (bottom) in Parque Nacional Alerce Andino is an impressive glacial lake lying in a deep trough, and can be visited in an easy three hour return trek.

Laguna Tonchek (top) and Laguna Jakob (bottom left) lie among the peaks of the Parque Nacional Nahuel Huapi. These lakes are fed by melting snow and ice, such as that from Glaciar Castaña Overo (bottom right).

the small settlement of **Quirrasco** after two to three hours, and follows the Río Nilahue to intersect with the Riñinahue-Lago Ranco road (ask locals about the shortcut to the main road via some small lanes between fields). Turn left and make your way to **Riñinahue**. The small township has one hostería and is well serviced by buses.

Camp Sites Along the first part of this section numerous tent sites can be found in the forest or clearings off the road. At Riñinahue, camping is possible at the south-eastern corner of Lago Ranco. Ask permission before camping on private property.

Other Treks in Parque Nacional Puyehue

PAMPA FRUTILLA
Pampa Frutilla, an attractive subalpine plateau at the north-eastern foot of Volcán Casablanca, can be visited in a two or three-day trek from Anticura. An unsignposted 4WD track (closed to non-CONAF traffic) leaves from 100m above where the Ruta 215 (highway) passes the waterfall known as Salto de los Novios, several kilometres east of Anticura. Follow this rough road for about 18km to pass an open CONAF refugio not far before it terminates at several small lakes. Pampa Frutilla (Spanish for 'strawberry field') is so-called because the native Chilean strawberry, or quellén, grows here in great abundance, its sweet little red berries ripening from late January (when the tábanos are also out in force). Trekkers with good route-finding abilities can ascend eastwards from Pampa Frutilla via the open volcanic ridges to Volcán Casablanca (see the description which follows). Two Chilean IGM 1:50,000 sheets, *Volcán Puyehue* (Section H, No 27) and *Volcán Casablanca* (Section H, No 36) cover the trek.

VOLCÁN CASABLANCA
Volcán Casablanca is a relatively low (2240m) volcano whose slopes have been developed for skiing. From Aguas Calientes a path leads for 11km south-eastwards to the Refugio Bertín, a small rustic CONAF hut at around 1500m near a tarn. The route winds its way on up south-eastwards to meet a rough road near the Crater Rayhuén above the tiny ski village of Antillanca. From this small side crater the climb to the summit of Volcán Casablanca takes a relatively easy half day return. Trekkers with sound navigational skills can make a descent to Pampa Frutilla by traversing northward from Volcán Casablanca, before descending north-east via a spur and crossing the Río Antillanca (see the preceding description).

Use the 1:50,000 Chilean IGM sheet *Volcán Casablanca* (Section H, No 36) – ideally together with the 1:250,000 CONAF map of Parque Nacional Puyehue. From Osorno, there are regular direct buses or colectivos only as far as Aguas Calientes, which is on the same road 18km before Antillanca. People with private transport can drive directly to Antillanca, but motorists should note that uphill traffic to Antillanca is permitted only from 8 am to 12 pm then from 2 until 5.30 pm, while downhill traffic from Antillanca is permitted only from 12 to 2 pm, then after 5.30 pm.

Parque Nacional Vicente Pérez Rosales

Created in 1926, the 2510 sq km Parque Nacional Vicente Pérez Rosales is the second oldest national park in Chile and the largest in the Chilean Lake District. The park fronts the Argentine border, where it meets the even larger Parque Nacional Nahuel Huapi, and together with the adjoining Parque Nacional Puyehue this area forms the largest tract of trans-Andean wilderness in the Lake District.

GENERAL INFORMATION
Geographical Information

Situated at roughly 41°S, Parque Nacional Vicente Pérez Rosales is centred around the 221 sq km Lago Todos los Santos, which at only 184m above sea level is the park's lowest point. This fjord-like lake is ringed by some of the highest and most prominent volcanic peaks of the southern Lake District. They form an arc running eastwards from the perfect cone of Volcán Osorno along the volcanic peaks of Puntiagudo, Cenizas and Casablanca to the majestic Monte Tronador at the lake's extreme eastern end. Ranges also extend back westwards along the southern side of Lago Todos los Santos as far as Volcán Calbuco.

Apart from Lago Pirehueico some distance to the north, Lago Todos los Santos is the only major low-level lake on the Chilean side that stretches deep into the Andes. The lake lies deep within a glacial trough, not at the termination of a former glacier's path (like nearby Lago Llanquihue). Immediately following the last ice age, Lago Todos los Santos was joined with Lago Llanquihue in an enormous body of water, but subsequent eruptions of Volcán Osorno and Volcán Calbuco divided them into separate lakes. Todos los Santos is unique among the larger lakes because, apart from the access road to Petrohué at its outlet, no roads penetrate its wild, densely forested shoreline.

Natural History

The heavy rainfall and mild weather in Vicente Pérez Rosales support dense, lush Valdivian rainforest whose predominant trees are coigüe, tepa, mañío, ulmo, canelo, olivillo (or teque), lingue and avellano. Less common tree species include the lleuque *(Prumnopitys andina)*, a podocarp related to the mañío that grows on the moist slopes above 600m; its small yellow fruit have the appearance of tiny lemons. Another is the fuinque *(Lomatia ferruginea)*, a small tree of the proteaceae family with yellow flowers.

The maqui *(Aristotelia chilensis)* is a very small tree typically found in stands (so-called *macales)* at the edge of the forest. It has oval leaves on a reddish stem and produces edible purple berries (from which the Mapuche made an alcoholic drink called *tecu)*.

The rainforest understorey harbours a great botanical diversity. The park is an important refuge for the ciprés enano *(Dacrydium fonckii)*, an extremely rare dwarf member the podocarp family that is almost identical to the pygmy pine *(D. laxifolium)* of New Zealand. This tiny prostrate conifer grows in montane swamps, often largely hidden by other nearby plants. More common is the quilquil *(Blechnum chilense)*, a common species of tree fern typically found growing in stream gullies. The quilquil looks like a small palm, hence its other common name of palmilla. In small clearings you'll find several species of ñipa (members of the genus *Escallonia)*, recognisable by their red or pinkish tubular flowers that end in five out-turned petals. Another distinctive bush (sometimes growing to a small tree) is the chaquihue (also called polizonte, *Crinodendron hookerianum)*, whose large leafy twigs produce bright-red, rounded pod-like flowers. The chaquihue prefers wet sites such as along streams or wetlands.

The park's lush vegetation makes it a veritable paradise for birds, of which parrots and nectar-eating hummingbirds are especially plentiful. The choroy *(Enicognathus leptorhynchus)*, a large green parakeet most easily identified by its long curved beak, dwells in these forests. The run run *(Hymenops perspicillata)* is a species of tyrant flycatcher that typically frequents wetlands, lake shores and riverbanks; apart from its yellow beak the male run run is black, while the female has a coffee-coloured upper body and a pale-yellow breast with darker longitudinal stripes. The yeco, also called bigua, *(Phalacrocorax olivaceus)*, a large black cormorant widely distributed throughout moist coastal areas of southern South America, often visits Lago Todos los Santos, where it finds plenty of fish and small amphibians. This large waterbird is an excellent diver and can often be seen perched on a log or rock with its wings outstretched.

The llaca *(Dromiciops australis)*, also known as the monito del monte, a tiny brown opossum, inhabits these temperate rainforests along with its marsupial cousin, the rincholesta, or comadrejita trompuda, *(Ryncholestes raphanurus)*. The rincholesta is a rare nocturnal insectivore that was only discovered by science – although the indigenous Mapuche people certainly knew about it – in the 1950s. Other mammals common to the forests of Vicente Pérez Rosales include the pudú, coipo, huiña, zorro culpeo and puma.

Numerous native fishes are found in the park's lakes and rivers. The main species are pejerrey *(Basilichthys microlepidotus)*, puyen *(Galaxia* species), Patagonian perch and peladilla, along with tollo, lamprea, huaiquil and lisa. More plentiful are introduced salmon and trout. A peculiar species of frog, the sapo partero *(Rhinoderma darwinii)*, first zoologically classified by Charles Darwin, also inhabits the ponds, lakes and rivers. After fertilisation, the male sapo partero ('midwife' in Spanish) incubates and hatches the eggs inside his own mouth, from which the fully developed froglets – not tadpoles – emerge after three weeks.

Climate
In this extremely wet coastal climate, annual rainfall averages 2500mm at Ensenada on the park's western extreme, but rainfall rises steadily towards the east. Precipitation levels around the Paso de Pérez Rosales on the Chile-Argentina frontier reach over 5000mm – the highest levels in the Lake District. Moderated by the lake's low elevation and proximity to the Pacific coast, average annual temperatures around the shore of Lago Todos los Santos are a relatively high 12°C. The hottest summer days rarely exceed 30°C. Conditions are less mild at the higher altitudes in the surrounding ranges, where winters regularly bring heavy snowfalls.

Place Names
The national park's name is a homage to the Chilean businessman and mining magnate Vicente Pérez Rosales, who was also an accomplished writer and the founder of Puerto Montt. Lago Todos los Santos ('all saints lake') was named by Jesuit missionaries, who from the early 17th century – a time when the whole of the Lake District was still under the control of hostile Mapuche tribes – journeyed across its waters en route from Argentina to Chiloé. The lake is called Lago Esmeralda, because of the emerald-green tint of its water. Numerous features, including the village of Peulla ('buds, sprouts'), the bay of Cayutúe ('the six grounds') and the thermal springs of Callāo ('spike, lance'), have graphic Mapuche place names.

PRACTICAL INFORMATION
Information Sources
The park administration centre is at Petrohué at the western end of Lago Todos los Santos, where there is a CONAF information centre (Centro de Informes) with a museum with information on local fauna and flora. Also see Trekking Bases at the beginning of this chapter for CONAF's offices in Puerto Montt.

Permits & Regulations
There are few restrictions on trekking in Parque Nacional Vicente Pérez Rosales. No permit is required, but where possible inform the park authorities of your intended route and the names of all members in the party. There are a number of small enclaves of freehold land within the park, and although the trekking routes are public rights of way, trekkers should respect private property. Wild camping is permitted, but use discretion when choosing your camp site.

When to Trek
Unless you're planning to go above the tree line, treks in Parque Nacional Vicente Pérez Rosales can generally be done between early November and early May. The hot weather between mid-December and late January usually brings out the tábanos, which can be a particular nuisance in locations below the tree line.

Termas de Calláo

> **Duration** 3 days
> **Distance** 44km
> **Standard** Easy-Medium
> **Start** Petrohué/El Rincón (or Puerto Calláo)
> **Finish** El Poncho (on Lago Rupanco)
> **Entry** Free, no permit needed
> **Season** November-May
> **Summary** This gentle trek from the shores of the fjord-like Lago Todos los Santos leads past idyllic farmlets in the lush Valdivian rainforest to natural thermal springs and on to the picturesque Lago Rupanco.

The relatively remote Termas de Calláo lie hidden behind Volcán Puntiagudo in the Valle Sin Nombre. The Termas de Calláo are delightful natural hot springs that emerge from the ground just beside the small Río Sin Nombre, which flows into Lago Todos los Santos. Small farms blend into the dense temperate rainforest along the river.

MAPS

Two Chilean IGM sheets cover this walk: *Volcán Casablanca* (Section H, No 36) and *Peulla* (Section H, No 44). These maps show the walking track, though unfortunately there are omissions and errors regarding the exact route.

DAYS REQUIRED

The trek can be done in three easy days, although an additional day could be spent enjoying this attractive area.

TREKKING STANDARD

The trek takes a low-level route along two river valleys and reaches its highest point at a forested pass around 800m. Because of its low elevation and relatively sheltered aspect, the Termas de Calláo can be visited from late spring until late autumn (late October to early May) when other walks may be out of condition. However, the summer months

(December to February) are the best time to do the trek.

The trek generally follows horse trails kept in condition by the local inhabitants, and all larger streams are bridged. Along the central section of the route between the Termas de Calláo and Laguna de los Quetros, however, fallen trees obscure the way in places, so careful route-finding is often required. Trekkers are strongly advised to walk in a south-to-north direction, as there is no reliable way of getting out from El Rincón (on the remote northern shore of Lago Todos los Santos) once you arrive.

The trek is rated *easy*. The total walking distance is 44km.

ACCOMMODATION & CAMPING

There is only one refugio along the route. Although it is possible for fit and fast parties to do the trek without carrying a tent, this is not recommended. The Refugio Termas de Calláo, an excellent hut constructed on private land from native timbers, has a wood stove, bamboo furniture and a sink; it sleeps six people and charges US$6 per person.

At Petrohué, the *Hotel Petrohué* (☎ 25 8042) offers tourist-style accommodation from around US$35 per night. On the other side of the Río Petrohué is an organised camping ground with facilities (which charges US$7.50 per site) a hostería (with beds from around US$10) and one or two casas de familia. Boats from the dock at Petrohué shuttle backpackers across the river for a small fee.

There is a mid-range hotel at El Islote, several kilometres west from El Poncho, at the end of the trek. There is a basic free camping area at Puerto Rico on the south-eastern shore of Lago Rupanco.

SUPPLIES

Farm produce and home-baked bread can often be bought at farms along the route, though trekkers should not rely on this. There is a small store at Petrohué where you can buy last-minute snacks, but Puerto Montt and Puerto Varas (on Lago Llanquihue) are the most convenient places to buy supplies.

GETTING TO/FROM THE TREK

The trek begins at El Rincón (also known as Puerto Calláo), in an inlet on the northern shore of Lago Todos Los Santos about halfway across the lake.

There is no regular direct transport to El Rincón, so it is necessary to charter a boat there. Access is easiest from Petrohué, a tourist village at the western end of the lake. You can get to Petrohué by one of the direct minibuses, which throughout the day leave from behind the main bus terminal in Puerto Montt (US$4), or on a short return day tour from Puerto Montt (from US$8.50 per person); all buses run via Puerto Varas on Lago Llanquihue. In summer an assortment of boats (of varying size and seaworthiness) wait for customers at the dock in Petrohué. The lowest asking price to charter a boat to El Rincón is US$35, so try to find other trekkers to share the cost. The trip takes about two to three hours, depending on the type of boat as well as the direction and speed of winds. It should also be possible to charter a boat to El Rincón from Peulla, a village on the lake's remote eastern shore. Remember, once you reach El Rincón the only way out is the route described below.

The walk finishes at El Poncho, a small scattering of holiday houses on the southern shore of Lago Rupanco. From El Poncho there are once-daily (sometimes twice-daily) buses to Osorno; the timetable is posted at the bus stop in El Poncho. The bus sometimes departs from El Islote, another small holiday village several kilometres farther west around the lake. If possible check bus departure times in Osorno before you begin the trek.

Stage 1: El Rincón to Termas de Calláo
12km, 3¼ to 4 hours

From the tiny sandy beach of El Rincón where your boat lands, head for one minute uphill to a broad trail running across the slope. Turn right here and make your way over a minor crest overlooking Lago Todos los Santos, then through semi-cleared fields past a turn-off (signposted 'Puerto Calláo') going back down to the lakeside. A good horse track sidles down northwards through ulmo forest above the **Río Sin Nombre** which rushes through a deep gully on your left to cross the **Río La Junta** side stream after 40 to 50 minutes. If you don't trust the rickety suspension bridge wade the shallow water slightly downstream.

Follow the often muddy path for 20 to 25 minutes to cross the Río Sin Nombre itself on another precarious suspension bridge and continue upstream. The path dips and rises along the river's steep-sided western bank before it climbs away left past a farm and crosses a sturdy log bridge over a large side stream after a further 1¼ to 1½ hours. Proceed on through the rainforest to a trail fork, where 'Termas' signs direct you off right through a bamboo-scattered clearing back across the Río Sin Nombre to reach a farmhouse 30 to 40 minutes on.

The farmhouse (where you can buy farm produce) stands in full view of the majestic volcanic plug summit of **Volcán Puntia-gudo** to the west. You should pick up the key to the refugio and hot springs at the farm-house. Inclusive prices are as follows: use of the refugio US$6 per person; camping US$7.50 per tent site; use of hot baths only US$2.50. You can arrange to leave the key in the refugio to save backtracking to the farm.

The route leads along the eastern bank of the river, recrossing a final time before it passes an abandoned shingled wooden cottage to arrive at the **Termas de Calláo** (see Accommodation & Camping) after a final 25 to 30 minutes. The thermal baths are just down by the river in a little shed with two private interior tubs. The water is piping hot and very relaxing. The scenic valley is enclosed by high, densely rainforested granite peaks on either side, and makes an excellent spot to stop for a day.

Camp Sites Nice camp sites can be found above El Rincón on grassy spots overlooking the lake. There is also good camping on the scenic flats where the Río Sin Nombre enters Lago Todos los Santos, 15 to 20 minutes west around the lakeside via a good trail. Further up the track, fair camp sites can be found in occasional small clearings by the

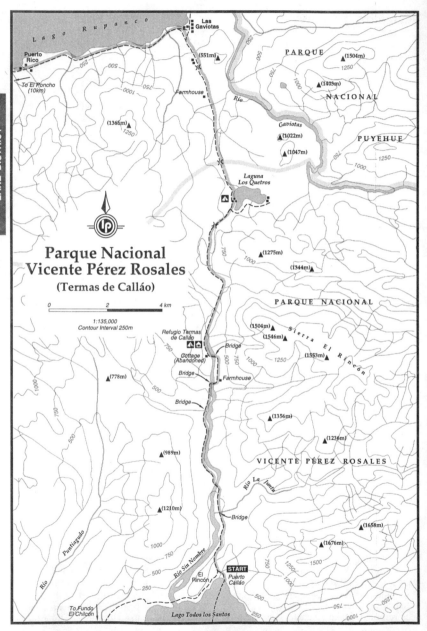

Parque Nacional
Vicente Pérez Rosales
(Termas de Callão)

0   2   4 km

1:135,000
Contour Interval 250m

river where the banks are not too steep. There is a very attractive camping area at the Termas de Calláo in the trees just below the refugio, but a fee is charged to camp here.

Stage 2: Refugio Termas de Calláo to Las Gaviotas
16km, 4 to 5¼ hours

From the refugio make your way upvalley through scrubby pastures along the river's western bank before rising into the rainforest. Bear leftwards at the second (probably dry) stream you come to, carefully following the route through an area of fallen trunks then on via tiny grassy patches. A large landslide on an adjacent mountainside has exposed a sheer rock face.

After 40 to 50 minutes the path turns away from the Río Sin Nombre and then begins climbing gently north-north-west beside a cascading stream through a forest of gnarled mañío and fragrant-leafed tepa.

Cross the stream and ascend along a steep spur through dense thickets of bamboo until the gradient eases, 50 minutes to 1¼ hours on. The path briefly follows the ridge top northwards through montane coigüe and ulmo forest, dropping down steeply then climbing again before it makes a proper descent north-east into fire-cleared pastures to reach the south-western corner of **Laguna Los Quetros** after a further 40 to 50 minutes. Continue for a final 15 minutes around the lake's reedy western shore to some camp sites beside a small stand of alerce trees. There is a picturesque farm cottage on the opposite side of Laguna Los Quetros, which lies in a basin that drains subterraneously through the porous volcanic soil.

Follow the prominent horse track up around the north-west side of the tranquil lake into the forest. The route passes by a small lily-covered lagoon to cross a low watershed. Here, where the earth is composed of friable pumice, the path rapidly erodes to form deep trenches, revealing the history of previous local volcanic eruptions in the layers of the soil. In places where the trenches have become too deep the path has been rerouted. Make your way down beside

a stream (a small tributary of the **Río Gaviotas**) towards the snowy cap of Volcán Casablanca. The path descends steadily through clearings, giving way to open hillsides to pass the first farmhouse at the edge of a broad green bowl after 1¼ to 1½ hours. Horses, cattle and flocks of noisy bandurrias graze on these choice Lake District pastures.

Skirt north-north-west through a gate in the middle of the fields into a minor saddle high above **Lago Rupanco**. With the volcano and shimmering lake ahead of you, drop down past wooden cottages and neat vegetable gardens to reach a trail fork on golden grassy slopes scattered with blackberry bushes after 30 to 40 minutes. Five minutes further down the left-hand branch meets a wide track along the black-sand shore of Lago Rupanco, while the right-hand path goes a short way down to the village of **Las Gaviotas** at the lake's south-eastern corner. There is really no reason to go to Las Gaviotas, as there is no accommodation or store.

Camp Sites There are no recommended camp sites until Laguna Los Quetros, where the best spot to pitch your tent is near the ruins of a wooden shack on the lake's western shore. Be extremely careful if you light a campfire. Camping is not recommended on the section from Laguna Los Quetros to Las Gaviotas, but there is nice camping along the black-sand beach a short way from where you meet Lago Rupanco.

Stage 3: Las Gaviotas to El Poncho
16km, 2¾ to 3½ hours

Follow the dark sandy shore west through the front yards of lakeside holiday houses. The wide graded track rises and dips around the often very steep banks of Lago Rupanco past rustic farm shacks and through patches of forest fringed by blackberry bushes. Cross a large dry gully (or the suspension footbridge up to the left if the stream is in flood) just before you come out onto a lovely lakeside pasture at the locality of **Puerto Rico** after 1¼ to 1½ hours.

The trail climbs away left over scrubby slopes high above the lake, bringing into

LAKE DISTRICT

view the bare volcanic ridges surrounding Volcán Puntiagudo to the south. Drop down past more holiday houses around the broad tranquil bay to cross the **Río Callảo** on a sturdy log bridge, 40 to 50 minutes on. The route cuts along cliffs above the aqua-blue water to reach the end of a dirt road, following this past the exclusive **Bahía Escocia Fly Fishing Lodge** to reach the tiny settlement of **El Poncho** after a final 50 minutes to one hour. There is a store here and a bus stop.

Camp Sites There is a basic free camping area at Puerto Rico. There are other potential camp spots along the Lago Rupanco shoreline, including beside the Río Calláo. Always seek permission before camping on private property or near houses.

Other Treks in Parque Nacional Vicente Pérez Rosales

VOLCÁN PUNTIAGUDO LOOKOUT

Puntiagudo is a spectacular sharp volcanic plug whose distinctive form makes it easily recognisable from many places in the southern Lake District. A long return day walk from Bahía Escocia (near the southern shore of Lago Rupanco – see Stage 3 of the Termas de Calláo trek) follows a path south via a steep spur to a lookout point on the prominent volcanic ridge coming down from Puntiagudo's north-eastern side. Two Chilean IGM 1:50,000 sheets, *Cerro Puntiagudo* (Section H, No 35) and *Volcán Casablanca*

(Section H, No 36), cover this trek but do not show its route.

VOLCÁN OSORNO – REFUGIO PICADA

This short one to two-day trek from Petrohué on Lago Todos los Santos follows a marked trail around the north-eastern slopes of Volcán Osorno (2652m) to the Refugio Picada. Ascents of Osorno are usually made from the Refugio Teski Club (see Other Treks in the Lake District at the end of this chapter). The Chilean IGM 1:50,000 sheet *Petrohué* (Section H, No 44) covers this area of the walk but does not show the path.

RALÚN TO ENSENADA CAYUTÚE

This easy return trek to Ensenada Cayutúe, an isolated southern arm of Lago Todos los Santos, takes around three days. The route begins at a prominent road turn-off 2km east of the village of Ralún on Seno Reloncaví. The road passes farms before it terminates at a logging camp, from where a path climbs northwards through the valley of the Río Reloncaví to the low pass of Portezuelo Cabeza de Vaca. From here you descend to the lovely Laguna Cayutúe, then continue down the Río Concha to Ensenada Cayutúe. The recommended place to camp is at Laguna Cayutúe on the other side of the inlet stream. The land fronting Ensenada Cayutúe is private property and camping there is not permitted.

Two Chilean IGM 1:50,000 sheets, *Petrohué* (Section H, No 44) and *Cochamó* (Section H, No 53), cover the trekking route. Ralún is about 95km east of Puerto Montt by road and can be reached by daily bus or ferry.

Parque Nacional Nahuel Huapi

Parque Nacional Nahuel Huapi (pronounced 'nah-well WAH-pee'), lies to the west of the popular tourist centre of Bariloche in the southern Argentine Lake District. Formally established in 1922, Nahuel Huapi is the

oldest of Argentina's national parks. The original park (whose title was simply 'Parque Nacional del Sur') comprised a vast tract of land first granted to the pioneering explorer Francisco Pascasio Perito Moreno for his services to the Argentine Boundary Commission. Perito Moreno donated it back to the nation on the condition that it be turned into a national park. Additional areas were later incorporated into Parque Nacional Nahuel Huapi to create what remains by far the largest national park on either side of the Andes in northern Patagonia.

The area of the modern-day park formed a large part of the Mapuche heartland, and tribes lived around the eastern shores of the great lake. There are several low Andean passes in the park, such as the Paso Vuriloche (near Pampa Linda) and the Paso de Pérez Rosales, which linked the many local Mapuche tribes on either side of the Cordillera. These passes were later used by Christian missionaries as a safe route to Chiloé. Today Nahuel Huapi's wild rugged interior is more easily accessible via an extensive network of well-maintained pathways – as well as numerous rougher unmarked routes – supported by many excellent alpine refugios. The park is a wonderfully scenic area of forests and lakes set among impressive craggy ranges.

GENERAL INFORMATION
Geographical Information

Parque Nacional Nahuel Huapi stretches from its northern boundary, fronting Parque Nacional Lanín, southwards to the southern edge of the Argentine Lake District at roughly 42°S. The park includes 7580 sq km of prime wilderness, whose heart and hub is the 557 sq km Lago Nahuel Huapi itself. With its numerous fjord-like branches (that reach a maximum depth of 454m), Lago Nahuel Huapi is unquestionably the finest example of a major glacial lake anywhere in northern Patagonia. This enormous lake lies at 765m above sea level – the lowest point within the northern four fifths of the park, which is drained by the Río Limay and is therefore part of the Atlantic basin.

There are numerous other sizeable lakes lying in the deep valleys surrounding Lago Nahuel Huapi. The largest of these are Lago Traful and Lago Espejo to the north, and Lago Mascardi in the park's most southerly

zone, which drains westwards via the Río Manso and Río Puelo into the Chilean Pacific. Approximately 20% of the park's area is covered by water. Alarmingly, this figure would be increased if a hydroelectric dam proposed for the upper Río Limay, 16km downstream from where it flows out of Lago Nahuel Huapi, is built. The dam would raise the lake level by around 2m, flooding its sandy beaches and killing trees around its beautiful natural shore, though it is now unlikely go ahead thanks to vehement opposition from the local population.

The other dominating feature of Parque Nacional Nahuel Huapi is the icy crown of Monte Tronador. At 3554m above sea level – at least according to most Argentine maps – Monte Tronador is the highest point within the entire Lake District, and stands almost 1000m above its nearest rivals. The loftiest of Monte Tronador's several summits, Pico Internacional, marks the Argentina-Chile frontier. This massif is smothered by some 60 sq km of névés, glaciers and icefalls, and is the only significant glacially active area found in the park. The mountain's geological origins were the subject of some argument in the past, but Monte Tronador is now believed to be a long-extinct volcano that was probably considerably higher in the past.

Parque Nacional Nahuel Huapi is one of the few areas in Patagonia where the Andes are more extensive and rugged on the Argentine side than on the Chilean side. (Although individual volcanoes do form higher summits in Chile, the ranges surrounding them are relatively low.) This is particularly evident in the mountains to the south of Lago Nahuel Huapi, where the 2388m Cerro Catedral – the highest non-volcanic peak in the Lake District – rises up in craggy steeple-like columns. Many other peaks in the area surpass 2000m. There are no real glaciers left on this eastern side of the park, but in many places intense frost shattering has formed large scree slides on the higher slopes.

Natural History
Flora Three main types of forest are found in Parque Nacional Nahuel Huapi: the wet

LAKE DISTRICT

temperate (or 'Valdivian') rainforest in the park's most westerly valleys, the deciduous alpine forest at higher elevations, and the coniferous forest in the drier eastern sectors of the park.

Of these, the rainforest is easily the most species-diverse, with several dozen different types of trees forming the forest canopy, including alerce (or lahuén), arrayán, avellano, canelo, ciprés de las Guaitecas, coigüe (spelt coihue in Argentina), laurel, mañío, olivillo (or teque), tineo, and ulmo. The deciduous forest of the highland valleys is dominated by lenga mixed with ñirre (spelt ñire in Argentina) and occasional luma blanca *(Myrceugenia chrysocarpa)*, a bush of the myrtle family. The lenga forest is interspersed with areas of *mallín* country where the local drainage is poor, but the mountainsides are barren and sparsely vegetated above 1700m.

Parque Nacional Nahuel Huapi has some of the best-preserved coniferous forests in the southern Andes. These are composed of cípres de la cordillera *(Austrocedrus chilensis)*, a graceful cypress species that forms pure stands on the drier and exposed ranges around the eastern side of the Lago Nahuel Huapi.

Parque Nacional Nahuel Huapi is renowned for its alpine and subalpine wild flowers. One of the most lovely and widespread species is the amancay, or liuto, *(Alstroemeria haemantha)*, which is typically found in forest clearings, where its orange blooms carpet the ground. Various members of the *Mutisia* genus collectively known by the popular name of clavel del campo (literally 'carnations of the countryside'), are climbing opportunists that produce orange, pinkish-white or purple daisy-like flowers. They often grow along sunny roadsides or where forest has been disturbed.

Hidden among the rocks on drier slopes, you may spot the estrellita de la cordillera *(Perezia* species), a small composite perennial whose flowers have numerous white clustered petals. Capachitos, various herblike plants of the genus *Calceolaria* with yellow flowers, are also found here. The

cuye colorado *(Oxalis adenophylla)* is a small alpine shrub with clam-like leaves; its white flowers have pink-tipped petals around a yellow centre. Other common wild flowers include the coxinea *(Collomia biflora)*, an annual that grows as a single reddish stalk crowned by a clustered head of tubular yellow flowers with five crimson petals, and *Chloraea magellanica*, a ground orchid whose flowers have a bluish tinge. The chupa sangre *(Maihuenia patagonica)*, is a spiky cushion-like plant, found still farther to the east where the park fringes the semi-arid Patagonian steppes.

Fauna Ground-dwelling birds, such as the chucao, churrín and huet-huet, inhabit the forest floor, where hummingbirds *(picaflores)* flutter madly around nectar-yielding flowers. The forests also provide the habitat for the carpintero negro, or black woodpecker, which can often be seen chipping away at tree trunks; the torcaza (or conu), a large grey pigeon; and the cachaña, an alpine parakeet. Countless water birds, including native ducks like the quetru, pato cuchara *(Anas platalea)* and the pato real *(Anas sibilatrix)*, live in the park's extensive lakes and rivers.

Mammals sometimes spied in the rainforest are the shy pudú, the world's smallest species of deer, and the marsupial llaca (or monito del monte). The puma and the far smaller huiña are the main terrestrial predators, while the amphibious coipo and the carnivorous huillín inhabit the waterways in the park. North American red deer have multiplied greatly since their introduction early in the 20th century, a major factor in the increasing rarity of the huemul, or Andean deer.

Parque Nacional Nahuel Huapi is the only place where the rare tuco-tuco colonial *(Ctenomys sociabilis)*, which was only discovered by science in 1983, is known to exist. It is a small rat-like creature, and unlike other members of this large South American genus (see Fauna in the Facts about the Region chapter), it lives in large colonies. On the rare occasions when it leaves the warren, the tuco-tuco gives out a peculiar cheeping call that sounds more like that of a bird than a mammal. Two other species of tuco-tuco also inhabit the park.

Climate

Because of the park's relatively high elevation and isolation from the Pacific (whose nearest point is roughly 150km from Llao Llao on Lago Nahuel Huapi) a cool and dry 'continental' climate prevails. At lower elevations mean winter temperatures are around 2°C and in summer around 18°C. Summers tend to be relatively dry and most of the annual precipitation occurs in the winter and spring, when areas above 1000m are covered by a thick mantle of snow.

The high ranges on the international frontier – most of all Monte Tronador – cause a typical 'rain shadow' effect, with steadily diminishing precipitation levels towards the east. It is very wet close to the main continental divide, and in the eastern sectors of Parque Nacional Nahuel Huapi it is semi-arid. For example, Puerto Frías on the border with Chile has an annual average rainfall of around 4000mm, while the Cerro Catedral area receives under 2000mm and the eastern outskirts of Bariloche less than 800mm.

Place Names

The indigenous Mapuche language is less well represented in the names of the major topographical features of Parque Nacional Nahuel Huapi than it is in other parks of the Araucanía and Lake District. The name Nahuel Huapi is usually translated from the Mapuche as 'island of the tiger', which actually refers to the spotted South American jaguar or yaguarete, whose vast range once included north-eastern Patagonia. Vuriloche, the name of a trans-Andean pass, is a variant of the Mapuche word *bariloche* and means 'people on the other side'.

The Spanish-language nomenclature is largely derived from the names of Argentine or European explorers (eg Lago Perito Moreno), early settlers (eg Arroyo Goye), or CAB members (eg Lago Tonchek, Refugio Meiling). More descriptive are names like Cerro Catedral ('cathedral mountain') and Tronador ('thunderer'), a reference to the noise caused by repeated snow and ice avalanches that crash down from the latter mountain's extensive névés. Interestingly, the Mapuche people knew Monte Tronador by the name of Anon, whose meaning is almost identical to the Spanish.

PRACTICAL INFORMATION
Information Sources

A visit to the Club Andino Bariloche (☎ 0944-24531; fax 24579) is recommended before you begin any trek in the Nahuel Huapi area. The CAB, which is one of the largest mountain clubs in Latin America, is a quaint stone building at 20 de Febrero 30 (just above the APN Intendencia).

It may also be worth seeking the much smaller but well organised Club Andino Villa La Angostura (contact address: CC:11, 8407, Río Negro), in the town of Villa La Angostura on the north-western shore of Lago Nahuel Huapi.

The APN Intendencia administration centre (☎ 0944-23111; fax 22989) of Parque Nacinal Nahuel Huapi, is in Bariloche on San Martín 24 (opposite the Centro Cívico); its opening hours are from Monday to Friday between 9 am and 2 pm.

The Asociación Argentina de Guías de Montaña can be contacted through Nicolas de la Cruz (☎ 0944-24807; fax 24818) at Guemes 750 (C.P. 584) in Bariloche. The association can give advice on (guided) mountaineering in the Nahuel Huapi region as well as elsewhere in the Argentine Patagonian Andes.

Several publications of interest to trekkers who can read Spanish are available from bookshops in Bariloche. *Fauna del Parque Nacional Nahuel Huapi*, by Claudio Chehébar and Eduardo Ramilo (Guías Regionales Argentinas, 1993) is a booklet dealing with the animals, birds and reptiles found in the park. *Las Montañas de Bariloche*, by Toncek Arko and Raúl Izagirre (Administración de Parques Nacionales & Asociación Amigos

LAKE DISTRICT

del Museo de la Patagonia), is a locally produced guidebook covering treks in the mountains around Bariloche. *Trekking en Bariloche* (Club Andino Bariloche, 1995) gives a history of mountain rescue in the Nahuel Huapi region and includes information on trekking routes.

Permits & Regulations

A permit (available free of charge) is required for all overnight treks in Parque Nacional Nahuel Huapi. Trekking permits are issued by the CAB and/or the park administration (see Information Sources) in Bariloche as well as by local ranger stations (guarderías) in the park.

A fee of US$5 is levied when visitors enter Nahuel Huapi via an official park entrance gate. (This fee does not apply if the road is a public right of way, as in the case of the Villa Catedral and Llao Llao roads, but visitors to the park's Pampa Linda, Río Manso or Lago Steffen sectors will have to pay it). Before they may cast their line anglers must have a fishing licence, which can be purchased from leading angling stores in Bariloche or at the APN Intendencia.

Camping within the park is now allowed only at designated camping areas. In most cases these are clearly indicated on trekking maps and by official signs at the park-approved camping areas themselves. Away from the more travelled trails, however, wild camping is generally tolerated as long as trekkers take heed of the minimum-impact code.

When to Trek

As most scenic routes in Parque Nacional Nahuel Huapi take you well up into the mountains, there's not much scope for trekking before mid-November or any later than the first half of May. Early and late-season trekkers are cautioned that if there is any breakdown in the weather it is likely to bring snowfalls on the ranges. In the main summer tourist season (January and February) the trails and refugios are crowded with trekkers.

Nahuel Huapi Traverse

Duration 5 days
Distance 40km
Standard Medium-Hard
Start Villa Catedral
Finish Colonia Suiza
Entry US$5, permit needed
Season November-May
Summary An excellent pass-hopping route through the rugged glaciated ranges west of Bariloche.

Hopping over passes and mountain ridges that separate tiny wild valleys in the rugged ranges to the west of Bariloche, this classic trek introduces some of the finest country in the Argentine Lake District. The route offers ever-changing scenery of craggy mountain summits, lovely alpine lakes, waterfalls and beautiful forests. Not surprisingly, it's one of the most popular treks in Argentina.

MAPS

The best map for this trek is a 1:50,000 small-format sheet of the Refugios, Sendas y Picadas series titled simply *Trekking 1*. This contoured map is recommended and sold by the CAB, but is also available at bookstores and/or kiosks in Bariloche for US$6. Also useful is a larger-format 1:100,000 colour sheet of the same Refugios, Sendas y Picadas series, titled *Parque Nacional Nahuel Huapi*, which sells for US$12. Unfortunately, both these maps don't show the trekking route accurately in a few short (but very important) sections.

Two 1:100,000 Argentine IGM sheets also cover the area, but these are hopelessly out of date and don't even show the trekking route. These are *Llao Llao* (Neuquén, No 4172-22), and *San Carlos de Bariloche* (Neuquén, No 4172-23).

DAYS REQUIRED

The full traverse can be done in four to five days. A further one or two days will allow you time to rest or do short side trips. You can also do many shorter variations of the trek. These include the so-called Circuito Catedral (a three-day route combining Stage 1A or 1B, Stage 2 and Stage 3B), the Circuito Chico (Stage 1B *and* Stage 1A walked in reverse order either as a long day walk or in two short days), and the exit route via the Arroyo Goye (Stage 4A, which makes a trek of three or four days length). A description of these alternatives follows.

TREKKING STANDARD

Most sections of the route are well-marked and well-trodden, and route-finding is relatively straightforward. The exception to this is the central section of the Nahuel Huapi Traverse between Refugio Jakob and Refugio Segre, where trekkers must navigate carefully, or places where the terrain is too rocky and/or steep to hold a proper path. The deep and steep-sided valleys often require heavy climbs and descents between the passes through loose rock or scree; wearing gaiters will make the going far more comfortable.

Many sections of this trek are well above the tree line. The route's relatively high altitude generally makes it unsuitable for inexperienced parties until around the beginning of December, though in places snow may remain well into January. The area is somewhat sheltered by the mountains to the west (chiefly Volcán Tronador), and bad weather tends to be slightly less extreme than on the adjacent side of the Andes. Nevertheless, many parts of the route are very exposed to the elements, so if conditions are poor you should wait for the weather to improve.

Many other tracks intersect with the traverse route, allowing you to shorten or vary the walk as you like (see Days Required). On all stages of the trek it is possible to walk out in one day. Less experienced parties are advised to opt for the shorter and easier variation of the trek known as the Circuito Chico (doing only Stage 1A or 1B, Stage 2 and Stage 3B).

The recommended direction in which to do the trek is clockwise from Villa Catedral.

Apart from the section from Refugio Jakob to Refugio Segre (Stage 3A, rated *hard*), all sections are of a *medium* trekking standard. The total length of the traverse is around 40km.

ACCOMMODATION & CAMPING

There are four trekkers' refugios along the route, which makes it possible to do the hike without carrying a tent. Nevertheless, for greater safety and in case huts are overcrowded, trekkers are advised to carry a tent. Particularly during spells of poor weather in January and February, the refugios can quickly fill to (over) capacity as young local trekkers (whose own tents tend to be less waterproof) seek dry shelter. All of the refugios are open at least from early December until mid-April.

The refugios offer basic dormitory accommodation, with little or no bedding apart from, perhaps, a mattress. Trekkers must therefore bring a sleeping bag. With the exception of Refugio López, the refugios belong to the Club Andino Bariloche (CAB), although they are generally run by a private concessioner who acts as a hut keeper *(refugiero)*. The refugios all charge an overnighting fee of US$6, but there's an additional charge of US$3 if you use the hut's cooking facilities. Simple meals, refreshments and supplies – at least chocolate, biscuits and yerba mate – are usually available from all of the refugios.

At Villa Catedral there are a number of ski lodges, including the CAB's own ski hostel, which may accept individual guests in summer. (Ask at the CAB information booth in Villa Catedral for possible accommodation options in the village.)

At Colonia Suiza (at or near the end of Stages 3B, 4B and 5) are two public camping grounds (both with hot showers). The *Camping Goye* (☎ 0944-48627) near the No 10 bus stop charges US$4 per person (or US$6 in the dormitory); it's very cramped and dusty. Far better and only slightly more expensive is the *Hueney Ruca*, a spacious camping ground where you can pitch your tent under ciprés trees right on the lakeshore;

its facilities are also far superior and it has a dining room.

There are also good (national park approved) camp sites along all sections.

SUPPLIES

The most practical base for the trek is Bariloche itself, where there is an enormous range of accommodation in all price ranges. Bariloche also has several large and modern supermarkets and is the best place to buy all necessary provisions. Villa Catedral is OK for a few last-minute supplies – like chocolate and film – and the small holiday village of Colonia Suiza also has a small store and a restaurant.

GETTING TO/FROM THE TREK

The trek begins at Villa Catedral, a ski village about 20km by road from Bariloche. Throughout the trekking season there is an hourly bus service from Bariloche to Villa Catedral run by two bus companies, Tres de Mayo and Buses Codao. All buses depart at alternate two-hourly intervals from the bus/train station (Estación Terminal de Omnibus y de Ferrocarril) at the eastern edge of town, but Tres de Mayo buses run via Avenida de los Pioneros while Buses Codao buses run via Avenida Bustillo.

The first bus leaves Bariloche at about 7 am and the last at around 8 pm, all returning almost immediately from Villa Catedral. The trip takes 30 to 40 minutes.

Trekkers who hike Stage 1B have the option of taking one of the mountain cableways that run from Villa Catedral up to the start of the trek on the Cordón Catedral. There are two possibilities: the cable car/chair lift combinations to Refugio Lynch or the chair lift to Piedra del Cóndor. The Lynch cable car/chair lift runs from Tuesday to Sunday between 9 am and 4 pm. The single child/adult fare for the cable car (cable-carril) is US$11/16, while the short chair lift ride on from the upper cable-car station costs an extra US$2. The Piedra del Cóndor chair lift (aerosilla) runs on Mondays or when winds or repairs force the cable car to close; the fares are virtually

the same as for the cable car – in other words, outrageously expensive.

The walk ends at Puente López, a picnic area and kiosk on the road between Llao Llao and Colonia Suiza, 22km west of Bariloche. The Tres de Mayo company's No 10 bus to Bariloche passes this point approximately every two hours throughout the day.

THE TREK
Stage 1A: Villa Catedral to Refugio Frey (via Arroyo Van Titter)
12km, 3½ to 4½ hours

This stage is longer and there are no cableways to haul you up the mountain as on Stage 1B, but the ascent is leisurely and more sheltered. It is the only safe route when the high-level traverse of Stage 1B is snowed over or icy.

From the CAB lodge at the southern edge of Villa Catedral, cut across the car park below a minor ski tow and take an old (unsignposted) road up left through a weedy field to a signpost at the trail head. The broad foot track goes southwards through ñirre and quila scrub on a kind of wide terrace above Lago Gutiérrez, then rises gently into the forest below overhanging cliffs to a fork 1½ to two hours from the village.

Continue up right here (the left-hand route leads down to the lake), turning up northwest through moist forest and cross the **Arroyo Van Titter** on a footbridge. Ascend at a leisurely pace through the tall lenga forest with an understorey of herbs and wild flowers to pass the **Refugio Piedritas** after 50 minutes to 1¼ hours. This quaint little refugio belongs to the local Club Andino Esloveno and has been constructed by building a log wall across the opening of a large boulder just to the right of the path. The Refugio Piedritas only has space for about eight people, and is basic.

Climb on through the forest, which soon changes into lower and denser lenga scrub granting views of the peaks on the Cordón Catedral. The route crosses the now much smaller stream on stepping stones a short way before you reach **Refugio Frey** after a final 50 minutes to 1¼ hours. The refugio stands at 1700m in a particularly scenic location on the eastern shore of **Laguna Tonchek** looking out across the lake to the craggy north and south peaks of Cerro Catedral.

The neat two-storey hut is built of local stone, and upstairs there is sleeping space for 40 people. The refugio has a wood stove for cooking, but meals are usually available. Simple supplies and refreshments can also be bought. Refugio Frey is normally open from December until the end of April, when the surrounding granite crags attract many rock climbers. It can get very crowded, particularly during periods of poor weather in the main tourist season.

Camp Sites The first authorised camping area passed along Stage 1A is by the Arroyo Van Titter just after you cross the footbridge. A similar camping area exits a short way up at the Refugio Piedritas. At both these camping areas you can find numerous good tent sites in the forest.

Camping is also officially permitted at Laguna Tonchek, where there are sheltered sites in the lenga scrub on the southern side of the lake. Campers here are not allowed to light fires (and firewood is a bit scarce anyway), so use your camp stove. In January and February the Laguna Tonchek camping area can get crowded.

Stage 1B: Piedra del Cóndor/Refugio Lynch to Refugio Frey
8.5km, 2¾ to 4 hours

This excellent alternative route to Stage 1A may be impassable because of snow and ice early (and sometimes late) in the season, in which case 1A will be the only safe way of reaching Refugio Frey. Fortunately, much of Stage 1B is exposed to the sun so the snow tends to melt away fairly early. If in doubt, enquire in the Club Andino office in Bariloche or at the CAB's information booth in Villa Catedral regarding the current condition of this route.

If the exorbitant cableway fares put you off, you can hike to Refugio Lynch via a foot track that spirals up below the cable car. The trail is steep and exposed to the sun (carry water), and the climb takes around three hours. This route is only recommended for saving money or building character.

On some days the chair lift rather than the cable car operates from Villa Catedral. This chair lift heaves you up into the stony and sparsely vegetated alpine zone to **Piedra del Cóndor**. At 1759m this is the northernmost point of the Cordón Catedral, and makes an excellent lookout offering an unbroken panorama across Lago Nahuel Huapi. The restaurant here is closed in summer. A rough road can be followed for 25 to 30 minutes around to **Refugio Lynch** (2042m).

Otherwise a cable car/chair lift combination heaves you up to Refugio Lynch (closed in summer). Head south-westwards along, or just to the left of, the bare ridge top, following yellow and/or red paint markings (lots of spots and dots on rocks) that quickly lead up to the hump of **Punta Nevada**, where winter snowdrifts linger well into summer. There are fine views down to your right into the tiny valley of the Arroyo Rucaco, whose stream meanders peacefully into alpine moors before entering a gorge, and beyond to the great glaciers of Monte Tronador, which rises up on the western horizon. The route dips down to reach a small saddle, not far from the upper station of another cableway, after 1 to 1¼ hours.

Sidle rightwards off the ridge to cross a scree slide, then make your way around below the rock spires of **Punta Princesa**. On your right the land falls away almost directly into the valley. Minor hand climbing is necessary as the route picks its way through short sections of rock blocks with small chrysanthemum bushes sheltering in the crevices. Keeping to this western side of the range, make your way on to reach the **Cancha de Fútbol**, 60 to 80 minutes from the small saddle. At this sandy shelf surrounded by the boulders, the 2388m Cerro Catedral Sur comes into view over to the south.

Stage 1B merges into Stage 2 here. The way to **Refugio Frey** is explained (in reverse sequence) at the beginning of Stage 2. The walking time from the Cancha de Fútbol down to the hut is 40 to 50 minutes.

Camp Sites There is nowhere at all to camp until you reach Laguna Tonchek (see Camp Sites under Stage 1A). Alternatively, from the Cancha de Fútbol trekkers can continue down to a camping area on the Arroyo Rucaco, as described in Stage 2.

Stage 2: Refugio Frey to Refugio Jacob (San Martín)

Make your way easily around Laguna Tonchek to the north-western side on the lake, then begin ascending to the right (ie north-west). The path winds up the loose-rock slopes beside a splashing stream to **Laguna Schmoll**, a smaller and shallower lake that occupies a sparsely vegetated terrace opposite the impressive craggy columns of Cerro Catedral. Cross the tiny outlet and climb on more steeply into a rock gully. Early in the season, snow here may make this section dangerous. Look back for a final view of the lovely upper valley behind you, then continue up through a small sandy basin to reach the **Cancha de Fútbol** after one to 1½ hours.

A sign ('Refugio Jakob') and an arrow painted on a boulder indicate where the route descends into the next valley. Follow red splashes on rocks down a short way to the right, then traverse back briefly leftwards. Now begin a long and very steep descent more or less straight down through dusty, raw talus, continuing down via a dry gully into the scrub. As the gradient eases, head off to the left along a good trail where the beautiful lenga forest fringes the grassy valley floor. The path ducks in and out of the trees to cross a refreshing stream below a tiny cascade at the official camping area, 50 minutes to one hour from Cancha de Fútbol.

Make your way on gently upvalley through the forest, avoiding the soggy open area to the right. The route soon moves out into sporadic ñirre scrub, where the **Cascada Rucaco** (waterfall) comes into sight, then crosses a stream coming down from the left. Red markings guide you on up to a flat stony

ridge dividing the upper valley. Behind you on the adjacent range the now familiar multi-steepled form of Cerro Catedral rises up, looking just as spectacular from this angle. Where the small ridge ends, make a final strenuous 250m climb west-north-west up through steep loose rock to reach the **Paso Brecha Negra** after one to 1½ hours. This is the broad ridge that connects Cerro Tres Reyes with Brecha Negra. There are superb views from here (better from a few paces downhill), with the refugio on Laguna Jakob clearly visible below to the south-west.

Sidle quickly down towards the lake to a small outcrop, then descend steeply via (or beside) a loose chute of coarse gravel back below the scrub line. Turn left where the route meets the main trail coming up through the valley, and follow this through a few boggy areas to cross the small **Arroyo Casa de Piedra** on stepping stones just below where it leaves the **Laguna Jakob**.

A short way on the route intersects with the main path coming up through the valley, and follow this briefly to the left to the **Refugio Jakob (San Martín)** at 1600m, 45 minutes to one hour from the Paso Brecha Negra. This timber and stone refugio stands near a tiny peninsula of the lake. It has a wood stove and can sleep around 30 people. You can buy a few basic provisions and sweet luxuries from the hut warden. The one to 1½-hour return side trip up to Laguna de los Témpanos is not to be missed. The way up to this impressive lake is described at the beginning of Stage 3A.

Camp Sites Some trekkers risk a scenic but unsheltered camp on the shore of Laguna Schmoll, where there is, of course, no firewood. Excellent sites can be found in the forest at the camping area in the upper Valle Rucaco. At Lago Jakob, camping is permitted a few minutes up from the refugio; collect water from the spring water tap at the hut.

Campers should remember it's their responsibility to prevent forest fires and to carry out all rubbish. Always use the toilets provided (even though their state of sanitation leaves a lot to be desired).

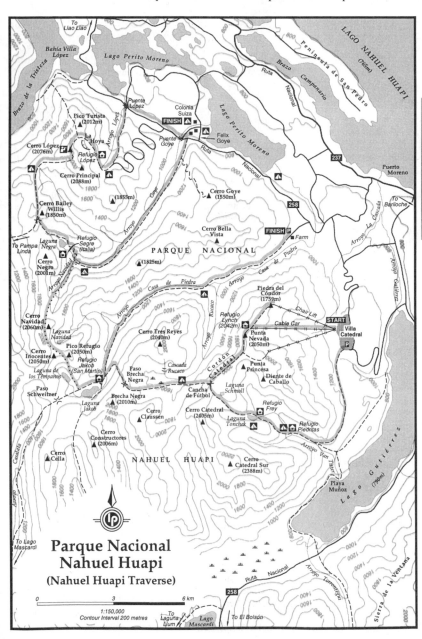

LAKE DISTRICT

Parque Nacional
Nahuel Huapi
(Nahuel Huapi Traverse)

0   3   6 km

1:150,000
Contour Interval 200 metres

Stage 3A: Refugio Jakob (San Martín) to Refugio Segre (Italia)
8.5km, 5 to 7 hours

This section of the trek following a high-level route is harder and more hazardous than other stages. It should not be attempted unless the weather is very good. Early in the season (until about mid-December) crampons and ice axe are likely to be needed to do the route safely.

The hut warden at the Refugio Jakob (who has photographs that clarify the route) can give further advice.

From the camping area head up the steep ridge, then sidle on around westwards over polished limestone slabs (note the scratch marks left by ice age glaciers) to reach **Laguna de los Témpanos** after 25 to 30 minutes. This spectacular little lake lies within a south-facing cirque with sheer rock walls that tower 500m above its icy-blue waters. (An additional route alternative from this point is to continue south-west over **Paso Schweitzer**, then down the valley of the **Arroyo Casalata** to **Lago Mascardi**; the trekking time is around five hours.)

Backtrack along the path (just past where you lose sight of Laguna de los Témpanos) to a rocky spur that comes down from **Pico Refugio**. After carefully studying the route from this point, follow occasional cairns north-north-east to the edge of the steep rock. Ascend a short way around to the left, then move up diagonally rightwards through a steep couloir (rocky chute) involving some hand-climbing, before you ease back left over small snowdrifts to gain the top of the ridge.

Taking care when negotiating more patches of old snow, head north-west along the ridge. After a short distance a rocky pinnacle blocks the way. Avoid this by descending around to the right, and traverse the slopes below the rock face. Continue through a stony area of gully cracks towards an obvious gap in the craggy range ahead, two to three hours on from Laguna de los Témpanos, then move over onto the loose scree slopes on the eastern side of the range above **Laguna Navidad**. This leads to a low point in the main ridge line between **Cerro Inocentes** and **Cerro Navidad**. Make your way 500m up a spur to reach the summit of Cerro Navidad.

Head 400m down the ridge on the northern side of Cerro Navidad. From here a rough route can be followed north-east down more steep and unstable slopes into the narrow canyon at the head of the **Arroyo Navidad**. Early in the season old winter snows may make this section tricky to negotiate. Crossing the cascading stream wherever necessary, follow this down to meet the main path coming up the **Arroyo Goye**, two to three hours on.

Follow red paint markings up through lenga scrub, before beginning a steep spiralling ascent adjacent to waterfalls where the Arroyo Goye spills over 300m cliffs. The path sidles on around westwards over a low rock crest, from where **Laguna Negra** comes into view. Laguna Negra lies in a little trough directly below Cerro Negro, and was evidently named for its proximity to the black-rock mountain as its water is blue. To the north lies the paler brown shale rock of Cerro Bailey Wills (1850m). Cut gently down leftwards across the tiny lake outlet to arrive at **Refugio Segre (Italia)** after a final 60 to 80 minutes.

This two-storey concrete construction (whose bunker-like design can withstand heavy winter snows and small avalanches) is situated at 1650m just across the tiny lake outlet below the towering peak of Cerro Negro (2001m). The refugio has bed space for 60 trekkers and is normally open from mid-November until mid-April.

Camp Sites After leaving Laguna Jakob, no suitable camp sites exist along the route until you come to some grassy areas along the Arroyo Navidad. Ten minutes down from this stream's junction with the Arroyo Goye is the official camping area (see Stage 4B), but it can get overcrowded in high season. There are a few semi-sheltered camp sites in the scrub where you come over the rock crest just before arriving at Refugio Segre, but firewood is very scarce.

Stage 3B: Refugio Jakob (San Martín) to Colonia Suiza
13km, 5 to 7 hours

This is the normal access to Refugio Jakob and is the quickest exit route from the hut. It is also the final stage of the shorter three-day trek known as the Circuito Chico.

Follow the well travelled path down the left (ie west) side of the **Arroyo Casa de Piedra**, crossing the stream just above a waterfall. Descend steeply in a series of switchback curves (known as Las Serpentinas) into the lenga forest, then on more gently down past a side valley that ends in a large cirque at Laguna Navidad (see Stage 3A). From here the route enters the drier central part of the valley (which apparently lies in the rain shadow of ranges to the west). The path leads through mogotes, calafate bushes and ñirres – typical dry land vegetation – to cross the stream on a rickety suspension bridge, two to three hours from the refugio.

Continue down the stony riverflats past where the Arroyo Rucaco flows into the main stream, then climb away left to avoid steeper banks before sidling gradually down into pleasant stands of coigüe trees by the Arroyo Casa de Piedra after 50 minutes to 1¼ hours. The route soon leaves the riverside again, ascending briefly through the forest onto slopes covered by thickets of retama *(Diostea juncea)* as it goes over into a 4WD track. Ahead of you across Lago Nahuel Huapi are the snowcapped mountains of the Sierra Cuyin Manzano. Pass by a tiny car park beside a rustic farm, after which a proper road brings you down to intersect with the Ruta Nacional 258 after 30 to 45 minutes.

Trekkers doing Stage 3B in the reverse direction should watch out for a crude sign ('Refugio San Martín, Laguna Jakob') at the turn-off; going uphill the trekking time is around six hours.

Go left, following the dusty road northwest. The roadsides are fringed by stands of ciprés de la cordillera draped with clavel del campo, a climbing plant that produces attractive daisy-like flowers with a yellow centre and pinkish-white petals. The final section along the road winds around the often steep

southern side of **Lago Perito Moreno**, before turning right (ie off the Ruta Nacional 258) into Felix Goye to reach the holiday village of **Colonia Suiza**, 1½ to two hours from the trail head.

Originally settled by Franco-Swiss farming families in the first decades of the 1900s, today Colonia Suiza is a modest lakeside holiday village with a restaurant, a small store and several camping grounds (see Accommodation & Camping at the start of this trek description). A number of the original houses remain, and the locals even sell homemade fruit preserves and traditional chocolates.

The No 10 bus to Bariloche passes through Colonia Suiza approximately every two hours until around 9 pm.

Camp Sites Once you pass the steep switchbacks of Las Serpentinas, there are camp sites near the route for most of the way until the stream. Thereafter the only good camping is among the coigües before the path climbs up from the Arroyo Casa de Piedra.

Stage 4A: Refugio Segre (Italia) to Refugio López
7.5km, 4 to 5½ hours

Head along the slope's eastern lake shore dotted with chrysanthemum bushes and yellow daisies, making your way on around the northern side of Laguna Negra over cracked rock and snowdrifts persisting well into January. There is a short section of rock here (probably with a fixed rope to hang on to) that requires some careful downclimbing. When you get to the far end of Laguna Negra, climb a short distance up to the right beside the small inlet stream and continue ahead towards a low point in the ridge at the termination of this tiny valley.

First cut up right along gravelly ridges, then double back left through steep and loose rock (guided by a few red paint markings) to reach a gap on the southern side of **Cerro Bailey Willis**, 45 minutes to one hour from Refugio Segre. From here the now familiar form of Cerro Catedral can be made out to the south-east beyond Laguna Negra. Sidle northwards for a further 15 to 20 minutes across a slope of coarse talus above a snow basin to reach a small pass.

From here you get an unobstructed panorama of the magnificent mountain scenery along the Chile-Argentina frontier. The great white rump of Monte Tronador (3478m) is smothered by sprawling glaciers, completely dominating the views of the western horizon. The pointed peak visible to the north of Monte Tronador is Volcán Puntiagudo in Chile, and the highland lake perched in a depression to the south-west is Laguna Lluvú (CAB), (see Other Treks, following).

Drop down north-east, descending briefly rightwards through loose rock before you sidle along the left side of a green boggy gully. In places the foot track is less definite, but the route is well marked with cairns and occasional red paint splashes on rocks. Follow these down left onto moist grassy meadows to cross a brook at the head of a tiny valley (the northern branch of the Arroyo Goye), 40 to 50 minutes from the pass. There is a small (national park-approved) camping area here among low lenga forest.

Head on over a marshy clearing and up out of the ñirre scrub. The indistinct path leads north-east gently up the sparsely vegetated slopes to cross a small stream coming from an obvious rocky gap to the north. From this point begin a very steep ascent up to the right via a gully of frost-shattered rock, whose loose, sharp, plate-like fragments make the going strenuous (and slightly dangerous), passing to the right of a rocky knob to reach a small dip in the range some way north of **Cerro Principal** (2088m). Continue for a short way north-west along the top of this ridge to the 2076m summit of **Cerro López**, 1½ to two hours from the camping area.

Cerro López offers another great panorama, which now includes Volcán Osorno (the perfectly symmetrical snowcapped cone visible beyond Monte Tronador in Chile), while to the north there are sweeping views across the islands, peninsulas and isthmuses that separate Lago Perito Moreno from Lago Nahuel Huapi. For a somewhat fuller view of the lakes below, make your way north along the range for 15 minutes to the slightly lower summit of **Pico Turista**. Trekkers are often thrilled by the sight of condors soaring around these mountain tops.

Following white and red arrows, drop down east along a rocky spur and skirt along the left side of a small glacial cirque known as **La Hoya**. After snowy winters when the spring thaw is rapid a shallow meltwater tarn forms here, but by autumn this basin is normally dry and snow-free. Descend more steeply toward the refugio visible far below you, downclimbing repeatedly at short sections of rock, to arrive at **Refugio López** after a final 50 minutes to 1¼ hours.

The privately owned Refugio López is the most popular and accessible hut on this trek, and sits at around 1600m in a very scenic location overlooking Lago Nahuel Huapi. This two-storey red-brick building has modern amenities (but no hot showers) and there is sleeping capacity for 100 people. Refugio López stays open for the entire trekking season.

Camp Sites The only permitted (and only recommended) camp sites along Stage 4A are at the camping area among the lengas at the head of the Arroyo Goye (northern branch).

Stage 4B: Refugio Segre to Colonia Suiza
12km, 3½ to 4½ hours

This is the usual access to Refugio Segre. It's also an easier alternative route out for trekkers who don't feel confident enough to tackle the high-level traverse of Stage 3A.

Head back down the switchbacks as described at the end of Stage 3A to cross the Arroyo Goye and the Arroyo Navidad just above their confluence. The path dips down into the lenga forest beside the cascading stream to the official camping area (see Camp Sites) after 40 to 50 minutes. Head gently downstream below almost vertical 500m rock walls fronting the opposite side of the valley, crossing through a small area of ñirre and quila before you pass a side valley of the Arroyo Goye (barely visible through the trees).

Continue along the (true) right bank, gradually moving down into evergreen forest dominated by coigüe to where the route joins a rough disused road, 2 to 2½ hours down from the official camping area. At this point you'll see a signpost ('Picada a Laguna Negra/Refugio', which indicates the way back up to the hut). Another unsignposted trail branches off right (south-east) from here up to the 1550m lookout peak of **Cerro Goye**, a side trip of 3½ hours return.

Sidle down above the rushing stream through patches of exotic North American fir trees (which are spreading rapidly at the expense of the native forest), then turn right off the vehicular track at a gate and make your way along the right-hand side of a fence. The last part of this route takes you through stands of ciprés de la cordillera, before dropping down steeply through the coigüe forest to reach the Ruta Nacional 258 after 40 to 50 minutes. Go left along this road, turning left into Felix Goye to arrive in **Colonia Suiza**, a further 10 to 15 minutes on. (For more information on Colonia Suiza, see the final paragraph of Stage 3B). Trekkers hiking from Colonia Suiza up to Refugio Segre will find the trail head at a group of pine trees, 400m east of the road bridge over the Arroyo Goye.

Camp Sites A few poor sites can be found in the scrub just up the slope from Refugio Segre. The only place trekkers are officially permitted to camp anywhere between Refugio Segre and Colonia Suiza is the camping area among the lengas, 10 minutes down from where the path crosses the Arroyo Goye. Numerous other (often used) camp sites can be found along the banks of the Arroyo Goye, but if you decide to camp at any of these you should at least refrain from lighting a fire. See Accommodation & Camping for details of camping grounds in Colonia Suiza.

Stage 5: Refugio López to Colonia Suiza
3.5km, 1½ to 2 hours

Take the path starting from just below the terrace of the refugio. This broad track winds down around to the right over grassy slopes grazed by cattle, crossing two small streams at the source of the **Arroyo López** to meet the end of a road after 15 to 20 minutes.

Follow the road past a small car park, then turn off left onto a foot track leading steeply down into the forest. The route twice crosses the road at hairpin bends, then leads down through previously fire-cleared slopes now regenerating with ñirre scrub and thickets of spiny crucero. Here avoid picking up trails which diverge rightwards back onto the road, and continue on down north into the forest.

The last section of the route follows the right side of the Arroyo López before coming out at a picnic area and kiosk at the **Puente López** (bridge) after a final 1¼ to 1¾ hours. (If you follow the road, you'll end up about halfway along Ruta Nacional 258 between the Puente López and Colonia Suiza). The No 10 bus back to Bariloche passes here roughly every two hours until around 9 pm. From here you can walk to Colonia Suiza in 30 to 40 minutes by following the bitumen 150m along to the right, before turning off south-east (ie to the right) along an unsurfaced road.

Trekkers who do this stage in reverse order should reckon on taking around 3½ hours to reach the Refugio López from Puente López.

Camp Sites Along stage 5 camping is permitted only on lawns below the waterfall 15 minutes down from the Refugio López.

Paso de las Nubes

> **Duration** 3 days minimum
> **Distance** 23 km (51km with side trips)
> **Standard** Medium
> **Start** Pampa Linda
> **Finish** Puerto Frías or Peulla
> **Entry** US$5, permit needed
> **Season** November-May
> **Summary** Explores the area on the eastern side of the glacier-smothered Monte Tronador; the trek can be extended by continuing across the border into Chile.

The 1335m Paso de las Nubes (literally 'pass of the clouds') lies among saturated rainforest and hanging icefalls at the eastern foot of the mighty three-summit massif of Monte Tronador. This aptly named pass lies on a continental watershed, sending its waters into the Pacific on its southern side, via the Río Manso and Río Puelo, and into the Atlantic on its northern side, via Lago Nahuel Huapi. The route over the Paso de las Nubes is often done as a 'trans-Andean trek' by continuing over the Paso de Pérez Rosales to the isolated village of Peulla on Lago Todos los Santos.

MAPS

Recommended is the contoured trekking map of the Refugios, Sendas y Picadas series titled *Trekking 2* and produced by the CAB at a scale of 1:50,000; it's available from the Club itself or from bookstores and kiosks in Bariloche for US$6. The larger-format 1:100,000 colour sheet of the same series titled simply *Parque Nacional Nahuel Huapi* is available for US$12, and is quite a good alternative.

The Argentine IGM 1:100,000 sheet *Llao Llao* (Neuquén, No 4172-22) completely covers this area. This map (also used for the Nahuel Huapi Traverse trek) gives poor topographical detail and doesn't shown the trekking route correctly.

A Chilean IGM 1:50,000 sheet, *Monte Tronador* (Section H, No 46), includes a good part of the frontier area on the Argentine side and is especially useful for trekkers who continue on to Peulla in Chile.

DAYS REQUIRED

The average trekking time from Pampa Linda to Puerto Frías is two full days, but the recommended side trips to the Salto Garganta del Diablo and Refugio Otto Meiling will lengthen the trek by one day each. Extending the trek by continuing on to Peulla requires at least one additional (very long) day.

TREKKING STANDARD

The trek follows a much travelled but often poorly marked path for most of the way. Apart from a short section on top of the Paso de las Nubes and the side trip to the Refugio Otto Meiling, the route is completely within the shelter of the forest. Snow often lies on the pass well into January. The section between the upper camp near the Glaciar Frías and Laguna Frías is not maintained and there are numerous fallen logs and quila (bamboo) canes over the path; here the going is especially slippery and tiresome after rain. Carry a stove as dry firewood is scarce at most camp sites along the way.

From Puerto Frías many trekkers continue on into Chile via a good dirt road to Peulla on Lago Todos los Santos. This isolated 27km section across the Paso de Pérez Rosales is not accessible to outside traffic, and is travelled only by a regular bus service and occasional border control vehicles.

The walk can be done in either direction, although for transport reasons south-to-north will probably be the most convenient. As this is a frontier area, be sure to carry proper identification. The trek has an overall rating of *medium*. The trekking distance from Pampa Linda to Puerto Frías is 23km (or around 51 with the side trips of Stage 1A and Stage 1B).

ACCOMMODATION & CAMPING

Except for the Refugio Otto Meiling, which is on an optional side trip route, there are no refugios for walkers along the Paso de las Nubes route and all trekking parties must therefore carry a tent.

At Pampa Linda there's a large free camping area *(camping agreste)* without facilities. Opposite is the very large CAB-run camping ground, which has facilities (including hot showers) and costs US$4 per person. Almost opposite the guardería is the *Albergue Pampa Linda*, which has dormitory accommodation for US$8 per person. Next door is the more up-market *Hostería Pampa Linda* (☎ & fax 0944-27049 in Bariloche, or direct by radio-telephone on ☎ 0944-23757), which offers rooms for US$45/60 single/double. The hostería has a good restaurant.

Puerto Frías has no accommodation (although personnel of the Gendarmería Nacional occasionally invite trekkers to stay at their quarters), but the *Hostería Blest* (☎ 0944-94224) at Puerto Blest offers double rooms from US$65 with half pension. For those continuing on to Chile, there are several hospedajes for budget travellers in the village of Peulla (on Lago Todos los Santos in Chile) as well as the rather more up-market *Hotel Peulla* (☎ 258041) with rooms from about US$20. There are several pensiones in Peulla where meals are served, and a CONAF-run camping ground (without facilities).

SUPPLIES

Bariloche is the best place to buy your provisions. The CAB camping ground at Pampa Linda has a well-stocked kiosk which sells most of the things needed by campers and trekkers; no other supplies are available on the way.

Trekkers continuing on to Peulla should remember that raw agricultural products and dairy foods may not be taken across the border into Chile. The only possibility of buying provisions in Peulla is a tiny shop at the back of the Hotel Peulla.

GETTING TO/FROM THE TREK

The trek begins at Pampa Linda, 77km by road from Bariloche via Villa Mascardi. From late December to the end of February Trans RM (☎ 23918) runs a daily bus to Pampa Linda (although the billed destination on the buses is 'Cerro Tronador') leaving at 9 am from the CAB office in Bariloche. Cerros Patagónicos (☎ 24975) at Perito Moreno 1160 also runs buses to Pampa Linda. The fare on both buses is US$12, and the trip takes 2½ hours (there is sometimes a delay at the park entrance gate at the Río Manso). The buses return from Pampa Linda at 5 pm.

During the extended summer tourist season (late November to mid-April), various companies run daily excursions to Pampa Linda. Tours normally leave at around 8 am from Bariloche and arrive at around 1 pm. The return fare is about US$30, which usually includes a boat trip across Lago Mascardi. Hitchhiking to Pampa Linda is only advisable in the busy tourist season.

The walk finishes at Puerto Frías. From here a tourist boat across Laguna Frías to Puerto Alegre connects with a bus to Puerto Blest on a branch of Lago Nahuel Huapi. At Puerto Blest catamarans run across Lago Nahuel Huapi to Puerto Pañuelo (at Llao Llao), from where you catch the frequent local (No 20) bus for the final stretch back to Bariloche. The combined cost of these fares comes to around US$22.

There is an alternative exit route into Chile that takes you from Puerto Frías to Peulla. An extremely expensive (US$37!) bus service operates along the very scenic and otherwise untravelled 26km international road linking these tiny settlements, so most trekkers opt to walk (as described here in Stage 3). Remember that it is prohibited to bring most unprocessed agricultural foodstuffs into Chile. From December to February there are two daily launches from Peulla to Petrohué, departing at 8 am (but no boat on Mondays) and 4 pm. The trip across Lago Todos los Santos costs about US$7 and takes 2½ hours. At Petrohué minibuses to Puerto Montt meet arriving boats.

THE TREK
Stage 1A: Pampa Linda to Salto Garganta del Diablo/Piedra Pérez
17km return, 3½ to 4½ hours return

Although it follows an often dusty road for most of the way, the return side trip into the head of the Río Manso at the foot of Monte Tronador should not be missed. For safety reasons the road is open only to upward traffic until 2 pm, and to downward traffic after 4 pm. If you arrive with a return day bus tour from Bariloche, the trip up to the Salto Garganta del Diablo will probably be included.

From Pampa Linda, walk north-west along the road past the guardería and hostería. Five minutes on you pass the signposted path turn-off to the Saltillo de los Nalcas (which is also the trail head for the route to Refugio Tronador – see Other Treks following). The road rises steadily beside the upper Río Manso, crossing the (northern branch) of the river shortly before it comes to a car park at a lookout point, 1 to 1½ hours on.

From here you get a sensational view up to the **Glaciar Manso**, which ends abruptly at a hanging icefall above a 750m high precipice on Monte Tronador. Enormous blocks of ice continually drop off the icefall and are smashed to pieces as they hit the ground, where the pulverised ice re-forms as a glacier. This lower section of the Glaciar Manso is known as the **Ventisquero Negro** (or 'black glacier') because large quantities of moraine and broken rock are mixed in with the ice. A short trail leads down to the edge of the Ventisquero Negro.

Head on for 15 to 20 minutes to the **confitería** (see Side Trip following) at the end of the road; snacks and refreshments are available here. A foot track from the upper end of the car park here continues for a further 20 to 25 minutes up to the stream at the base of an impressive cirque at the head of the valley. Up to your left the long and spectacular waterfall known as the **Salto Garganta del Diablo** shoots down from the side of the Glaciar Manso, while numerous other high cascades emerge from the icefalls up to the right. The agile can climb up to where the Salto thunders into a tiny chasm, spraying out mist that settles on the mossy rocks.

Trekkers who visit the Salto Garganta del Diablo should be mindful that there is a risk, although relatively low, of ice breaking off the hanging glaciers directly above and falling into the upper valley.

Side Trip to Piedra Pérez/Filo Clerk Trekkers who decide they still haven't had their fill of breathtaking scenery (and who don't mind a strenuous climb) can do a rewarding side trip to a lookout point up on the ridge to the north. It takes an additional two to three hours return.

Pick up the (unsignposted) path behind the *confitería* and head 50m down right across makeshift bridges over small channels in the glacial stream. A graded foot track snakes its way up through the coigüe forest, with the odd fallen trunk to clamber under or over. The route steepens as it rides a narrow spur covered with lengas up to the top of a broad ridge known as **Filo Clerk** (which is sometimes used by andinists as an alternative route to the summits of Monte Tronador).

Follow white paint markings a few hundred metres left (ie north-west) along the scrubby ridge past **Piedra Pérez**, a small but prominent tooth-shaped pinnacle visible from down in the valley, to reach a lookout point 60 to 80 minutes from the confitería.

This part of the ridge offers a classic close-up view of the **Glaciar Castaño Overo**. The crevasses and seracs of the glacier terminate in an impressive icefall that – like the Glaciar Manso – hangs over a mighty precipice. A dozen or so meltwater cascades spill out from the edge of the ice. Visible on the ridge beyond the glacier is the path going up to Refugio Otto Meiling (see Stage 1B), while to the south-west you should just be able to make out the old Refugio Tronador (see Other Treks following) on a high rock ridge just left of the Glaciar Manso icefalls. From up here you also get an excellent view back into the upper valley of the Río Manso.

The return to the confitería is via the ascent route.

Camp Sites Camping is permitted only at the two camping grounds at Pampa Linda.

Stage 1B: Pampa Linda to Refugio Otto Meiling
21km return, 5 to 6½ hours return
This is another highly scenic return day or overnight side trip that is recommended to all trekkers.

After signing in at the guardería, take the vehicle track heading roughly north past a signposted trail diverging rightwards up to Laguna Ilón (see Pampa Linda to Refugio López in the Other Treks section following). This 4WD road brings you through coigüe forest and small clearings intermittently strewn with the striking orange flowers of the amancay to reach the camping area at the **Río Castaño Overo** after 30 to 40 minutes. Cross the small glacial river on a makeshift footbridge and continue a short way ahead to a trail junction, where the way to the Paso de las Nubes departs right.

Bear left along the more prominent 4WD road, which soon begins a steady winding ascent through attractive mature coigüe

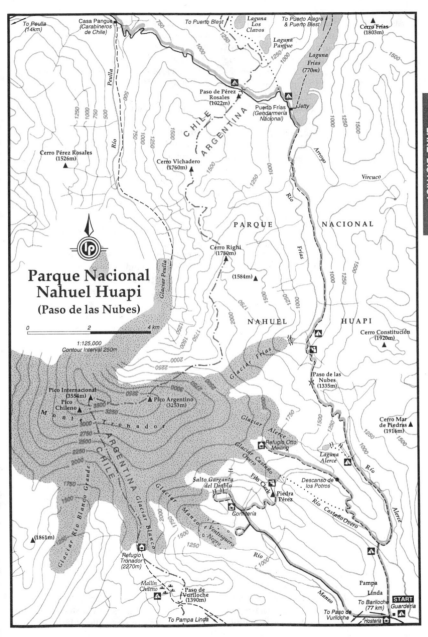

Parque Nacional Nahuel Huapi
(Paso de las Nubes)

0   2   4 km

1:125,000
Contour Interval 250m

forest. Following the vehicle track only for short sections, shortcut between the long switchback curves to pass a path turn-off going to the Glaciar Castaño Overo. The side trip to this glacier, which ends in a spectacular icefall, takes around one hour return. The final section climbs steeply through lenga forest to reach the top of the ridge, 1¼ to 1¾ hours from the camping area.

Make your way gently up along this broad ridge top to **Descanso de los Potros**, where the 4WD track ends at a grassy area near the upper limit of the lenga scrub. A well-marked path sidles on around to the left above high bluffs on the southern side of the ridge, giving wonderful views across to the adjacent Glaciar Castãno Overo and the various summits of Monte Tronador behind it. Cross back up to the right over a small snowfield, before following large cairns and marker stakes up the bare rocky ridge top to arrive at the **Refugio Otto Meiling** after 60 to 80 minutes.

Refugio Otto Meiling stands at an altitude of around 2000m, a short way below the permanent snow line. The refugio's upstairs loft has sleeping capacity for 60 mountaineers and trekkers and offers gas-cooked meals and simple refreshments. In summer, the Refugio Otto Meiling serves as the base for courses in snow and ice climbing organised by the Club Andino Bariloche. Its location offers a superb panorama taking in Pampa Linda, the Paso de las Nubes and Cerro Catedral directly to the east. Descend via the same route.

Camp Sites At Pampa Linda there is a camping ground with modern facilities run by the CAB, as well as the national park's free camping area. There are a dozen or so camp sites at the officially approved camping area along the true right bank of the Río Castaño Overo. There is space for four or five tents in the shelter of rocks near Refugio Otto Meiling, where trekkers may camp with the permission of the hut warden in reasonable weather (this side of Monte Tronador is sheltered from the westerlies).

Stage 1C: Pampa Linda to Upper Río Frías
13km, 4 to 5½ hours

As described in Stage 1B, walk 30 to 40 minutes along the vehicle track from Pampa Linda to the **Río Castaño Overo**. Cross the river and turn right at the path junction (where the route up to the Refugio Otto Meiling continues left) and follow the remains of an ancient road north-eastwards to meet the **Río Alerce**. Apart from a short section where you have to climb over fallen logs at a tight bend in the river (where the old vehicle track simply fords and re-fords the milky waters), the route continues on gently up along the western bank through pleasant coigüe and lenga forest to reach the camping area at the edge of a mallín after a further 1¼ to 1½ hours.

From the camping area, an excellent side trip taking around two hours return can be done to **Laguna Alerce**. Head up the true right bank of the Río Alerce to the base of a cliff on the left side of the gushing meltwater cascade. A steep climb over rock slabs leads into a tiny moraine-filled upper valley, which is followed (crossing the stream where necessary) to this impressive glacial lake lying directly under the hanging glacier known as **Glaciar Alerce**.

Make an easy ford of the small Río Alerce and cut directly north across the sodden ground covered with scattered ñirres and thickets of chapel *(Escallonia virgata)*, a small shrub with fragrant white flowers. Pick up the path at the edge of the forest and begin a steadily steepening climb, making a few quick zigzags into the lenga scrub before the gradient softens. The route continues up more gradually, following cairns and paint on rocks northwards over grassy alpine meadows to reach the **Paso de las Nubes** after 1½ to 2 hours.

The 1335m pass is too scrubby to give any real vistas, but as you descend you pass small lookout points which grant a clear view down through the glacially formed valley ahead as far as the sombre-looking Laguna Frías. The descent is much steeper on this side of the Paso de las Nubes. The path takes you directly down into the forest to cross a fast-flowing stream on stepping stones before coming out onto a small rocky outcrop.

Here you stand immediately opposite the **Glaciar Frías**, an amazing icefall sprawling down from the névés on the eastern side of Monte Tronador. This glacier feeds a surging waterfall and numerous other smaller cascades that form the **Río Frías**, and drops the occasional car-sized chunk of ice over a high cliff face. Drop down along the small rocky ridge into the valley floor, then recross the gravelly stream to arrive at the official camping area, 50 minutes to 1¼ hours from the pass.

Camp Sites There is an official national park camping area on the upper Río Alerce just before where the route fords the stream. The scenic grassy meadows on the southern side of the pass are a more tempting place to camp, but choose a dry and well-sheltered site. The camping area at the end of Stage 1C is in a spectacular location opposite the Glaciar Frías, and it has about a dozen scattered sites under the coigües. As most trekking parties that cross the Paso de las Nubes camp here, firewood can be hard to find.

Stage 2: Upper Río Frías to Puerto Frías
10km, 3¼ to 4½ hours
Pick up the trail below the camping area and begin the long trek downvalley. This route avoids the open waterlogged ground near the banks of the river by maintaining a slightly higher course along slopes on the eastern side of the valley through wet temperate rainforest dominated by coigüe, mañío and laurel. The moist conditions favour climbing epiphytes such as the botellita and the estrellita, whose delicate crimson flowers stand out on trunks.

The foot track is unmaintained, leading through dense thickets of quila and colihue bamboo and over, under or around numerous trees that have fallen across the way. The going is tiresome, slow and monotonous, with only the occasional glimpse through the trees of the (usually snowcapped until mid-summer) range on the adjacent side of the valley. The path improves gradually, however,

with logs laid along boggy sections. It passes small camp sites and old bridges shortly before it meets the Río Frías, 2½ to 3½ hours from the camping area at the head of the valley.

Follow the true right (eastern) bank of the river for 15 to 20 minutes, then cross its deep, murky waters on a large fallen log secured by sturdy hand wires. This improvised bridge (which the former Mapuche inhabitants of this area would have called a *cuy cuy*) dips into the river, and at times of high water it may be better to cross by another, slightly higher, double-log bridge about 10 minutes downstream. Head on now to the left of the Río Frías through stands of lengas and large alerces, coming onto a long-abandoned road just before you pass a memorial to members of the Argentine Gendarmería Nacional who died in a plane crash here in 1952.

The route soon skirts the south-western side of **Laguna Frías** to arrive at the small landing jetty and an outpost of the Gendarmería Nacional at **Puerto Frías** after a final 30 to 40 minutes. Laguna Frías is a superb example of a glacial trough. The lake is surrounded by sheer-sided mountains that rise directly from the shore, giving Laguna Frías a dramatic fjord-like appearance. All trekkers (even those returning to Bariloche) must notify the Gendarmería Nacional when they arrive. Trekkers continuing to Peulla in Chile pass through customs here (if you want to leave early it's possible to have your passport exit-stamped the night before).

Trekkers not going on to Chile begin the long trip back to Bariloche by catching a boat to Puerto Alegre (at the northern end of Laguna Frías). In summer boats leave for Puerto Alegre at approximately 10.30 am, 1.30, 4 and/or 6 pm, and passengers are shuttled on directly by bus to Puerto Blest (the western-most point of Lago Nahuel Huapi). From Puerto Blest, catamarans leave for Puerto Pañuelo (at Llao Llao) at around 9 am, 4.30 and 6 pm, but with the morning boat/bus combination there is usually no *direct* onward connection to Bariloche.

A worthwhile way to use any spare time at Puerto Blest is to do the 1½-hour return walk to the **Lago Los Cántaros**, whose outlet stream cascades in several picturesque waterfalls. The lake is fringed by stands of ancient alerces, of which one specimen is believed to be around 1500 years old.

Camp Sites Camping is possible, though not recommended, in the damp forest along the first half of Stage 2. Better sites can be found along the true right bank of the Río Frías. There is a camping area at Puerto Frías, just up from the boat jetty (fetch water from the tap outside the Gendarmería Nacional). There is also free camping at Puerto Blest.

Stage 3: Puerto Frías to Peulla
26km, 6 to 9 hours
Be sure to have your passport exit-stamped at the gendarmería building before setting out.

Follow the good dirt road around the south-west side of Laguna Frías. The road climbs steadily in switchbacks to reach the **Paso de Pérez Rosales** after 45 minutes to one hour. The pass lies in the lush rainforest at 1022m above sea level on the Argentina-Chile border.

Begin the descent into Chile past tiny pampas and an abandoned farmhouse on your left, which now serves as an apparently free refugio. The road gradually winds down through more dense forest of coigüe and arrayán to reach **Casa Pangue** after two to three hours. This post of the Carabineros de Chile looks out up the valley towards the spectacular snowbound northern slopes of Monte Tronador. From here trekkers can opt to do the long (20km return) day hike up the gravelly east bank of the Río Peulla to the snout of the receding **Glaciar Peulla**.

Follow the road 3km downstream and cross to the southern side of the Río Peulla on a suspension bridge. The road heads west across the flat valley floor for two to three hours, before swinging around through a wide expanse of soggy grassland. Continue south for another 1½ to two hours to the Chilean customs post just outside **Peulla**. Passports must be presented here and luggage may be inspected.

Peulla has a CONAF guardería and several moderately priced places to stay as well as

the more up-market *Hotel Peulla*. While in Peulla stroll around to the **Cascada de los Novios** waterfall, or do the three-hour return hike up to the **Laguna Margarita**. The tiny harbour is 1km on from the village. Throughout the tourist season (December to March) launches running across the lake to Petrohué leave at 8 am (but there's no boat on Monday) and 4 pm. The trip takes about 2½ hours.

Camp Sites There are excellent camp sites on little meadows 10 to 15 minutes down from the Paso de Pérez Rosales. Camping is also possible (but discouraged by the park authorities) in many places along the Valle Peulla. There is also a CONAF-run camping area (without facilities) at Peulla. At Petrohué a CONAF camping ground charges a fee per tent site.

Other Treks in Parque Nacional Nahuel Huapi

The Club Andino Bariloche (CAB) and the staff at the APN Intendencia in Bariloche can advise you on other treks in the Nahuel Huapi area. The local publication *Las Montañas de Bariloche* by Toncek Arko also has many other good route suggestions.

Sebastián de la Cruz, a mountain guide based in Bariloche, was kind enough to contribute information to several of the following trek descriptions.

CERRO OTTO
Situated little more than 5km west from the centre of town, the 1405m Cerro Otto is Bariloche's 'backyard mountain'. The two to three-hour walk up to Cerro Otto makes a pleasant introduction to the Nahuel Huapi area. Take the road turn-off from Avenida Los Pioneros, following sections of foot track that shortcut the hairpin bends to Refugio Berghof. This CAB hut standing beside a mountain tarn is open all year and has sleeping space for 30 people. A path continues west along the ridge to Cerro Otto,

which grants nice views over the lake. The descent can be made either by taking the cable car (which operates daily), by returning on foot the way you came, or by continuing south-west via the lookout point of Piedra de Habsburgo to Lago Gutiérrez.

REFUGIO TRONADOR (REFUGIO VIEJO)

The Refugio Tronador was the first refugio built by the CAB on Monte Tronador. Today this small arched-stone building (with a capacity for 10 people) is also known as the Refugio Viejo ('old refugio'), because it has largely been superseded by the newer and larger Refugio Otto Meiling (see Stage 1B of the Paso de las Nubes trek). The CAB restored this historic hut in the southern summer of 1996. Standing on a high ridge of the main Cordillera, the Refugio Tronador offers superb views of both sides of the Lake District.

Five minutes west of Pampa Linda, the path (signposted 'Cascada de las Nalcas') leads off the road and across the young Río Manso. The route soon passes the left-hand path going to the waterfall, then follows the Río Cauquenes past another turn-off going to Cerro Volcánico (see following section) up across the Paso Vuriloche. This pass was a favoured trans-Andean crossing route of the indigenous Mapuche people, and today marks the Argentina/Chile frontier. The path continues to **Mallín Chileno**, a beautiful alpine meadow, then follows a rocky ridge north-west to the refugio, which is inside Argentine territory – just a few paces east of the international border – at 2270m.

The best map to use is the 1:50,000 sheet of the Refugios, Sendas y Picadas series titled *Trekking 2*. The trek is recommended as an overnight trip, but remember that (especially in January and early February) the hut may already be full of andinists and trekkers when you arrive. Mallín Chileno is a good place to camp.

CERRO VOLCÁNICO

The climb to the 1861m summit of Cerro Volcánico is another excellent long day (or overnight) return trek from Pampa Linda.

The route fords the Río Cauquenes where it leaves the path to Refugio Tronador (described previously) and follows a large side stream southwards. A gentle climb eastwards leads to Laguna La Rosada, from where the trail continues south-west through mallín meadows then on steeply through lenga forest onto a flat, windy ridge that gradually brings you up to the summit. Cerro Volcánico offers a fine view down to Lago Fonck and Lago Hess in the upper basin of the Río Manso between Cerro Cretón and Cerro Granítico. Use the CAB's 1:50,000 *Trekking 2* map.

REFUGIO NEUMEYER

This is an easy and very well-sheltered area that makes a good option for two or three days trekking if the weather looks unstable. From the main Ruta Nacional 258 on the way to El Bolsón, a turn-off heads south-west up the Arroyo Ñirecó, before entering the broader side valley of the Arroyo Challhuaco. The road leads to Refugio Neumeyer, a well-equipped CAB hut, from where you can do a variety of nice day walks.

Where the road crosses the Arroyo Ñirecó a foot track turns off to the right (west). A path continues along the eastern bank of the stream to the Refugio Ñirecó located beside a mallín at the head of the Valle Ñirecó. From the refugio a rough and more difficult route leads west up to a pass and follows the range north for a way before descending via the Arroyo Melgurejo to the eastern shore of Lago Gutiérrez.

The best map to use is the 1:50,000 sheet *Trekking 3* of the CAB's Refugios, Sendas y Picadas series. Refugio Neumeyer is accessible from Bariloche by private vehicle or tour bus (ask at the CAB office); you can walk to the trail head in half a day.

PAMPA LINDA TO REFUGIO LOPEZ

This excellent four or five-day trek is similar to the Nahuel Huapi Traverse featured earlier, but offers much wilder scenery and is suited to more experienced parties. An old road leads from near the Guardería Pampa Linda across the Río Alerce (a knee-high wade), then climbs up between Cerro del Viento and Cerro Punta Negra to a minor pass (which is nevertheless on the Pacific-Atlantic watershed). The descent dips north to Laguna Ilón, a lovely alpine lake with a basic refugio on its northern shore. The route continues eastwards through a gap between Cerro Capitán and Cerro Punta Negra, then descends past the tiny Laguna Jujuy to Laguna Callvu (Azul). From Laguna Callvu you go north-east via another gap in the ridge south of Cerro Cristal, before dropping down to Laguna Lluvú (or CAB) where there is also a basic refugio.

From Laguna Lluvú (or CAB) the route descends to the Arroyo Lluvunco and over the Bailey Willis range to connect with the Refugio Segre to Refugio Cerro Villa López route (see Stage 4A of Nahuel Huapi Traverse). Another route possibility is to continue down the Arroyo Lluvunco to intersect with a path (an old road) leading north-east along the southern shore of Brazo Tristeza to Bahía López on Lago Nahuel Huapi.

See the Paso de las Nubes and Nahuel Huapi Traverse treks earlier in this chapter for transport details. Two maps of the 1:50,000 Refugios, Sendas y Picadas series *Trekking 1* and *Trekking 2* cover the trekking route. You can also use the larger-format colour map of this series titled *Parque Nacional Nahuel Huapi* scaled at 1:100,000.

AROUND LAGO MASCARDI

Lago Mascardi has a rough 'U' shape formed by two unequal twin arms on either side of a peninsula. From the north-eastern side of Lago Mascardi (near the Pacific-Atlantic watershed) a path leads around the lake's western shore, cutting off the peninsula as it climbs to Laguna Llum, a tranquil lake surrounded by rainforest. The route continues over the main ridge north of Cerro General Justo, then drops back down to the lakeside. The route follows this western arm (Brazo Tronador) around to cross a suspension footbridge over the Río Manso 1.5km before meeting the Pampa Linda road. Alternatively, trekkers can make their way up the Arroyo Callvuco (or Azul) to Laguna Callvu (or Azul) to meet the Pampa Linda to Bahía López route described earlier.

Use the large format 1:100,000 colour map of the Refugios, Sendas y Picadas series titled *Parque Nacional Nahuel Huapi*. This is a two-day trek with a camp at Laguna Llum. The most reliable access is by daily CAB-organised bus to and from Pampa Linda (see the Paso de las Nubes trek for details) and Bariloche.

Parque Nacional Alerce Andino

Ostensibly a reserve for the giant alerce, an extremely slow-growing native conifer (known to the Mapuche as lahuén), Parque Nacional Alerce Andino is in the *precordillera*, or Andean foothills 25km to the east of the Chilean Lake District city of Puerto Montt. Despite its proclamation as a national park in 1984, the area still attracts a surprisingly low number of visitors.

GENERAL INFORMATION
Geographical Features
Comprising 392 sq km, Parque Nacional Alerce Andino occupies much of the prom-

ontory between the broad bay of Seno Reloncaví and its elongated eastern arm known as the Estuario de Reloncaví. Here, the Pacific coast begins to break up into the maze of islands, fjords and channels that typify western Patagonia.

At the hub of the park, two small valleys (of the upper Río Lenca and the Río Chaica) run between granite ranges whose highest summits surpass 1500m. Although this rugged landscape bears the unmistakable signs of intensive glaciation during past ice ages – most notably its dozen or so beautiful glacial lakes – there are no glaciers left in Alerce

Andino. On its north-eastern side the park almost touches Lago Chapo, a natural lake whose water level has recently been raised as part of a hydroelectric project.

Natural History

Luxuriant montane rainforest grows – at an almost visible speed – at all but the highest elevations. Two trees particularly favoured by Andino Alerce's moist and mild climatic conditions are the tiaca *(Caldcluvia paniculata)*, whose elongated, serrated leaves bear a superficial resemblance to those of raulí (a beech species absent from the park), and the ulmo *(Eucryphia cordifolia)*, which is found up to an altitude of 500m. When flowering in January and February, the ulmo is covered by fragrant blossoms. Hummingbirds, or picaflores, thrive on such nectar-bearing flowers, and because of their surprising lack of timidity these delicate birds can often be observed from close range. Unfortunately, horseflies known as tábanos also gain strength feeding on nectar, but soon start to crave the protein-rich blood of passing trekkers.

Other common tree species found in Alerce Andino include coigüe de Chiloé, tepa, tineo, canelo, arrayán, avellano, ciprés de las Guaitecas – and, of course, the majestic alerce tree, or lahuén. The area's relative inaccessibility has prevented major exploitation of its stands of giant alerces. The trees are now saved from the woodcutters, and the most ancient and massive specimens may exceed 4m in diameter and reach several thousand years of age.

Among the numerous creepers and vines of the rainforest understorey are the copihue, whose beautiful large crimson flowers are the floral emblem of Chile. The related coicopihue *(Philesia magellanica)* has somewhat less exuberant red flowers, which are nevertheless quite lovely. Less discreet climbers are the pilpil de canasta *(Campsidium valdivianum)*, recognisable by its pinkish tubular flowers, and the voqui, or lilinquén *(Grisenlinia ruscifolia)*, a small bushy plant with alternate tear-shaped leaves that yields clusters of tiny (but unpalatable) deep purple, cherry-like fruit. A similar-looking (though unrelated) species is the quilineja, or azahar *(Luzuriaga radicans)*.

Native fauna is much less conspicuous, but the shy pudú, the world's smallest species of deer, and the marsupial llaca, also called monito del monte, are occasionally spotted in the forest. The vegetarian coipo and the carnivorous huillín are probably inhabitants of Andino Alerce's lakes and streams. Catty cousins, the puma and the far smaller huiña, are the largest terrestrial predators.

Climate

Its proximity to the coast gives the area a mild maritime climate, but also high annual rainfall. Precipitation ranges from 3300mm in the lower sectors to maximum levels of 4500mm on the highest ranges, usually falling as snow down to 800m (or lower) in winter.

Place Names

As usual, Mapuche names figure abundantly in the nomenclature. The local Mapuche communities held collective meetings in the area of Reloncaví (the name of both the sound and long fjord-like estuary that surround the park on three sides), whose name translates as 'valley of the festivities'. Pangal means 'grove of nalcas', a reference to the giant Chilean rhubarb *(Gunnera tinctoria)* that grows prolifically in Alerce Andino. Chaica means 'raft' in Mapuche (perhaps an allusion to a crossing point on this river), while Quilaleu means 'stream of bamboo'. Sargazo was a Chilean hermit settler who established a little farm on the Río Sargazo.

PRACTICAL INFORMATION
Information Sources

There are three ranger stations in Parque Nacional Alerce Andino. The administrative office is at the Guardería Chamiza, at the park's northern entrance gate, and the Guardería Sargazo is 8km farther on along the road. The southern sector of the park is managed by the Guardería Chaica.

See also Trekking Bases at the beginning of this chapter for CONAF's main regional offices in Puerto Montt.

LAKE DISTRICT

Permits & Regulations

Parque Nacional Alerce Andino is one of the least restrictive parks in Chile. There is no entrance fee, and wild camping is permitted provided trekkers exercise extreme caution with fire and carry out all rubbish.

When to Trek

You are best to trek in Parque Nacional Alerce Andino between late November and mid-April. In January the tábanos are a nuisance.

Laguna Fría

Duration 2 days minimum
Distance 34km
Standard Easy-Medium
Start/Finish Correntoso
Entry Free, no permit needed
Season November-April
Summary A short return trek past highland lakes amongst luxuriant rainforest where ancient alerces grow.

This delightful trek leads into the heart of the park, where several charming lakes nestle in the cool temperate forest.

MAPS

Two 1:50,000 IGM sheets cover the central part of the park: *Correntoso* (Section H, No 52) and *Lenca* (Section H, No 61). These maps do not accurately show local roads and trekking routes, but are otherwise reasonably accurate (note that on these sheets the Río Lenca is incorrectly given as the Río Chaica and vice versa).

The guardaparque at the Guardería Chamiza has free CONAF maps of Alerce Andino which indicate trekking routes quite accurately.

DAYS REQUIRED

If you trek from the Guardería Chamiza (via the Pangal route – see Stage 1), the trek takes about 3 days return, but from the Guardería

Sargazo (ie Stage 2) the return trekking time is only two days.

TREKKING STANDARD

Although the guardaparques do their best to keep Alerce Andino's foot tracks open, the ferocious growth rate of the southern Lake District vegetation makes this a difficult task. Occasional fallen tree trunks have to be ducked or climbed over, and vigorous quila (native bamboo) leans over the route in many places. Heavy winter snowfalls can flatten the quila canes, completely obscuring the path. From time to time enthusiastic parties of volunteers (organised by CONAF, the Chilean scouts, or Operation Raleigh International) recut the trails, so the trek's level of difficulty will depend largely on how recently such work has been done. Trekkers can help to keep the trails open by removing overhanging vegetation – but don't overdo it.

CONAF's plans to cut a foot track from Laguna Fría through to Laguna Triángulo (in Alerce Andino's southern Chaica sector – see Other Treks) have been abandoned, so trekkers must backtrack via the same route.

The Laguna Fría trek is rated *easy to medium* and has a total distance of some 34km return.

ACCOMMODATION & CAMPING

See Trekking Bases for a few tips on places to stay in nearby Puerto Montt.

There is little or no accommodation near the start of the trek at Correntoso. The park has four refugios: at Río Pangal, Río Sargazo, Laguna Sargazo and Laguna Fría; these refugios are left open and their use is free of charge. There is also a free camping area (without facilities) known as *Campamento Pangal* just off the road between the Guardería Chamiza and the Río Chamiza bridge. Wild camping within the park is permitted, but trekkers should choose their camp sites carefully, with consideration to the minimum-impact code.

SUPPLIES

The village of Correntoso has a small grocery store selling basic provisions, which is likely

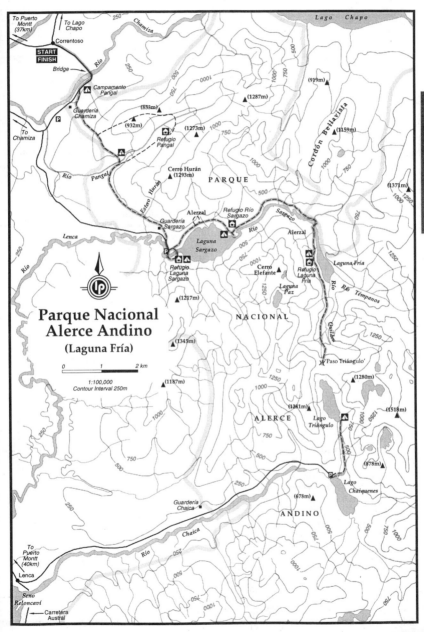

to be your last option after leaving Puerto Montt.

GETTING TO/FROM THE TREK

For those without private transport, the trek begins and ends at the village of Correntoso, 37km east by road from Puerto Montt. Together the two companies Buses Fierro and Buses Río Pato run five daily buses to Lago Chapo, which pass through Correntoso, 14km before the lake. The last bus leaves the Puerto Montt bus terminal at around 5 pm. The fare is US$1.50 for this pleasant one-hour trip through green farming country and patches of rainforest. The buses begin the return journey to Puerto Montt shortly after arriving at Lago Chapo.

Private vehicles can be left at the Guardería Chamiza or at the end of the road at the upper Río Lenca.

THE TREK
Stage 1: Correntoso to Guardería Sargazo
8km, 2½ to 3½ hours

From the bus stop in Correntoso (on the main road to Lago Chapo), take the turn-off (signposted 'El Salto') leading past wooden houses to cross the **Río Chamiza** bridge. Because water has been diverted for the hydroelectric scheme on Lago Chapo, the once-powerful cataract known as the **Salto Chamiza** is now little more than a pitiful trickle. Continue along the road past the **Campamento Pangal** (see Camp Sites) to reach the **Guardería Chamiza** at the park entrance gate after 40 to 50 minutes. All visitors should sign in here; the friendly and knowledgeable resident guardaparque can advise you on the trail conditions.

The road continues for about 7km on to the Guardería Sargazo, but the trekking route takes the foot track leading up south-east into the forest to reach a signposted fork after 1¼ to 1¾ hours. The left-hand path follows a high-level circuit route along the Cordón Pangal, leading back onto the main trail by way of a refugio above the **Río Pangal**. This is a strenuous two to three-hour side trip that

is almost entirely without views. Continue upward a short way before dipping down to cross the small Río Pangal; the Pangal circuit route rejoins the main foot track on the opposite bank. The path now contours the slopes below Cerro Hurán, turning slowly around south-east to reach the **Guardería Sargazo** after 1¼ to 1¾ hours.

Side Trip to Refugio Laguna Sargazo This 45-minute return side trip to the south-western corner of Laguna Sargazo is worth doing even if you don't want to stay at the hut. Follow the road for 1.5km until it ends at a tunnel sealed by a locked gate; private vehicles can be parked here. A path leads off right to meet the **Río Lenca** after a minute or two. Cross the river a short way downstream from here – an easy ford, since a weir just upstream diverts most of its water into the nearby tunnel. The path climbs up roughly eastwards through the damp forest of tepa and mañio to reach the refugio. This quaint, shingled wooden shack stands just above a tiny beach on Laguna Sargazo. It sleeps up to 10 people, and has a fireplace in the middle with a smoke outlet in the roof. Rough anglers' trails lead around the lake shore before petering out.

Camp Sites The Campamento Pangal is a free CONAF camping area without facilities a short way off the road (accessible via a signposted trail), 700m on from the Río Chamiza bridge. There are few good camp sites on the trail between the Guardería Chamiza and the Guardería Sargazo, though there's reasonable camping by the Río Pangal. Campers at the Refugio Laguna Sargazo often pitch their tents right on the tiny beach in front of the hut.

Stage 2: Guardería Sargazo to Refugio Laguna Fría
8.5km, 3½ to 4¾ hours

Follow the road 500m past the Guardería Sargazo and pick up the (possibly unsignposted) path leading off left into the trees. The route climbs up past a forestry observation tower over a low ridge, then dips gently around the rainforested northern slopes just above **Laguna Sargazo** to pass a left-hand turn-off to an **Alerzal** after 40 to 50 minutes. This is a rewarding short side trip to a small stand of particularly massive ancient alerces.

Make your way on through damp groves of leafy tiacas *(Caldcluvia paniculata)*, which grant only the occasional unobstructed glimpse of the lake, and cut down across a small wash full of boulders. After finding the trail again in the scrub just up from the tiny rocky beach, climb on some way above the lake before you drop down again to the reedy eastern shore of Laguna Sargazo after one to 1¼ hours.

Pick up the path in the scrub on the far side of this flat, boggy area and continue walking past a right-hand turn-off to the **Río Sargazo** (the lake inlet). The route leads north-eastwards through the remains of an old orchard to arrive at the **Refugio Río Sargazo**, 10 to 15 minutes on. Built by a long-since evicted local settler, this extremely basic wooden shelter nevertheless offers dry sleeping space for a maximum of eight people.

Proceed gently upvalley along the northern bank of the Río Sargazo through quila thickets, crossing small side streams and ducking under fallen trunks across the path to cross the small Río Sargazo on a log bridge after 50 minutes to one hour. The foot track, in places very prone to overgrowth of vigorous bamboo, leads on up past another stand of (somewhat smaller) alerces to reach the lovely **Laguna Fría** after a further 50 minutes to 1¼ hours.

The **Refugio Laguna Fría** is an excellent refugio, has a fireplace and bunk-space for four people, and is situated 300m on around the western side of the lake. Despite its name, which means Lake Cold, Laguna Fría is fine for swimming, and is enclosed by various granite peaks visible only from the middle of the lake. A difficult and strenuous side trip can be made by following the rough path around the lake shore and on up the western side of the **Río Quilaleu** to **'Paso Triángulo'**.

This pass overlooks **Lago Triángulo**, an impressive glacial lake in a forested cirque (see also Other Treks in Parque Nacional Alerce Andino below).

Camp Sites There are few really good places to camp along Stage 2. The nicest spot (with good swimming here in hot weather) is near where the Río Sargazo enters Lago Sargazo, but there are only one or two sheltered sites by the lake shore. At Laguna Fría the best sites are near the refugio or at the southern end of the lake by a small pebble beach on the other side of an inlet stream.

Other Treks in Parque Nacional Alerce Andino

LAGO TRIÁNGULO
Lago Triángulo lies in a deep fjord-like trough fronted by massive smooth granite walls in the southern (Chaica) sector of Parque Nacional Alerce Andino. This impressive glacial lake can be visited in an easy three-hour return hike through the rainforest from the car park at Lago Chaiquenes. The path leads briefly around the northern shore of Lago Chaiquenes, then follows the east bank of the Río Triángulo northwards to the southern end of Lago Triángulo. Unfortunately, plans to cut a path over **'Paso Triángulo'** at the head of Lago Triángulo to connect with the Laguna Fría route have not yet been realised.

Lago Chaiquenes is accessible via a 17km road from Lenca, a scattered village on Seno Reloncaví; there is a CONAF guardería 4km before Lago Chaiquenes. Lenca is on the Carretera Austral, and can be reached from Puerto Montt by several daily buses (the trip takes approximately 1½ hours). There is no public transport to Lago Chaiquenes, which makes a pleasant but long 4½-hour uphill walk from Lenca. The 1:50,000 Chilean IGM sheet *Lenca* (Section H, No 61) covers the route; also refer to the map of Parque Nacional Alerce Andino in this guidebook.

Parque Nacional Chiloé

Despite centuries of gradual colonisation, large parts of the great island of Chiloé remain virtually untouched wilderness. The 430 sq km Parque Nacional Chiloé, on Chiloé's windswept western side, offers wonderful coastal scenery of sandy beaches and estuarine lagoons set before a backdrop of densely forested hills.

GENERAL INFORMATION
Geographical Features

Parque Nacional Chiloé consists of two separate sectors, the northern Chepu sector (with around 78 sq km) and the southern Anay sector (with around 352 sq km), which are divided by a large parcel of forest earmarked for logging that lies outside the park boundaries. The only two roads that penetrate Chiloé's wild west coast – to the small villages of Chepu and Cucao – give access to each sector of the national park.

Along this Pacific coast, sheltered sandy beaches alternate with rugged cliffs and rocky headlands. Small rivers drain westwards from the low range of hills known as the Cordillera de Puiche, flowing through brackish tidal lagoons into the surf-beaten sea. During the devastating 1961 earthquake (before which Lago Cucao and Lago Huelde were wholly fresh-water lakes) much of this coastline suddenly subsided by around 2m. Today the stumps of trees killed in the wake of the ocean's advance can still be seen in many places along the beaches. Near Cucao work has been done to stabilise the coastal sand dunes to prevent the sea advancing further.

Natural History

Most of Parque Nacional Chiloé is covered by rich coastal rainforests. The island is the stronghold of the evergreen coigüe de Chiloé (*Nothofagus nitida*), an evergreen beech species identifiable by its broad, diamond-shaped leaves. Another particularly common species is the arrayán, whose reddish-brown bark stains the local streams the colour of tea.

The tepú grows to be a large bush whose small white five-petalled flowers bloom late in the summer. The tepú forms often impenetrable thickets (called *tepuales* in the local Spanish), which provide a protective environment well suited to the dwarf deer, pudú. Canelo, a member of the magnolia family with distinctive white, sweet-scented flowers, and ciprés de las Guaitecas also do well in the moist mild climate of the island, and in places both of these tree species form pure stands.

An interesting epiphyte member of South American's large Bromeliaceae family, the chupallita (*Fascicularia* species) looks like a thick tuft of grass. The chupallita does not need soil to grow in, but lashes its tiny roots onto the upper branches of rainforest trees. An endemic species of lizard, the largartija verde (*Leolaemus chiloensis*), lives almost exclusively in the shelter of the long saw-like leaves of the chupallita, camouflaged by its green colouration. Other local species of bromeliads have a pineapple-like foliage and a form similar to Australian and New Zealand pandanuses. The vigorous nalca, or pangue, often grows beside streams, producing giant leaves at the end of a succulent thorny stem. Submarine groves of kelp grow in the storm-tossed coastal waters.

The zorro chilote (*Pseudolopex rufipes*), is a small species of fox endemic (except for a small population in the Nahuel Buta area of the Cordillera de la Costa) to the island of Chiloé. There are no other fox species or pumas on Chiloé, so the zorro chilote is the only land predator, although healthy colonies of the chungungo (*Lutra felina*), a sea otter, exist along Chiloé's rocky Pacific coastline. Another small mammal is the amphibious coipo, which can sometimes be spotted (though more likely heard) swimming in the coastal lagoons in the evenings.

Over 100 species of birds live in or regularly visit the park, many of them aquatic ducks and geese or water birds such as herons and pelicans. Typically seen picking over the tidal debris washed up by the surf are sandpipers and various species of oystercatcher known as pilpilén. Along this wet coastline you may also spot the pidén *(Rallus sanguinolentus)*, a species of rail, which is olive-brown to grey with long yellow legs and beak. Easy to recognise is the martín pescador *(Ceryle torquata)*, a kingfisher that has a blue head, tail and upper wings with a white collar separating its orange-brown breast. The martín pescador is typically seen perched on a branch along lake shores and river banks surveying the waters for signs of surfacing fish.

Climate
Facing out towards the South Pacific, Parque Nacional Chiloé has a decidedly maritime climate. This often makes weather unstable and blustery, with sea squalls regularly moving along the coast. Annual precipitation levels in Cucao reach 2200mm but this rises to 3000mm in the low ranges of the island's interior. The coastal aspect does, however, moderate the temperatures considerably.

Place Names
In the language of the Huilliche (or Cunco, a Mapuche people), Chiloé means 'land of the Andean gull' *(Larus serranus)*, a fitting symbol for an island whose environment and culture are so intricately connected with the sea. Similarly, the name Cucao (the village at the southern end of Parque Nacional Chiloé) translates as 'water with seagulls'. Cole Cole, a river in the park, means 'reddish', an apparent reference to its dark, arrayán-stained waters, while Lago Huelde's name may be a variant of the Mapuche word *huele*, meaning 'sinister' or 'unfortunate'.

PRACTICAL INFORMATION
Information Sources
There is an excellent modern visitors' centre (Centro de Informes) at the Guardería Chanquín, reached 10 minutes after crossing the footbridge at Cucao, which includes a small museum and an audiovisual room. The CONAF office in Castro (☎ 2289) is also helpful, and can advise you on other treks on Chiloé. It is on the 3rd floor of the provincial

government building (Edificio Gobernal Provincial) at O'Higgins 549 (on the Plaza de Armas).

Permits & Regulations
No special permit is required to trek in Parque Nacional Chiloé, but there is a park entry fee of around US$2.50. Camping is permitted only at private camping grounds and the free park-authorised camping areas at the Río Cole Cole, Río Anay, Río Abtao and Río Lar.

When To Trek
Because of its low elevations and mild coastal climate, Parque Nacional Chiloé has one of the most extended trekking seasons in Patagonia. You can trek virtually any time apart from the winter (June to September), although in January and early February the trails and camping areas can get crowded.

Río Anay Trek

> **Duration** 3 days
> **Distance** 48km return
> **Standard** Easy
> **Start/Finish** Cucao
> **Entry** US$2.50, no permit needed
> **Season** October-May
> **Summary** A return trek along the wild Pacific coast and through coastal rainforest of Parque Nacional Chiloé.

This trek along lovely sandy beaches fringed by rainforest passes through tiny isolated settlements in the southern (Anay) sector of the park. Here descendants of the indigenous inhabitants derive an austere existence from farming, fishing and collecting edible kelp, called *cucho yuyo*, which they roll into bundles and pack out on horseback. This tough seaweed grows abundantly in the cold coastal waters of southern Chile, forming thick clusters many metres long that cling to the surf-buffeted rocks before breaking off and stranding in the shoals.

LAKE DISTRICT

MAPS

The area is covered by two Chilean IGM sheets scaled at 1:50,000: *Río Anay* (Section H, No 86), and *Cucao* (Section H, No 95). These maps indicate the route fairly accurately to the Río Cole Cole, after which no path is shown. A good brochure map scaled at 1:125,000 is given to visitors (at either the park entrance gate or the Guardería Chanquín) upon payment of the park entrance fee.

DAYS REQUIRED

Three days is the recommended minimum trekking time for this route. This allows you to reach the Río Cole Cole at a leisurely pace on the first day. From there the section north to the Río Anay can be done as a short day trek.

TREKKING STANDARD

Following well-trodden paths around rocky headlands between small bays, the route involves a great deal of beach walking, but there are enough rough and muddy paths to justify wearing more robust boots on this trek. The coast is blustery and prone to sudden squalls, so carry you rain gear in the top of your pack.

The trek is graded *easy*. The total return distance (ie to the Río Anay and back) is 48km.

ACCOMMODATION & CAMPING

In Cucao village, at the start of the trek, there are several lower-budget places to stay, including the *Hostería Darwin* and *Hospedaje Pacífico*. The Lago Cucao area has many private camping grounds, which in the peak summer season are teeming with Chilean campers and backpackers. Just across the footbridge from Cucao is the well-equipped *Flor del Río*, which offers nice riverside sites. At the north-western end of the brackish Lago Cucao (little more than five minutes from the CONAF guardería) is *Camping Chanquín*; sites here cost US$12 (including firewood and hot showers). There are several other privately run camping grounds along the first section of the route, which are cheaper, if somewhat basic.

There are two free CONAF refugios on the

trekking route at the Río Cole Cole and Río Anay (see the route description for details).

SUPPLIES

Although range and prices are better in Castro (see Trekking Bases) – or in one of the other larger towns on Chiloé – you can buy food, wine and other basic supplies in Cucao. There is a good lower-budget restaurant where the bus terminates (near the Río Cucao suspension footbridge). Some of the farms passed en route sell fresh home-made bread, *empanadas* (filled pastries) or other edibles.

GETTING TO/FROM THE TREK

The trek begins at the village of Cucao, 55km from Castro. During the busy summer holiday months of January and February, the two companies Buses Arroyo and Ocean Bus run five or six buses out to Cucao each day. These leave from the municipal bus terminal (Terminal Municipal), four blocks north of the Plaza de Armas. The trip takes a bit less than two hours and the fare is US$2.50. The road is unsurfaced after you leave the Panamerican Highway. Outside the holiday period the service is much less frequent, but there is at least one bus most days in the off-season.

This route can also be done as a return day trip by mountainbike or on horseback (the latter may only go as far as the Refugio Cole Cole); a number of farms or camping grounds around Cucao rent out horses.

The trek ends at the Río Anay, from where you must return to Cucao via the same route.

THE TREK
Stage 1: Cucao Village to Refugio Cole Cole
18km, 4 to 5¼ hours

Where the bus terminates in Cucao village, cross the suspension footbridge spanning the Río Cucao and follow a broad sandy road for 10 minutes to the national park gate. After paying the entrance fee, take the short right-hand trail leading to the **Guardería Chanquín**. Fresh drinking water can be hard to find along the way, so fill your canteen at the tap here. Two rewarding short trails from the Guardería Chanquín lead to **Playa Cucao**, a

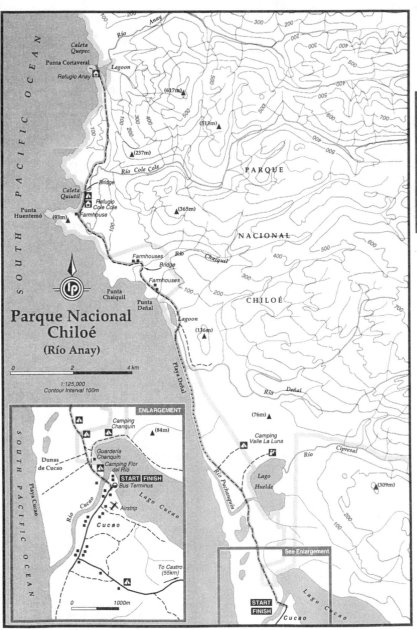

LAKE DISTRICT

Parque Nacional
Chiloé
(Río Anay)

0   2   4 km

1:125,000
Contour Interval 100m

PACIFIC OCEAN

SOUTH

Caleta
Quepec
Punta Cortaveral
Refugio Anay
Lagoon

Río   Anay

(617m)

(513m)

(237m)

Río Cole Cole

PARQUE

Bridge
Caleta
Quiutil
Refugio
Cole Cole
Farmhouse

(93m)
Punta
Huentemó

(365m)

NACIONAL

Farmhouses   Río   Chaiquil

Bridge

Farmhouses

Punta
Chaiquil

Punta
Deñal

CHILOÉ

Lagoon

(136m)

Playa Deñal

Río   Deñal

(76m)

Camping
Valle La Luna

Río   Cipresal

(309m)

Lago
Huelde

Río Puchanquín

See Enlargement

Lago Cucao

START
FINISH

Cucao

ENLARGEMENT

SOUTH PACIFIC OCEAN

Playa Cucao

Dunas
de Cucao

Río Cucao

Camping
Chanquin

(84m)

Guardería
Chanquín
Camping Flor
del Río
START   FINISH
Bus Terminus

Airstrip

Cucao

Lago Cucao

To Castro
(55km)

0   1000m

white sandy ocean beach, and to some high sand dunes called the **Dunas de Cucao**. Another nice walking route goes (via Camping Chanquín) around the northern shore of **Lago Cucao**.

Follow the broad sandy trail past farm cottages and several camping grounds amid marshy coastal moors, crossing the bridge over the **Río Puchanquín**, the outlet of nearby **Lago Huelde**, after 35 to 45 minutes. For a view of this brackish lake (which you otherwise don't see), pick up a trail leading off to the right just after the bridge. Head on northwest between grassed-over sand dunes on your left and higher, older, scrub-covered dunes up to your right. The route climbs around a tiny head (only necessary at high tide) to reach the broad ocean beach known as the **Playa Deñal**, a further 40 to 50 minutes on.

With the salty wind in your face, make your way along the firm, moist sand scattered with strands of kelp washed ashore by the crashing breakers until you reach the suspension footbridge over the **Río Deñal** after 50 minutes to 1¼ hours. Once across continue alongside the river's narrow tidal lagoon to cross a small stream just up from where its brownish waters mingle with the waves. From here a wide path climbs up between woven wooden fences past rustic cottages atop **Punta Deñal**, then drops directly down into a lovely little cove after another 25 to 30 minutes.

Walk almost to the far end of the sheltered beach and pick up a trail leading off right to cross the **Río Chaiquil** on a bridge a few hundred metres from where it enters the sea. Head past more simple farms among green riverside lawns to a football field, here breaking away north-west up into the forest behind **Punta Chaiquil**. The often muddy foot track (which in places has eroded to form a shoulder-high trench) takes a spectacular rising-and-dipping course along the edge of cliffs high above the rocky, wave-pounded coast, before descending to several wooden cottages on a broad grassy saddle behind the headland of **Punta Huentemó**, one to 1½ hours on.

Pick up the path to the right of the first

cottage here and then drop down north through a seaside pasture scattered with pineapple-like bromeliads to come out onto the beach of **Caleta Quiutil**. Follow walking pads just above the sandy shore of this beautiful bay to arrive at the **Refugio Cole Cole** after a final 15 minutes. This free hut has a wood stove and basic sleeping space for around 10 people. During the summer the friendly and helpful CONAF warden is often present.

Camp Sites See Accommodation & Camping for options around Cucao. There are several basic camping grounds near the path between the Guardería Chanquín and the Río Puchanquín bridge; the *Camping Valle La Luna* is reached via a signposted foot track on the right about 25 minutes after crossing the Río Puchanquín.

Camping is not permitted anywhere else along this coastline until you reach the northern end of the Caleta Quiutil. Here you'll find numerous semi-sheltered sites hidden in the tepu scrub behind the beach front. The tiny brackish lagoon at the mouth of the Río Cole Cole is regularly flooded by the tide, so it is necessary to fetch water from farther upstream.

Stage 2: Refugio Cole Cole to Refugio Anay
6km, 1½ to two hours
This short section can be done as a simple return day trek from Cole Cole.

Head across the footbridge over the **Río Cole Cole** and into the forest. Vines, grassy-looking epiphytes and parasitic plants grow on the trunks and branches of the arrayan, tepa and coigüe de Chiloé trees, while delicate maidenhair ferns, luminescent mosses, lichens and pandanus-like bromeliads cover the wet forest floor. The foot track (which has deteriorated considerably since the last edition of this guidebook) turns northwards away from the river after 20 to 25 minutes, repeatedly crossing a tiny swampy side stream as it rises gently over a low watershed. Continue closely beside another (also north-flowing) streamlet to come out at an overgrown clearing beside the **Río Anay** after a further one to 1½ hours.

Make your way left along the steep river banks for five minutes to reach the **Refugio Anay**, an unsophisticated construction in a quila thicket at the edge of **Caleta Quepec**. The refugio has a fireplace in the middle (with an opening in the roof to let out the smoke) and offers extremely basic shelter for a maximum of six people. The lovely wild beach on the other side of the Río Anay can only be reached by swimming across the tiny brackish lagoon at the river's mouth.

Camp Sites There is very poor camping beside the Refugio Anay, but reasonable sites can be found where the forest fringes the small riverside clearing less than 10 minutes from the refugio. The small lagoon where the Río Anay meets the beach is slightly brackish, so fetch your water from the last small stream passed on the way.

Other Treks on Chiloé

CHEPU SECTOR
The interesting northern Chepu sector of the Parque Nacional Chiloé is renowned for its rich marine wildlife. From the village of Chepu a good trail can be followed south along beaches and the rainforested coast to a

refugio and guardería at the Río Lar. Seal colonies inhabit the numerous rocky islets just offshore.

The Chilean IGM 1:50,000 sheet *Chepu* (Section H, No 75) covers the trekking route, and the national park has produced a useful brochure map of the Chepu sector. Chepu is accessible by daily bus from Ancud.

ABTAO SECTOR
The central Abtao sector of Parque Nacional Chiloé is often visited by Chilean sport fishers. The three or four-day trek first follows a 4WD track west from the village of Piruquina (22km north of Castro) along the Río Grande, then continues over the low Cordillera de Piuchén to an isolated beach and coastal lagoon at the mouth of the Río Abtao, where there is a basic CONAF refugio.

Two Chilean IGM 1:50,000 sheets, *Castro* (Section H, No 87) and *Río Anay* (Section H, No 86), cover this area but do not show the hiking route.

SOUTH OF CUCAO
From Cucao (see the Río Anay Trek) at the southern end of Parque Nacional Chiloé, 4WD tracks and foot trails can be followed south along the Pacific coastline to wild sandy beaches outside the national park. The Chilean IGM sheet *Río Catiao* (Section H, No 104) covers this area.

Other Treks in the Lake District

VOLCÁN CHOSHUENCO – CHILE
Choshuenco (2415m) and Mocho (2413m) rise from a small volcanic range south-west of Lago Panguipulli (Mapuche for 'puma slopes') and Lago Riñihue ('place of the foxes') in one of the more remote parts of the Chilean Lake District. You can follow a road to a small ski field on the lower south-western slopes to above the tree line, from where you can spend several days exploring the trackless open slopes. Higher up, the

mountains are covered by glaciers and only experienced trekkers equipped with proper climbing equipment are advised to trek in this area.

The two Chilean IGM 1:50,000 sheets, *Choshuenco* (Section G, No 122) and *Neltume* (Section G, No 123) cover the Choshuenco area. Buses on the international route to Argentina via Lago Pirehueico pass near the village of Choshuenco, from where it is 23km to the ski field.

RÍO BUENO TO VALDIVIA – CHILE

This is a long four to six-day trek along the wild and sparsely settled Pacific coastline south of Valdivia. At the village of Trumao, 6km south-west of La Unión, take a ferry down the Río Bueno to the tiny outpost of Venecia. From here the route follows paths and roads north through coastal rainforest, along sandy beaches and across several rivers. A number of isolated fishing villages are passed on the way where you can buy basic supplies. The trek finishes in Corral at the mouth of the Río Valdivia from where there are boats upriver to Niebla and Valdivia.

Three Chilean IGM 1:50,000 sheets, *Corral* (Section G, No 117), *Chaihuin* (Section G, No 116) and *Río Colun* (Section H, No 1) cover the trek, but do not always indicate the route.

ASCENT OF VOLCÁN OSORNO – CHILE

One of the great landmarks of the southern Chilean Lake District, the perfect white cone of Volcán Osorno attracts considerable attention from serious mountaineers. Volcán Osorno's last major eruption occurred in 1835, and released a series of catastrophic floods and lahars (mud avalanches). The volcano has been more or less dormant since then, allowing extensive glaciers to re-accumulate around its upper slopes.

The climb to the summit, which takes two or three days, is normally undertaken from the refugio at 1180m on the western slopes of Volcán Osorno (outside Parque Nacional Vicente Pérez Rosales). At all times of the year crampons and ice axe are required, and inexperienced climbers are strongly urged to make the ascent of the volcano with a professional local mountain guide.

A service road leads off the main Puerto Octay-Puerto Varas road, 2km north of Ensenada on the eastern shores of Lago Llanquihue up to the Refugio Los Pumas and on to the refugio. The Chilean IGM 1:50,000 sheet *Las Cascadas* (Section H, No 43) covers the west side of Volcán Osorno and most of the ascent route. The adjoining sheet *Petrohué* (Section H, No 44) is also very useful.

VOLCÁN CALBUCO – CHILE

The 2015m Volcán Calbuco is the central feature of Reserva Nacional Llanquihue, a roughly 300 sq km reserve on the southeastern corner of Lago Llanquihue. A two-day return trek from the Guardería Chapo, at the northern end of Parque Nacional Alerce Andino, follows a path up the Río Blanco to a rustic refugio on the volcano's southern side. From here experienced climbers can tackle Volcán Calbuco, whose flat-topped summit is capped by a thick layer of glacial ice. The 1:50,000 Chilean IGM sheet *Correntoso* (Section H, No 52) covers the trek.

Central Patagonia

The Central Patagonian Andes are remote, often extremely wet and have considerable problems of accessibility. Fewer roads (which are generally smaller and little-travelled) penetrate the Cordillera of Central Patagonia, and especially on the Chilean side, trekking is limited by the lack of paths and by dense, impenetrable temperate rainforest. Despite this, trekkers adventurous enough to visit this thinly settled region will be rewarded for their perseverance by its wild and untamed nature.

TREKKING BASES
Esquel (Argentina)

This dusty, windswept town of 23,000 lies on the Ruta 40 at the edge of the dry Patagonian pampa in northern Chubut Province, and makes a good base for trips into Parque Nacional Los Alerces. The local mountain club is the Club Andino de Esquel (☎ 2962; fax 4502), whose mailing address is CC 625, 9200 Esquel, Chubut. Fishing permits are available from the office of the Recursos Naturales (☎ 2503) at Roca 751.

Transportes Esquel, Minibus Lago Verde and Zabala-Daniel all run buses from Esquel to Parque Nacional Los Alerces. Esquel is connected with El Bolsón and Bariloche by many regular daily buses. El Trochita, a romantic narrow-gauge steam train familiar to English speakers (and readers) as the 'Old Patagonian Express' – the title of a South American travel narrative by Paul Theroux – connects the junction town of Jacobacci (where another line continues to Bariloche) with Esquel via El Maitén. A number of airlines fly in and out of Esquel; most are flights to/from Buenos Aires, but there are several per week to/from Bariloche and Comodoro Rivadavia. Esquel's area code is ☎ 0945.

El Bolsón (Argentina)

Situated in the south-western corner of Río Negro province in a basin enclosed by high mountains, El Bolsón has long attracted alternative lifestyle seekers (whom Argentinians call *hippis*). As the self-appointed 'capital' of the so-called Comarca Andina region this small laid-back town of just 3500 souls offers a laid-back atmosphere ideal for relaxing after a hard week's trekking in the surrounding ranges.

El Bolsón's tourist office (☎ 92604) is at the northern end of the Plaza Pagano, the town's central park. The very helpful local mountain club, the Club Andino Piltriquitrón, or CAP (☎ 92600), has its office on the corner of Roca and Sarmiento (almost directly west of the tourist office), El Bolsón 8450. A good place for backpackers to stay is the *Campamento Ecológico* (☎ 92954), about 1km south of the town centre on the banks of the Río Quemquemtreu; it has well organised camping for US$5 per person and a 40-bed hostel where you can stay for US$8.

El Bolsón is connected by regular buses north to Bariloche and south to Esquel. Zabala-Daniel (☎ 92145) operates daily minibuses to Lago Verde in Parque Nacional Los Alerces, leaving at 12.30 pm and 5 pm (US$15). LADE (☎ 92206) has weekly flights to both cities as well as Comodoro Rivadavia (on the Atlantic coast); Sapse also has a weekly flight to Bariloche and to Buenos Aires and Viedma. El Bolsón's area code is ☎ 0944.

Coyhaique (Chile)

The regional capital of Chile's remote XI Región, Coyhaique (pronounced 'coy-AI-kay', meaning 'landscape of lakes' in the Tehuelche language) sits in a sheltered valley behind ranges to the west. Although a small city of 40,000 people, Coyhaique is nevertheless home to around half the region's population.

Coyhaique marks the line of climatic transition between moister western Patagonia and the drier eastern steppes. The mountains surrounding the city, which reach altitudes of almost 2000m, are green, forested and often snowcapped to the west, but become dry and barren a short distance to the east.

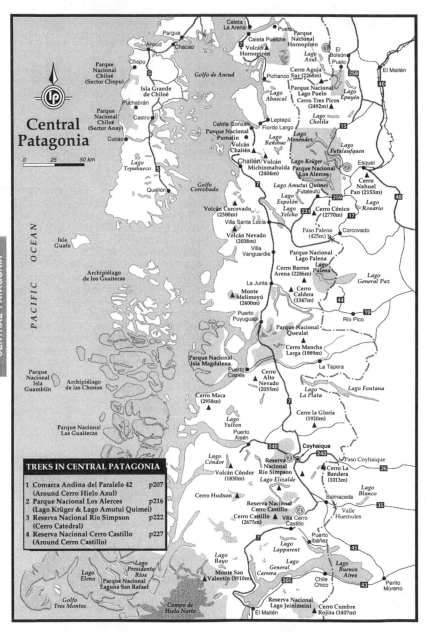

Central Patagonia

Parque Nacional Chiloé (Sector Chepu)

Parque Nacional Chiloé (Sector Anay)

0   25   50 km

Lago Tepuhueco

PACIFIC OCEAN

Isla Guafo

Archipiélago de los Guaitecas

Parque Nacional Isla Guamblín

Archipiélago de las Chonos

Parque Nacional Las Guaitecas

Golfo Tres Montes

Lago Elena

Lago Presidente Ríos

Parque Nacional Laguna San Rafael

Campo de Hielo Norte

Parque Nacional Chiloé (Sector Chepu)
Chepu
Ancud
Chacao
Pargua
Isla Grande de Chiloé
Puchabrán
Castro
Cucao
Quellón
Golfo de Ancud
Golfo Corcovado

Caleta La Arena
Caleta Puelche
Puelo
Parque Nacional Hornopirén
Volcán Hornopirén
Lago Azul
El Bolsón
Puelo
El Maitén
Pichanco
Cerro Aguja Sur (2268m)
Lago Abascal
Parque Nacional Lago Puelo
Cerro Tres Picos (2492m)
Lago Epuyén
Leptepú
Caleta Gonzalo
Fiordo Largo
Parque Nacional Pumalín
Lago Reñihue
Lago Cholila
Volcán Chaitén
Lago Menéndez
Lago Futalaufquen
Esquel
Chaitén
Volcán Michinmahuida (2404m)
Lago Krüger
Parque Nacional Los Alerces
Cerro Nahuel Pan (2153m)
Lago Amutui Quimei
Futaleufú
Lago Espolón
Lago Yelcho
Cerro Cónico (2770m)
Lago Rosario
Volcán Corcovado (2300m)
Villa Santa Lucía
Paso Palena (425m)
Corcovado
Volcán Nevado (2038m)
Villa Vanguardia
Parque Nacional Lago Palena
Cerro Barros Arena (2286m)
Lago Palena
Lago General Paz
La Junta
Cerro Caldera (1347m)
Monte Melimoyú (2400m)
Río Pico
Puerto Puyuguapi
Parque Nacional Queulat
Parque Nacional Isla Magdalena
Cerro Mancha Larga (1989m)
Puerto Cisnes
La Tapera
Cerro Alto Nevado (2035m)
Lago Fontana
Cerro Maca (2958m)
Lago Yulton
Lago La Plata
Cerro la Gloria (1920m)
Puerto Aisén
Lago Cóndor
Coyhaique
Paso Coyhaique
Reserva Nacional Río Simpson
Volcán Cóndor (1830m)
Lago Elizalde
Cerro La Bandera (1013m)
Lago Blanco
Cerro Hudson
Reserva Nacional Cerro Castillo
Balmaceda
Valle Huemules
Cerro Castillo (2675m)
Villa Cerro Castillo
Puerto Ibáñez
Lago Lapparent
Lago Bayo
Monte San Valentín (3910m)
Lago General Carrera
Lago Buenos Aires
Perito Moreno
Chile Chico
Reserva Nacional Lago Jeinimeini
Cerro Cumbre Rojiza (1407m)
El Maitén

TREKS IN CENTRAL PATAGONIA

1 Comarca Andina del Paralelo 42   p207
   (Around Cerro Hielo Azul)
2 Parque Nacional Los Alerces   p216
   (Lago Krüger & Lago Amutui Quimei)
3 Reserva Nacional Río Simpson   p222
   (Cerro Catedral)
4 Reserva Nacional Cerro Castillo   p227
   (Around Cerro Castillo)

Coyhaique is the only large trekking base for trips into national reserves such as Cerro Castillo and Río Simpson. Day walks in the scenic Reserva Nacional Coyhaique, 5km north of town, are worthwhile. The small local museum, the Museo de Patagonia Central, is on the pentagonal Plaza de Armas.

The regional CONAF office (☎ 23 2599; fax 23 1065) is at Avenida Ogana 1060 on the southern road out of town. Contact Peter Hartmann through the office of Codeff (☎ 23 4451) at Dussen 357 for information on trekking and mountaineering possibilities in the region. The helpful SERNATUR office (☎ 23 1752) is at Bulnes 35. Anglers will find the nearest SERNAP office (☎ 33 2546) in Puerto Aisén at Alfredo Bustos 181. Accommodation in Coyhaique is relatively expensive, but one reasonable lower-budget place to stay is the hospedaje at Avenida Almirante Simpson 571.

Air transport is increasingly important in this remote region. LAN Chile's standard one way fare to Puerto Montt is US$55, and to Santiago it is around US$115. The small national airline ALTA, whose office is on the corner of Avenida General Belgrano and Condell, has the only direct flights (19-seat Beechcraft) south to Puerto Natales ($US100, 1¾ hours) and Punta Arenas. ALTA flights depart from Coyhaique Airport (not from Balmaceda) almost daily in either direction, and in (relatively rare) fine weather there are superb views of the mountains and enormous glaciers of the Hielo Norte and Hielo Sur. ALTA also flies the northern route to Puerto Montt, Temuco and Valparaíso.

The regional transport company Don Carlos (☎ 23 1500), at Cruz 63, has flights to Chile Chico (five days a week), to Cochrane (US$55, Monday and Wednesday), and to Villa O'Higgins (Wednesday), all returning the same day. Don Carlos also runs buses to/from Puerto Aisén (eight times daily) and Cochrane (US$25, twice weekly). Buses Pudú (☎ 23 1008) also run three or four weekly buses to Cochrane. There are also four or five weekly buses north along the Carretera Austral to Chaitén, but buses to

Puerto Montt run via Argentina rather than the Carretera Austral. Navimag and Transmarchilay have ferries to/from Puerto Chacabuco and Puerto Montt departing on alternate days; the fare is US$50. In summer the Navimag ferry goes on to Laguna San Rafael. Coyhaique's area code is ☎ 67.

Chile Chico (Chile)

Situated on the southern shore of Lago General Carrera (called Lago Buenos Aires on the Argentine side), the small, sleepy town of Chile Chico enjoys a mild microclimate due to the moderating influence of the enormous lake. (The townspeople boast that they grow the best fruit in Chile south of Puerto Montt, although little locally produced fruit is on sale in Chile Chico's shops). Trekkers sometimes pass through Chile Chico on their way to the nearby Cueva de los Manos (where there are prehistoric Indian cave paintings), the Reserva Nacional Jeinimeini (see Other Treks in Southern Patagonia) or to Los Antiguos and Perito Moreno in Argentina.

CONAF has a helpful office at Alberto Blest Gana 121. The recent opening of a gold mine 20km west of the town has provided a boost to Chile Chico's economy, but this has also raised local accommodation prices. The *Hostería Austral* (☎ 41 1274; fax 41 1461) at O'Higgins 501 has rooms and organises excursions to Reserva Nacional Jeinimeini. Car/passenger ferries run six days a week in both directions across Lago General Carrera to Puerto Ibáñez, a tiny port on the lake's northern shore which has direct minibus connections to Coyhaique. Turismo Padilla runs buses several times daily between Chile Chico and the nearby Argentine town of Los Antiguos (US$11), and the new road from Chile Chico to Puerto Guadal (just off the Carretera Austral) offers an exhilarating minibus ride around the precipitous southern side of Lago General Carrera hundreds of metres above the lake. Don Carlos also has one or two flights per week to Coyhaique and Balmaceda. Chile Chico's area code is ☎ 67.

Comarca Andina del Paralelo 42

Centred around the town of El Bolsón, the Argentine region known as the Comarca Andina del Paralelo 42 straddles the country's mountainous frontier with Chile. Meaning literally the 'Andean District of the 42nd Parallel', its Spanish name is a reference to the latitudinal line 42°S, which passes several kilometres south of El Bolsón and delimits Río Negro from Chubut. The term unites the small, closely linked communities in the isolated corners of both provinces, who refer to the region simply as the Comarca Andina.

GENERAL INFORMATION
Geographical Features
Although it is not an official geographical term, the Comarca Andina more or less corresponds to the upper basin of the Río Puelo. The Comarca Andina lies entirely to the west of the Pacific-Atlantic watershed, and, had it not been for the efforts of the great Argentine explorer, Francisco Perito Moreno, the whole region would almost certainly have become part of Chile. Moreno convincingly argued that the international border should follow the line of the highest Andean peaks, rather than the more facile solution of following the east-west drainage pattern.

Culminating in the névés and small glaciers of the Cordón Nevado on the Argentina-Chile frontier, the Comarca Andina forms a relatively narrow band of rugged ranges on the eastern side of the Andes in central Patagonia. Narrow, but deep and surprisingly long lateral valleys descend eastwards from the highest summits, which easily top 2000m and are covered with névés and small glaciers.

Natural History
Tall evergreen forest dominated by coigüe, spelt coihue in Argentina, grows in the moister valleys of the Comarca Andina, becoming increasingly species-rich closer to the Chilean frontier. Here large pockets of typical 'Valdivian' rainforest species such as avellano, canelo, luma and giant alerces grow.

The ranges' drier eastern slopes are covered by fragrant stands of ciprés de la cordillera. This tree is locally known as cedro del sur (literally 'southern cedar'), although it is, in fact, a member of the cypress family. The ciprés understorey consists largely of thickets dominated by scrubby species like retama *(Diostea juncea)* and leafless crucero *(Colletia ulicina)*, whose countless green stalky branchlets end in sharp spines.

Beautiful open forests of deciduous lenga mixed with ñirre are found above 1100m. Despite the apparent biological paucity of these forests, the understorey harbours species such as alpine quila or tihuén *(Chusquea tenuiflora)*, and traro *(Olvidia andina)*, a bush with clusters of large drooping dog-eared leaves at the ends of its branches. The lenga forest also provides an ideal habitat for the zorro culpeo, usually called zorro colorado in Argentina, a fox common in the Comarca Andina, and the gato montés *(Oncifelis geoffroyii)*, a native cat that measures up to 1m from head to tail.

Two adaptable bird species, the small silvery-grey diuca *(Diuca diuca)* and the chincol, or red-collared sparrow, also dwell in these highland forests. The chunco *(Glaucidium nanum)*, is a southern pygmy owl that makes up for its small size by its audacious (and occasionally aggressive) temperament. Larger birds of prey are the Andean condor and the águila mora, a species of eagle.

Climate
Visitors arriving from the nearby Argentine Lake District will notice the dry, crisper continental climate. The high range of the Cordón Nevado acts as a surprisingly effective climatic barrier, filtering out much of the Pacific moisture carried by the westerly winds. Except for these loftier peaks close to the frontier, where rain and snowfall may exceed 3000mm annually, precipitation levels are relatively modest. Beyond the thin strip of mountains along the Cordillera, annual precipitation drops dramatically – in

the valley of El Bolsón to as little as 700mm. Summer temperatures are warm, but the frequent winds tend to prevent oppressively hot weather. In winter snow covers all areas above 800m, generally reaching a depth of a metre or so in early August, when El Bolsón's humble (compared to Bariloche's) skiing industry is in full swing.

Place Names

The town of El Bolsón, which in Argentine Spanish means 'handbag', gets its name from the broad basin of the Río Quemquemtreu, which is bordered by high ranges on both sides. Piltriquitrón, a high mountain on the eastern side of El Bolsón, means 'peak in the clouds' in the Mapuche language. Epuyén comes from the Mapuche for *epu*, two, and *yen*, meaning 'they who came', an allusion to the two largest lakes in the Comarca Andina, Lago Puelo and Lago Epuyén. Puelo itself, which combines the Mapuche *puel*, east, and *o*, a shorter form of *co*, meaning water, could be roughly translated as 'flowing from the east', while Currumahuida, the name of a peak to the south of Lago Puelo, means 'black mountain'.

PRACTICAL INFORMATION
Information Sources

The Club Andino Piltriquitrón (or CAP; ☎ 0944-92600) at Roca and Sarmiento in El Bolsón, is open daily in summer; the obliging club staff, some of whom speak Italian, can advise trekkers on the best routes in the Comarca Andina. El Bolsón also has one of Argentina's most helpful tourist offices (☎ 0944-92604), who produce an excellent free tourist booklet to the Comarca Andina that includes tips for trekkers.

Permits & Regulations

Except for Parque Nacional Lago Puelo (see Other Treks in the Comarca Andina), trekking permits are not required in the Comarca Andina. Anglers can purchase fishing licences from the several outdoors stores in El Bolsón. Where possible camp at established camp sites. Many popular walking routes cross private property, where trekkers should be on their best behaviour.

When To Trek

The trekking season in the Comarca Andina runs from November until the end of April. January and February can be hot and the *refugios* crowded, but – unlike areas with moister climes to the north and on the other side of the Cordillera – there are few or no *tábanos* (horse flies) then.

Around Cerro Hielo Azul

Duration 4 days
Distance 43km
Standard Medium
Start El Criado farm
Finish Warton homestead
Entry Free, no permit needed
Season November-April
Summary A route linking two small valleys that includes a climb to a natural lookout adjacent to the 'blue ice' glacier of Hielo Azul and a hike along the deep and narrow chasm of the Cañadón del Azul.

This is an excellent trek linking two of the Comarca Andina's loveliest alpine valleys in the ranges that are visible from El Bolsón. The route leads up to a lookout summit opposite 'blue ice' glaciers on Cerro Hielo Azul, then on into the Cajón del Azul, a deep gorge of the wild upper Río Azul.

MAPS

Although it does not show the trekking route itself, the Argentine IGM's 1:100,000 sheet *El Bolsón* (4172-34, Río Negro) is relatively new and covers the area of the trek. The *Mapa de El Bolsón y su Zona*, prepared by the CAP in 1973 at a scale of approximately 1:125,000, does show trekking routes (although some have changed since publication) and is also worth having; it's available for US$3 from the CAP or at newspaper kiosks in El Bolsón.

CENTRAL PATAGONIA

DAYS REQUIRED

This is a four-day trek, which could be lengthened by several days by trekking on up the Río Azul from the Refugio Cajón Azul.

TREKKING STANDARD

The CAP has marked most of the route with red and white paint stripes on rocks and trees, but the more difficult section from the Refugio Hielo Azul up to Barda Negra (Stage 2A) is unmarked. Route-finding is generally easiest in the direction described below. The trails are scrubby in places and often dusty, so wearing protective gaiters (or at least long trousers) will make your trek more comfortable.

Although technically a relatively straightforward climb, the ascent of Cerro Hielo Azul involves crossing a small glacier with dangerous crevasses and is suited only to parties with mountaineering experience and ice-climbing equipment.

The trek has an overall rating of *medium* and covers a total distance of around 43km.

ACCOMMODATION & CAMPING

For places to stay in El Bolsón see Trekking Bases. There are two refugios on this route, so it is possible to do the trek without a tent – though this is not advisable in January, when the refugios are often full. The Refugio Hielo Azul belongs to the CAP, and following a recent extension it has sleeping space for up to 30 people. The overnight fee is US$6, but it costs US$4 extra if you use the hut's cooking facilities. Simple meals (cooked on a wood stove) are available; breakfast costs US$4 and dinner is US$6. Depending on seasonal snow conditions, the refugio is generally staffed from November until the end of April, but is left open when the warden is absent. Run and inhabited (all year round) by a hippie family, the 20-bed *Refugio Cajón del Azul* offers beds for US$8 per night (hot showers are extra). Meals, including fresh garden vegetables and home-made bread, are available here for reasonable prices, and for a small fee trekkers can camp near the refugio.

The *Camping Río Azul*, 6km by road from El Bolsón by the eastern bank of the river, is an organised camping ground with good facilities; it's also the start of the Cerro Lindo trek (see Other Treks in the Comarca Andina). The *Camping Doña Rosa*, on lovely grassy riverflats by the Río Azul (about halfway between the Camping Río Azul and El Criado), has very cheap primitive camping (with tent sites costing just US$1 per day). Farther upstream is the *Camping Puente del Arco Iris* (☎ 93142), a short way down from the Río del Encanto Blanco footbridge (see Stage 3).

SUPPLIES

Buy whatever you'll need for the trek in El Bolsón, as only a few basic provisions (like chocolates and beer) and simple meals are available at the refugios en route.

GETTING TO/FROM THE TREK

The trek begins in the valley of the Río Azul at the farm known as El Criado, 10km by road from El Bolsón. The trek finishes at Warton (also spelt as Wharton), a farmstead 10km farther north along the Río Azul road.

During January and February, the CAP runs three minibuses each day along the Río Azul road to and from Refugio Perito Moreno (see under Other Treks) and to the club office in El Bolsón (see Trekking Bases). Most of the CAP minibuses pass El Criado on the way, but one of these services enters the Río Azul road via a turn-off at Warton. Although the following timetable may change, the departures are currently at 7.15 am (Warton turn-off), 9 am and 8 pm; these return from Refugio Perito Moreno at 11.30 am, 6 pm (Warton turn-off) and at 9 pm.

Outside these times trekkers can charter a taxi *(remise)* to take them to and from El Criado and Warton for around US$10/20. The friendly locals often pick up hitchhikers, so you could also try thumbing a ride there and back.

THE TREK

Stage 1: El Criado to Refugio Hielo Azul
14km, 3¾ to 4¾ hours

There is no definite sign at El Criado, so if you arrive on foot keep a careful watch out for this minor turn-off – or ask a local. Otherwise, the CAP-run minibus will drop you off here.

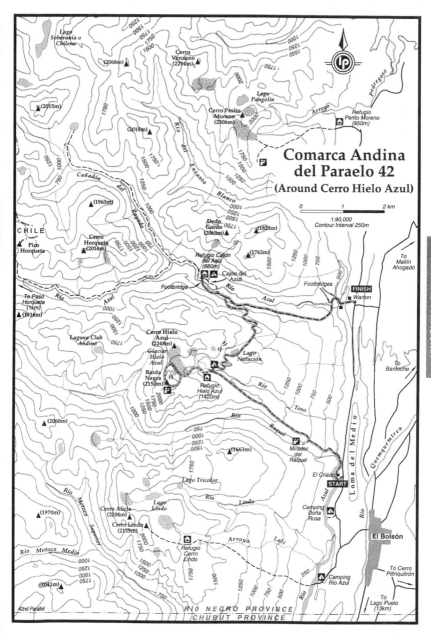

Comarca Andina
del Paraelo 42
(Around Cerro Hielo Azul)

CENTRAL PATAGONIA

Follow the private road down around past the farmhouse to the banks of the **Río Azul**. A broad horse track leads on upstream through attractive stands of coigües to a suspension bridge a short way above the river's confluence with the **Río Raquel**, allowing a rickety but safe crossing. Fill your water bottle here for the thirsty section ahead, then pick up the red and white marked route a few paces downstream. The path climbs steeply, easing up rightwards along the slope to meet a wire fence at the edge of a grassy clearing, scattered with rose bushes, after 40 to 50 minutes.

At this point trekkers can opt to do a short and rewarding side trip to an impressive lookout above the Río Raquel. First follow the left-hand side of the fence, then, after crossing another older ramshackle fence made of logs, ease rightwards until you near a graceful old coigüe tree. Here pick up markings guiding you down left to the high precipitous bluff known as the **Mirador del Raquel**, which grants a fine view down into the river gully.

Back on the main track, cut up rightwards through the clearing and sidle past a derelict wooden hut, before beginning another ascent up steep slopes of ciprés de la cordillera to gain a small spur covered with low ñirre woodland and retama *(Diostea juncea)* scrub. The path soon brings you up onto a broader ridge with small rocky outcrops (giving the first good views back eastwards to Cerro Piltriquitrón), then climbs onward roughly north-west past a small scrubby *mallín* to meet the small **Río Teno** after 2½ to three hours. This is a pleasant spot to rest.

Continue along the true right (ie southern) bank of the stream, rising gently through the open lenga forest. The route passes a riverside camping area not long before arriving at the **Refugio Hielo Azul** (see Accommodation & Camping earlier in this section), a final 40 to 50 minutes on. Built in 'log cabin' style with trunks cut from the surrounding forest, the Refugio Hielo Azul stands at around 1420m in the beautiful upper valley of the Río Teno, enclosed by the high rock walls of a glacial cirque above which small

névés are visible. The refugio is frequently visited by local inhabitants such as the zorro culpeo, a native fox, and the occasional puma has even been known to pass by.

Camp Sites The CAP discourages camping anywhere along Stage 1 apart from the camping area five minutes down from the Refugio Hielo Azul; the sites on the true left bank of the Río Teno are nicest. Trekkers should resist any temptation to camp on the (otherwise ideal) riverflats along the Río Azul, as this is private property.

Stage 2A: Refugio Hielo Azul to Barda Negra
7km return, 3½ to 5 hours return
This excellent return day trek from the refugio (or the nearby camping area) is the highlight of the trek, but it should only be done in fine weather. The ascent of **Cerro Hielo Azul** is a relatively straightforward climb that is nevertheless exclusively for people who come with mountaineering experience and ice-climbing equipment.

Cross a tiny wooden bridge over a streamlet at the edge of the lenga forest just a few paces on from the refugio. Head out directly into the amphitheatre through alluvial rubble and cross a second somewhat larger stream, following this up until red markings on rocks lead off to the right through a gravelly chute. The route leads on up a rocky moraine ridge to the base of cliffs rounded and smoothed by the action of glaciers. Here trekkers may spot the white estrella de la cordillera and the red bottle-shaped voqui, two hardy Andean wild flowers that grow sporadically on these otherwise bare slopes.

Sidle briefly left back to the now cascading stream, climbing on steeply through the rock. Make your way over polished slabs littered with glacial debris to a milky-green meltwater lake at the snout of the small glacier known as the **Glaciar Hielo Azul**. Cross the turgid stream (the nascent Río Teno) to reach a waterfall spilling down from the left, one to 1½ hours from the refugio. From here the summit of Cerro Hielo Azul (2248m) is more clearly visible up to the right, above the broken-up ice on the upper part of the glacier.

Skirt the left-hand side of the Glaciar Hielo Azul, then cut up over the ice around a rock outcrop (marked by a prominent cairn) and climb on via the minor spur behind it into a snowy basin. (Alternatively, you can head directly up to the left of the waterfall through steep scree, but this is a route better taken on your way down). The route ascends beside the small stream, crossing and recrossing as it rises steeply through (probably snow-filled) gullies and loose rock. Where the stream ends, move rightwards over persistent snow drifts to gain the ridge top (about 500m to the right of white veins of rock in the reddish-brown ridge forming a cross), continuing north-westwards along the snowy ridge to reach the 2150m summit of **Barda Negra** after one to 1½ hours.

Barda Negra offers a superb alpine panorama that takes in Cerro Piltriquitrón to the east beyond El Bolsón; Monte Tronador almost directly to the north; the perfect cone of Volcán Osorno to the north-west in Chile; and the distinctive triple summits of Cerro Tres Picos – the major landmark of the Comarca Andina – to the south. Laguna Club Andino can be seen in a deep glacial hollow to north-east, and another unnamed lake is visible to the south-west. Trekkers also have an excellent chance of seeing condors swooping around the nearby mountain tops.

Descent Via Glaciar Hielo Azul Although from below it looks quite difficult, this alternative descent is fairly straightforward. It calls for more care, however, and should not be done before mid-February because winter snows generally still hide the few (otherwise small and harmless) crevasses before then.

Head north over a tiny plateau, then follow the ridge through rock gaps to a low point between Cerro Hielo Azul and Barda Negra. Descend onto permanent snow fields, making your way down over a minor brown rock rib above a small lake dammed by the ice. From here continue along the right-hand (ie southern) side of Glaciar Hielo Azul, keeping well away from the more crevassed

ice over to your left. After you pass the large cairn on the rocky outcrop (mentioned earlier), cut down right off the ice and follow the edge of the glacier back to the waterfall near its snout.

Camp Sites No sensible trekker would want to pitch their tent anywhere along Stage 2A – use the free camping area five minutes down from the Refugio Hielo Azul described in Stage 1.

Stage 2B: Refugio Hielo Azul to Refugio Cajón del Azul
10km, 3¼ to 4¼ hours

Cross the small Río Teno on a makeshift bridge to the camping area, then head 250m down the left bank to a (normally dry) stream bed. Follow red markings off left up the steep slope, moving gently rightwards higher up to reach a small dirty lagoon among lenga scrub. The route, which is confused in places by diverging animal trails, dips back into the forest and continues north-westwards just left of a long mallín. You should come out at a lovely green lawn where a snow-fed waterfall splashes over the precipice of a tiny cirque, 60 to 80 minutes from the refugio.

Pick up a rough horse trail at the remains of an old corral, following it eastwards around the right-hand side of a small lake with a rocky islet. The foot track drops gently down through lengas mixed with bamboo to cross the tumbling brook (flowing from the cirque waterfall). Watching out carefully for waymarkings as the path here is overgrown and obscured by fallen trees, make your way up diagonally left (roughly east-north-east) away from the stream. The route crosses over a minor crest onto high scrub-covered slopes that overlook the broad valley of El Bolsón towards Cerro Piltriquitrón, 50 minutes to 1¼ hours on.

Begin your gradual descent north-westwards into the lovely **Valle Azul**, alternating between long sidles up the valley and short, sharp switchbacks. The path drops down through fragrant stands of ciprés de la cordillera towards **Cerro Horqueta** and **Dedo Gordo** (the 2069m 'fat finger' peak on the opposite side of the valley) to meet a 4WD track after one to 1¼ hours. (Trekkers going the other way should note that this inconspicuous trail turn-off is signposted simply 'H. A.' and is visible only from its upvalley side.)

Proceed left through the tall coigüe forest for five minutes to meet the **Río Azul**. The road fords the river here, but a good foot track continues upstream along its wild southern bank past small alerces and turquoise pools to cross the impressive 3m wide, 40m deep gorge known as the **Cañadón del Azul** on a footbridge. Skirt the left side of a wooden stockade, then cut through a grassy orchard to arrive at the **Refugio Cajón del Azul** (see Accommodation & Camping earlier in this section) after a final 20 to 25 minutes. This homy hut stands at the foot of Dedo Gordo in a small open area of the valley, which is enclosed by incredibly steep rock walls. The refugio serves as an excellent base for return treks up through the alerce forests along the Río Azul as far as the Cañadon del Rayado or Paso Horqueta (on the Argentina/Chile frontier).

Camp Sites The grassy meadow at the base of the cirque passed midway along Stage 2B is the only recommended place to camp en route. Campers at the Refugio Cajón del Azul can use the hut's facilities for US$4 per person.

Stage 3: Refugio Cajón del Azul to Warton

12km, 2½ to 3¼ hours

Retrace your steps to the 4WD track and continue on down along the Río Azul, skirting its coarse-pebble bed where the road fords and refords the river. After passing isolated buildings (including a kiosk selling natural juices and bread), the road climbs away right over a high crest before descending steeply to cross the Río Azul on a suspension footbridge just above its confluence with the smaller **Río del Encanto Blanco**. Cross the latter stream on a second (rather rickety) bridge to reach a cottage just downstream, which is connected with the homestead of Warton by a 1km dirt road.

For trekkers walking the other way, there are several signs at this intersection (the most prominent of which reads 'Confluencia del Río Azul y Blanco'); the upriver time is less than 30 minutes longer than the (downward) time quoted above.

Other Treks in the Comarca Andina del Paralelo 42

CERRO PERITO MORENO

This five-hour return trek begins from the Refugio Perito Moreno, a ski lodge situated at 950m, 25km by road north of El Bolsón (see Trekking Bases). Refugio Perito Moreno (☎ 93912) belongs to the local Club Andino Piltriquitrón (CAP), and during January and February the CAP runs minibuses out to the refugio (see the Getting to/from the Trek section of Around Cerro Hielo Azul). The route first climbs to the upper end of the winter ski lifts, then heads westwards into the lenga scrub and crosses a plateau (at around 1600m) to reach the snout of the glacier on the side of Cerro Perito Moreno. The 2206m summit can only be reached by experienced climbers with proper mountaineering equipment, but from a lookout point on a spur a short way over to the left trekkers get an excellent view southwards across the valley of the Río Encanto Blanco to the peaks around Dedo Gordo.

The *Mapa de El Bolsón y su Zona* scaled at roughly 1:125,000 and the 1:100,000 Argentine IGM sheet *El Bolsón* (4172-34, Río Negro) cover this area, but neither properly shows the route itself; also refer to the 'Barda Negra & Cajón del Azul' map in this guidebook.

CERRO PILTRIQUITRÓN

Another of the Comarca Andina's key landmarks, the rump ridge of Cerro Piltriquitrón (pronounced 'pill-tree-kay-TRON') rises up directly from the flat valley floor on the eastern side of El Bolsón. The two to three-day return trek to this 2260m panoramic summit can be shortened by chartering a taxi to Platforma del Piltriquitrón, a lookout point at the end of the 10km access road (the turn-off is several kilometres south-east of El Bolsón on the road to El Hoyo). From here you climb for one hour up to the Refugio Cerro Piltriquitrón (☎ 92024). This large CAP refugio, which stands at around 1400m, below an old ski field (now superseded by the newly developed ski field around the Refugio Perito Moreno), offers beds for US$7 a night and meals are available. A marked trail ascends beside a disused ski lift, skirting away eastwards before it makes a final steep climb through loose scree to reach the summit. From here there are superb views south across Lago Puelo to Cerro Tres Picos as well as northwards to Volcán Osorno and Monte Tronador.

The Argentine IGM's 1:100,000 sheet *Cuesta del Ternero* (Río Negro, 4172-35) covers the trek.

CERRO LINDO

The glacier-crowned 2135m Cerro Lindo, which stands just under 15km directly west of El Bolsón, can be climbed in a moderate three-day return trek. The path crosses the suspension bridge near the *Río Azul* camping ground (see Accommodation & Camping) and climbs north-westwards through the forest. After descending steeply to cross the small Arroyo Lali (the last water until the refugio) continue up westwards to reach the Refugio Cerro Lindo, at the foot of a waterfall. This CAP hut has sleeping space (US$7 per night) for up to 35 people and meals are available; in January the refugio can get crowded. From here a rougher trail leads up to the summit of Cerro Lindo; the return trip takes around three hours. Recommended maps are as for the Around Cerro Hielo Azul trek described earlier; also refer to the 'Barda Negra & Cajón del Azul' map in this guide-book.

PARQUE NACIONAL LAGO PUELO

This small (237 sq km) national park is 15km south-west of El Bolsón in the province of Chubut. As its name suggests, the park's central feature is Lago Puelo itself, a roughly 40 sq km glacial lake which is the source of the Río Puelo. The park administration centre (Intendencia, ☎ & fax 0944-99064) is at the north-eastern end of Lago Puelo near where the Río Azul enters the lake. There is tourist accommodation at the nearby village of Villa Lago Puelo (several kilometres north on the access road from El Bolsón), and a camping ground with good facilities (US$5 per person) near the boat jetty.

All of the longer treks starting in Parque Nacional Lago Puelo eventually lead outside the park boundaries. In addition to the routes outlined below, refer to the Up The Río Puelo trek described under Other Treks in Central Patagonia at the end of this chapter.

The best single-sheet map covering almost all of the park is the *Mapa de El Bolsón y Su Zona* published by the Club Andino Piltriquitrón in El Bolsón. Two Argentine IGM 1:100,000 sheets, *Cordón del Pico Alto* (Chubut, No 4372-3) and *Lago Puelo* (Chubut, No 4372-4), cover all of the park. From Monday to Saturday there are half a dozen buses to Lago Puelo from El Bolsón (get on at the bus stop near the post office or opposite the ACA service station), but on Sunday there are only three buses. A taxi *(remise)* to Lago Puelo costs US$12.

LAGUNA HUEMUL

Although it lies some distance outside the borders of Parque Nacional Lago Puelo, the pretty alpine lake of Laguna Huemul makes an excellent full day's trek from the Intendencia (park administration centre).

The Río Azul can be crossed on a bridge several kilometres upstream from where it runs into Lago Puelo. The route climbs past a road under construction (which will eventually connect to the Río Puelo road in Chile) to a farmhouse, where trekkers should ask permission to cross this private property (and perhaps for route directions as well). Continue northwards mostly along 4WD tracks through patches of coigüe forest across a first stream, then follow a foot track up near a second stream to a lookout point with views along the Valle Azul to El Bolsón. The route heads on over the ridge past a tarn, before descending roughly north-west to Laguna Huemul.

The 1:100,000 Argentine IGM sheet *Lago Puelo* (Chubut, No 4372-4) covers the trek (but does not properly show the route).

CERRO CURRUMAHUIDA

You can climb this peak (about 1200m) in around 6 hours return from the Intendencia. The route sidles along slopes on the eastern side of Lago Puelo, then climbs through stands of coigüe and ciprés de la cordillera (higher up the forest has largely been destroyed by the fires of 1987) to the top of the range. A trek along (or near to) this ridge top to the summit of Cerro Currumahuida offers you great views across Lago Puelo to Lago Inferior (in Chile), to Cerro Tres Picos to the south-west and Cerro Piltriquitrón to the north-east.

RIO TURBIO & CERRO PLATAFORMA

The day hike to the Río Turbio leaves from the free camping area at El Desemboque, where the Río Epuyén runs into Lago Puelo; this is some 16km from El Hoyo, which is roughly 14km south of El Bolsón. The trail begins at the southern end of the beach, sidling up through burnt forest on the western slopes of Cerro Durrumbe before descending again to an APN guardería at the south-eastern corner of Lago Puelo. From here launches run back across the lake to the jetty near the Intendencia on the north-eastern shore.

Cerro Plataforma, a flat-topped mountain well outside the park boundaries where ancient marine fossils are found, can be reached in a three-day return trek from the guardería. The route turns south-westwards, crosses the Arroyo Derrumbe and climbs steadily up past little farms high above the valley of the Río Turbio; a final climb following red paint markings leads to the Cerro Plataforma. Two Argentine IGM 1:100,000 sheets, *Lago Puelo* (Chubut, No 4372-4) and *Lago Rivadavia* (Chubut, No 4372-10), are needed for this route.

Parque Nacional Los Alerces

Parque Nacional Los Alerces lies to the west of the small city of Esquel in the north of Argentina's Chubut Province. Established in 1937 (concurrently with Parque Nacional Los Glaciares in southern Patagonia), the park protects – not always successfully, unfortunately – one of the largest and most beautiful tracts of Andean wilderness in central Patagonia. The scope for overnight trekking trips in Los Alerces is fairly limited, however, because public access to the park's interior is restricted.

GENERAL INFORMATION
Geographical Features

Occupying an area of 2630 sq km, Parque Nacional Los Alerces is a vast lakeland created during the Pleistocene Ice Age. The landscape in the northern half of the park is dominated by three major glacial lakes, Lago Rivadavia, Lago Menéndez and Lago Futalaufquen, whose fjord-like arms stretch deep into the Cordillera; they are surrounded by several other smaller, yet still quite sizeable lakes, including Lago Cisnes and Lago Krüger. The large lakes all lie at over 500m above sea level, and drain southwards into another even bigger – and far younger – lake, Lago Amutui Quimei (formerly called Lago Situación), a huge reservoir built in the early 1970s to generate hydroelectricity for an aluminium smelter in Puerto Madryn on the Atlantic coast. The dam inundated four beautiful lakes stretching along what had been one of the wildest larger valleys on the Argentine side of the Patagonian Andes.

Although situated east of the main range of the Cordillera, Parque Nacional Los

Alerces lies entirely within the Pacific watershed, and the outlet of Lago Amutui Quimei, the Río Futaleufú, therefore flows westwards into Chile. Los Alerces' major lakes form a natural division between the dry, almost steppe-like eastern fringe of the park and the increasingly wet sector towards the west. Roads run along the eastern sides of Lago Rivadavia and Lago Futalaufquen, but there is no access to Los Alerces' wild interior apart from the navigable waterways of the lakes and rivers. The highest peaks in the park, such as Cerro Torrecillas, Cerro Situación and Cerro Piramides, are not on the frontier with Chile but in lateral ranges that extend eastwards between the lakes. Although none of these mountains comes close to reaching 2500m, their impressive rock walls rise up almost 1000m from the tangled lengas at the tree line to glacier-clad summits.

Natural History

Parque Nacional Los Alerces (like the national park of Alerce Andino in Chile) conserves some of the southern Andes' most majestic stands of giant alerces. The most eminent representative of the so-called Valdivian rainforest, the alerce grows throughout the southern Lake District, but only occasionally reaches the enormous size for which it is so famous. The main prerequisites for this – mild conditions, deep and perpetually wet soil, absence of fire and lots of time – are fulfilled by several locations in the remote interior of the park. In the stand known as the Alerzal Milenario, on the extreme northwestern arm of Lago Menéndez (see Other Treks), are alerces aged well over 2000 years, but a single ancient specimen found on the lake's south-western arm is believed to be over 4000 years old!

Alerces are typically found growing in association with other rainforest trees. One species is the olivillo *(Aextoxicon punctatum)*, also known by its Mapuche name of teque. It has pointed oval leaves whose undersides are lighter and often red-speckled, and as its Spanish name suggests, the olivillo produces small, round fleshy fruit. Also present are avellano *(Gevuina avellana)*, a member of the proteaceae family with shiny serrated leaves and white-spotted ash-grey bark, and tineo *(Weinmannia trichosperma)*, instantly recognisably by its serrated, paired leaves. The holly-leafed taique *(Desfontainia spinosa)*, traumén *(Pseudopanax laetevirens)* and tepú *(Tepualia stipularis)*, a myrtle bush with small white flowers, are typical plants of the Valdivian forest understorey.

The lower, drier foothills on the park's eastern edge have some fine stands of coniferous ciprés de la cordillera, also called lahuán, often growing in loose association with the maitén *(Maytenus boaria)*, a very attractive willow-like tree. The maitén, which was sacred to the local Mapuche people, is also an important winter fodder tree for wild animals such as huemul and guanaco. Bordering the lakeshores and the riverbanks are some superb examples of arrayán *(Myrceugenella apiculata)*, a myrtle species that is recognisable by its striking reddish orange bark and numerous twisted trunks. In summer the arrayán is covered by a profusion of white flowers.

Los Alerces' large lakes provide a habitat to many water birds. Visitors may spy the huala, a large brownish-grey grebe. The huala has a long reddish neck and white underbelly, and feeds on a rich diet of fish, molluscs and aquatic insects in the many freshwater lakes in the park. It's often found with the tagua, a black coot with a yellow beak that builds a floating nest on lakes and still-water streams. The pato torrentes, or torrent duck, is well adapted to fast-flowing rivers and streams, and is occasionally seen diving into white water in search of food. Other species of native duck include the colourful pato anteojillo, or bronze-winged duck *(Anas specularis)*, which builds its nest on small islands, and the pato juarjual, or crested duck *(Lophonetta specularioides)*.

In the forest trekkers will hear the distinctive chuckling warble of the chucao, which hides among the canes of the colihue bamboo, and may see the tiny picaflor, a nectar-eating hummingbird that gorges itself on the nectar of the notro and the chilco. The cachaña, a green parakeet with a yellowish-red under-belly, is usually observed in pairs.

Predators found in the park include the puma, huiña and two native foxes, the reddish-brown zorro gris and bluish-greyish zorro culpeo. The very lucky might even chance to spot the amphibious huillín, a carnivorous mammal that lives along the banks of the larger rivers and lakes.

Climate
Parque Nacional Los Alerces is in a rain shadow, which is typical for areas in the lee of the Andes. Annual precipitation peaks at almost 4500mm in the ranges along Argentina's frontier with Chile, but declines progressively to a minimum of just under 800mm at the park's north-eastern boundary near Lago Rivadavia. A continental climate prevails, with occasional hot summer weather and crisp winters that can bring heavy snowfalls.

Place Names
Surprisingly, little of Los Alerces' nomenclature is derived from the language of the indigenous Mapuche people; the only important exceptions are Lago Futalaufquen (also spelt Futalafquen), which simply means 'big lake', and the Río Futaleufú, or 'big river'. Most other place names in the park are of Spanish origin, and either descriptive, such as the Cordón de los Piramides ('pyramid range') and Cerro Dedal ('thimble peak'), or honour local settlers and explorers, including the Río Frey and Cerro Meiling (a peak near Cerro Torrecillas, first climbed by members of the Club Andino Bariloche).

PRACTICAL INFORMATION
Information Sources
The APN has an office in Esquel (☎ 0945-71015; fax 0945-4315), but the administration centre (Intendencia) for Parque Nacional Los Alerces is at Villa Futalaufquen, 67km by road from Esquel (and 12km on from the park's southern entrance gate). The information centre (Centro de Informes; ☎ 0945-75015; fax 0945-71020) is open daily from 9 am until 6 pm (until 9 pm in January and Febru-

ary). There are also guarderías at Lago Verde and Lago Rivadavia.

Permits & Regulations
All visitors to Parque Nacional Los Alerces must pay a US$5 entrance fee (collected at the park's northern or southern gates, or *portadas*). Fishing permits can be purchased at the APN information centre in Villa Futalaufquen, as well as from the Camping Ecológico Lago Verde (see Accommodation & Camping).

Apart from organised camping grounds and park-authorised camping areas, camping is not permitted – or tolerated – anywhere in the park. Fines are imposed for serious infringements of this rule.

When To Trek
Since all (permitted) treks in Los Alerces are either lower-level routes or return day walks in the ranges on the park's less more sheltered eastern side, trekking can normally be undertaken somewhat earlier and/or later in the season – from around mid-November until early May.

Lago Krüger & Lago Amutui Quimei

Duration 3 or 4 days
Distance 46km (65km if you return on foot)
Standard Medium
Start/Finish Villa Futalafquen
Entry US$5, permit needed
Season November-May
Summary A return route that leads around the wild southern shores of Lago Futalaufquen to the beautiful secluded Lago Krüger then on to a scenic lookout above Lago Amutui Quimei.

This pleasant trek leads past little lakeside beaches fringed by luxuriant forests on the southern shores of Lago Futalaufquen and Lago Krüger, then down beside the wild cataracts of the Río Frey to a lookout on the northern side of Lago Amutui Quimei.

MAPS

Two sheets 1:100,000 produced by the Argentine IGM, *Lago Rivadavia* (Chubut, No 4372-10) and *Villa Futulafquen* (Chubut, No 2372-16) cover the trekking route.

DAYS REQUIRED

The trekking time to Lago Amutui Quimei is two days, but if you return via the same route (rather than taking the launch back – see Getting to/from the Trek) this becomes a three or four-day trek.

TREKKING STANDARD

This trek follows well-trodden paths for most of the way and route-finding is fairly straightforward. Winds can be very strong on the low west-facing pass (at roughly 1050m) crossed about halfway, but there are no other exposed sections. Along the section between Playa Blanca and Lago Krüger, however, numerous fallen logs and overgrown thickets of colihue bamboo will slow you down. The route between Lago Krüger and Lago Amutui Quimei leads along a disused road, where the odd collapsed bridge is a minor inconvenience.

The trek is rated *medium* and has a total distance of 46km (or 65km return if you trek both to and from Refugio Lago Krüger).

ACCOMMODATION & CAMPING

This short trek can be done without a tent by staying at the *Refugio Lago Krüger* (☎ 3380; fax 2086). The refugio has 30 bunks with blankets (but take a sleeping bag if possible), and the overnighting charge per person is US$8. Simple cooked meals, basic supplies and liquid refreshments are available from the canteen. Trekkers can also camp by the lake a short way from the Refugio Lago Krüger for US$5 per person. There's a toilet/shower block (with wood-heated water) in the forest between the camping ground and the refugio.

The *Los Maitenes* camping ground 400m down to the right from the Intendencia at Villa Futalaufquen, has attractive grassy

sites for US$4 per person under the maitén trees; there are hot showers and laundry facilities. About 1.5km along the road to El Bolsón is a free camping area (known as Las Lechuzas) by the lake shore. The up-market *Hostería Futalaufquen* (☎ 0945-71008), at the end of the road 500m on from Puerto Limonao, has doubles from US$140.

Around the eastern shore of the Lago Futalaufquen are half a dozen or so hosterías and camping grounds with cabins, including: the *Hostería Quime Quipán* (☎ 0944-4134, or 0945-22272), the *Cabañas Los Tepúes*, the *Hostería Pucón Pai*, the Cabañas Tejas Negras (☎ 0944-22272), the *Hostería Cume Hue* (☎ 0944-3639) and *Cabañas Bahía Rosales* (☎ 0945-3622).

Two organised camping grounds in the northern sector of the park are the excellent *Camping Ecológico Lago Verde* on the eastern shore of Lago Verde and the *Autocamping Bahía Solis* on Lago Rivadavia.

Trekkers should note that camping is only permitted in Parque Nacional Los Alerces at organised camping grounds and the free park-authorised camping areas.

SUPPLIES

Basic provisions (including fresh bread, meat and fruit) are available from the grocery store in Villa Futalaufquen. The village also has also a postal service and a petrol (gasoline) station. All of the 10 organised camping grounds in Parque Nacional Los Alerces have stores *(proveedurías)* selling a narrow range of campers' supplies.

GETTING TO/FROM THE TREK

The trek begins and ends at the village of Villa Futalaufquen, which is most easily accessible from Esquel (see Trekking Bases). Throughout the trekking season Transportes Esquel (☎ 3529) runs daily buses from Esquel to Villa Futalaufquen, leaving at 8 am, 2 pm, 4.30 pm (January only) and 8 pm. The trip takes 45 minutes and costs US$4.50. The buses continue on to Lago Verde (one of these buses goes on as far as Lago Rivadavia). There are return buses at 9.30 am, 12.30pm, 5.30 pm (January only) and 8 pm.

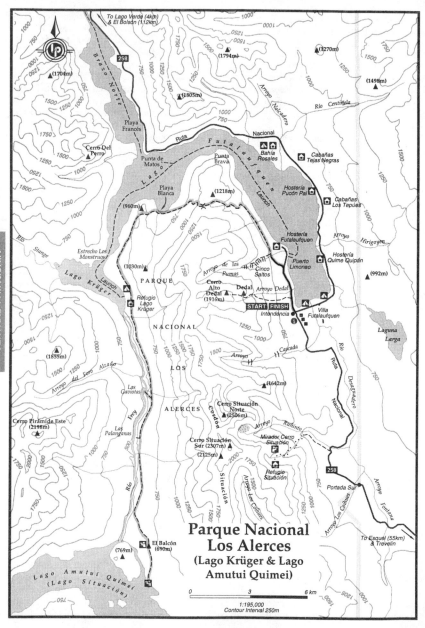

Parque Nacional Los Alerces
(Lago Krüger & Lago Amutui Quimei)

0   3   6 km

1:195,000
Contour Interval 250m

Two other smaller operators, Minibus Lago Verde and Zabala-Daniel, also run minibuses to/from Lago Verde and Esquel three times a week.

Another way of getting to/from the park is via El Bolsón (see Trekking Bases). Zabala-Daniel operates a minibus service between El Bolsón and Lago Verde/Río Arrayanes, from where you can catch another bus on to Villa Futalaufquen. The minibuses depart daily from El Bolsón at 12.30 pm and 5 pm and return from Lago Verde/Río Arrayanes at 11.30 am and 3.15 pm; there is sometimes another minibus to El Bolsón at 6 pm. The (rather dusty) trip takes around three hours and the fare is US$15.

Rather than backtracking on foot, it's recommended that trekkers do the return leg from Lago Krüger to Puerto Limonao by boat. From December to the end of March the Safari Lacustre company, which has an office at Puerto Limonao (☎ 0945-71009 or 394-3808), runs a small launch to Lago Krüger three days per week. At the time of research the launch left Puerto Limonao at 10 am on Saturdays, Tuesdays and Thursdays, returning from Lago Krüger at around 4 pm; the boat trip only takes around 1½ hours. Safari Lacustre charges trekkers the full US$25 return fare, even though they only travel one way. Note that the launch does not run on days when strong westerly winds make the lake too choppy, and trekkers may have to walk back out to Villa Futalaufquen or spend a day or two waiting at Lago Krüger (although it may also be possible to hitch a ride back on a speedboat). Private vehicles can be parked overnight at Puerto Limonao.

THE TREK
Stage 1: Villa Futalaufquen to Refugio Lago Krüger
19km, 6½ to 8 hours
This is a long and tiring day, so try to start early.

After signing in at the APN information centre, follow the road (or a path slightly closer to the lake) around the south-western side of Lago Futalaufquen. Go left at a short road turn-off several hundred metres before **Puerto Limonao** – if you want to buy a

ticket back on the launch, first continue ahead to the port – which soon ends at a small car park by the **Arroyo de los Pumas** after 30 to 40 minutes. Cross the small stream on a footbridge and head into the forest past a signposted trail leading off left to the **Cinco Saltos** (a series of waterfalls that can be visited in around 30 minutes return).

Continue walking behind the **Hostería Futalaufquen** to begin an undulating traverse up along the steep-sided lake through stands of coniferous ciprés de la cordillera that gradually go over into coigüe beech. The path then begins a steady winding climb away to the left through clustered thickets of overhanging colihue, sidling on rightwards over high slopes of ñirre and notro scrub, giving good views of Cerro Alto El Petiso and other peaks on the northern side of Lago Futalaufquen.

After turning west-north-west to cross a small stream, head up through a hollow covered with low, weather-beaten bamboo. The route skirts the lenga forest on the right-hand side of this shallow basin to reach a scrubby saddle (at roughly 1050m) overlooking a small cove in the lake immediately below to the west, 2½ to 3 hours from the Arroyo de los Pumas. Descend directly in steep, loose-earth zigzags before moving over to the left to reach **Playa Blanca** after a further 50 minutes to 1¼ hours. This idyllic little white-sand beach is fringed by lovely arrayán trees.

Pick up the route again at the reedy far end of the beach. The now poorly maintained path leads away from shore through tall coigüe forest, where the distinctive call of the tiny chucao rings out from the quila underbrush, and delicate white palomita orchids *(Codonorquis lessonii)* grow, thriving in the damp, humus-rich soil. After returning to the lakeside for some distance the route again moves away left, finally coming out onto a lovely pebble beach at **Lago Krüger** after three to 3½ hours. The **Refugio Lago Krüger** (see Accommodation & Camping earlier in this section) is 10 minutes on around past the camping ground and jetty at the lake outlet.

Camp Sites Although some trekkers disregard the rule, camping is no longer officially allowed at Playa Blanca. If you are tempted to pitch the tent at this idyllic spot, please refrain from lighting a fire and take all of your garbage with you. The camping ground at Refugio Lago Krüger costs US$5 per person, which includes use of the wood-heated hot shower.

Stage 2: Refugio Lago Krüger to Lago Amutui Quimei

27km return, 5½ to 7 hours return

Follow the path from the southern side of the small clearing in front of the refugio. After a short distance it goes over into a long-disused road which became obsolete after completion of the dam. This broad track leads smoothly down through tall coigüe forest into the valley of the **Río Frey**, which flows through a continuous series of white-water rapids, passing a signposted path turn-off leading down steeply to **Las Gaviotas**, a spot that is favoured by fly fishers, after 40 to 50 minutes.

Make your way on for 25 to 30 minutes past more anglers' pools known as **Las Palanganas**, proceeding smoothly through tiny meadows dotted with raspberry bushes and wild strawberries. Surrounding a glacial cirque up to your right stands the interesting jagged 2198m peak of **Cerro Piramide Este**. The old vehicle track climbs slightly over a crest, from where the great reservoir of **Lago Amutui Quimei** comes into sight, then descends briefly to reach **El Balcón** after a further 1½ to 2 hours. Pairs of condors often circle above this high open grassy shelf that looks out to the often snowcapped mountains on the southern end of the lake. For better views you can continue for another 15 to 20 minutes to a slightly higher knob on a minor peninsula.

Return to Refugio Lago Krüger via the same route.

Camp Sites Although anglers and trekkers sometimes camp along the banks of the Río Frey, camping is permitted only at the Refugio Lago Krüger.

Other Treks in Parque Nacional Los Alerces

CERRO ALTO DEDAL

The short trek up to Cerro Alto Dedal (1916m) is the most popular in the park, and takes around six hours return from Villa Futalaufquen. The signposted foot track leaves the road about halfway between the Intendencia and Puerto Limonao. The route soon crosses the Arroyo Dedal (carry water from this stream as it is the last) as it climbs steeply out of the forest and follows a spur over Dedal (a minor point at around 1600m) to Cerro Alto Dedal. The summit offers great views northwards across Lago Futalaufquen, east to Laguna Larga, south along the range to Cerro Situación and south-west to the Cordón de los Piramides. There is a rule in the park that trekkers must begin climbing before 10 am in order to return safely by nightfall.

The 1:100,000 Argentine IGM sheet *Villa Futulafquen* (Chubut, No 2372-16) covers the area (but doesn't show the route).

MIRADOR CERRO SITUACIÓN

The trek up to this lookout point, which gives excellent views of a small glacier in the cirque between the northern and southern summits of Cerro Situación, is best done as an overnight trip. An unsignposted foot track leaves from the road 10km south of Villa Futalaufquen, first following the southern side of the Arroyo Ruñinto. Head up left at the first large side stream you meet, crossing this several times as you climb steeply to reach a small refugio. (Situated among lenga scrub at roughly 1450m, this refugio belongs to the Club Andino Esquel; it has a fireplace and sleeping space for up to six people.) The route then sidles around northwards along the ridge to the Mirador. Use the same IGM map as for the Cerro Alto Dedal trek.

CERRO ALTO EL PETISO

The 1790m Cerro Alto El Petiso is the best lookout point in the park's northern sector, and you can visit it in a full day trek of medium difficulty taking around eight hours return. The trail head is at Puerto Mermoud (where there is an historic wooden farmhouse built by the first settler in this area) on the western shore of Lago Verde. As a rule, trekkers must set out before 10 am so that they have leave enough time to return safely by nightfall. The path climbs over a ridge, then follows the Arroyo Zanjón Honda up to its source at two tiny streamlets (the last running water). A final steep ascent along a spur leads to the summit, from where you get a superb panorama that includes Lago Menéndez, Lago Futalaufquen, Lago Rivadavia and the glacier-clad peak of Cerro Torrecillas. Use the same IGM map as for the treks mentioned earlier.

LAGO CISNE
The beautiful wild interior of Parque Nacional Los Alerces is essentially out-of-bounds to trekkers. The park authorities restrict public

access and there are almost no foot tracks in the impenetrable rainforest. The only way to visit the otherwise restricted zone close to the frontier with Chile is to do the boat trip (which is run by Safari Lacustre and costs US$35) from Puerto Chucao at the south-eastern corner of Lago Menéndez.

Puerto Chucao itself can be reached if you do a lovely 30-minute walk along the Río Menéndez (which is the lake outlet). The launch cruises past the hanging glaciers on Cerro Torrecillas before docking at the north-western end of Lago Menéndez. From here an APN guide leads you on a 1½ hour circuit tour through the forest past the beautiful emerald lake of Lago Cisne. The highlight of this 'trek' is unquestionably the ancient stand of alerces (known as the Alerzal Milenario), where one enormous tree is thought to be about 2500 years old. The Argentine IGM's 1:100,000 sheet *Lago Rivadavia* (Chubut, No 4372-10) covers the Lago Cisne area.

Reserva Nacional Río Simpson

Reserva Nacional Río Simpson is north-west of Coyhaique in Chile's IX Region. Taking in a good part of the snowcapped ranges visible from the city, the reserve was established in 1967 to protect an area close to Coyhaique in a region that has been very badly affected by environmental degradation caused by forest fires, which in turn have led to erosion. Reserva Nacional Río Simpson has largely returned to its previous wild state, and offers pleasant and readily accessible trekking.

GENERAL INFORMATION
Geographical Features
The reserve comprises an area of 404 sq km (although its exact boundaries have not yet been fully determined) and takes in much of the catchment area of the Río Simpson. From its source just to the north of Lago General Carrera, this river cuts through the Cordillera

to run into the Pacific at Fiordo Aisén, dividing the reserve into northern (Correntoso) and southern (Río Claro) sectors. Although the highest of these mountains scarcely reach 2000m, the sheer-sided, U-shaped valleys of unmistakable glacial origin are very impressive. The Aisén-Coyhaique road follows the broad green valley of the Río Simpson for over 50km. The Río Simpson's flow has an unusually high annual variation, often flooding during the winter months but normally diminishing to no more than a gentle stream in late summer.

Natural History
Damp forests dominated by moisture-loving trees such as coigüe, tepa, mañío, tineo and canelo are typical vegetation in the reserve (although numerous areas of charred trees are a reminder of the fire sensitivity of the native forest). Flowery thickets of notro,

tepu and chilco are found in clearings or at the edge of the forest along with colihue, the native bamboo. Here the pudú, a midget deer, finds an ideal habitat, and is preyed on by the puma. Birds commonly heard (and less commonly seen) in these forests include the tiny orange-red breasted chucao and the lechuza *(Tyto alba)*, the barn owl to bird lovers the world over. Also present is the queltehue austral, a black-breasted lapwing that frequents small clearings in the moist valley floors. Native ibis, known as bandurrias, as well as ducks like avutardas and caiquenes are found around the rivers and small lakes.

Climate
The Río Simpson area is considerably sheltered by coastal ranges (particularly the longitudinal Cordón de los Barrancos). The local climate shows the gradual fall in precipitation levels that typically occurs the further east you travel. While the rainfall on the coast less than 40km directly to the west is almost 5000mm, no parts of Reserva Nacional Río Simpson receive more than 3000mm annually.

Place Names
The Río Simpson is named after the Chilean naval officer Enrique Simpson who produced the first maps of the Aisén region in the early 1870s (although some attribute the name to George G Simpson, an American natural scientist who explored parts of Aisén in the early part of this century). The name Aisén itself appears to be a corruption of the Tehuelche word *athen*, which means 'worn' or 'abraded', perhaps a reflection of the region's glaciated topography.

PRACTICAL INFORMATION
Information Sources
The ranger at the Guardería Correntoso, where the Cerro Catedral trek starts, can give basic advice on route conditions in the reserve's Correntoso sector. The administrative centre for the reserve is near the CONAF information centre and camping ground at the Salto del Vírgen, 10km west (or 32km from Coyhaique) along the road to Puerto

Aisén. For the CONAF office in Coyhaique see Trekking Bases.

Permits & Regulations
No permit is required to trek in Reserva Nacional Río Simpson, but trekkers should leave details of party members and route intentions with the guardaparques. Wild camping is permitted in the reserve, but trekkers are again urged to take extreme caution when lighting campfires.

When to Trek
Because of the generally low level of the routes and sheltered climate in the reserve, treks can be undertaken over an extended summer period from October until late April.

Cerro Catedral

Duration 4 days
Distance 37km return
Standard Medium
Start/Finish Coyhaique-Puerto Aisén highway (Ruta CH 245)
Entry Free, no permit needed
Season October-April
Summary A return trek through lush forests of coigüe, tepa and mañío to a lovely alpine lake under the granite spires of Cerro Catedral; a side trip to a petrified forest is also possible.

The northern sector of Río Simpson consists of a compact series of steep and glaciated granite ranges. These surround Cerro Catedral, not to be confused with Cerro Catedral in Parque Nacional Nahuel Huapi, whose impressive citadel-like summit almost reaches 2000m. Small glaciers cling to the higher summits and several small glacial lakes lie in the forested valleys.

MAPS
A Chilean IGM 1:50,000 sheet, *Río Correntoso* (Section I, No 108), completely

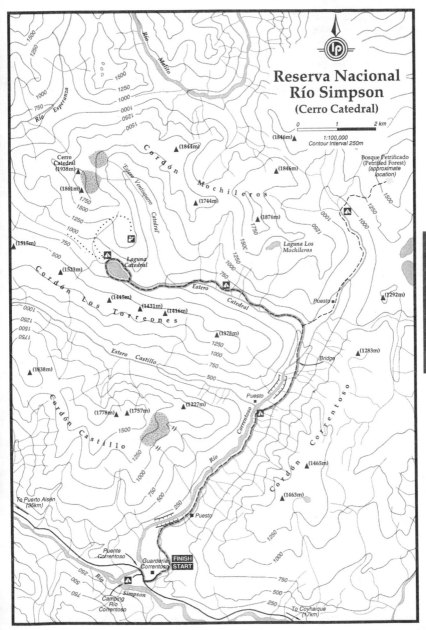

covers the area. This map does not show the trekking route, but is topographically accurate.

DAYS REQUIRED
The minimum time for a trek to Cerro Catedral is three days. An additional day or two could be spent doing the side trip to the petrified forest (described in the route description).

TREKKING STANDARD
The trek follows an often wet foot track providing access to a few tiny farms along the Río Correntoso. The route is poorly marked but relatively straightforward, although cattle and horses have left it very muddy and eroded in places – a real quagmire on the first section between the Guardería Correntoso and the Río Correntoso. Along the final section to Laguna Catedral vigorous rainforest growth may obscure the route in places, but the path was laboriously recut by an enthusiastic group of young Raleigh International volunteers in early 1996, and should remain easily passable for many years to come.

The trek is graded *medium*; the return walking distance to Lago Catedral is 37km.

ACCOMMODATION & CAMPING
There are no en route huts (although CONAF does plan to construct a refugio at Laguna Catedral at some time in the future), so trekkers must carry a tent. The Camping Río Correntoso, near the start of the trek, offers cabins and organised camping facilities beside the Río Simpson. There is also a CONAF camping ground near the CONAF visitors' information centre 10km west along the road.

SUPPLIES
There is no store near the start of the trek, so you should bring all you need from Coyhaique or Puerto Aisén.

GETTING TO/FROM THE TREK
The trek begins at the Puente Correntoso on the road to Puerto Aisén (Ruta CH 245), 22km from Coyhaique. Taxibus Don Carlos runs eight daily buses in both directions between Coyhaique and Puerto Aisén. You will probably have to pay the full-distance fare (US$6); make sure the driver knows where you want to get off. Traffic is reasonably constant and hitchhiking is a fairly reliable alternative. Private vehicles can be left at the Guardería Correntoso (but the short turn-off road is steep and muddy).

THE TREK
Puente Correntoso to Laguna Catedral
18km, 6½ to 8 hours
From the **Puente Correntoso** walk 500m east (towards Coyhaique) to where a signpost points up left along the dirt road leading you in five minutes to the **Guardería Correntoso**. Waterfalls stream down the sheer glaciated rock walls on the adjacent side of the Río Simpson valley.

After leaving all relevant details of your party at the guardería, follow the broad and initially very muddy track roughly northwest through regenerating coigüe forest to meet the **Río Correntoso** at a gorge. Make your way up the east bank past a puesto and small corral in a grassy meadow, proceeding smoothly on upvalley through attractive stands of mañío and tepa below a broad shelf glacier on the Cordón Castillo and interesting rock outcrops on the Cordón Correntoso to where the **Estero Castillo** meets the river after 2¼ to three hours.

Upstream of this confluence the valley narrows where the Río Correntoso rushes through a deep gully, which the path avoids by moving up to the right. After climbing briefly beside a mossy streamlet fringed by nalcas, walk high above the river along grassy terraces scattered with chilcos and clumps of resilient colihue, then gradually drop down again to cross a log bridge over the now small Río Correntoso just above its junction with the **Estero Catedral**, 1¼ to 1½ hours on. Ascend 15 minutes northwards via a steep, eroded trail to an indistinct turn-off on the slopes well above the junction.

From this point, a side trip taking five hours return can be made into the upper valley of the Estero Correntoso to the **Bosque Petrificado**, a recently discovered petrified forest of ancient ciprés de las Guaitecas trees.

Parque Nacional Los Alerces is scattered with lakes (top) and rivers like the Río Frey (bottom). River valleys provide ideal trekking routes, such as along the lightly settled Río Puelo (middle).

Top Left: Laguna Cerro Castillo, Reserva Nacional Cerro Castillo.
Bottom Left: Cerro Fitz Roy (3441m) from Laguna de los Tres, Parque Nacional Los Glaciares.
Bottom Right: Glaciar Moreno, Parque Nacional Los Glaciares.

After crossing the tiny stream near its source, the route climbs roughly north-east through the lenga scrub to the open ridge top site (which overlooks the Carretera Austral to the east). Move down north-west into the side valley of the Estero Catedral, then make your way on along the forested true left (north) bank below high rock walls (ignoring where the old route fords and refords the stream) to reach some small grassy clearings (all that remains of an old puesto) after 1¼ to 1½ hours. The path continues upvalley to cross the stream below its confluence with the **'Estero Ventisquero Catedral'**, then ascends past a waterfall to arrive at the **Laguna Catedral**, another 1¼ to 1½ hours further on.

Head around the scrubby southern shore for 15 to 20 minutes to an open meadow at the far end of the lake. CONAF has plans to construct a refugio (to replace the now completely ruined log hut) on this lovely spot directly below the spectacular summit of Cerro Catedral. A lookout can be reached by following the inlet stream up north onto a ridge descending from Cerro Catedral.

Camp Sites Good camp sites can be found along the central section of the Río Correntoso, particularly near its junction with Estero Castillo, as well in many places along the banks of the (lower) Estero Catedral. At Laguna Catedral there is good camping on clover lawns.

Other Treks In Reserva Nacional Río Simpson

RÍO CLARO SECTOR

The southern sector of the Reserva Nacional Río Simpson around the Río Claro begins just 10km directly west of Coyhaique and the ranges surrounding this small river valley overlook the city. The Río Claro sector is one of the best places to observe the endangered huemul. A long return day or overnight trek from the guardería goes up to Cerro Cono Negro. A longer and more difficult three-day trek can be made north-east over a low pass on the southern side of Cono Negro then down the Río Carácoles to the Río Simpson. The CONAF guardería at the Río Claro is only 16km by road from Coyhaique, but there is no public transport. The Chilean IGM's 1:50,000 maps *Coyhaique* (Section I, No 120) and *Lago Portales* (Section I, No 119) cover most of the Río Claro sector; for the route down the Río Carácoles you will also need the sheet *El Balseo* (Section I, No 107).

Reserva Nacional Cerro Castillo

The 1340 sq km Reserva Nacional Cerro Castillo (not to be confused with the settlement of Cerro Castillo near Parque Nacional Torres del Paine) is south-west of Coyhaique in Chile's XI Region. Its highest point and key feature is the 2675m peak of Cerro Castillo, at the southern edge of the reserve 90km south of Coyhaique.

GENERAL INFORMATION
Geographical Features
Situated at roughly 46° S, Reserva Nacional

Cerro Castillo extends south from the large elongated glacial lake of Lago Elizalde as far as the Río Ibáñez. The reserve is an area of heavily glaciated basalt ranges rising to over 2000m that are intersected by deep valleys. The higher peaks are covered by large névés and hanging glaciers, several of which creep right down into the valleys. The reserve's seemingly erratic boundaries exclude numerous small valleys farmed by local settlers, and some areas inside the reserve are also subject to cattle grazing over the summer months. The source of the Río Ibáñez, a major river on the reserve's southern side, is the extensive glaciers on Volcán Hudson, one of the Patagonian Andes' most unpredictably active volcanoes. Volcán Hudson erupted massively in August 1991, spewing vast amounts of ash across central Patagonia but leaving Reserva Nacional Cerro Castillo virtually unaffected.

Natural History

Reserva Nacional Cerro Castillo is one of five sanctuaries in Chile's XI Region established to protect the southern Andean deer, or huemul. Sadly, the numbers of this once common inhabitant of the southern Andes have dropped to alarmingly low levels, and the huemul is now an endangered species. Only a few of these graceful but generally shy animals remain in the Cerro Castillo area. The huemul is attracted by the remoteness of the central part of the reserve, where small herds graze in places where recent glacial recession has led to recolonisation by palatable plant species. Other mammals sometimes spotted in the reserve include the chingue, a Patagonian skunk, and the zorro gris, a small fox.

Although uncontrolled burning has scarred a large part the reserve's periphery, the interior remains a relatively unspoiled wilderness. Open forests of lenga mostly cover the subalpine areas up to almost 1200m, generally with little underbrush apart from the occasional thickets of calafate *(Berberis* species). Ground-hugging forest plants, such as the frutilla del diablo *(Gunnera magellanica,* or 'devil's strawberry'), the similar-looking frutilla de Magallanes, which produces pinkish edible berries, and the brecillo *(Empetrum rubrum)*, whose purple berries are a favoured food of foxes and other native fauna, can be found on moister places.

The pitío, or Chilean flicker, is an endemic Patagonian woodpecker typically seen in the somewhat drier lenga forests found in the eastern sector of the reserve. The pitío has a greyish crown and brownish-black bands, but its creamy yellow face and upper neck make it easy to recognise. The mero austral *(Agriornis livida fortis)*, is a coffee-grey coloured subspecies of the great shrike tyrant, endemic to the Aisén region.

Climate

Situated well inland and largely sheltered from the far wetter coastal climate by high ranges (including Volcán Hudson) to the west, Reserva Nacional Cerro Castillo has a continental type climate. Annual precipitation levels are relatively moderate by the standards of western Patagonia, generally not exceeding 3000mm on the higher peaks. In the Valle Ibáñez to the south, the reserve borders abruptly on the drier *monte* terrain so typical of the Andes' eastern fringes, where rainfall is generally under 1000mm. Summers in the reserve are generally mild, with January temperatures only occasionally rising above 30°C. Winter can bring locally heavy snowfalls above 500m, and the first patches of permanent snow are encountered at a little over 1200m.

PRACTICAL INFORMATION
Information Sources

CONAF's regional office (☎ 23 2599; fax 23 1065), at Avenida Ogana 1060 in Coyhaique, can give basic advice on the trek. There is also a CONAF guardería at Laguna Chiguay, 6km before the start of the trek at Las Horquetas Grandes.

Permits & Regulations

No permit is required to trek in the Reserva Nacional Cerro Castillo, but trekkers are advised to leave their route details at the guardería at Laguna Chiguay or at the CONAF office in Coyhaique. There is a nominal entry fee of US$1 (which does not apply to traffic merely passing through the reserve along the Carretera Austral).

A final section of this trek cuts through private property of an estancia in the Valle Ibáñez, where trekkers should be on their best conduct.

When to Trek

The best time to trek in Reserva Nacional Cerro Castillo is from early January to late

March. In the otherwise fair month of February, tábanos – those nasty horseflies familiar to all Patagonian patriots – are likely to be out in force. Stay high, stay cool.

Around Cerro Castillo

Duration 4 days minimum
Distance 62km
Standard Medium-Hard
Start Las Horquetas Grandes (on Carretera Austral)
Finish Villa Cerro Castillo
Entry US$1, no permit needed
Season January-March
Summary A wonderful back country trek into the upper valleys surrounding the 2675m basalt peak of Cerro Castillo where small herds of the rare huemul survive.

Towering over the Río Ibáñez and the Carretera Austral, Cerro Castillo is the most prominent peak of the compact Cordillera Castillo. The mountain's Spanish name comes from its many striking basalt turrets and craggy ridges, giving it a strong resemblance to a fortified medieval castle. As a landmark of the Aisén region, this striking peak regularly attracts international climbers.

The scenery along this trek is spectacular and varied, introducing some of the finest country in the central Patagonian Andes. The route follows charming gently forested upper valleys that lead up into the raw alpine landscape. Hanging glaciers cling precariously to the craggy mountainsides, disgorging waterfalls or thundering blocks of ice that plummet over sheer cliffs into stark highland lakes clouded by moraine sediment.

MAPS
The Chilean IGM 1: 50,000 series covers the area of the trek in three sheets: *Lago Elizalde* (Section I, No 132); *Balmaceda* (Section I, No 133); *Villa Cerro Castillo* (Section J, No 10). Although most of the route described

here is not shown on these maps, they are still very useful.

DAYS REQUIRED
Trekkers should allow a minimum of four days to complete this trek.

TREKKING STANDARD
Although the trek follows a largely unmarked route, reasonably fit and experienced walkers should experience few real difficulties in making their way through this country. Careful navigation is important in the more rugged central section. Here you will have to cross exposed terrain above the vegetation line, where until January you may encounter much snow. You also need to cross glacier-fed streams in several places, though these are not very large and can normally be easily forded. You should note that during sunny weather glacial streams generally reach their highest level in late afternoon.

CONAF's Guardería Chiguay, on the Carretera Austral 6km north of where the trek starts at Las Horquetas Grandes, can give advice on the trekking route. CONAF's regional headquarters are in Coyhaique on Avenida Ogana 1060 (on the left as you head south out of town).

By far the best direction to do this trek is north to south, as this makes access and route-finding much easier. The village of Villa Cerro Castillo also makes a rather more convenient place to end the trek than the bend in the road at Las Horquetas Grandes.

The trek has been rated *medium to hard* and has a total distance of 62km.

ACCOMMODATION & CAMPING
There are no huts or trekkers' refugios to speak of on any part of the trek, and it is essential for all parties to carry a tent. CONAF runs a camping ground at Laguna Chiguay, on the Carretera Austral, 6km north of Las Horquetas Grandes. In Villa Cerro Castillo, the *Residencial El Viajero* and the *Residencial El Castillo* offer basic accommodation (with hot showers) for around US$5 per person; but only the *Residencial El Castillo* is recommended.

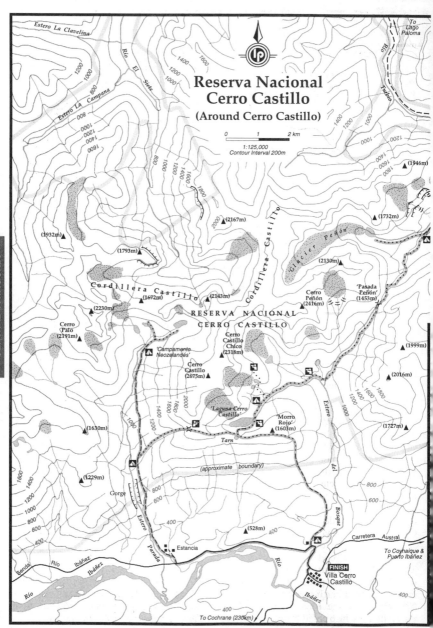

Reserva Nacional Cerro Castillo
(Around Cerro Castillo)

0   1   2 km

1:125,000
Contour Interval 200m

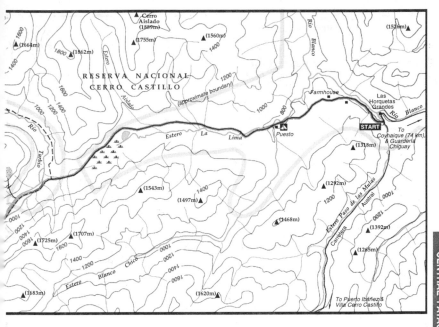

SUPPLIES

Villa Cerro Castillo, at the end of the walk, has several general stores. For the best range and price, Coyhaique is the place to pick-up supplies.

GETTING TO/FROM THE TREK

The walk begins at Las Horquetas Grandes, 75km south of Coyhaique. Las Horquetas Grandes is little more than a bend in the Senda Río Ibáñez (the name given to this section of the Carretera Austral) where two minor streams flow together. The Dirección de Vialidad has a small road works depot here on the west side of the road.

From Coyhaique you can take buses going to either Cochrane or Puerto Ibáñez. The road is relatively good and the journey takes a bit less than two hours. In summer there are five Cochrane buses per week in each direction, usually departing around 8 am. In Coyhaique private minibuses to Puerto Ibáñez often pick up passengers along Arturo Prat. Trekkers arriving from Cochrane or Puerto Ibáñez will disembark shortly after crossing the scenic Paso Las Mulas.

The trek ends at Villa Cerro Castillo, a tiny town on the Carretera Austral (almost below the majestic mountain itself) 98km south of Coyhaique. Minibus Cerro Castillo (☎ 23 2415) at Bilbao 736 in Coyhaique runs 12-seater buses in both directions between Villa Cerro Castillo and Coyhaique five days a week. Buses running between Cochrane and Coyhaique also pass by Villa Cerro Castillo. Going north they generally arrive at Villa Cerro Castillo at around 2.30 pm. In this region hitchhiking tends to be very good, but your chances of getting a ride back to Coyhaique are much better once you pass the Puerto Ibáñez turn-off 12km north of Villa Cerro Castillo. If you are going on to Puerto Ibáñez, head south once you reach this intersection.

Both public and private transport are gradually increasing as the road improves.

THE TREK
Stage 1: Las Horquetas Grandes to Upper Río Turbio
18km, 4 to 5 hours

Cross the bridge over the **Estero Paso de Las Mulas** just above where it enters the **Río Blanco**, and follow a dirt road down the left bank of the river. The road soon turns away westwards past a farmhouse, winding on through open lenga forest before it drops gently down onto grassy flats beside the **Estero La Lima** after one to 1¼ hours. Make your way past a rustic puesto and cross the small side stream of the **Estero Blanco Chico**, heading on upvalley through streamside pastures to easily ford the shallow Estero La Lima itself after a further 30 to 40 minutes.

After crossing the **Estero Aislado**, which drains another tiny side valley to the north, the increasingly rough vehicle track skirts above a reedy lagoon frequented by black-necked swans to reach a fork after 60 to 80 minutes. Here take the left-hand branch, which avoids a mallín stretching along the poorly drained valley floor before it (almost imperceptibly) crosses a watershed to meet the **Río Turbio** another 30 to 40 minutes on. This roaring white-water torrent flows through a wild upper valley below the **Cordillera Castillo**, whose towering peaks have been visible along much of your approach route.

Follow an indistinct 4WD track south-west along the broad gravelly valley floor below waterfalls spilling over sheer cliffs from hanging glaciers up to your right. Where the vehicle track finally peters out after 30 to 40 minutes, pick up a trail that continues into the lenga forest. The route crosses a clear brook before climbing gently rightwards onto an open field of glacial debris covered by snow grasses and chauras (which produce tasty white or red berries), a further 10 to 15 minutes on. Huemul sometimes graze around this pretty head of the Río Turbio valley.

The short side trip to the nearby **'Glaciar Peñón'**, which curls down from the heart of the Cordillera Castillo as the source of the Río Turbio, is recommended. The river's boulder-strewn banks can be followed for 20 to 30 minutes to a murky meltwater pool at the snout of the glacier, but only trekkers with the necessary experience should venture onto the ice itself.

Camp Sites Apart from the waterlogged area near the shallow lagoon, good camp sites can be found virtually right along the Estero La Lima. The most scenic camping is in the upper Río Turbio.

Stage 2: Upper Río Turbio to 'Laguna Cerro Castillo'
14km, 4¼ to 5¾ hours

Follow an initially prominent animal trail south-west beside the small clear brook (mentioned in Stage 1), crossing it where necessary as the terrain steepens and the forest goes over into scrub. Higher up there is no path at all, but the going is relatively easy close to the cascading stream. The route climbs on higher into a rocky gully, passing streamlets splashing down from a small névé up to the right before reaching **'Pasada Peñón'** (1453m) after 1½ to two hours. 'Pasada Peñón' is a long, narrow gap filled by frost-shattered rock and accumulated winter snow (which may remain well into February). From the southern end of the pasada a high turquoise lake visible to the south-south-west indicates the way ahead.

Descend cautiously onto steep and unstable scree covered slopes, directly opposite spectacular icefalls that grip the raw eastern flank of **Cerro Peñón**. The icefalls produce numerous meltwater cascades. Cut left across the glacial wash below to pick up random trails leading down the stream's forested left bank. After making an easy ford (best where the stream briefly divides into two channels), continue on downstream to arrive at the **Estero del Bosque** junction, just 1½ to two hours from Pasada Peñón.

Here, where the eastern branch of the Estero del Bosque merges with the somewhat larger western branch, much of the forest has been flattened by winter avalanches sweeping off the southern side of Cerro Peñón. Downstream from the junction the Estero del Bosque leads into a steep canyon, but trekkers should not be tempted to walk out via that impossible route.

Find your own way upstream through the mess left behind by the avalanches, then follow faint cattle trails up along the embankments on the true left (ie north-western) side of the stream. At a rocky streamway reached after 50 minutes to 1¼ hours, move a short way up right where the trail ducks back into the weather-beaten scrub. The path continues upvalley for 10 or 15 minutes to cross a side stream spilling down in a large cascade fed by an icefall on **Cerro Castillo Chico**. It's well worth climbing either moraine ridge to reach several tarns on the shelf behind the waterfall; more adventurous and energetic trekkers can climb the loose bare slopes on the right for more spectacular views.

Head on a final 15 to 20 minutes up through streamside meadows interspersed with lenga thickets to arrive at **'Laguna Cerro Castillo'**. A stunning sight, the lake lies at 1275m above sea level in a deep glacial basin which is directly under the imposing **Cerro Castillo**. Hanging glaciers periodically drop ice blocks onto the rock cliffs below, where they shatter and occasionally hit the water.

Camp Sites After you leave the upper valley of the Río Turbio there are no suitable camp sites until just above the Estero del Bosque junction. Trekkers will find excellent camps in the shelter of bushy scrub 20 to 30 minutes below 'Laguna Cerro Castillo'. The open stony ground around 'Laguna Cerro Castillo' offers scenic but extremely exposed camping, and firewood is scarce.

Stage 3: 'Laguna Cerro Castillo' to 'Campamento Neozelandés'
11km, 3½ to 4½ hours

Cross the lake's outlet stream on stepping stones and climb up diagonally left along coarse, bare moraines to a very narrow shelf high above the lake. Follow this around to reach a broad, flat saddle just west of **'Morro Rojo'** after 40 to 50 minutes. This spot offers a fine view to Cerro Castillo directly opposite (though you'll need a 28mm lens to get it all in one shot!). Walk a short way left across the saddle to a tarn, from where you can see the tiny town of Villa Cerro Castillo and down along the Valle Ibáñez as far as Lago General Carrera.

Direct Route to Villa Cerro Castillo A more direct (though not particularly rewarding) route down to Villa Cerro Castillo taking around three hours leaves from this saddle. First contour eastwards around the southern side of 'Morro Rojo', then descend 1km along a steep spur to a prominent cairn indicating where to move right. Pick up initially vague animal trails leading down roughly south-east through regenerating forest into a burn-cleared area then past a corral and a gate. Below this a 4WD track leads down past a farmhouse to the meet the Río Ibáñez road at the Estero del Bosque bridge (see Stage 4).

The longer and more scenic alternative continues westwards along a shelf opposite the basalt turrets of Cerro Castillo, before climbing easily over boulder rubble to reach a rocky gap after 40 to 50 minutes. This ridge top overlooks the wild, forested valley of the **Estero Parada**, which is enclosed by interesting jagged peaks. Drop directly into a steep, scree-filled gully, following this stream bed as it curves leftwards into the trees. Paint markings (visible only from above) indicate where this descent route intersects with the much more prominent path coming up through the valley, a further 30 to 45 minutes on.

Head upvalley through the lenga forest, passing some pleasant camp sites by the Estero Parada (not far downstream from where a large glacial tributary enters from an adjacent side valley) after 40 to 50 minutes. The increasingly less distinct path rises steadily onward, skirting around soggy bogs close to the stream before petering out at the head of the valley near **'Campamento Neozelandés'**, another 50 minutes to 1¼ hours on. This was where a small mountaineering party from New Zealand established its base camp in 1976, making a number of first ascents in the area.

The wild upper Valle Parada is enclosed on three sides by jagged summits of the Cordillera Castillo, and half a day or so might be spent exploring this area. A small tarn set in bare surroundings under Cerro Castillo Chico can be visited from 'Campamento Neozelandés' by heading up beside the narrow eastern branch of the Estero Parada. After the path peters out, continue over mossy slopes and glacial debris to the lake. On the west side of the valley two more lakes formed by end moraines are best reached by crossing the east stream and heading around underneath the cliff face.

Camp Sites There is no sheltered camping at all on Stage 3 until you reach the valley of the Estero Parada. 'Campamento Neozelandés' provides the most pleasant option, although there is a limited number of sites that are both dry *and* level.

Stage 4: 'Campamento Neozelandés' to Villa Cerro Castillo
19km, 4 to 5 hours
Backtrack downvalley to the rocky stream gully where you first encountered the trail (see Stage 3). After climbing over a minor ridge, follow the path across burnt-out slopes scattered with wild strawberries above where the Estero Parada races through a deep chasm. The route descends gently through pockets of lenga forest, before dropping rightwards to the banks of the stream at the point where it merges with the wide, open **Valle Ibáñez**. Now on private property, cut

down left across rocky pastures past an estancia sheltered by graceful poplars, 2¼ to three hours after you have left 'Campamento Neozelandés'.

Make your way east-south-east along a farm track across rich grassy flats grazed by flocks of sheep and long-beaked bandurrias (a gregarious species of ibis). A graded road leads on through ñirre scrub and calafate bushes to meet the **Río Ibáñez**, 40 to 50 minutes on. The glacial waters of this large, swift-moving river flow through deep channels whose course changes constantly. Head on through a sandy plain to cross the Estero del Bosque on a bridge (near where the short-cut route described in Stage 3 intersects), then continue a short way down the road to arrive at **Villa Cerro Castillo** after a final one to 1¼ hours.

Although the tiny town itself is not a very inspiring place, Villa Cerro Castillo is surrounded by beautiful, scenic ranges. There is a monument dedicated to the first European colonists who began settling the Valle Ibáñez in the early decades of the 20th century.

Camp Sites Apart from in the upper valley of the Estero Parada (see Stage 3), most of the good camp sites are on private property – so use discretion when pitching your tent. A nice and popular camping spot near to Villa Cerro Castillo is beside the Estero del Bosque road bridge.

Other Treks in Central Patagonia

UP THE RÍO PUELO – CHILE INTO ARGENTINA
The Río Puelo rises in Argentina, where several large rivers draining most of the Comarca Andina flow into Lago Puelo, but immediately crosses into Chile and begins its roughly 80km journey north-eastwards to meet the Pacific coast at the village of Puelo (100km south-east of Puerto Montt on Seno Reloncaví). Chilean colonists began settling

the Río Puelo at the beginning of the 20th century, and today perhaps a thousand people live on numerous small farms or scattered villages along the valley. Since then the Río Puelo has remained relatively inaccessible. No roads penetrated the valley and until quite recently the locals found it more convenient to journey on horseback upriver into Argentina to buy supplies.

This situation is about to change. A new

road is being constructed up the Río Puelo, and it is expected that by the year 2000 it will connect with another section of road now under construction on the Argentine side. This will make it possible to drive the whole way from Puelo to El Bolsón. The road will probably spoil most of the valley's remote charm, so enjoy the Río Puelo trek while you can.

The trek is best done in an upriver direction, beginning from Puelo (accessible by several daily buses from Puerto Montt). Trekkers may be able to get a ride (possibly with the Chilean corps of army engineers, who are building the road!) to Lago Tagua Tagua – or beyond. The section of road around Lago Tagua Tagua may be completed when you read this, but at the time of research it was still necessary to charter a boat to the lake's eastern shore. From there the route leads up the eastern bank of the river to its junction with the Río Manso, which must be crossed by a locally hired boat to the airstrip village of Llanada Grande (the only place where you can buy supplies).

At the south-eastern corner of Lago Totoral, not far on from Llanada Grande, there are two equally rewarding route variants. Trekkers can go *left* to Lago Azul, paying a local to ferry them across this beautiful lake before they continue around the *eastern* side of Lago Las Rocas to the Carabineros border post of Retén at Lago Inferior. The other route option is to head *right* from Lago Totoral, passing along the eastern side of Lago Blanco, the *western* side of Las Rocas Inferiores and the *eastern* side of Lago Mosquitos to Retén. Have your passport exit-stamped here.

The route crosses the Argentine frontier into Parque Nacional Lago Puelo at Los Hitos. From the nearby jetty ('Puerto Nuevo') trekkers again have the option of taking a tourist launch across the lake rather than continuing on foot around its northern side via the Gendarmería (Argentine border post). Trekkers will have to ford the Río Azul – a serious wade – or cross the bridge several kilometres north of the river's mouth to finish the trek at the boat dock and guardería on the north-eastern shore of Lago Puelo

(from where buses run up to six times daily to El Bolsón).

Trekkers should plan on taking a minimum of six days to hike up the Río Puelo. The route is ideal for a three or four day mountain bike trip, and you are likely to encounter as many MTB riders as other trekkers.

Five Chilean IGM 1:50,000 maps cover the Río Puelo trek: *Puelo* (Section H, No 62), *Lago Tagua Tagua* (Section H, No 63), *Río Traidor* (Section H, No 73), *Llanada Grande* (Section H, No 74) and *Lago de las Rocas* (Section H, No 84). See also Parque Nacional Lago Puelo above in the Other Treks in the Comarca Andina section.

PARQUE NACIONAL HORNOPIRÉN – CHILE

This small national park lies south-east of Puerto Montt near the village of Hornopirén on the Carretera Austral. The park is centred around the 1572m cone of Volcán Hornopirén whose name (a curious mixture Mapuche and Spanish) means 'oven of snow'. A two-day return trek from Hornopirén follows a good horse trail through the forest along the western side of Volcán Hornopirén to the eastern shore of Lago Cabrera, from where there are good views across the lake to the superb 2111m Volcán Yate. Volcán Hornopirén can be climbed from its eastern side.

The Chilean IGM's 1:50,000 map *Volcán Hornopirén* (Section H, No 72) covers virtually all of the park; the adjoining sheet *Volcán Apagado* (Section H, No 71) is also useful. Buses Fierro runs two daily buses from Puerto Montt to the village of Hornopirén leaving at 8 am and 3 pm (Sundays at 3 pm only). The bus trip includes a ferry crossing between Caleta Puelche and Caleta La Arena on Estuario/Seno Reloncaví. The ferry runs on a two or three hourly schedule in either direction. You can also reach Hornopirén by a direct ferry (operated by the shipping company Transmarchilay) which departs daily at 3 pm from Angelmó in Puerto Montt.

VOLCÁN CHAITÉN – CHILE

Volcán Chaitén, a tiny extinct volcano at the foot of the much higher and more majestic

Volcán Michinmahuida stands less than 10km directly north-east of the small coastal town of Chaitén, opposite the island of Chiloé. Volcán Chaitén's main peak is a lava plug that rises up 400m out of the volcano's 2km wide crater, which you can climb for excellent views of Chaitén township, the adjacent island of Chiloé and Volcán Michinmahuida. A grassy circular strip extends almost the whole way around the caldera between its rim and the central volcanic plug, providing a natural walking route. Within this grassy ring are two small murky lakes and an elusive mineral spring.

Volcán Chaitén can be visited in a strenuous two to three-day trek. There is no real trail, so a machete is recommended to clear away thick vegetation. The rough route begins 100m south of the Puente Gigios (bridge) on the Carretera Austral, 25km north of Chaitén. Head up through steep coastal rainforest, negotiating slippery fallen trees and clumps of quila until you reach the caldera rim. Walk 700m leftwards high above the crater before dropping down a steep ridge to a first lake in the crater floor. Return to the Carretera Austral via the ascent route.

The entire area is covered by a single 1:50,000 sheet produced by the Chilean IGM, *Chaitén* (Section H, No 110). There is no local public transport to the start of the trek, but buses run several times a week between Chaitén and Fiordo Reñihue (where there is a ferry to Hornopirén and hitchhiking is a fair prospect.

TERMAS EL AMARILLO TO LAGO ESPOLÓN – CHILE

This challenging route taking 4 or 5 days is for experienced trekkers only. The route starts from the small hot springs resort of Termas El Amarillo (also known as Termas Vuelta y Vuelta, 25km south of Chaitén on the Carretera Austral) and leads south-east via the Río Michinmahuida along the shore of Lago Espolón to the village of Villa Futaleufú near the Argentine border. Two Chilean IGM 1:50,000 IGM sheets are needed for the trek: *Puerto Cardenas* (Section I, No 9) and *Lago Espolón* (Section I, No 10). A homy and economical place to stay in Futaleufú is the *Posada*

Campesina La Gringa (☎ 25 6833, extension 260) a few minutes from Lago Espolón.

CERRO CÓNICO – ARGENTINA

Just south of Parque Nacional Los Alerces on the frontier with Chile, the 2271m summit of Cerro Cónico makes an excellent lookout point. At the Estación de Salmonicultura (salmon hatchery), 26km by road south-west of Trevelin on the Ruta Nacional 259 (which continues to Villa Futaleufú in Chile), a 4WD track leads 8km along the Arroyo Baggilt to Lago Baggilt. A rough foot track continues west around the lake shore, then over rocky slopes to Cerro Cónico. From the summit there are fine views over to the Chilean lakes of Lago Espolón and Lago Yelcho, and on clear days the Pacific coast is visible.

The trek is best done in two days; two 1:100,000 Argentine IGM maps cover the area of the trek: *Complejo Hidroeléctrico Futaleufú* and *Carrenleufú* (Chubut). The only way to get to the trail head is by hitchhiking or organising private transport.

PARQUE NACIONAL QUEULAT – CHILE

The 154 sq km Parque Nacional Queulat is a new park (established in 1983) near the village of Puyuguapi. Queulat is on the Pacific coast and has a wet, maritime climate that has produced vast glaciers and ice fields in the interior of the park, while the lower country is vegetated by dense coastal rainforest. The administrative guardería for the park is at the end of a 2km turn-off, 25km south of Puyuguapi along the Carretera Austral. The guardería looks out towards the Ventisquero Colgante, a spectacular hanging glacier that drops great blocks of ice over a precipice several hundred metres high. There's a better lookout about 15 minutes on past the CONAF camping area. A harder return day walk continues across the suspension bridge and follows an increasingly overgrown path along the Río Ventisqueros to Laguna Témpanos, a small lake directly below the Ventisquero Colgante. The Chilean IGM 1:50,000 sheet *Puyuguapi* (Section I, No 61) covers the central part of the park around Ventisquero Colgante.

Southern Patagonia stretches south from the Península de Taitao and Lago Carrera/ Buenos Aires as far as the Straits of Magellan. Dominated by the two vast continental icecaps, the Hielo Norte and the Hielo Sur, this region is the most intensely glaciated part of South America. Unquestionably one of the world's most ruggedly beautiful places, southern Patagonia includes the internationally renowned Los Glaciares and Torres del Paine national parks. Their towering granite peaks attract thousands of trekkers every year. There are also many other lesser known and less frequently visited areas. Wherever else you plan to go in the Patagonian Andes, be sure to include a trip to one of the superb parks of this region.

TREKKING BASES
Cochrane (Chile)

Cochrane is 70km south of Lago General Carrera and on the Carretera Austral. Although a very small and isolated town of 2000 people, Cochrane is the only reasonably sized settlement in the far south of Chile's IX Región (Aisén). The town is very sheltered by the Hielo Norte, the more northerly of the two Patagonian icecaps, which is roughly 60km to the west. The entire icecap and much of the surrounding country is within the huge and wild Parque Nacional Laguna San Rafael. Cochrane is only a few kilometres south of Reserva Nacional Tamango, and is a logical starting point for long treks south to Lago Brown and Monte Cochrane (called Monte San Lorenzo in Argentina).

Cochrane's tourist office is in a small booth in the Plaza de Armas. Contact the tourist office for the new address of the local CONAF office. Together the bus companies Pudu, Río Baker and Don Carlos run almost daily in both directions between Coyhaique and Cochrane. Don Carlos also has flights between Cochrane and Coyhaique on Monday and Wednesday in both directions (around US$42 one way). Sit on the eastward-looking

side of the plane for tremendous views of the northern continental icecap, if fine weather allows. Because of the low volume of traffic, hitchhiking on the Carretera Austral can be very slow. Both public and private transport are expected to increase as the roads are gradually improved.

El Calafate (Argentina)

El Calafate lies on the southern shore of Lago Argentino, and lives almost entirely from the booming tourism in the nearby vast Parque Nacional Los Glaciares. Day visits to Glaciar Moreno (including guided 'minitreks' on the ice), boat excursions across Lago Argentino to the snout of Glaciar Upsala and trips to the park's northernmost Fitz Roy sector all begin and end in El Calafate. Although quite a pleasant place, El Calafate has little else to offer the passing traveller.

The APN Intendencia (☎ 91005; fax 91755) for Parque Nacional Los Glaciares is at Avenida del Libertador 1302 (at the western end of the main road through town); it's open from 9 am to 3 pm. Calafate's tourist office (☎ 91090) is located at the new bus station (Terminal de Omnibuses) in the centre of town. The very informal local Club Andino Lago Argentino can be contacted through Claudio 'Gringo' Schurer (☎ 91280) or Susana Oteola at the Hospedaje Avenida (☎ 91159), Avenida Libertador 902.

Two good places for backpackers to stay in Calafate are the *Albergue del Glaciar* (☎ & fax 91243), at Los Pioneros, and the *Albergue Lago Argentino*, near the bus station at Campaña del Desierto 1050. The *Hotel La Loma*, also near the bus station at Roca 849, has rooms with private bath from US$15.

The companies Quebek Tours, El Pingüino and Interlagos all run daily buses between Calafate (via Río Gallegos airport); the fare is around US$25. Three bus companies, Cootra, Del Glaciar and San Cayetano have services to Puerto Natales in Chile (US$24, eight hours). Kaikén (☎ 23663) has almost daily

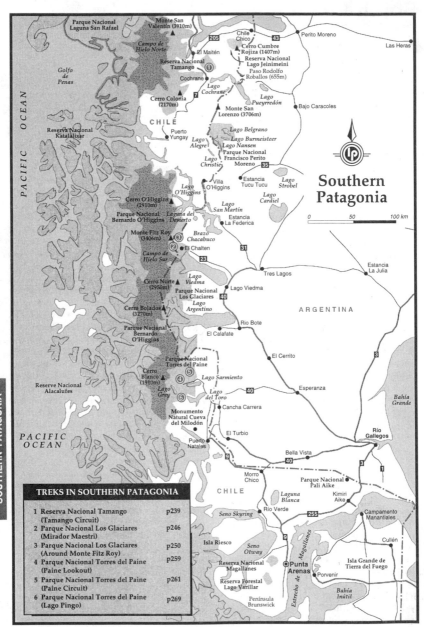

Southern Patagonia

| 0 | 50 | 100 km |

TREKS IN SOUTHERN PATAGONIA

flights to/from Ushuaia (US$95), and to Esquel and Bariloche (US$125) several times per week. LADE (☎ 21123) has one weekly flight to and from Ushuaia (US$55) as well as flights to/from other cities in Argentine Patagonia.

Refer to the Parque Nacional Los Glaciares section for details of transport to El Chaltén (the tourist village in the Fitz Roy sector). El Calafate's area code is ☎ 0902.

Puerto Natales (Chile)
Composed largely of imaginatively constructed corrugated iron buildings stretching along the eastern shore of Seno Última Esperanza (Last Hope Sound), the windy town of Puerto Natales is the gateway to Parque Nacional Torres del Paine. Visits to the local museum at Bulnes 285 and the Cueva de Milodon, 24km north-west of town, are recommended. Another way to fill in a day is to take the cold but rewarding boat trip over to Glaciar Balmaceda, which calves into the fjord at the northern end of Seno Última Esperanza.

Puerto Natales' tourist office (☎ 2125) is about 1km north of the docks on Costanera Pedro Montt; it's open Monday to Friday from 8.30 am until 7.30 pm, and on Saturday from 9.30 am to 4.30 pm (but closes over lunch). Puerto Natales has a CONAF office (☎ 14380) at Ignacio Carrera Pinto 566, but if you want information about Torres del Paine the staff will probably tell you to ask out at the park itself. Anglers can get a fishing permit from the local office of SERNAP (☎ 41 1350), on the corner of Eberhard and Tomás Roger.

Several stores along the streets south of the Plaza de Armas hire out quality trekking gear such as tents, cookers and rainwear. *Onas* (☎ 41 2707; fax 41 1938) at Bulnes 453, organises outdoor adventure trips in the region and rents equipment. The hardware store *(ferretería)* behind the Esso service station (which is diagonally opposite the tourist office) and the pharmacy on the Plaza de Armas both sell white gas *(bencina blanca)*. Two recommended places to stay are the *Residencial Dickson* (☎ 41 1218) and *Residencial Tequendama* at Ladrilleros 141.

Puerto Natales is the southern port for the *Puerto Eden*, a large vehicle/passenger ferry operated by NAVIMAG (☎ 41 1221), Costanera Pedro Montt 380. The *Puerto Eden* makes the long three-day trip through the spectacular Chilean fjord land between Puerto Natales and Puerto Montt three or four times per month. There are daily buses from the provincial capital of Punta Arenas, four hours south by road. A daily bus service operates between Puerto Natales and Calafate in Argentina between November and March; going from Puerto Natales to Calafate the fare is around US$18, but in the other direction it costs US$25. The small Chilean airline ALTA has almost daily flights (from Punta Arenas) via Puerto Natales to Coyhaique ($US100, 1¾ hours). Puerto Natales' area code is ☎ 061.

Punta Arenas (Chile)
With a population of just under 100,000, Punta Arenas is the largest city in southern Patagonia. Apart from some easy walking in the low ranges of the Península Brunswick, Punta Arenas makes a poor base for trips into the Cordillera, but there are plenty of interesting places to visit in and around this gust-prone city. The Salesian Museum (Museo Salesiano) at the corner of Bhories and Sarmiento, is one of the best in Patagonia and has good exhibits on local Indians – including the only surviving canoe built by the Alacalufe sea nomads – and wildlife. A visit to the Instituto de la Patagonia (opposite the duty-free zone, or *zona franca*), is well worthwhile. The institute has a zoo, an open-air museum and a good library specialising in Patagonian history, wildlife and geography. The day trip to the penguin colonies near the city is also recommended.

Punta Arenas' tourist office (☎ 22 4435) is at Waldo Seguel 689 (just off the Plaza de Armas) and the regional CONAF office (☎ 22 7845) is at Jose Menéndez 1147 (downhill from the main square between Quilota and Montt). Anglers can get a Chilean fishing permit at the office of SERNAP (☎ 24 1142), Maipú 1060. Two good budget place to stay are the *Lodging Guisande* (☎ 24 3295) at

Jose Miguel Carrera 1270 and the *Albergue Backpackers* (☎ 22 2554) at Pinto 1022. The Argentine Consulate is at Avenida 21 de Mayo 1878.

Punta Arenas is the regional transport hub, with flights and boats from Chile's far north and to Isla Navarino and Tierra del Fuego. The local airline DAP flies to the Fuegian destinations of Porvenir (daily, US$22), Puerto Williams (several times a week, US$68), and Ushuaia (almost daily, US$80). ALTA has almost daily flights via Puerto Natales direct to Coyhaique (US$110) then on via Puerto Montt and Temuco to Valparaíso. Together the larger airlines Ladeco, LanChile and Nacional have four or five daily flights to Santiago (most via Puerto Montt). Punta Arenas is connected with Puerto Natales by very frequent buses. The area code for Punta Arenas is ☎ 61.

Reserva Nacional Tamango

Comprising just 83 sq km, the Reserva Nacional Tamango is immediately north of Cochrane, a rapidly expanding town to the south of Lago General Carrera on Chile's Carretera Austral. The reserve occupies the western end of the Cordón Chacabuco, a range of low mountains overlooking Lago Cochrane. Because the park is isolated and virtually unknown, Tamango is visited by very few trekkers (local or foreign), yet this compact reserve is surprisingly wild and attractive.

GENERAL INFORMATION
Geographical Features
Much of Reserva Nacional Tamango is an undulating forested plateau averaging little more than 1000m but reaching its highest point of 1722m at the summit of Cerro Tamango. This rounded mountain rises abruptly from the Carretera Austral and the nearby Río Baker, which is the most voluminous river in Chile.

In the centre of the reserve there are two attractive lakes, and numerous small alpine tarns lie hidden in the forest. On its south-eastern side Reserva Nacional Tamango borders Lago Cochrane, a large, deep glacial lake whose western half lies within Argentine territory (where it is known as Lago Pueyrredón). Immediately north of Tamango lies the Valle Chacabuco, a vast (75,000 hectare) estancia which occupies the entire valley.

Natural History
Tamango is largely covered by light Magellanic forest of predominantly deciduous lenga. The ground cover often consists only of low herbs and mosses, giving the forest a very open appearance. In many places the tree branches are covered with growths of stringy lichen called barba del viejo *(Usnea* species), or 'old man's beard'. Where drainage is poor, boggy-grassy areas known as *mallines* create attractive clearings within the forest.

Chilcas, various species of native daisy-like shrubs of the genus *Baccharis*, grow in the forest or on moist sunny sites. Chauras *(Pernetya mucronata)* also thrive in these habitats, producing bountiful red berries from late January. On the reserve's eastern edge the forest gives way to a drier vegetation more typical of the Patagonian steppes, including tussock grasses and 'saltbush' type plants such as mogotes *(Mulinum spinosum)*.

Bird life is especially abundant here, and there are many species of ducks, swan and other waterfowl around the isolated lakes and marshes. A characteristic bird of central and southern Patagonia is the bandurria, a gregarious ibis invariably observed in flocks of a dozen or more. The bandurria has a long curved beak – the perfect tool for picking over moist grassy stream flats – and an ochre-coloured head and neck. The rayadito *(Aphrastura spinicauda)*, is a diminutive spinetail that lives and nests in Tamango's extensive lenga forests, and feeds on the plentiful insects that hide in the flaky bark of the lenga. The dormilona rufa *(Musci-saxicola capistrata)*, or cinnamon-bellied tyrant, inhabits the drier scrubland on the eastern side of the reserve.

Like other reserves in Chile's XI Region, Tamango is a sanctuary for the endangered huemul, or Andean deer. Other wildlife includes guanaco, ñandú, native foxes and the mara (or Patagonian hare). Trekkers may also be lucky enough to spot the piche *(Chaetophractus pichii)*, a shy species of Patagonian armadillo, which digs its burrow in soft earth. Decidedly less native are the 60 or 70 head of cattle that are driven up to the Tamango plateau for the summer season (from about early January until mid-April).

Climate
Reserva Nacional Tamango occupies a zone of climatic transition. The vegetation changes noticeably as rain/snowfall drops away as you move eastwards. The Hielo Norte, the smaller and more northerly of Patagonia's two vast ice sheets, largely shelters Reserva Nacional Tamango from the savage weather typical of the coastal ranges. Tamango barely manages to catch the last moisture of the Pacific winds, and annual precipitation levels average no more than 1500mm even on Cerro Tamango itself.

PRACTICAL INFORMATION
Information Sources
Tamango's remaining guardería is often unstaffed, so the CONAF office in Cochrane (contact the tourist office for the new address) is the only reliable local source of current information regarding the reserve.

Permits & Regulations
No special permit is necessary to trek in Reserva Nacional Tamango, but it's recommended that trekkers inform CONAF of their intentions before setting out. Exercise extreme caution if you light a campfire.

When to Trek
Because of the relatively sheltered geograph-

ical position, Reserva Nacional Tamango generally offers good trekking conditions throughout the warmer period between November and mid-April.

Tamango Circuit

Duration 2 days minimum
Distance 33km
Standard Easy-Medium
Start/Finish Cochrane
Entry Free, no permit needed
Season November-April
Summary Features a circuit through a small and little-visited reserve comprising an undulating forested plateau of numerous small alpine tarns overlooking the large glacial lake of Lago Cochrane.

This rewarding little trek takes you right through Reserva Nacional Tamango. In the middle of this small pocket of wilderness are several tranquil lakes visited only occasionally by trekkers.

MAPS
Reserva Nacional Tamango is covered by one Chilean IGM 1:50,000 sheet, *Valle Chacabuco* (Section J, No 57). The map does not indicate the reserve or the walking route, but is otherwise quite accurate.

DAYS REQUIRED
The Tamango Circuit takes a minimum of two long days to complete, but taking at least one additional day in order to better explore the reserve is recommended. People with less time might consider visiting the area on a long return day trek from Cochrane to Lago Tamango and Lago Elefantita or the CONAF guardería above Lago Cochrane.

TREKKING STANDARD
The circuit follows paths and small roads for most of its distance, but the central 4km section after Lago Elefantita is scrubby in

SOUTHERN PATAGONIA

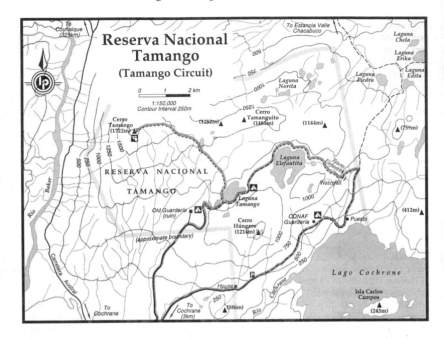

Reserva Nacional Tamango (Tamango Circuit)

parts. Livestock still graze in and around the reserve, and in places the route actually follows cattle trails. There is usually little underbrush, however, and off-track walking is relatively easy except where fires have destroyed the forest. The route is largely unmarked, but with some care navigation should not be a major problem.

The Tamango Circuit is rated *easy to medium*, and has a total length of 33km.

ACCOMMODATION & CAMPING
CONAF has established an irregularly staffed guardería on the slopes high above Lago Cochrane. There are no huts within the reserve, so all trekkers must carry a tent.

For places to stay in Cochrane see Trekking Bases.

SUPPLIES
Although the town has no true supermarkets, all basic supplies can be bought in Cochrane. Prices reflect the town's relative isolation so,

if possible, do your shopping in Coyhaique or Puerto Aisén.

GETTING TO/FROM THE TREK
The trek begins directly from Cochrane, 340km by road south of Coyhaique (see Trekking Bases for further details).

Stage 1: Cochrane to Laguna Tamango
10km, 2¾ to 3¾ hours
From the Plaza de Armas in Cochrane, walk north along Luis Baez B (street) past the town cemetery. The road winds up beside a pine plantation then on over slopes of ñirre scrub to reach a fork after 45 minutes to one hour. Here take the left branch and continue up past a farmhouse in a little green meadow, climbing a bit more steeply into light lenga forest. Locals cut timber and collect firewood in these forests, carrying it down to Cochrane in mule-drawn carts with solid-wood wheels (each made from a cross section of a tree trunk). After crossing a minor crest,

where Cerro Tamango comes into view to the north-west, descend a few paces to another fork, a further 60 to 80 minutes on.

The left-hand turn-off leads you for five minutes down across a small footbridge to a disused CONAF **Guardería**. The building is now in ruins, but the surrounding grassy forest clearing is attractive.

Follow the road on along to the right past two *mallines* until it finally peters out. Here pick up a foot track leading north-north-east past two large attractive ponds in the lichen-covered lenga forest to reach **Laguna Tamango** after 60 to 80 minutes. Head around the lake's south-eastern shore, which is largely covered by snow grass, heath and alpine wild flowers.

Side Trip to Cerro Tamango The 1722m summit of Cerro Tamango can be climbed from Laguna Tamango in five to seven hours return. There is no trail to speak of, but although the route is relatively straightforward, Cerro Tamango should not be visited by inexperienced trekkers. From the western end of Lago Tamango head north-north-west through the forest to a wide saddle with several scattered tarns between Cerro Tamango and Cerro Tamanguito. From here pick your way along the mostly bare ridge of glacier-smoothed rock leading to the summit. In fine weather there are excellent views west towards the northern continental icecap. The great snowcapped massif 60km to the south-west is Cerro Cochrane (called Monte San Lorenzo in Argentina), the second highest mountain in southern Patagonia. The western slopes of Cerro Tamango are dangerously steep. Don't try descending to the Carretera Austral from the summit, but return via the ascent route.

Camp Sites The first recommended camping along Stage 1 is at the old CONAF Guardería, but nicer camp sites can be found on moist lawns dotted with daisy bushes near the eastern end of Laguna Tamango. At Laguna Elefantita there are scenic but exposed sites near the inlet stream.

Stage 2: Laguna Tamango to Lago Cochrane
9km, 3½ to 4½ hours
Make your way on north-eastwards through moist clearings, where guanaco (but more often cattle) sometimes graze, to arrive at the western shore of **Laguna Elefantita**, 40 to 50 minutes on. The best route leads around the northern side of the lake. Depending on the water level, either follow the narrow rocky shore line or make your way through the sometimes scrubby forest. As some clearings appear near the lake's eastern end, pick up faint trails leading south-east to reach **'Estero Elefantita'**, the tiny lake outlet stream, after 50 minutes to 1¼ hours.

Continue through the strip of open heathland around the streamlet, passing left (north) around a shallow, reedy lagoon before moving up rightwards to avoid thick scrub. Traverse through the lenga forest along the southern side of 'Estero Elefantita', then drop down via a steep burnt-out spur to recross below a waterfall. The route now circles gradually around north-east to east over fire-cleared slopes to the left of several deep gullies before intersecting with a broad and well-trodden horse trail, about 1½ hours on from Laguna Elefantita.

Descend steadily southwards along a prominent ridge towards **Lago Cochrane**, whose turquoise waters are scattered with a dozen or so large and small islands. The path dips through pockets of regenerating coigüe forest before coming out onto the lake shore after 40 to 50 minutes. On this open field covered with calafate bushes stands a small adobe hut with a roof of wooden shingles (a shelter that serves as a *puesto* for the nearby Estancia Valle Chacabuco).

Camp Sites Good camp sites can be found on grassy clearings in various places around the shore of Laguna Elefantita. There is little good camping thereafter until you reach the flat field on the shore of Lago Cochrane.

Stage 3: Lago Cochrane to Cochrane
14km, 3¾ to 4¾ hours
Find the onward trail turn-off near a corral

SOUTHERN PATAGONIA

just above the hut and follow it across the 'Estero Elefantita'. The route sidles up in steep switchbacks onto chaura slopes dotted with notro bushes to reach the **CONAF Guardería** perched on a small terrace above Lago Cochrane after 45 minutes to one hour. The guardería has become rather run-down and is staffed only irregularly.

From here a well-graded foot track makes a scenic rising-and-dipping traverse several hundred metres above the lake, eventually coming out at a car park after a further 1¼

to 1¾ hours. Follow the road south-westwards for one to 1¼ hours to the reserve boundary gate and past old wooden barns to the road fork described in Stage 1, before proceeding on downhill to arrive back in Cochrane after a final 40 to 50 minutes.

Camp Sites The CONAF Guardería makes a reasonable camp site, and there are also camping possibilities beyond the guardería on level shelves above Lago Cochrane.

Parque Nacional Los Glaciares

Often considered the greatest single tract of remaining wilderness in the country, Argentina's vast Parque Nacional Los Glaciares in the south of Santa Cruz Province straddles the Hielo Sur, the largest icecap outside the earth's polar regions. Created in 1937 to protect a unique landscape totally dominated by ice age glaciation, Los Glaciares continues to exhibit a variety of remarkable and spectacular glacial phenomena. Parque Nacional Los Glaciares was declared a UNESCO World Heritage area in 1982, and public access is tightly controlled and restricted to specific areas. The Fitz Roy sector at Los Glaciares' northern end is the only significant area where trekking is permitted.

GENERAL INFORMATION
Geographical Features
Comprising an area of 4460 sq km, Parque Nacional Los Glaciares stretches 200km north to south along the eastern edge of the vast Hielo Sur, or southern continental ice sheet, between about 48°S and 51°S. Over a dozen major glaciers slide down eastwards from the Hielo Sur into Lago Viedma and Lago Argentino. These two enormous low-lying (roughly 200m above sea level) lakes extend well into the Argentine pampa, indicating the eastern extent of the ice age glaciers. Particularly in the case of Lago Argentino, the lakes' numerous fjord-like

arms reaching westwards deep into the Andean Cordillera give them the form of giant squids. Approximately a quarter of Los Glaciares' area – just how much is a contentious issue, since Argentina and Chile disagree vehemently as to where the line of the international border should run – is covered by glacial ice.

One of Argentina's most famous natural landmarks, the spectacular Glaciar Moreno, lies in the southern sector of the park. Until recently, this glacier would periodically block off a major branch of Lago Argentino, creating a natural dam that built up behind the icy wall until the immense pressure of the backwaters eventually broke through it in a marvellous show of natural forces. Glacial recession (apparently caused by global warming) now seems to have stopped Glaciar Moreno's advance, however, and most Argentine glaciologists consider it unlikely that the glacier will return to its former behaviour in the near future.

At the far northern end of Los Glaciares lies one of the most magnificent and famous mountain areas in the Andes. Here the legendary diorite peaks of Cerro Torre and Monte Fitz Roy (3441m) rise abruptly from the flat Patagonian steppes, attracting climbing expeditions from all over the world. Short lateral valleys lead into the ranges to the base of these peaks, giving trekkers relatively straightforward access to the finest scenery. This so-called Fitz Roy area includes the northernmost sector of Los Glaciares as well as the private land (largely belonging to the Estancia Ricanor) just outside the park's northern boundaries.

Natural History

Virtually all of Parque Nacional Los Glaciares' forests are a blend of two deciduous beech species, lenga and ñirre. Playing the role of post-glacial colonisers (similar to that of birches in the northern hemisphere), lenga and ñirre have moved into new terrain left vacant by the receding glaciers. Growing sporadically in the forest are hardy wild flowers, including the topa topa *(Calceolaria biflora)* and the zapallito *(C. uniflora)*, two low-growing, closely related annuals that produce one or two surprisingly large 'pea-like' flowers of a yellowish-red colour. Land orchids *(Chlorea* species) and species of *Oxalis* may also be found. The lenga/ñirre (so-called 'Magellanic') forest forms a thin strip close to the Cordillera, which recedes into dry steppeland towards the east. This is because of the dehydrating effect of the incessant westerly winds that whip across the valleys and plains, carrying off moisture even as it falls as rain.

Scattered around the steppes are woody bushes such as neneo rojo *(Anarthrophyllum desideratum)*, a dull-green, rounded shrub that brightens up the steppes with thousands of red flowers when in bloom, and algarrobo patagónico *(Prosopis* species). Hierba negra or mata barrosa *(Mulinum spinosum)*, a misshapen umbelliferous small shrub that looks like scraggy fennel, is usually found growing in matted, windswept bushes known as mogotes. Hierba negra is often mixed with tough native tussock grasses called coirones, of the genus *Stipa*. Other common steppeland species include the native Patagonian cactus *(Pterocactus australis)* and the maihuén *(Maihuenia* species), a more atypical member of the cactus family that grows in small mounds like spiny lawns.

Parque Nacional Los Glaciares boasts bountiful bird life, including Patagonia's two largest bird species. The flightless, ostrich-like ñandu (generally called the choique in Argentina, but known to English-speakers as Darwin's rhea) is sometimes glimpsed streaking across the steppes. More often spotted by trekkers is the great Andean condor, gliding with ease around the loftiest summits buoyed by mighty wings that have a span of over 2m. On the steppes you'll also find the martineta copetona *(Eudromia elegans)*, a black-crested

Southern Beech *(Nothofagus)*

Southern Beech belong to the genus *Nothofagus*, and are closely related to the 'true' beech species (of the genus *Fagus*) found throughout the northern hemisphere. Southern beech – with literally the same common name in Spanish, *haya del sur* – are represented across the entire South Pacific, with several species of *Nothofagus* in Australia, five in both New Zealand and the island of New Caledonia, and well over a dozen species in the temperate highland forests of New Guinea.

The 10 species of southern beech that grow in South America are all endemic to the southern Andes, and do not grow north of the subtropical zone above 30°S. The distribution of southern beech is determined by factors such as climate and elevation, but although many other tree species may also be present, southern beech forms the basis of the forest in virtually all areas.

Most of these Patagonian species of *Nothofagus* are deciduous – a feature shared only by one other member of the genus outside South America, the Tasmanian tanglefoot bush *(N. gunnii)*, which bears a remarkable resemblance to lenga *(N. pumilio)*. Deciduous species of southern beech are found with increasing altitude or distance south. In April and May, mountainsides all over Patagonia turn golden-red with the autumn colours of the southern beeches, giving the landscape a peculiarly 'northern hemispherical' feel.

See under the Trees heading in the Flora section for descriptions of the seven species of southern beech found in the Patagonian Andes. ■

ground-dwelling partridge whose plumage of fine black and ochre stripes camouflage it well. The loica *(Sturnella loyca)* is a meadowlark; the male is readily recognisable by his red breast and white slash above each eye. The cometocino, or fringilio cordillerano *(Phyrgilus gayi)*, a grey-hooded finch of the steppeland zone, typically builds its nest among the protective thorny branches of the calafate bush.

Another finch species, the yal cordillerano *(Melanodera xanthogramma)*, is also generally found on the flat, dry lowlands, but prefers the highland environment. The tordo *(Curaeus curaeus)*, or austral blackbird, inhabits the Magellanic forests on the park's moister western side, retreating to the milder climate of the nearby Pacific coast for the winter. The tucúquere *(Bubo virginianus)* is a species of forest owl with twin crests above its eyes that look like feathery horns. Flocks of cachañas *(Microsittace ferruginea)*, a colourful and boisterous Patagonian parakeet that feeds on seeds, fruit and shoots, also visit Los Glaciares over the summer.

The guanaco mostly forms herds on the open steppes (where it can keep a look out for pumas), but individuals sometimes move up into the mountains. The huemul, a stout species of Andean deer once present in large numbers throughout the Patagonian Andes, survives in small remnant herds in certain areas of the park. Another gravely endangered native mammal is the mara, commonly known as the Patagonian hare, which still manages to survive despite the steady encroachment of introduced European rabbits into its steppeland habitat. The adaptable zorro culpeo, feeds mainly on these newcomers, and the numbers of this reddish-brown fox are consequently quite high. The zorro culpeo also preys on native animals like the chingue, or zorrino, a Patagonian skunk with the characteristic black coat and white dorsal stripe.

Climate

Parque Nacional Los Glaciares has a similar climate to that found farther north at the eastern rim of the Argentine Patagonian Andes. A major difference is that the Hielo Sur, or southern continental ice sheet, completely blocks out the maritime influence, leaving a much more frigid continental climate. Closer to the great lakes of Lago Viedma and Lago Argentino a milder microclimate exists.

At El Chaltén, the average minimum/maximum in February (summer) is 5/22°C. In August (winter), it is around 1/9°C. On the great icy expanse of the Hielo Sur, the average annual level of precipitation (falling almost entirely as snow) reaches 5000mm in places; this figure drops to little more than 1500mm on the forested Andean foothills, and to less than 400mm on the steppes on the park's eastern fringe.

The strong westerly winds are chilled and dry out as they blow over the Cordillera and continue in blustery gusts across the steppes. Except for minor 'wind shadows' at the foot of the Cordillera, blustery winds blow almost incessantly throughout the summer. The cool, windy conditions prevent the development of summer thunderstorms, and the infrequent rain that falls often quickly evaporates again in the wind. Winter conditions are not as severe as you might think, because the harsh Patagonian winds that constantly blow throughout the summer months drop away from around May to the beginning of September.

Place Names

The local Tehuelche tribes venerated Monte Fitz Roy, whose prominent form must have been a key landmark during their annual migrations from the Atlantic to the Cordillera. Francisco 'Perito' Moreno gave the peak its present (Celtic) name after Captain Fitzroy of the Beagle, who in 1834 accompanied Charles Darwin up the Río Santa Cruz to within 50km of the Cordillera. Fitzroy (the original spelling of his name) and Darwin were presumably the first Europeans to view Monte Fitz Roy's classic 3441m summit of smooth frost-polished granite. The Tehuelche called the mountain Chaltén ('peak of fire'), apparently in the mistaken belief that Monte Fitz Roy was a volcano.

The slightly less spectacular 'needles' on either side of the Monte Fitz Roy bear the names of members of the 1952 French expedition who first climbed it: Saint Exupery, Mermoz, Guillomet and Poincenot. Other local nomenclature commemorates local pioneering families, such as Cerro Madsen, named after Andreas Madsen, a Danish settler who established Estancia Fitz Roy on the Río de las Vueltas in 1903.

PRACTICAL INFORMATION
Information Sources
In Calafate, the APN Intendencia (☎ 91005; fax 91755) at Avenida del Libertador 1302 (at the western end of the main road through town) has a helpful visitors' information office open from 9 am to 3 pm.

The Guardería Chaltén (☎ 93004), at the southern end of the new tourist village of El Chaltén in the park's northern Fitz Roy sector, has an information centre (Centro de Informes) with displays introducing aspects of Los Glaciares' ecology; it's open daily from 9 am until 3 pm. El Chaltén's small tourist office is also open from 9 am to 3 pm.

Several English-speaking trekking/mountaineering guides are based at El Chaltén over the summer months, including Alberto del Castillo (☎ 93017), Jorge Tarditti (☎ 93013) and Oscar Pandolfi; Paula Marechal (☎ 93017) is a local French-speaking guide. Contact the tourist office for other trekking/mountaineering guides based at El Chaltén.

The Comisión del Auxilio Club Andino El Chaltén carries out emergency rescues (mainly for mountaineers); the emergency VHF radio frequency is 150.390.

Permits & Regulations
In order to protect the park's delicate environment, public access to Parque Nacional Los Glaciares is restricted by the APN authorities. The only part of the park that is open for trekking is the northernmost Fitz Roy sector. Apart from supervised tourist launch excursions across Lago Argentino, venturing into the heart of Los Glaciares is not encouraged.

There is no charge to enter Los Glaciares'

Fitz Roy sector (because the road also serves estancias to the north outside the park). All trekking parties in the Fitz Roy sector are required to fill out a simple form at the Guardería Chaltén giving names of party members and details of their trekking itinerary (including which camping areas they intend to use). Trekkers may not stay longer than seven days at Campamento Bridwell and Campamento Poincenot. Note that lighting campfires (or using firewood) anywhere within the park is now banned, so all overnight trekkers must carry a portable stove.

Climbing permits (for mountaineers) are available without charge and are valid for 30 days (after which they may be renewed once only).

When to Trek
Since large parts of Los Glaciares receive heavy winter snowfalls, the recommended time to visit the park is during the summer season from November to April. If possible avoid visiting the park in January and the first half of February, when trails and camping areas often become overcrowded.

Maps
Most recommended is Zagier & Urruty's contoured colour trekking map scaled at 1:50,000 titled *Monte Fitz Roy & Cerro Torre*, which is available in Calafate (and many other cities in Argentine Patagonia) for around US$12. Otherwise four Argentine IGM 1:100,000 sheets are needed to get full coverage of the Fitz Roy sector: *Estancia Kaiken Aike* (No 4972-26, Santa Cruz), *Laguna del Desierto* (No 4972-20, Santa Cruz), *Glaciar Viedma* (Nos 4972-25 & 4975-30) and *Monte Fitzroy* (No 4972-19). Although these IGM maps are reasonably accurate topographically – the Zagier & Urruty map is actually drawn from them – they do not show trekking routes.

Accommodation
El Chaltén There are more than half a dozen reasonable places to stay in El Chaltén, the administration village of Los Glaciares' Fitz Roy sector.

For budget-range accommodation try the *Ruca Mahuida* (☎ 93018), the *Albergue Patagonia* (☎ 93091), the *Posada Lago del Desierto* (☎ 93010) or the *Albergue Los Ñires* (☎ 93009), some of which also offer camping and kitchen facilities. The *Cabañas Cerro Torre* (☎ 93061), *Casa de Piedra* (☎ 93015) and *Cabaña de Miguel* (☎ 93063) have small self-contained cabins for four to six people.

More up-market accommodation is available at El Chaltén's new *La Aldea Apart Hotel*La Aldea Apart Hotel, the *Fitz Roy Inn* (☎ 93062, which also has camping facilities and a good restaurant), and the *Hostería Fitz Roy* (☎ 0966-22436 or 20968 in Calafate). The *Hostería La Quinta*, a recently renovated former estancia several kilometres before the Guardería Chaltén, also offers rooms of a better standard.

Camping

Camping is allowed only at the park-authorised camping areas.

El Chaltén has two free camping areas: the *Campamento Confluencia*, across the road from the Guardería Chaltén; and the less crowded *Campamento Madsen*, several kilometres north along the road from the guardería. Both are without facilities (even toilets), and become quite busy (and noisy) in January and early February. Trekkers should select tent sites with maximum shelter from the often very strong winds that sweep through the valley. Lighting fires is prohibited at both camping areas.

Several free en route camping areas (without facilities) are described in the trail notes. The *Refugio Los Troncos* at Piedra del Fraile in the upper Río Eléctrico offers organised camping (see Stage 2 of the Around Monte Fitz Roy trek).

Supplies

Although the price difference is not as great as you'd expect, supplies are cheaper in El Calafate, where there are two well-stocked supermarkets and a bakery. El Chaltén has two small grocery stores *(proveedurías)* as well as a post office and petrol (gasoline)

station. There are also several small restaurants in El Chaltén.

Access to the Fitz Roy Area

The Fitz Roy area is accessible from the rapidly growing tourist town of El Calafate. The 220km access route is north via the bitumen Ruta Nacional 40, then north-west via the unsurfaced Ruta Provincial 23 to the village of El Chaltén. In summer two bus companies, Cal Tur (☎ 91117) and Los Glaciares (☎ 91753), run daily services from El Calafate to El Chaltén. Both buses depart Calafate at 6 am (picking you up from your hotel or hostel) and return from El Chaltén at 4 pm. The trip takes four hours each way and costs around US$50. There is no problem breaking the journey, even if you want to stay a few weeks or more in the Fitz Roy area. The Los Glaciares bus terminates at the Restaurante Senyera in El Chaltén, while the Cal Tur bus continues to the Fitz Roy Inn (about 1km farther north). After late April/early May, Cal Tur operates a reduced service several times a week to El Chaltén.

Hitchhiking to El Chaltén outside the busy summer months is a lonely and unpredictable prospect.

Mirador Maestri (Cerro Torre Lookout)

> **Duration** 2 days
> **Distance** 19km
> **Standard** Easy
> **Start/Finish** El Chaltén
> **Entry** Free, permit needed
> **Season** November-April
> **Summary** A spectacular return trek to a lookout close to the stunning granite tower of Cerro Torre.

This recommended short walk takes you to an exhilarating lookout opposite the 3102m Cerro Torre. The polished, vertical rock walls of this classic granite needle were for decades considered impossible to climb. The eventual conquest of Cerro Torre in 1970 by Cesare Maestri provoked the most bitter controversy in climbing history, when it became known that the Italian alpinist and his party had used a portable compressor drill to fix a line of bolts to reach the summit.

DAYS REQUIRED

The trek is often done as a long return day walk from El Chaltén, but a more leisurely two days is recommended with a night at Campamento Bridwell. The park authorities have closed the shortcut path (described in the previous edition of this guidebook) between Campamento Bridwell and Campamento Poincenot, so trekkers are now obliged to return to El Chaltén (or at least to the valley of the Río de las Vueltas).

TREKKING STANDARD

The path to Laguna Torre is well marked and easily followed. The trek is 19km return and has an *easy* rating.

THE TREK

El Chaltén to Campamento Bridwell

19km return, 5 to 6½ hours return

After signing in at the ranger station, proceed north across the Río Fitz Roy bridge through El Chaltén. From the **Albergue Los Ñires**, follow a bulldozed track west to pick up a foot track leading high above the river past a tiny hydroelectric dam that supplies power to the village. The route rises on through scattered lenga and ñirre woodland (with the odd wire fence to step over) before merging with a more prominent (signposted) path coming in from the right after 45 minutes to one hour.

On their way back, trekkers can turn off here rather than returning directly to El Chaltén. It leads first north-east past a mallín, before winding down eastwards around large boulders on slopes covered with typical Patagonian dryland plants. The path comes out at the **Ruta Provincial 23**, the main road through the Valle Río de las Vueltas, several kilometres north of the Guardería Chaltén

and just south of Campamento Madsen, after 35 to 45 minutes.

Continue up past a rounded bluff to the **'Mirador Laguna Torre'**, a lookout crest giving you the first clear view up the valley to the extraordinary rock needle of Cerro Torre standing above a sprawling mass of intersecting glaciers. The trail dips down gently through beautiful stands of stout ancient lengas, before cutting across open scrubby riverflats and old revegetated moraines (past a now off-limits shortcut route to Campamento Poincenot) to reach a signposted fork, 45 minutes to one hour on. Bear left and climb over a forested embankment to cross a small alluvial plain, following the fast-flowing glacial waters of the Río Fitz Roy to arrive at **Campamento Bridwell**, after a further 20 to 25 minutes.

Mirador Maestri

The wonderful walk up to this lookout is best done as a return loop from Campamento Bridwell. First head up north-west through barely vegetated glacial rubble to the top of the moraine wall damming **Laguna Torre**, a stark lake fed directly by Glaciar Torre, from which blocks of ice break off continually and beach around the shore.

Make your way up northwards along the narrow ridge to about halfway around the frigid lake, then begin zig-zagging up diagonally leftwards past the **Refugio Maestri**, a tiny A-frame 'bivouac' refugio on a little terrace of dwarf lengas. This lovely spot once served as a base camp for mountaineers, but the park authorities now prohibit overnight stays here. The route climbs on a way to reach the **Mirador Maestri**, 50 minutes to 1¼ hours from Campamento Bridwell. From up here you get much enhanced views of the Cordón Adela, a serrated ridge that includes half a dozen snowcapped peaks between Cerro Grande (2751m) and Cerro Torre (3102m).

To reach the signposted fork first passed on the way to Campamento Bridwell, descend again along the moraine ridge to where an inconspicuous route marked only by cairns darts off left down into the forest.

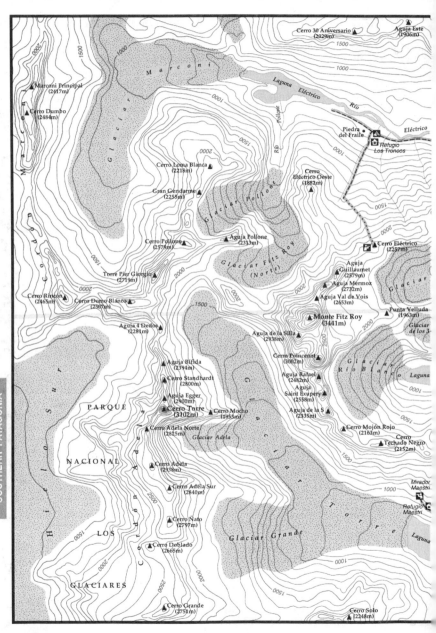

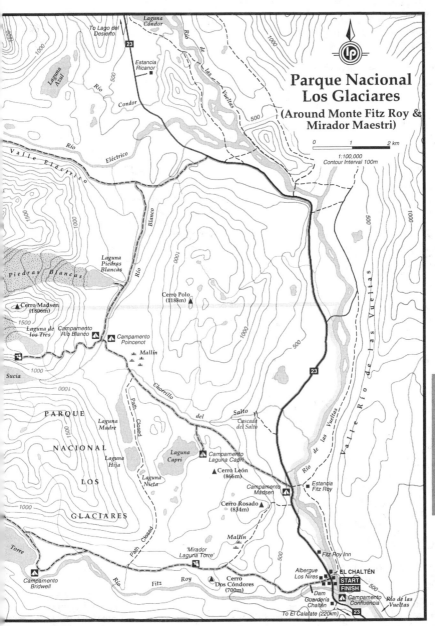

Parque Nacional
Los Glaciares
(Around Monte Fitz Roy &
Mirador Maestri)

0   1   2 km
1:100,000
Contour Interval 100m

This foot track passes large boulders, then rises and dips roughly south-east to reach the fork after 25 to 30 minutes.

Camp Sites Although some trekkers still pitch their tents near the refugio below the Mirador Maestri, the only park-authorised place to camp is at Campamento Bridwell. This free camping area (without facilities) is in a pleasant grove of riverside lengas below Cerro Solo. Campers should use a fuel stove for cooking rather than light a fire.

Around Monte Fitz Roy

> **Duration** 4 days
> **Distance** 50km
> **Standard** Easy-Medium
> **Start/Finish** El Chaltén
> **Entry** Free, permit needed
> **Season** November-April
> **Summary** A circuit trek to lookouts breath-takingly close to Monte Fitz Roy.

Easily the highest peak in the area, Monte Fitz Roy was first climbed in 1952 by a French expedition based at Campamento Poincenot. This trek takes you into the valleys surrounding this classic Patagonian peak, where Monte Fitz Roy can be viewed close-up from two high-level lookouts.

DAYS REQUIRED
This trek can be done as a circuit (returning to El Chaltén via the Ruta Provincial 23) in about three days. Backtracking via Camp-amento Poincenot or doing the side trip up to the Cerro Eléctrico lookout each add an additional day.

TREKKING STANDARD
The well-trodden path up to Campamento Poincenot is marked with yellow-painted stakes and occasional red splashes on rocks, and – except for the short section leading out

of the Río Blanco into the Valle Eléctrico – the remainder of the trek is easy to follow.

The trek has been given a grading of *easy to medium* and covers a distance of 50km. The 8km return side trip up to the lookout near Cerro Eléctrico, which is a high-level route, is graded *medium to hard*.

ACCOMMODATION & CAMPING
For places to stay in El Chaltén refer to Accommodation and Camping. For places to stay in El Calafate see Trekking Bases earlier in this chapter.

The only en route accommodation is the Refugio Los Troncos at Piedra del Fraile, so all trekkers must carry a tent. The Refugio Los Troncos is open throughout the trekking season and charges US$5 per camp site, US$10 per bed, or US$15 per night for a four-person cabin. The hut also has toilets and hot showers plus a small proveeduría (store). A cooked evening meal costs around US$15.

The only other authorised places to camp en route are the Campamento Laguna Capri and Campamento Poincenot, which are without facilities and free of charge. It is strictly prohibited to camp anywhere else in the Fitz Roy area, either within the national park or on private property.

THE TREK
Stage 1: Guardería Chaltén to Campamento Poincenot
10km, 2¾ to 3¾ hours

Follow the road for several kilometres north through El Chaltén to **Campamento Madsen**, and take the signposted path just above the camping area. Climb to the right of a large rock outcrop onto open slopes of mogotes (*Mulinum spinosum*) and tussock grasses (*Stipa* species) giving fine views of the adjacent **Cordón de los Cóndores**. The route sidles on steadily upwards high above the braided gravelly channels of the Río de las Vueltas through pockets of lenga and occasional coigüe de Magallanes (or guindo). After swinging around north-westwards through a minor saddle, head up beside the ravine of the **Chorillo del Salto** to reach the signposted turn-off to Laguna Capri after 1¾ to 2¼ hours.

This recommended short side trip leads up to the lake's northern shore, then dips left through the forest to reach the free camping area of **Campamento Laguna Capri** after just 10 minutes. A tranquil lake with lovely little beaches, Laguna Capri sits before the jagged backdrop of the Fitz Roy Massif.

Make your way on upvalley through heathland scattered with stunted ñirre scrub past a well-trodden but unsignposted trail diverging up left. (This shortcut route to Campamento Bridwell has now been closed by the park authorities as it leads through a sensitive habitat of the endangered huemul, or southern Andean deer). Skirt along the left side of a broad boggy mallín, hopping across the tiny clear stream and following yellow-tipped marker stakes north-westwards through a band of Magellanic lenga forest. You will arrive at **Campamento Poincenot**, 50 minutes to 1¼ hours from the turn-off to Laguna Capri.

Named in memory of a French mountaineer who died 1952 while attempting to cross the Río Fitz Roy, this charming spot along the grassy (eastern) bank of the **Río Blanco** looks up directly to the spires of the Fitz Roy Massif.

Monte Fitz Roy Lookout

The obligatory three-hour return hike up to the foot of Monte Fitz Roy will be another major highlight of your Patagonia trip – a pre-dawn start will get you there for the scenic sunrise. From Campamento Poincenot cross the small river on a makeshift bridge to the mountaineers' base camp of **Campamento Río Blanco** , and there pick up a foot track leading off leftwards. The route spirals up increasingly steeply west-south-west out of the trees and on over loose rocky ground to reach a low crest.

From here you get a sudden and stunningly close-up view of Monte Fitz Roy towering over 2000m above the picturesque **Laguna de los Tres**, which lies in a glacial hollow immediately in front of you. Away to the south-east, beyond the nearby Laguna

Madre and Laguna Capri, the enormous Lago Viedma spreads out into the dry steppes. Another wonderful viewing point can be easily reached by heading around the shore of Laguna de los Tres to its outlet stream, then leftwards to a high precipice far above the cloudy-green Laguna Sucia.

For more superb vistas of Monte Fitz Roy, Cerro Madsen can be climbed in a somewhat more difficult four-to-five hour return route that follows the spur just north of Laguna de los Tres.

Laguna Sucia

This spectacular lake can be reached in around two hours return by following the bouldery bed of the Río Blanco. Laguna Sucia lies in a deep trough-like cirque under the towering granite 'needles' of **Aguja Poincenot** and **Aguja Saint Exupery**. Frozen white chunks periodically tear off the **Glaciar Río Blanco** icefall and plummet over 300m into the lake.

Camp Sites The only places trekkers are permitted to pitch their tents along Stage 1 are Campamento Laguna Capri and Campamento Poincenot, both free camping areas with space for around 20 tents. Although Laguna Capri has no outlet its water is considered safe to drink, so please don't pollute the lake with detergents or soap, and defecate well away from the shore. Campamento Poincenot is most recommended, but it can get crowded and supports a population of audaciously voracious mice.

Campamento Río Blanco, on the opposite side of the river from Campamento Poincenot, is a base camp normally reserved for mountaineering parties.

Stage 2: Campamento Poincenot to Refugio Los Troncos
11km, 2¾ to 3½ hours

Cross to the **Campamento Río Blanco** and find the signposted path at the lower end of the camping area. The often vague route goes downstream along the western banks of the Río Blanco over eroding embankments and small gravel washes to meet a rubble-filled side valley after 40 to 50 minutes. From here, moderately agile trekkers can make a very worthwhile 30-minute return side trip by following cairns that lead up left around and over white granite boulders to **Laguna Piedras Blancas**. The heavily seraced **Glaciar Piedras Blancas** curves around from the eastern face of Monte Fitz Roy in a series of icefalls that sprawl down into this impressively bleak meltwater lake.

Back on the main route pick your way through the moraine debris and jump across the gushing lake outlet stream. The trail continues downvalley, skirting the edge of the rocky alluvial plain or occasionally dipping briefly left into the forest. Where the valley fans out at its mouth, move away from the river towards hanging glaciers on mountains to the north-west to intersect with a more prominent foot track (indicated by orange paint markings), 50 minutes to 1¼ hours from the Laguna Piedras Blancas turn-off.

Head left (west) over rolling wooded slopes and through small fire-cleared pastures sprinkled with calafate bushes to enter the enclosed upper valley of the **Río Eléctrico** below high glacier-sheered cliffs after 30 to 40 minutes. The path proceeds gently up beside the rushing, murky-grey river through open, cattle-grazed lenga forest before cutting across a broad grassy meadow to arrive at the **Refugio Los Troncos** (see Camp Sites), a further 40 to 50 minutes on.

The refugio and camping ground are at the eastern end of **Piedra del Fraile**, a large erratic block in the middle of the flat valley floor below the 2257m **Cerro Eléctrico**. The whole of the Valle Eléctrico is private property (belonging to the nearby Estancia Ricanor), and the owners only welcome trekkers who intend to stay or camp at the Refugio Los Troncos. Non-paying day visitors may be turned back when they get to Piedra del Fraile.

A short pathway climbs up to the top of the rock for a great view upvalley to **Lago Eléctrico**, a dramatically bleak lake exposed to the fierce and incessant winds blasting down from the nearby Hielo Sur. Lago Eléctrico can also be visited in around 1½

hours return by taking an easy trail across the moist river flats then over wave-like moraines to the lake's raw, glaciated south-eastern shore.

Side Trip to Cerro Eléctrico Lookout This much longer and more difficult side trip (involving an ascent of 1700m in altitude) takes you well into the realm of the mountaineers, and should only be attempted during stable weather. Take the well-worn foot track up the steep southern side of the valley between twin cascading streams until the gradient moderates, then continue ascending steadily southwards to reach the lip of an impressive cirque filled by a small glacier after 1¾ to 2¼ hours. Monte Fitz Roy can be seen towering above the back wall of this cirque.

The path leads slightly left, but after passing over a small spur it finally peters out. Head south along the bottom of reddish scree slopes with the glacier to your right for 30 to 40 minutes, bearing left where the cliffs up to your left suddenly change into black rock. Make your way up steeply to the right of the red rock over loose scree slopes into a small col, another two hours on. Head east from the col and traverse the steep boulder slopes below a huge wedge-shaped rock, then ascend gradually to reach the lowest point of the main ridge of Cerro Eléctrico, 40 to 50 minutes on. From here there are utterly stupendous views towards Fitz Roy, Cerro Pollone and south-west over the Hielo Sur.

Camp Sites The Refugio Los Troncos is the only place trekkers are permitted to camp along the whole of Stage 2. Here pleasant tent sites on watered lawns sheltered by the Piedra del Fraile cost US$5 per night (including firewood), while simple cabins can be rented for US$15 (or US$10 per bed); showers are also available. The resident caretaker (a likeable eccentric named Ricardo, who backpacks supplies in during winter) sells essential items like beer and biscuits at reasonable prices.

Stage 3: Piedra del Fraile to Guardería Chaltén (Via Valle Río de las Vueltas)
22km, 4¾ to 6 hours

This is an alternative to backtracking to El Chaltén via Campamento Poincenot (ie Stages 1 and 2 in reverse order).

Retrace your steps to the trail junction on the lower Río Blanco and head on eastwards through boulders and regenerating ñirres to cross improvised bridges over the river's several channels. (After rain, however, crossing the Río Blanco may require a more serious wade). The route continues along the edge of the rocky stream bed to meet a 4WD track that leads down quickly to intersect with the **Ruta Provincial 23**, the main road through the Valle Río de las Vueltas, 1¾ to 2¼ hours from the refugio. (This turn-off is signposted and 1.2km south of the Río Blanco road bridge).

Follow the gravel southwards around a tight, cliffed bend beside the river, edging on along a wide plain – your pace accelerated by gusty tailwinds – back into the national park. After two to 2½ hours the road passes the signposted trail to the **Cascada del Salto**, a waterfall spurting out of the gorge up to your right (reached in around one hour return). Proceed another 30 to 40 minutes past **Campamento Madsen** and on through the village to arrive back at the **Guardería Chaltén** after a final 30 to 40 minutes.

Other Treks in the Fitz Roy Area

LAGO TORO
Lago Toro (not to be confused with the Laguna Torre) may not be as pretty as other lakes in the park but its impressive, raw glacial setting makes it the worthy objective for this two-day return trek, graded *medium*. The often poorly marked route begins from behind the Guardería Chaltén, leading southwards across a small footbridge then southwest through a series of clearings to a shallow lake on a little plateau looking out towards Cerro Huemul. From here you drop down to a simple shack (a private puesto, or outstation hut) on the grassy northern bank of the milky Río Tunel, and follow the trail upstream to Lago Toro, a small turgid meltwater pool at the snout of the Glaciar Río Tunel below high craggy peaks. There is a tiny A-frame refugio (identical to the hut near the Mirador Maestri) near where the river leaves Lago Toro. Camping is permitted at the refugio, although there are nicer camp sites on the banks of the Río Tunel farther downstream.

The heavily glaciated area behind Lago Toro is interesting to explore, but requires fording the river and heading around the lake's exposed southern side. Experienced trekkers can continue up to the Paso del Viento at the edge of the Hielo Sur (the huge southern continental ice sheet), a difficult trackless route that takes another long day.

Cross a short section of the lower Glaciar Tunel (there are no crevasses on this part of the glacier), continuing around a tiny lake at the snout of a second glacier before you ascend steeply south-west over scree slopes leading up to the pass. The proximity of the continental ice sheet makes weather extremely unpredictable, and only parties with a sound knowledge of mountaineering techniques and adequate equipment should venture onto the Hielo Sur itself. A refugio (constructed for scientific research) stands on a nunatak ridge within the ice of the Hielo Sur 4km south of the Paso del Viento, but it can be hard to find in bad weather.

LAGO DEL DESIERTO
The narrow, 12km long lake known as Lago del Desierto, is outside Parque Nacional Los Glaciares 37km from El Chaltén along a newly constructed extension of the Ruta Provincial 23. It is the source of the Río de las Vueltas (whose waters flow into the Río Santa Cruz via Lago Viedma and Lago Argentino). Until recently, the lake (which the Chileans call *Laguna* del Desierto) was also the source of a long-running border dispute, but this ended in 1995 when a special

SOUTHERN PATAGONIA

international tribunal accepted Argentina's claim to the whole Lago del Desierto area.

The two or three-day trip to this lovely 'deserted lake' surrounded by pristine lenga forests is recommended to all trekkers in the Fitz Roy area. The route begins where the road currently terminates near the Estancia Lago del Desierto at the lake's southern end. A foot track crosses a bridge over the outlet and leads around the eastern shore to the Refugio Lago del Desierto (☎ 01-331 0191), a large privately run hut at the northern end of the lake with electricity and 24-hour hot water.

Plans exist for the further extension of the Ruta Provincial 23 north as far as Lago San Martín, which would make the Refugio Lago del Desierto accessible to regular vehicles.

From the Refugio Lago del Desierto, trekkers can continue up to a very rustic refugio on the shore of Lago Diablo, thereby lengthening the trek by two days.

Two new Argentine IGM 1:100,000 sheets, *Península MacKenna* (Santa Cruz, No 4972-14) and *Laguna del Desierto* (Santa Cruz, No 4972-20) cover the Lago del Desierto area, but more convenient is Zagier & Urruty's special trekking map, *Monte Fitz Roy & Cerro Torre*, which includes a 1:100,000 insert showing the trekking route itself.

In January and February the Los Glaciares company runs minibuses from El Chaltén to Lago del Desierto, leaving daily at around 11 am (US$12). The service otherwise operates on demand (minimum of 12 passengers).

Parque Nacional Torres del Paine

Parque Nacional Torres del Paine lies some 100km directly north of Puerto Natales in far southern Chile. Rising up from the flat steppes with breathtaking abruptness, the craggy mountains of Torres del Paine present an astonishing sight even when viewed from far off on the park's south-eastern approach road. For over 60 years before the establishment of the national park in 1959, the Torres del Paine area had been subject to often highly destructive grazing practices from which it is still recovering. The uniqueness of the area was fully recognised in 1978, when Torres del Paine was declared an international biosphere reserve by UNESCO.

In recent years tourism has boomed in Torres del Paine, bringing infrastructure development, including new refugios and hotels. Increasing numbers of visitors have forced the park authorities to restrict public access to certain areas and tighten camping regulations, but this superb park unquestionably offers some of the best trekking in the world.

GENERAL INFORMATION
Geographical Features
At roughly 51°S, Parque Nacional Torres del Paine takes in a remote area of 1814 sq km at the south-eastern end of the Hielo Sur, Patagonia's massive southern continental icecap. To the north Torres del Paine borders on Argentina's vast Parque Nacional Los Glaciares, and on its south-western side it meets the much smaller Chilean Parque Nacional Balmaceda.

Torres del Paine was landscaped by the great glaciers of the Hielo Sur, which during the recent Pleistocene Ice Age extended right down to cover all but the highest ground or the park's most easterly areas. The great streams of ice have largely receded to the Hielo Sur, but today four major glaciers, Dickson, Grey, Zapala (or Pingo) and Geikie – which are all appendages of this colossal block of ice – creep down into the park to terminate in deep meltwater lakes. The largest is the 17km-long Ventisquero Grey, which disgorges huge icebergs into the turquoise waters of Lago Grey. The entire area of Torres del Paine lies within the basin of the Río Serrano, which drains southwards into the fjord-like Seno Ultima Esperanza.

Rising out of the largely flat and barren plains barely 300m above sea level, the roughly quadrilateral massif known as the Macizo Paine forms the park's core and displays many of its most unique and spectacular features. Numerous glacial lakes surround the Macizo Paine, principally Lago Grey, Lago Pehoe and Lago Nordenskjöld along its southern foot, while the somewhat smaller lakes of Lago Dickson, Lago Paine and Lago Azul lie on the northern side of the massif. The park's largest lakes are Lago del Toro and Lago Sarmiento on its south-eastern edge. The Macizo Paine is penetrated by the short but very deep valleys of Río Francés and Río Ascensio, which flow south into Lago Nordenskjöld.

At the south-western end of the Macizo Paine stands the 3248m *cumbre principal* (main summit) of Cerro Paine Grande, the park's highest point and its only peak over 3000m. Cerro Paine Grande is capped by so-called *hongos de hielo* (ice mushrooms) a phenomenon seen in few areas outside the Patagonian Andes. Ice mushrooms form only at high elevations in subpolar regions, where moisture in the extremely intense winds freezes directly onto alpine rock. Just east of Cerro Paine Grande are the Cuernos del Paine, jagged turrets of a resistant layer of sedimentary shale covering the granite base. At the eastern end of the Macizo Paine are three magnificent frost polished 'towers' of pink granite, the Torres del Paine, from which the park gets its name.

Natural History

Until the declaration of the national park in 1959 a large portion of the Torres del Paine area was grazed by cattle and sheep. Old fences and puestos are visible in places, and a local estancia still runs some cattle – though not sheep, because they crop grass too close to the ground – in a small part of the park. The graziers' past use of fire to clear forest has greatly modified the landscape, and regeneration is occurring only slowly – another reminder of the destructive effect of fire in the Patagonian Andes.

Forests of lenga, a southern beech, cover the moister interior areas of the park. On steeper slopes the trunks of these trees often take on a bow-like form, perhaps caused by the downward force of the heavy winter snows or the young trees' continual search for light. At lower elevations coigüe de Magallanes, can also be found in the forest, although it rarely challenges the dominance of the lenga anywhere within the park boundaries.

Ñirre, yet another southern beech species, covers drier and well-drained slopes in the central part of Parque Nacional Torres del Paine. Daisy bushes including the romerillo (*Chiliotrichum rosmarinifolium*), whose foliage has something of the appearance and the aromatic smell of the rosemary bush, grow where the moist natural pasture meets the drier steppeland. Another daisy species found in this transition zone is the chilco de Magallanes (*Baccharis magellanica*), not to be confused with the common native species of fuchsia known simply as chilco.

The easternmost third of the park is covered by the *monte* vegetation characteristic for the lee of the Patagonian Andes. Here plants well adapted to the dry and extremely windy conditions, such as tumbleweeds, or mogotes (*Mulinum spinosum*), spinifex-like maihuén (*Maihuenia* species), the cacto patagonico or yerba del guanaco (*Austrocactus patagonicus*), the world's most southerly cactus, and clumps of native tussock grasses known as coirón (*Festuca* species) are typical. A subspecies of butterfly, *Etcheverrius chilensis magallanicus*, lives among these steppeland plants, somehow managing to avoid being blown away.

The bird life in Torres del Paine is abundant and diverse. The park's lakes (particularly the saltwater ones such as Lago Sarmiento and Laguna Amarga) provide an ideal habitat for the flamenco chileno (*Phoenicopterus chilensis*), or Chilean flamingo. The only flamingo species found in Patagonia, the flamenco chileno eats aquatic insects and small molluscs (whose pigments are responsible for the striking pink colour of its plumage). Even more common is the cisne de cuello negro, a large white swan with a black neck and a red tip under its ill.

Ducks such as the quetru volador, or flying steamer duck, and the caiquén or upland goose, are other water birds often seen on Torres del Paine's lakes. In the fast-flowing rivers (such as the Río de los Perros), the now rather rare pato de torrentes, or torrent duck, may occasionally be spotted swimming against the current in search of its prey, chiefly invertebrates and their larvae. Several species of heron, including the garza grande are also found in lagoons and rivers.

Particularly on the drier eastern sectors of the park, several species of chorlos (plovers) can be sighted from time to time. These dry steppes are also the home of the ñandu or rhea, a Patagonian relative of the ostrich that runs in a fast, zig-zagging gait to outrun potential predators.

Condors are frequently sighted gliding effortlessly around the peaks. Identifiable in flight by their enormous size and distinctive white wing tips, these superb Andean vultures nest in inaccessible cliffs on the eastern side of (or even outside) the park. Condors will sometimes take small live mammals, and although they may attack a dying guanaco they prefer to feed on carrion. Other birds of prey that trekkers may observe are the águila mora *(Geranoaetus melanoleucus)*, a handsome species of eagle, and hawks, harriers and falcons such as the peuquito *(Accipiter bicolor)* and the traro *(Polyborus plancus)*, a species of caracara.

Guanaco graze on the grasslands in the eastern sector of Torres del Paine, and the park's less accessible western interior provides a refuge for small numbers of the shy Andean deer, or huemul. Such rich game sustains the puma, although trekkers are rarely lucky enough to catch even a fleeting glimpse of this discreet predator.

Climate
Abutting the Hielo Sur, the western sectors of Parque Nacional Torres del Paine experience extremely unstable and often localised weather. Precipitation levels vary enormously over relatively short distances, and it is not uncommon to experience heavy downpours in areas closer to the continental icecap while sunshine is visible on the steppes just a few kilometres to the east. The highest precipitation levels, exceeding 4000mm, occur on the Hielo Sur (slightly west of the park's borders), dropping to about 2000mm around the Refugio Pehoe and under 800mm at Laguna Amarga. The mean annual temperature at Lago del Toro is only around 6°C, and summer days never rise much above 20°C. From October to April, but particularly from December to February, winds are almost unremitting and often extremely strong. The chilling effect of the freezing winds that blow off the great glaciers should not be underestimated.

Place Names
The origins of the park's name are in some doubt. The word *paine* (pronounced 'pienee') means 'pale blue' in Tehuelche and may be a reference to the colour of the area's half dozen or so large glacial lakes. The local Andean nomenclature often carries the names of andinists who achieved first ascents, and another theory says that Paine was the name of an early Welsh climber. The 2850m Torre De Agostini, the highest and most southerly tower of the Torres del Paine was named in honour of Father Alberto De Agostini in the 1930s. Lago Skottsberg and Lago Nordenskjöld carry the names of early 20th century Patagonian explorers. More graphic is the Río de los Perros ('River of the Dogs'), which is supposedly named after a herder's dogs who drowned in its fast-flowing waters.

PRACTICAL INFORMATION
Information Sources
CONAF has an office in Puerto Natales (see Trekking Bases), but staff are not interested in answering questions about Torres del Paine. The Torres del Paine administration headquarters is at Lago del Toro, beside the ruins of the original Estancia Paine building (which was destroyed in a fire in 1982). For information about (or to reserve beds in) the refugios in the park, contact Andescape (☎ & fax 061-41 2592) at Pedro Montt 308 in Puerto Natales. Andescape also has an office in Santiago (☎ & fax 02-235 5225) at Santa Beatriz 84-A Providencia.

Top: The stunning granite columns of the Torres del Paine.
Middle: Deciduous trees add colour to the moorland below the peaks of Parque Nacional Los Glaciares in southern Patagonia.
Bottom: Isla Carlos Campos and others in Lago Cochrane, Reserva Nacional Tamango.

Tierra del Fuego offers some of the most rugged and challenging terrain in South America, but the trekking is rewarding. Bare eroded hills at the Laguna Tres Marías (top) and on Isla Navarino (bottom) attest to a harsh climate inhospitable to vegetation. *Mallines*, or marshes and bogs (middle), are common on the poorly drained lowlands near Lago Kami.

Permits & Regulations

All visitors to Parque Nacional Torres del Paine are required to register with the CONAF authorities at the park entrance gate. Trekkers should leave details of intended routes and party members. An entrance fee of US$12.50 for adult foreigners is payable at the park entrance gate (citizens and residents of Chile pay only US$5). In the past, visitors were required to deposit their passports at the park entrance and collect them when they left, but this practice has been discontinued.

In order to protect the environment the park authorities have introduced restrictions on where you can trek and camp. Public access to many parts of the park is not permitted, and trekkers must not leave the official pathways. Camping is now only allowed at designated camping areas, and trekkers caught pitching their tent outside these park-approved sites are likely to be fined. Trekkers who for whatever reason decide to camp 'wild' should at least observe the minimum-impact code and refrain from lighting a fire. Given the continual rise in the number of trekkers visiting Torres del Paine it is important to follow these simple rules.

When to Trek

The summer and early autumn – that is from early December to late March – is the best time to trek in Parque Nacional Torres del Paine. Outside these months, areas above 500m (or lower) are subject to unpredictable and heavy snowfalls. The overwhelming number of visits to this extremely popular national park are during the busy summer holiday season (January to mid-February), when the refugios are prone to overcrowding and camping areas can get cramped. Surprisingly, during the winter season (from around May to the middle of September), the severe Patagonian winds drop away almost completely, making winter trips to the park less extreme than might otherwise be expected. Nonetheless, winter trekking should be confined to shorter low-level routes.

Maps

The recommended map is a contoured 1:100,000 sheet titled *Parque Nacional*

Father Alberto De Agostini

Father Alberto De Agostini (1883-1960) was unquestionably Patagonia's most accomplished and respected early andinist. From his arrival in Punta Arenas as a newly ordained priest in 1910 until he finally retired to his native Turin almost 50 years later, the indefatigable De Agostini explored the Patagonian Andes, climbing, photographing and mapping these wild peaks and ranges. Somehow managing to coordinate his expeditionary activities with his clerical responsibilities, De Agostini made numerous first ascents throughout the Patagonian and Fuegian Andes, including in the Nahuel Huapi, Torres del Paine and Fitz Roy areas.

In 1930 he accompanied a small group of andinists on a first east-to-west traverse of the vast Hielo Sur, the southern Patagonian icecap. In 1941 De Agostini and two members of the Club Andino Bariloche, Hemmi and Schmoll, became the first climbers ever to set foot on the summit of the mighty 3706m Monte San Lorenzo (known as Cerro Cochrane in Chile). De Agostini was fascinated by the 2404m Monte Sarmiento – the third highest summit of the Fuegian Andes – and had made an early attempt on this majestic 'sphinx of ice' in 1913; in 1956 a climbing party organised by De Agostini finally achieved the first ascent of Monte Sarmiento.

De Agostini was also a skilled photographer whose extensive collection of photographs provides the earliest photographic record of the landscape and indigenous peoples of many parts of Patagonia and Tierra del Fuego. Today quite a number of geographical features in Patagonia and Tierra del Fuego (including a fjord, a peak and even a national park) have been named in his honour. De Agostini wrote half a dozen books based on his experiences in the southern Cordillera, culminating in his outstanding *Andes Patagónicos* (listed in the Books section in Facts for the Trekker), which was the first serious mountaineering work ever published on the region. Unfortunately, all of his books have long been out of print, but most larger libraries in southern Chile and Argentina stock them. ■

SOUTHERN PATAGONIA

Torres del Paine, which is published by Sociedad Turistíca Kaoniken (but printed by the Chilean IGM). It very accurately shows topographical detail, trekking routes with average times as well as the location of refugios and park-authorised camping areas. Alternatively, trekkers can use the *Torres del Paine Trekking Map*, a similar colour sheet also scaled at 1:100,000 which is published by Juan Luis Mattassi A Producciones. Both maps cost around US$10 and are available at small bookstores *(librerías)* or newspaper stands in Puerto Natales and other towns throughout Patagonia.

Accommodation & Camping

There are currently nine refugios for trekkers in Parque Nacional Torres del Paine, but it is possible that the construction of new refugios will be approved by the park authorities in the coming years. The route possibilities for parties who don't carry a tent are still fairly limited, so all serious trekkers are strongly advised to bring a tent with them. Remember that camping is allowed only at park-approved camping areas and in organised camping grounds.

The best refugios are those run by Andescape (see Information Sources) at Lago Dickson, Lago Grey and Lago Pehoe. These are modern and well-equipped wooden constructions offering such luxuries as (sometimes hot) showers, electricity and cooked meals. The charge at Andescape refugios is US$14.50 per night for a bed; camping at the refugios costs US$3 per site. In addition Andescape runs the camping ground on the upper Río de los Perros. All the Andescape refugios have radios for emergencies.

There are two other good refugios where a fee is charged: CONAF's Refugio Lago del Toro near the park administration centre (US$5 per night, hot showers US$1.50 extra), and the concessionised Refugio Pudeto at the launch landing jetty on Lago Pehoé near Salto Grande. Refugio Pudeto has recently been expanded and renovated, and now offers accommodation similar to the Andescape refugios. The remaining refugios are free and extremely basic: Refugio Laguna Amarga near the Guardería Laguna Amarga, and Refugio Pingo and Refugio Zapata in the valley of the Río Pingo.

There are also two organised camping grounds at Lago Pehoe and on the Río Serrano with hot showers (both US$6 per site).

Five establishments within Parque Nacional Torres del Paine currently offer hotel-style accommodation. These are as follows:

The *Hostería Las Torres* (☎ 24 7050), accessible by road from the Guardería Laguna Amarga, has rooms for US$85/110 single/double (including breakfast). The hostería (which is passed on the trek to the Torres del Paine Lookout) also has a small shop and a medium-range restaurant.

The *Hostería Pehoe* (☎ 41 1390, or 24 1373 in Punta Arenas), on a tiny island in Lago Pehoe connected by a bridge, which has singles/doubles for US$85/110.

The *Hotel Explora* (☎ 41 1247, 562-699 2922 in Santiago), a rather ugly building at the Salto Chico, has up-market accommodation for around US$300 per person with full board.

The Posada Río Serrano, in the administration village at Lago del Toro charges US$85 per double.

The *Hostería Lago Grey* (☎ 24 8220/ext 29) is on the southern shore of Lago Grey; the launch to Ventisquero Grey and Refugio Grey leaves from near the hostería.

Supplies

Buy all your supplies in Puerto Natales – there are two or three grocery stores or small supermarkets in the streets east of the Plaza de Armas – as prices are exorbitantly high and the range of items is very limited in the park. The Andescape refugios all have small stores (proveedurías) with essentials like wine, soft drinks, spaghetti, biscuits (cookies), canned tuna, dehydrated soup, cigarettes, candles and soap. White gasoline (Shellite) is available in Puerto Natales from the pharmacy on the Plaza de Armas or the hardware store near the tourist office. The Posada Río Serrano, near the administration centre, also has supplies. It's usually possible to leave well-packaged food at the administration centre or guarderías for later treks, but during the busiest months (January and February) CONAF staff may be reluctant to store anything because of lack of space.

Access to the Park

Access to Parque Nacional Torres del Paine is via the junction at Cerro Castillo (on the international road linking Puerto Natales to El Calafate) on the south-eastern side of the park. The main park entrance gate *(portería)* is at the Guardería Laguna Amarga, 116km by road from Puerto Natales; the park administration centre *(sede administrativa)* at Lago del Toro is a further 29km on from the Guardería Laguna Amarga. The road is unsurfaced but well-maintained gravel. A much rougher alternative southern approach road leading around the western side of Lago del Toro is closed to public traffic, although local mountain-bikers often use it.

Turismo Zaahj, Buses JB, Cayetano and Servitur run buses from Puerto Natales to the Torres del Paine administration centre, leaving at 7 am from each company's office (all near the Plaza de Armas) and arriving at the administration centre around 11.30 am. The return fare is US$14 and you can stay in the park for as long as you wish before returning. Not all companies have a service outside summer, but from late October until late April there is at least one daily bus to Torres del Paine. The bus companies have different return departure times, but the earliest bus leaves the administration centre at 12:30 pm.

There is a daily launch across Lago Pehoe between Refugio Pudeto (near Salto Grande) and the Refugio Lago Pehoe. The launch departs at 1 pm and returns from Refugio Lago Pehoe at around 2.30 pm, and the hour-long single trip costs US$12.50. All buses call in at the Refugio Pudeto dock en route to/from the park administration centre; trekkers coming from Puerto Natales will have plenty of time to catch the 1 pm launch, but the earliest bus back to Puerto Natales doesn't reach Refugio Pudeto until after the launch has left.

Another launch runs across Lago Grey between the Hostería Lago Grey and the

Refugio Lago Grey; the 1½ to 2-~ trip costs US$15 (US$25 return). O hostería (☎ 24 8220/ext 29) for deta

Torres del Paine Lookout

> **Duration** 1 long day
> **Distance** 34km return
> **Standard** Easy-Medium
> **Start/Finish** Guardería Laguna Amarga
> **Entry** US$12.50, permit needed
> **Season** December-March
> **Summary** A superb return trek to several magnificent granite towers sitting dramatically above a turgid glacial lake.

This short trek is the most spectacular in the park and should not be missed. The Torres del Paine stand just north of the Cuernos peaks within a deep valley of the Paine Massif. The 'torres' themselves are three and a half distinctive pinnacles of hard Andean batholith rock, and are all that remain of a great cirque that has been sheared away by the relentless forces of glacial ice. The summit of the tallest tower, the Torre De Agostini, stands some 2850m above sea level and imposingly overlooks the intensely glaciated and barren surroundings 1500m below.

DAYS REQUIRED

The trek can be done as a long return trip from Guardería/Refugio Laguna Amarga or as a medium-length day walk from the Hostería Las Torres. Alternatively, trekkers could camp along the Río Ascencio and spend an additional half-day hiking up to Campamento Japonés.

The trek is easily combined with the Paine Circuit.

TREKKING STANDARD

Apart from some minor rock-hopping on the final climb, this return trek follows a good and well marked path for the whole way.

The trek up to the Torres del Paine Lookout is rated *easy to medium*.

GETTING TO/FROM THE TREK

For details of how to reach the park see the Access to the Park heading above. Unless you continue via the Paine Circuit to the administration centre, the Torres del Paine Lookout trek begins and ends at the Guardería Laguna Amarga. All of the scheduled bus services enter and exit Parque Nacional Torres del Paine via the Guardería Laguna Amarga.

The Hostería Las Torres, a large privately owned hotel and camping ground at the end of the road roughly halfway along the trekking route, runs its own shuttle minibus to and from the Guardería Laguna Amarga. The minibus meets the buses from Puerto Natales (which arrive at around 9.30 am). Trekkers staying at the Hostería Las Torres can ask permission to leave private vehicles there.

THE TREK

Guardería/Refugio Laguna Amarga to Torres del Paine Lookout

34km return, 9 to 12 hours return

The Guardería Laguna Amarga is the main entrance gate for Parque Nacional Torres del Paine. The Refugio Laguna Amarga, just 70m down from the guardería, is very basic, with a simple fireplace and sleeping space (on the floor) for a maximum of 10 people.

Walk down to cross the **Río Paine** on two new bridges, then immediately take a signposted left-hand short-cut trail that soon crosses the road once or twice. The route thereafter mostly follows the winding road as it leads west-north-west through ñirre scrub then down into a grassy basin and across a small clear stream just below the **Camping Las Torres** to reach the **Hostería Las Torres** (see Accommodation & Camping) after 2½ to three hours. The hostería and camping ground sit below the 2640m glacier-crowned summit of Cerro Almirante Nieto.

Proceed until the road peters out before dropping down to cross the **Río Ascencio** on a suspension footbridge. Continue across a small alluvial plain to where the 'Paso de los Cuernos' path diverges left (via the northern side of Lago Nordenskjöld to the Río Francés – see Stage 7A of the Paine Circuit). From here begin climbing north-westwards up an ancient heath-covered moraine ridge that lends a fine view south across Lago Sarmiento. Over to your right (and never really visible unless you make a brief side trip), the stream rushes through a gorge of layered black shale. The path traverses on into the valley along steep slopes high above the Río Ascencio, before moving down to meet the river again at the **Campamento Chileno**, 1¼ to 1½ hours from the hostería.

Continue up the western bank, gradually rising leftwards away from the river. Crossing several streams on stepping stones, the trail brings you up through lovely dwarf stands of lengas (untouched by the fires that destroyed much of the forest farther down the valley) to arrive at the **Campamento Torres** (see Camp Sites) after 50 minutes to 1¼ hours. This is the main camping area for trekkers and mountaineers in the valley.

Take the path (signposted 'Mirador') from the southern side of the small gully just *before* you reach the camping area. First follow the tiny clear stream up the left side of the regenerating glacial rubble, then follow orange paint spots leading rightwards over bare boulders to arrive at the **Torres del Paine Lookout** at the top of the moraine wall after 40 to 50 minutes. This often windy spot lies immediately below the Torres del Paine, mighty columns of grey granite ringed by shelf glaciers that occasionally drop icy blocks into a turgid lake in the foreground – one of the Patagonian Andes' classic scenes.

Trekkers not continuing to Puesto Serón (on the Paine Circuit) make the return to the Guardería Laguna Amarga via the same route.

Side Trip to Campamento Japonés The 8km return side trip into the wild upper valley of the Río Ascencio takes less than three hours. Pick up the initially vague trail at the lower edge of Campamento Torres, following cairns leading out over boulder rubble and across several channels of the cloudy glacial stream that descends from the lake at the foot of the Torres. The route rises mostly gently along the western side of the Río Ascencio before coming out onto an attractive forested flat after 50 minutes to 1¼ hours. Here you'll find **Campamento Japonés**, an old climbers' camp with a small makeshift hut and various improvised plaques made from tin lids nailed to trees. From here much less distinct routes continue up as far as the head of the valley.

Camping Las Torres to Puesto Serón For trekking parties walking the Paine Circuit, this easy (and scenic) shortcut route will avoid backtracking the whole way to the Guardería Laguna Amarga, saving several hours.

Take a 4WD track five minutes up the eastern side of the stream opposite the Camping Las Torres past a wooden refugio. From here a path leads off to the right over grassed-over moraine mounds through a tiny gap, then climbs on gently across mostly open slopes scattered with notro bushes. From there Laguna Amarga and Lago Nordenskjöld are visible to the south-east and south-west, respectively. Follow wire fences running below the steeper forested slopes up to your left, traversing high above the valley of the Río Paine as the route gradually turns from a north to a north-westward direction.

As you approach a broad flat plain beside the river, begin a northward descent to intersect with the main path after two to 2½ hours. (There is no signpost here, so trekkers going the other way will have to watch out carefully for this trail junction). Refer to Stage 1 of the Paine Circuit for further route directions.

Camp Sites Free camping without facilities is available at the Refugio Laguna Amarga. The spacious Camping Las Torres is an organised camping ground passed five minutes before you reach the Hostería Las Torres. It offers ideal sites among attractive green lawns scattered with ñirres, with nearby toilets and hot showers. There is reasonable camping along the banks of the Río Ascencio at the Campamento Chileno, though most sites

there tend to be a bit stony. The Campamento Torres, in the shelter of the lenga forest below the Torres del Paine Lookout, has the best and most abundant camp sites in the valley of the Río Ascencio. There are also several small and ramshackle huts at the Campamento Torres, but trekkers should not rely on these for shelter. The Campamento Japonés has pleasant camping in a much less frequented location.

Paine Circuit

> **Duration** 7 days minimum
> **Distance** 100km (excluding side trips)
> **Standard** Medium-Hard
> **Start** Guardería Laguna Amarga
> **Finish** Lago del Toro (Park Administration Centre)
> **Entry** US$12.50, permit needed
> **Season** December-March
> **Summary** A classic trek that circumnavigates the Paine massif, passing by large glacial lakes and enormous glaciers.

Truly one of the world's classic treks, the Paine Circuit circumnavigates the Macizo Paine. It is the longest and wildest route in the park, following the course of the Río Paine up to the Paso John Garner before descending the Río Grey to the park administration centre. The Paine Circuit offers constantly changing views of this extraordinary massif as it leads through dry steppes, moist alpine forests, highland moors and past enormous glaciers and deep turquoise lakes strewn with icebergs.

DAYS REQUIRED

The full circuit is normally done in around seven days, although side trips and rest days might stretch out the trek to 10 days or more. Do not underestimate your trekking times, and be sure to carry enough supplies for a safe, comfortable trip.

If you are unable to do the entire Torres

circuit, a shorter return trek to Ventisquero Grey (basically Stage 5 to Stage 7 in reverse), taking around three days, is a recommended alternative. The day walk to Campamento Británico would take an additional day.

TREKKING STANDARD
In most places the Paine Circuit is well enough marked (with orange stakes and paint) and trodden that serious navigational difficulties should not arise. The trail is less well maintained along the central section of the route, however, where fallen logs and boggy terrain make the going slower and more strenuous in places. Reliable bridges now provide safe crossings of all larger streams.

For safety reasons, the park authorities discourage anyone from undertaking the Paine Circuit alone, so lone trekkers are advised to find a companion for the trek. The circuit involves crossing the approximately 1180m Paso John Garner in its remotest central section. Although technically very straightforward, this pass is exposed to the frigid westerly winds, which bring sudden snowfalls even in midsummer; before December and after March snow may close the pass completely. Even in recent years, inexperienced and/or poorly prepared trekkers have come to grief on Paso John Garner, so the crossing must be taken very seriously. Less dangerous but extremely bothersome (particularly during occasional windless moments in December and January) are the plagues of mosquitoes at some of the camping areas along the Paine Circuit – carry some insect repellent.

Despite the reconstruction of new refugios in the park in recent years, it is still not possible to trek the Paine Circuit safely without carrying a tent. This is because there is no proper shelter along the most difficult and remote stretch of the circuit between the Refugio Lago Dickson and Refugio Grey. In January and February the refugios are often very full. Campers should note that park authorities have now prohibited the lighting of camp fires along the entire Paine Circuit; trekking parties must use a portable stove or cooker.

Most parties trek the Paine Circuit in an anti-clockwise direction, which is how the route is described in this guidebook. One disadvantage of an anticlockwise trek, however, is that it requires a steep, slippery descent from Paso John Garner. The Paine Circuit is rated *medium to hard* and covers a total distance of 100km, but optional long side trips to the Torres del Paine Lookout (34km return) and Campamento Británico (30km return) would considerably lengthen the walk.

GETTING TO/FROM THE TREK
The walk begins at the Guardería Laguna Amarga, the main entrance point to Torres del Paine. Transport details to Laguna Amarga are described in the Access to the Park section. The last section (Stage 7B) can be avoided by taking the launch from Refugio Pehoe to Refugio Pudeto.

THE TREK
Stage 1: Guardería/Refugio Laguna Amarga to Puesto Serón
20km, 4 to 5 hours
The Refugio Laguna Amarga is just down from the guardería. There is no charge for its use, but the refugio is very basic and has sleeping space for a maximum of 10 trekkers.

The highly recommended side trip to the Torres del Paine Lookout (described earlier as a separate trek) can easily be combined with Stage 2.

Cross the two road bridges over the Río Paine (as previously described) and walk a few minutes along to the right until you come to where a signpost indicates where the path leaves the road. Marked with orange-painted stakes and rocks, the trail moves well away from the Río Paine as it heads roughly north-north-west across the rolling grassy floor of the valley. After 1¼ to 1½ hours you pass an unsignposted and indistinct route leading off right. (This side trip takes less than 1½ hours return and leads almost directly east to the **Cascada Paine**, where the cloudy waters of the Río Paine drop 4m.)

The main path meets the Río Paine again 2km on, then continues upstream some distance above the river's steepening banks to reach the unsignposted trail junction (where the shortcut route coming from the Torres del Paine intersects) after two to 2½ hours. Cut over left through a fence gate to ford a shallow stream, then make your way approximately north-west across broad grassy riverflats scattered with ñirre woodland to arrive at **Puesto Serón** after a final 50 minutes to 1¼ hours.

Camp Sites The only authorised camping along Stage 1 is at Puesto Serón, which charges US$3.50 per person (including firewood and use of hot showers). This pleasant private camping ground has good sites among the ñirres at the edge of a large windy pasture.

Stage 2: Puesto Serón to Refugio Lago Dickson
19km, 4¾ to 6 hours

Head past the toilet and shower block (the old puesto building), cutting briefly rightwards beside a fence before you continue upvalley. The path first skirts broad waterlogged riverflats, where caiquenes (upland geese) and other water birds congregate in the marshy overflow ponds. It leads on immediately beside the swift-flowing milky-blue river, then starts climbing away northwestwards through ñirre woodland to reach **Laguna Alejandra** after 45 minutes to one hour.

Make your way around the southern shore of this tiny horseshoe-shaped lake, before continuing up in a few wide switchbacks. A more gentle climb roughly westwards brings you into an indistinct saddle after 30 to 45 minutes. From this often gusty spot there is a wonderful panorama of Lago Paine, several hundred metres below you, as well as the impressive arc of jagged peaks along the Chile-Argentina frontier behind **Lago Dickson** at the head of the valley.

Begin a very gradual traversing descent high above Lago Paine, rising and dipping continually as you head towards the glacier-crowned summit of Cerro Paine Chico 20km to the west. Because of their continual exposure to the wind and sun, these steep north-facing

slopes are mostly covered with battered calafate bushes, mogotes and other well-anchored plants. After sidling gently down through the light forest above boggy mallines where the Río Paine enters the lake you arrive at **Campamento Lago Paine (or Coirón)**, one to 1¼ hours on.

Follow the path on roughly west-south-west through stands of ñirres and open grassland dotted with wild daisies, keeping a good distance from the Río Paine to avoid marshy areas along its banks. Magnificent views of the mountains ahead, from the 2197m Paine Medio in the Cordillera Paine to Cerro Ohnet to the north-west, open out as you go. After crossing through previously burnt-out lenga forest now slowly regenerating, the path climbs an old moraine ridge, suddenly bringing Lago Dickson into sight. The ridge top offers a wonderful view across the lake to Ventisquero Dickson, whose white icy mass sprawls down from the Hielo Sur to calve in its greenish-grey waters.

On a lovely lakeside meadow immediately below you stands **Refugio Lago Dickson**, which should be reached 2½ to three hours after leaving Campamento Lago Paine. The amenities of this modern 33-bunk refugio include hot showers, flush toilets, a proveeduría, electricity and two-way radio; cooked meals and hot drinks are served. The old refugio, a rustic corrugated-iron construction nearby, is used only when the new hut is full.

Camp Sites The only place en route where trekkers are permitted to camp is Campamento Lago Paine (Coirón). This is a free camping area whose best sites are mainly on the other side of the stream. There is also a small primitive open-sided tin shack here, which provides basic shelter only. Thanks to the unsound sanitary practices of previous visitors, it's advisable to boil your water unless you fetch it from well upstream. If you find no toilet here (despite CONAF's promises to construct one), please go well downstream – ie *not upstream* – to defecate.

For a fee, trekkers can camp on the grassy lawn around the Refugio Lago Dickson, but lighting campfires is not permitted.

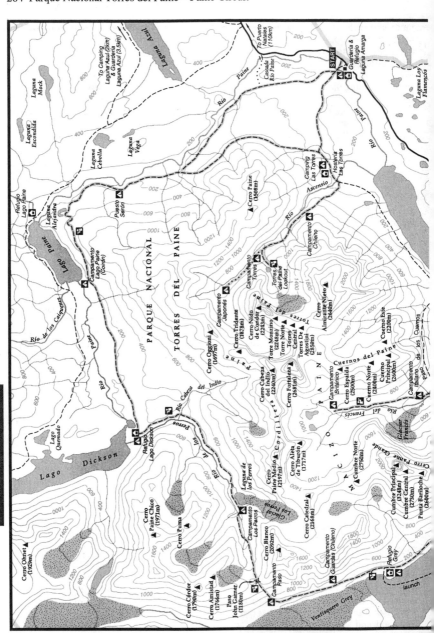

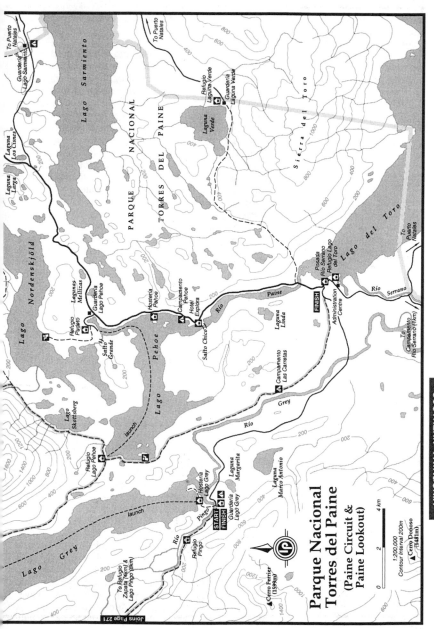

Parque Nacional
Torres del Paine

(Paine Circuit &
Paine Lookout)

1:200,000
Contour Interval 200m

0   2   4 km

▲ Cerro Donoso
(1441m)

Stage 3: Refugio Lago Dickson to Campamento Los Perros
9.5km, 3¼ to 4¼ hours

Follow the trail as it loops around south-westwards through low forest onto the steep embankment of the **Río de los Perros**. Make your way on upwards well above the rushing river (which is initially heard but not seen), remembering to look back for your last views across the lake to the Ventisquero Dickson, whose snout is ringed by floating ice debris. Shortly after passing a tiny peat bog, from where you get the first views ahead upvalley into the wildest and least accessible section of the Paine Circuit, the route comes to the **Río Cabeza del Indio**. Cross this large side stream on an improvised log bridge 60 to 80 minutes from the refugio.

The path undulates south-westwards through stands of coigüe de Magallanes to pass a thunderous chasm after 25 to 30 minutes, where delicate ground orchids such as the tiny white 'dove-shaped' palomita *(Codonorquis lessonii)* thrive in the moist conditions and rich humus. Continue on upvalley through attractive open lenga forest in long, virtually flat stretches interrupted only by very short steeper climbs to cross a suspension bridge spanning the Río de los Perros, a further 60 to 80 minutes on.

Head up through old regenerating glacial debris, then climb the end-moraine forming a natural dam wall that created **Laguna de los Perros**. A small glacier calves directly into the lake, noisily dropping blocks of ice that float around its frigid waters. The route now mainly follows the top of the moraine wall before leading off rightwards through pretty stands of lengas to arrive at the **Campamento Los Perros** after 30 to 40 minutes.

Camp Sites The only authorised place to camp along Stage 3 is at Campamento Los Perros, an organised camping ground in the forest near the confluence of the valley's two uppermost stream branches. Operated by Andescape, Campamento Los Perros charges US$3 per person, which includes eventually hot showers and toilets. The small and expensive proveeduría stocks basic supplies.

Stage 4: Campamento Los Perros to Campamento Paso
7km, 3¼ to 4½ hours

Stage 4 takes you into very exposed terrain well above the tree line. Trekkers should not cross the pass alone or in poor weather.

Not far above where the large side stream (coming from a glacier between Cerro Paine Chico and Cerro Puma) enters, recross the main stream on a small bridge. Make your way upvalley along an often muddy path through stunted forest, avoiding a prominent trail that continues some distance ahead before petering out to recross the stream at a little chasm, 40 to 50 minutes up from the camping ground.

Follow the stream briefly to the tree line, then pick up cairns leading away to the left (roughly west-south-west) up over sparse alpine grasses. The route then ascends more steeply to cross a tiny tumbling brook, climbing on over minor snowdrifts and tiny shallow tarns in the barren rock slopes. To the north a small crevassed glacier, which is the source of the valley's uppermost stream, descends from Cerro Amistad. Watching out carefully for marker stakes and/or occasional paint markings, ease leftwards to reach the **Paso John Garner** after 1¼ to 1¾ hours.

The pass lies at around 1180m above sea level, and is the highest point on the Paine Circuit. From up here trekkers get their first awe-inspiring view across **Ventisquero Grey**, whose enormous fractured mass of ice chokes the valley ahead, while in the other direction you can see back down the valley towards Lago Paine. The almost gale-force westerlies that frequently blast through this low point in the range may make it hard to enjoy the views for long.

Head a short way down from the pass, then follow trail markings that lead diagonally down left into the uppermost wind-whipped lengas. The route first drops sharply through this robust alpine scrub, whose resilient trunks have a curved, bow-like form (caused by the sharp gradient, severe winds and heavy winter snowfalls), then moves steadily downward through evergreen coigüe forest. A final, extremely steep descent almost directly downhill – a very slippery section after recent rain – brings you to **Campamento Paso**, 1⅓ to two hours from Paso John Garner. Cachañas, chatty parakeets found throughout Andean Patagonia, frequent this area during the summer.

Camp Sites The only sensible place to camp after you leave Los Perros is at Campamento Paso, a free, park-approved camping area completely without facilities. Occupying a tiny forested terrace high above Ventisquero Grey, space is limited. A trickling brook here provides your water source, but – as there is no toilet – water must be boiled or otherwise sterilised. Trekkers are again reminded that they should never leave campfires unattended and should properly extinguish campfires before departing. Be sure to carry out all your rubbish.

Stage 5: Campamento Paso to Refugio Grey
9km, 4 to 5½ hours
Begin contouring roughly south-east through the forest to reach the first ravine, which is being heavily eroded by a small torrent. In the past metal railings and/or fixed ropes have been erected here to help trekkers cross, but since these aids don't hold for long in the loose eroding rock you'll probably have to make your way through this somewhat dangerous obstacle on your own wits.

Continue on, rising and dipping along the steep slopes high above Ventisquero Grey to meet a second ravine, which should be easier to cross than the first. Along much of this section recent fires have killed most of the young trees which had been slowly regenerating after the original forest was burnt out decades ago, but the route gradually leaves the fire-damaged area behind as it leads through pleasant coigüe forest to arrive at **Campamento Guardas** (formerly called Campamento Chileno), three to four hours on from Campamento Paso. A short, unmarked trail leads from Campamento Guardas to a scenic lookout that offers wonderful views across the glacier.

The route now takes an undulating course

past Ventisquero Grey, whose mighty snout (divided into two sections by a large rock outcrop, a so-called nunatak) forms the northern end of **Lago Grey**. The unstable, 200m-thick wall of ice continually sends large blocks – some as big as a house – plunging into the freezing waters. Driven by the strong winds, these icebergs sail across the lake before stranding around the shoreline. The best vantage point to view this spectacle can be reached via a short side trail passed just before the main path cuts up behind a minor peninsula.

Descend gently to a signposted path junction, proceeding briefly right to arrive at the **Refugio Grey**, one to 1½ hours down from Campamento Guardas. This modern Andescape-run refugio (which is very similar in design and amenities to the Refugio Lago Dickson) looks out towards Ventisquero Grey from a lovely little lakeside meadow with its own pebble beach. Unless strong winds or icebergs make the trip too dangerous, a daily tourist launch operates from the dock near the Hostería Lago Grey (at the southern end of the lake) to Ventisquero Grey, calling in at Refugio Grey; the one-way/return fare is US$15/25.

Camp Sites Campamento Guardas, another free camping area without facilities, offers the only authorised camp sites between Campamento Paso and Refugio Grey. A pretty cascade on the lower side of the camping area provides uncontaminated water.

Trekkers can also camp at the Refugio Grey for a fee, which includes the use of the hut's facilities.

Stage 6: Refugio Grey to Refugio Lago Pehoe
13km, 3 to 4 hours
Return to the junction a few minutes up from the refugio, following the main path on behind a long rock rib. After descending slightly past a large waterfall to cross its raging torrent on a log bridge over a tiny gorge, the route continues leftwards up a steep, muddy slope with a steel cable. Accompanied by the sharp ice-shrouded peaks of

SOUTHERN PATAGONIA

Cerro Paine Grande jutting up to the left, you now begin a steady upward traverse via narrow glacial terraces covered with the prostrate, heather-like brecillo *(Empetrum rubrum)* high above Lago Grey to cross a saddle after two to 2½ hours.

Make your way on around the left side of a little lake scenically perched above Lago Grey, then descend south-eastwards through a broad dry gully vegetated with maihuén and mogote bushes to reach a small bay at the north-western shore of **Lago Pehoe**, one to 1½ hours on. In this attractive grassy plain looking out across the brilliant turquoise lake stands Andescape's Refugio Lago Pehoe, a large modern hut offering dormitory beds and (eventually) private rooms. It has hot showers, flush toilets, electricity and a two-way radio. Cooked meals and hot drinks are also available and there is a proveeduría. The old refugio several hundred metres away is not for use by trekkers except as an 'overflow' shelter when the new hut is full.

Except when strong winds or mechanical breakdowns stop it from operating – which can happen for several days in a row – a launch runs between Refugio Pudeto/Salto Grande and Refugio Lago Pehoe (see Access to the Park); the one-way fare is US$12.50.

Camp Sites Camping is *not permitted* anywhere along the route between Refugio Grey and Refugio Lago Pehoe. Camp sites at Refugio Lago Pehoe are over near the old refugio and cost US$3 per person (including hot showers). Wind barriers shield each site from the strong gusts that would otherwise flatten many tents. Campfires are not permitted at the Refugio Lago Pehoe.

Stage 7A: Refugio Lago Pehoe to Campamento Británico
30km return, 5½ to 8 hours return

This superb side trip into the amazing valley between the Cuernos del Paine and Cerro Paine Grande is not be missed – not even by trekkers who've almost completed the Paine Circuit and think they've seen all of the park's wild wonders!

Pick up the path near the old refugio,

heading around the steepening lakeside before you break away north-north-east through an area of burnt-out notro to reach **Lago Skottsberg**. The route gently rises and dips around the western side of this wind-swept lake under small hanging glaciers that slip down the southern flank of Cerro Paine Grande. Climb over a minor crest and continue past a smaller lake on your right to cross the sturdy suspension footbridge over the **Río Francés** after two to 2½ hours.

Go on five minutes upstream through the popular camping area known as **Campamento Italiano**, then follow paint markings leading through boulder rubble up to your right to gain a lateral moraine ridge. The route traces this forested ridge top, drops down leftwards past where the Río Francés shoots through an awesome water slide, before climbing on through the woods to reach an open area that serves as a natural lookout.

From up here you get exciting views of the adjacent **Glaciar Francés**, whose hanging icefalls cling to the sheer black-rock east face of Cerro Paine Grande. At the least predictable moments whopping hunks of ice dislodge and crash noisily into the valley, their shattered fragments then reforming into a small glacier which finally melts into two murky pools at this glacier's snout. Looking southwards, the view stretches beyond Lago del Toro on the park's southern periphery.

Head on into the upper valley, rising more gently now beside the stream through lovely alpine lenga forest. After crossing a water-logged grassy area, from where you get a fine view of the ice-formed 'horns' of the Cuernos del Paine up to your right, the path re-enters the forest to reach the **Campamento Británico**, 1½ to two hours further on from Campamento Italiano.

From Campamento Británico a rough foot track leads up to two attractive tarns near the tree line at the head of the valley, a trip taking an additional 1½ hours return. The only trekking route out is backtracking down the Río Francés.

Alternative Route: Paso de los Cuernos
After exploring the valley of the Río Francés,

trekkers can opt to do a moderately difficult route along the northern side of Lago Nordenskjöld to the Hostería Las Torres (see Stage 1B). The path begins at the signposted turn-off on the eastern bank of the river near the footbridge. This five to seven-hour alternative stage requires crossing several large streams coming down from the southern side of the Cuernos del Paine and Monte Almirante Nieto, where winds can be very strong. No camping is allowed along the way.

Camp Sites The only permitted camping along Stage 7A is at Campamento Italiano (space for several dozen tents) and Campamento Británico (about a dozen sites). Both are free but without facilities.

Stage 7B: Refugio Lago Pehoe to Lago del Toro (Administration Centre)
22km, 4¾ to 6 hours
Climb steeply over a minor ridge at the western edge of the grassy plain, sidling up and down around the mostly steep lakeside to reach a tiny bay opposite some islets after 45 minutes to one hour. Rising up dramatically from the brilliantly turquoise waters of Lago Pehoe, the black slate and granite summits of the Cuernos del Paine now appear from a particularly scenic aspect.

Cut south-eastwards away from the lake, first over ancient moraine mounds now covered with grasses and light scrub, then across a broad pampa to meet the cloudy-green waters of the **Río Grey** (the outlet of Lago Grey). Follow the undulating path downstream along the river's often steep banks, climbing high to avoid cliffs before you drop down to the riverside to reach the **Campamento Las Carretas** after two to 2½ hours.

The route now breaks away from the Río Grey, turning gradually around eastwards as it crosses a wide expanse of windy steppes, where small groups of ñandú may occasionally be observed. (Trekkers heading in the other direction are almost certain to encounter strong north-westerly headwinds along this section). Where the path brings you to a road (going to Lago Grey), turn left and walk

along the dusty roadway (or on trails not far to its left) to arrive at the administration centre (sede administrativa) at **Lago del Toro** after a final two to 2½ hours.

About 400m on straight ahead is the **Refugio Lago del Toro**, one of the park's few huts still run by CONAF. The refugio, which has electricity and a gas stove, charges US$5 per mattress in its simple upstairs dorm; hot showers cost an extra US$1.50. The **Posada Río Serrano**, diagonally opposite, offers more up-market accommodation. The posada also has a small store selling basic supplies at premium prices (but generally cheaper than at the Andescape refugios).

Camp Sites The only place trekkers are permitted to camp along Stage 7B is at Campamento Las Carretas, a free camping area in a slight depression (giving shelter from winds) on the banks of the Río Grey. It's not all that nice, since past fires have killed off the ñirres here. Unfortunately, camping is currently not possible at Lago del Toro.

Lago Pingo

Duration 3 days
Distance 36km
Standard Easy
Start/Finish Guardería Lago Grey
Entry US$12.50, permit needed
Season December-March
Summary A trek through the pretty valley of the Río Pingo to a remote lake fed by a glacier that calves directly in its frigid waters.

SOUTHERN PATAGONIA

This trek takes you to Lago Pingo, an impressive glacial lake beyond Lago Grey in the wild western sector of Parque Nacional Torres del Paine. Here the Ventisquero Zapata (or Pingo) spills down to calve in the freezing waters of Lago Pingo, the source of the Río Pingo. The valley of the Río Pingo is forested with attractive stands of open Magellanic forest, and along the undulating riverbanks are thickets of calafate bushes which in February and March produce abundant berries. Small numbers of the shy Andean deer, or huemul, thrive in the isolation of the Pingo area.

DAYS REQUIRED

The Lago Pingo trek takes one full day in each direction (ie a minimum of two days), but taking an extra day to explore this lovely area is time well spent. Since there is usually no public transport, it may be necessary to walk to/from the trail head, further increasing the trekking time by up to two days.

TREKKING STANDARD

The simple return trek to Lago Pingo follows a marked and very well trodden path up the Río Pingo, and presents little route-finding difficulty. The gradient rises very gently along the course of the river, and there are no really strenuous sections. Mosquitoes can be quite a problem along this trek in late December and January.

At the time of research, a crucial footbridge over the Río de los Hielos had still not been replaced after it was destroyed by a flood some years previously. The park authorities (or, more likely, a group of young and enthusiastic Raleigh International volunteers) will eventually rebuild this bridge, but – although some intrepid trekkers wade the icy waters – until then the Río de los Hielos should be considered unsafe to cross. Ask the advice of CONAF staff at the administration centre or the Guardería Lago Grey before setting out.

The trek has an *easy* rating, and the return distance to/from Guardería Lago Grey is 36km.

ACCOMMODATION & CAMPING

There are two very basic (and free) refugios en route, the Refugio Pingo and the Refugio Zapata, and for the time being the park authorities have no plans to hand the refugios over to private concessioners. Although it is possible to do the trek without a tent, this is not recommended (especially during January and February) as the small refugios get crowded very easily.

The *Hostería Lago Grey* (☎ 24 8220/ext 29), a hotel at the southern shore of Lago Grey offers accommodation.

GETTING TO/FROM THE TREK

The trek begins from the car park of Guardería Lago Grey, at the southern end of Lago Grey 18km on from the Lago del Toro administration centre (Sede Administrativa – see Access to the Park). Follow the road south across the Río Grey bridge and continue right (east) along the road on the river's southern side. There is no public transport to the trail head, but in summer you may be able to arrange a lift to Lago Grey; ask CONAF staff or call the Hostería Lago Grey. You can walk out to Guardería Lago Grey in 4 to 5½ hours – depending largely on the strength of the (invariably westerly) winds; getting a ride *to* the trail head will at least save you from having to walk into the wind.

THE TREK
Guardería Lago Grey to Refugio Zapata
14km, 3¾ to 4¾ hours

It's worth making the short side trip – either before you set out or upon your return – to the **Hostería Lago Grey** (see Accommodation & Camping). Simply cross the **Río Pingo** bridge and follow the road. From the hotel at the southern end of Lago Grey there are views to the distant Ventisquero Dickson and icebergs at the head of the lake. The launch to the Ventisquero Grey and Refugio Grey leaves from near the hostería.

From the guardería take the signposted foot track upstream along the western side of the river to reach the **Refugio Pingo** after 30 to 40 minutes. This tin cottage has a wood stove and sleeping space for eight trekkers. Continue on upvalley, climbing away from the Río Pingo through a long series of grassy meadows (granting views of Cerro Paine Grande to the north-east) and numerous thickets of thorny calafates (that in March are laden with sweet, seedy berries). The trail returns to the riverside just before it passes the (probably unsignposted) turn-off to the **Cascada Río Pingo**, 2½ to 3¼ hours on from the Refugio Pingo; this waterfall on the

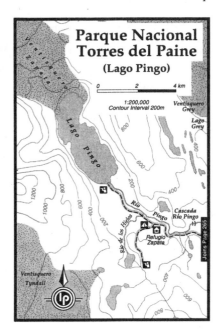

the river now and again before rising over a low terminal moraine 'dune' to arrive at Lago Pingo, 1¼ to 1½ hours from Refugio Zapata.

From this blustery southern shore there is a chillingly awesome view of the spectacular **Ventisquero Zapata**. This glacier slides down directly from the Hielo Sur into Lago Pingo, its icebergs driven across the lake by the incessant winds to strand on the sandy beach near the outlet.

Camp Sites

Although there are numerous temptingly attractive spots to pitch the tent all along the Río Pingo valley, the only park-approved camping areas are at the Refugio Pingo and the Refugio Zapata. Camping is strictly prohibited everywhere else.

Other Treks in Parque Nacional Torres del Paine

LAGUNA VERDE

This is an easy two-day trek to a large shallow lake where bird life and guanacos can be observed. Just north of the Río Paine bridge (2.5km north of the administration centre) a foot track leads north-east across the windy steppes to Laguna Verde. At the south-eastern corner of the lake are a CONAF guardería, a hostería and an extremely rustic refugio (which is barely suitable for habitation).

LAGUNA AZUL TO LAGO DICKSON

This four or five-day return trek leaves from the Guardería Laguna Azul (or you can take a shortcut north from the Guardería Laguna Amarga) and largely follows a 4WD track (used to transport goods to the Refugio Dickson). The track goes to a refugio on the northern side of Lago Paine and continues to a lookout near the north-eastern head of Lago Dickson, from where you can view the spectacular Ventisquero Dickson from quite close up. This route gives far better views of the Macizo Paine than the Paine Circuit

Río Pingo can be visited as a 15 minute side trip.

Make your way on for 30 to 40 minutes to the **Refugio Zapata**, a cosy wooden hut (which once served as a puesto for the Estancia Paine) at the edge of a grassy open riverflat. The refugio has an efficient stove and sleeps about four people. (Unfortunately, the Refugio Zapata also accommodates an extended family of mice, so keep your food out of reach of these rodents overnight). A rewarding two-hour return hike from the refugio follows a marked route southwards up to a lookout point giving views of **Ventisquero Tyndall**.

The route to **Lago Pingo** goes on up-valley, crossing a bare gravel plain to reach the **Río de los Hielos**, a narrow but deep and swiftly flowing glacial stream. At the time of research there was still no bridge here (see Trekking Standard). Once across the Río de los Hielos, however, the path leads on through endless calafate shrubbery, meeting

(which leads via the river's southern banks along the foot of the massif), but requires backtracking.

SALTO PAINE & CUERNOS LOOKOUT

From the Refugio Pudeto a two-hour return walk leads via the nearby surging falls of Salto Grande (where the Río Paine enters Lago Pehoe), to a lookout point from where there are classic views across Lago Nordenskjöld to the Cuernos del Paine, which rise imposingly immediately north of the lake.

Other Treks in Southern Patagonia

RESERVA NACIONAL JEINEMENI – CHILE

Reserva Nacional Jeinemeni (pronounced 'hey-ni-MAY-ni') lies in the forested ranges between the semi-arid country around Lago General Carrera to the north and the equally dry steppes of the Valle Chacabuco to the south. Lago Jeinemeni lies in the heart of this large reserve, approximately 60km by road south of Chile Chico (see Trekking Bases in the Central Patagonia chapter for further information).

From north of the guardería on the northern end of Lago Jeinemeni a trek can be made west to Lago Verde, a spectacular lake enclosed by high glaciated cliffs. From Jeinemeni's eastern shore another much longer track leads south up the Estero San Antonio to an attractive pass, then continues down the Estero La Leona to eventually reach the Valle Chacabuco, which is run as a vast estancia. At present the road ends at Lago Jeinemeni, but in time it will be extended along the route of the present foot track so that it connects with the Cochrane/Paso Rodolfo Roballos road.

The Chilean IGM 1:50,000 sheet *Lago Verde* (Section J, No 49) covers the key area around Lago Jeinemeni. There is no regular public transport up to Reserva Nacional Jeinemeni, although it is often possible to get a lift with a local who is licensed to collect firewood in Jeinemeni (ask at the local CONAF office) or on a logging truck. In January and February there are sometimes day tours up to Jeinemeni, when you may also be able to hitch a ride with the occasional private 4WD tourist.

RÍO PINTURAS – ARGENTINA

The Río Pinturas is 185km by road southeast of Perito Moreno in northern Santa Cruz Province. The river is best known for its ancient rock paintings found at the small Cuevas de las Manos reserve, but 150m-high canyons and gorges within the area also provide a backdrop for interesting treks lasting perhaps several days. The surrounding country is largely grazing land set among semi-arid steppes and rugged *mesetas* (small tablelands), and is best suited to more experienced trekkers.

Four 1:100,000 Argentine IGM sheets cover the Río Pinturas area. These are *Arroyo Telken* (Santa Cruz, No 4772-18), *Cerro Negro* (Santa Cruz, No 4769-13) *Río Pinturas* (Santa Cruz, No 4772-24) and *Cañadon Charcamac* (Santa Cruz, No 4769-19). There is a local bus from Perito Moreno township to the reserve several times a week during the summer months.

COCHRANE TO VILLA O'HIGGINS

This approximately 170km trek taking around 10 days follows horse tracks through the remote back country along the Chile-Argentine frontier. The route leads south from Cochrane (see Trekking Bases) past Lago Esmeralda and Monte Cochrane (3706m), then follows the Río Salto to cross a pass. It continues down the Río Bravo before heading off south-east past Lagos Alegre, Guitarra, Cristie and Riñon to the Río Mayer and on to Villa O'Higgins. Occasional settlers' farms are passed but most of the country is uninhabited. Unfortunately, fires in the 1940s destroyed large stands of forest in places. This trip is for experienced back country trekkers only and might be better done on horseback.

Two 1:250,000 colour sheets of the Chilean IGM's *Carta Terrestre* series cover the trekking route fairly accurately: *Cochrane* (No SL-18-12) and *Lago O'Higgins* (No SM-18-3). The Chilean IGM also has most or all of the necessary sheets scaled at 1:50,000. Two Argentine IGM 1:250,000 colour sheets, *Lago Belgrano* (No 4772-III) and *Monte Tetris* (No 4972-I) also cover the area but do not show the route.

Villa O'Higgins will eventually be the termination of the Carretera Austral, but at present this village can only be reached by a once-weekly Don Carlos air service from Coyhaique (around US$75 single fare). It is, therefore, recommended that parties fly in to Villa O'Higgins (with plenty of supplies) and do the trek south-to-north.

PARQUE NACIONAL PERITO MORENO

The 1150 sq km Parque Nacional Perito Moreno is a superb wilderness area roughly 250km directly south-west of the provincial town of Perito Moreno in Argentina's Santa Cruz Province. Lying on both sides of the continental watershed, the Perito Moreno area is enclosed by eight major lakes which reach out into the Patagonian steppes from the park's mountainous interior. Just north of the park is the mighty San Lorenzo Massif, whose major summit, Monte San Lorenzo (known as Cerro Cochrane to the Chileans), is the second highest point in southern Patagonia. In the late 1930s the area was explored by the famous ecclesiastical andinist Father Alberto De Agostini, who returned in 1941 with two members of the CAB, Schmoll and Hemmi, to make the first ascent of Monte San Lorenzo.

Until quite recently this isolated park was visited only by determined climbers and trekkers with their own transport. This is changing with the upgrading of the access road (Ruta 37 from Las Horquetas on the Ruta 40 turn-off) and the development of a modest tourist infrastructure. The APN administration centre near Estancia Lago Belgrano

was reopened several years ago, and now has a permanent resident guardaparque. The *Estancia La Oriental* (☎ 0962-2196/2445), which takes in a good part of the area fronting the park, offers accommodation in the medium price range. The Estancia La Oriental sells some basic supplies, but ideally visitors should bring everything they need with them.

Dirt roads and rough musterers' tracks give access to the eastern sectors of the park, but unbridged fast-flowing streams and sheer glaciated lake shores make it more dangerous and difficult to reach the interior. One relatively easy four-day return trek from the park administration centre (Intendencia) goes to an andinists' base camp. A foot track leads north past the abandoned Estancia El Rincón, then up via the Río Lácteo (shown on IGM maps as 'Río Late') to a refugio well outside the park boundary at around 1000m. From here a more difficult route leads up to two high glacial lakes known as Lagunas Los Tempanos.

Two relatively recent Argentine IGM 1:100,000 sheets, *Lago Belgrano* (Santa Cruz, Nos 4772-33 & 4772-32) and *Monte Tetris* (Santa Cruz, No 4972-3), cover all of the park. An adjoining northern sheet, *Cerro Pico Agudo* (Santa Cruz, No 4772-27), includes the nearby Monte San Lorenzo, and will also be useful to trekkers and climbers in this area.

Visitors without their own transport will still find Parque Nacional Perito Moreno a difficult place to get to. It may be possible to charter (or hire) a vehicle from either Perito Moreno or Gobernador Gregores. The Estancia La Oriental might be able to help unmotorised trekkers.

RESERVAS NACIONALES MAGALLANES & LAGUNA PARRILLAR

These two small reserves are on the Península Brunswick west and south-west respectively from Punta Arenas. Both lie in pleasant – although generally unexciting – country of rolling hills covered in low Magellanic forest. There are modest skiing facilities at

Reserva Nacional Magallanes, and a trail leads to the Río de las Minas. At Reserva Nacional Laguna Parrillar you can camp by the lake, from where walks can be made into the surrounding area.

The CONAF office (and possibly also the tourist office) in Punta Arenas have the only maps of the reserves that are of any real use. They may allow you to borrow these for photocopying.

Reserva Nacional Magallanes can be reached on foot or by chartered taxi from Punta Arenas. A travel agency in Punta Arenas, Turismo Pali Aike (☎ & fax 223301) at Lautaro Navarro 1129, runs day tours out to Reserva Nacional Magallanes (costing US$13 per person) four or five times a week throughout the summer. Reserva Nacional Laguna Parrillar is difficult to reach without private transport.

Tierra del Fuego

The largest of South America's islands, Tierra del Fuego is a southern extension of the Patagonian mainland. Its northern half is covered by arid steppeland devoted to sheep grazing and oil production, but farther south this dry, flat land gradually changes into undulating terrain of shallow lakes and extensive peat bogs before meeting what remains of the Cordillera in the south of the island. Rising at the mighty Darwin Range,

these so-called Fuegian Andes form a narrow line of mountains that becomes progressively lower with increasing distance to the east.

The Isla Grande (or 'great island') is divided into more or less equal Chilean (western) and Argentine (eastern) sections by an arbitrary north-south border that cuts across the Fuegian Andes at right angles. Only the northernmost part of Chilean Tierra del Fuego has been

TREKS IN TIERRA DEL FUEGO

1 Sierra Valdivieso Circuit — p279
2 Montes Martial Circuit — p283
3 Isla Navarino (Dientes Circuit) — p289

settled to any extent, and the far south remains an almost completely uninhabited and virtually inaccessible wilderness. Argentine Tierra del Fuego, on the other hand, has a much higher population, with roads penetrating all but its more remote corners.

TREKKING BASES
Ushuaia (Argentina)

Ushuaia, whose name means 'bay that runs to the west' in the language of the indigenous Yaghan people, stretches along the Beagle Channel directly below the snowcapped summits of the Fuegian Andes. As the capital of Argentine Tierra del Fuego, Ushuaia has experienced extremely rapid growth over the last two decades. The small Museo del Fin del Mundo at the corner of Maipú and Rivadavia has an interesting collection of natural and local history. Boat trips on the Beagle Channel to see marine life, and other tourist excursions, can be made from Ushuaia. Although the city is a free zone, prices for most things are still quite high.

Ushuaia's tourist office (Dirección Municipal de Turismo; (☎ 32000; fax 24550) is at San Martín 660 (next to the library). Another helpful tourist service is the Instituto Fueguino de Turismo/Oficina Antártica (☎ 21423; fax 30694) at Avenida Maipú 505 (under the Hotel Albatross), or in January and February at their office at the wharf directly across the road.

For information on Parque Nacional Tierra del Fuego, trekkers can visit the helpful ANP office (☎ & fax 21315) at San Martín 1395 (open Monday to Friday from 9 am to 3 pm). The Club Andino Ushuaia, Juana Fadul 58, 9410, Ushuaia, (contact Juan Carlos Begué) organises treks and climbs in the Fuegian Andes; the office is open daily from 4 pm to 9 pm. Caminante, a private guiding company at Don Bosco 319 (☎ & fax 22723) and Tempo Libre, at San Martín 863, organise outdoor-adventure activities (including overnight treks in otherwise restricted areas of the national park).

Lower-end accommodation is in short supply in Ushuaia, but backpackers are welcome at the central *Hospedaje Torres al Sur* at Gobernador Paz 1437, where bed and breakfast costs US$15 per night with cooking facilities.

As the bus ticket prices compare unfavourably with airfares, most people fly in and out of Ushuaia. Together two small airlines, Kaikén, (☎ 23663) at San Martín 857, and DAP, (☎ 31373) at San Martín 626, have almost daily direct flights between Punta Arenas and Ushuaia (around US$80 one-way). Kaikén has almost daily flights in either direction between Ushuaia and Calafate (the fare is around US$95), while LADE (☎ 21123) has one weekly flight in either direction (US$55) as well as several daily flights between Río Gallegos and Ushuaia (around US$50). Ushuaia's area code is ☎ 0901.

Puerto Williams (Chile)

This small settlement of no more than 1500 people, some of whom are descendants of the indigenous Yaghan people, is on the northern shore of Isla Navarino. Fronting the Beagle Channel – the only maritime border between Chile and Argentina – 60km east of Ushuaia, Puerto Williams is a Chilean naval base in strategic waters. It is also a minor fishing port (known for its king crabs, or *centollas*, which are caught in the surrounding sea canals) and the most southerly town in the world.

Puerto Williams' free Museo Martín Gusinde, honouring the German priest who worked among the Yaghans, has exhibits on local history. A good place to stay is the *Residencial Onashaga*, which has rooms from around US$15. The *Hostería Patagonia* is 2km west of Puerto Williams and offers up-market accommodation (around US$80 per night).

Aerovías DAP have up to three scheduled weekly flights in either direction between Puerto Williams and Punta Arenas; the one-way airfare is US$68. DAP and the Chilean airforce (FACh) also have occasional irregular flights between Punta Arenas and Puerto Williams. Airforce flights are generally on an at-short-notice basis and cannot, therefore, be reserved.

Chilean naval ships run irregularly between Punta Arenas and Puerto Williams, and there is a supply ship about once a month. The trip takes two days and follows the spectacular fjord-indented coast of southern Tierra del Fuego; the charge is around US$120 (including all meals).

Encouraging tourist links with neighboring Argentine Tierra del Fuego evidently has low priority for the Chilean navy. For years 'disagreements' between Argentine and Chilean maritime authorities have repeatedly interrupted the once-weekly return launch service operating between Ushuaia and Puerto Williams during the summer tourist season; when running the return fare is around US$65. If the launch is not running, boats can be chartered from Ushuaia (ask at the tourist office or the harbour) for around US$100.

Locals in Puerto Williams are not allowed to ferry people to Ushuaia – even the town's soccer team has been refused permission to cross the Beagle Channel to play in Ushuaia. During the summer, however, many private yachts on their way to and from Cape Horn or Antarctica pass through Ushuaia and/or Puerto Williams en route, and it is often possible to hitch (or pay for) a ride on one of these boats.

Argentine Fuegian Andes

The Argentine Fuegian Andes form an arc of rugged wilderness stretching around the regional capital of Ushuaia. Although they lack the altitude, extent and savage scenery of Chile's Cordillera Darwin, the mountains of Argentine Tierra del Fuego are far more accessible and enjoy a less extreme climate than the glacier-smothered ranges on the Chilean side. There are few true paths – once you leave the roads you are literally on your own – but adventurous trekkers will be excited by the numerous excellent off-track routes that make the Argentine Fuegian Andes such an excellent area to explore.

GENERAL INFORMATION
Geographical Features
Sandwiched between Lago Kami (also known by its European name, Lago Fagnano) to the north and the Beagle Channel to the south, the Argentine Fuegian Andes extend from the Chilean frontier, diminishing gradually in height until they peter out completely at the Estrecho de Le Maire, Tierra del Fuego's most easterly tip. Filling a 105km-long trough gouged out by Pleistocene glaciers, Lago Kami forms a natural division between the largely flat and much drier northern part of the island and this more rugged southern strip that extends west into the long peninsula formed by the Darwin Range.

While few of their summits exceed 1500m, intense ice age glaciations have so shaped these ranges that they resemble 'scaled-down' versions of far higher mountain massifs. As you trek through the deeply carved glacial valleys and over passes separating jagged peaks ringed with glaciers, it's easy to forget the Argentine Fuegian Andes' relatively low elevation. The upper limit of alpine vegetation is around 600m, and the permanent snow line is only several hundred metres above this.

Natural History
The moist Fuegian forests tend to be less dense than those farther north, with numerous kinds of low herb-like plants but little real underbrush. The southern beech species lenga is dominant higher up, where soils tend to be shallower, but lower down coigüe de Magallanes, known locally as guindo, is more common.

A typical herb-like plant found in these subantarctic forests is the frutilla del diablo (Gunnera magellanica), also called 'devil's strawberry'. It grows close to the ground, producing miniature, but inedible, bright-red berries on tiny brush-like branchlets. The frutilla de Magallanes is surprisingly similar in appearance, but is most easily distinguished by its 'real' berries, whose look and taste is actually more akin to that of raspberries. Thickets of calafate *(Berberis* species) and miniature ferns cover the ground in open, more well drained areas. Sundews *(Drosera* species) grow in the acidic soils low in nutrients, but these delicate plants are able to supply their needs by trapping small insects with their sticky, tentacle-like branchlets. Another carnivorous species is *Pinguicula antarctica*, which has violet flowers.

Numerous species of lichens and mosses are found growing on tree trunks, including the parasitic cabello de ángel *(Misodendron linearifolium)*, a member of the mistletoe family. The llao-llao *(Cyttaria harioti)*, a parasitic fungus, produces spongy yellow clustered balls on the branches of southern beech species, and was eaten by the indigenous peoples of Tierra del Fuego (hence its common Spanish name, *pan del indio*, or 'bread of the Indians'). The luminous orange jelly-like growths on fallen trees you see here are another interesting type of fungus, which accelerates the rotting of the dead wood.

The Fuegian Andes' poorly drained valley floors favour the development of sphagnum bogs, known locally as *mallines* or *turbales*. Mallines cover extensive areas of the lower valleys, where they are gradually colonised by encroaching forests. The bogs form beautiful, spongy red and gold peat mounds that are often dry enough to walk on. Thick deposits of peat have accumulated – in places to several metres in depth – and this material is cut commercially (for use as potting mix for plants).

Trekkers are most likely to see water birds on the numerous lakes and rivers. Although more at home on the open plains of northern Tierra del Fuego, the cauquén colorado (called canquén colorado in Chile, is found in the Fuegian Andes. This species of native goose has an orangey-brown head and upper neck and bluish-grey body plumage interrupted by brown stripes on its breast. Trekkers have a better chance of sighting the caiquén, or cauquén común. The female looks similar to (but is somewhat larger and darker than) the cauquén colorado, while the male has a white head, breast and underbelly. A common seabird is the gaviota austral *(Larus scoeresbii)*, a species of gull endemic to southern Patagonia and Tierra del Fuego.

Guanaco are common throughout the Argentine Fuegian Andes and their trails often provide excellent natural walking routes. The zorro fuegino is a subspecies of the zorro culpeo found on the Patagonian mainland. It is the only native Fuegian fox and lives its furtive existence in field and forest.

Regrettably, North American beavers now inhabit most forested streams all over Tierra del Fuego. The gnawed tree stumps and the animals' often surprisingly high dams are a constant hindrance and eyesore. Reindeer have also been introduced to the Fuegian Andes, but fortunately their numbers have stayed low enough (reportedly several dozen head) to keep them a novelty.

Climate

Somewhat sheltered by the much higher mountains to the west and by other lower ranges on the Chilean islands of Isla Hoste and Isla Navarino to the south, the Argentine Fuegian Andes have a relatively moderate maritime climate considering their subantarctic latitude. Average annual precipitation levels in the Argentine Fuegian Andes are 1500mm, though there is considerable variation between the higher ranges and the valleys. Subantarctic conditions concentrate the climatic zones into narrow altitude bands, which are reflected in the local vegetation and low permanent snow line. Because of the southerly latitude, the Fuegian winter (from late May until early September) brings heavy snowfalls – even down to sea level. Skiing, both cross-country and downhill, is a popular pastime, but most Argentinians prefer ski resorts with more clement climes.

Places Names

Many features of the Argentine Fuegian Andes still have no official nomenclature. In order to make the route description less confusing, however, I have given key features (particularly lakes and mountain passes) tentative place names. These appear between inverted commas (eg 'Paso Valdivieso') in the route descriptions to make it clear that the name is not official.

PRACTICAL INFORMATION
Information Sources
The Club Andino Ushuaia, at Fadul 50, organises treks and climbs in the Fuegian Andes; the office is open daily from 4 pm to 9 pm. Although they are only responsible for the national park, the helpful staff at the ANP office (☎ & fax 21315) at San Martín 1395 can advise trekkers on general conditions in the Argentine Fuegian Andes. Ushuaia's tourist office (Dirección Municipal de Turismo, ☎ 32000; fax 24550) at San Martín 660 has a free bilingual booklet offering a good basic outline of local history, flora and fauna.

Caminante, Don Bosco 319 (☎ & fax 22723), is a recommended outdoor-adventure company based in Ushuaia. Big Harbour Travel (☎ & fax 23551) at San Martín 625 is another good travel agency that organises short trekking and fishing excursions.

For other local sources of information in Ushuaia see Trekking Bases.

Permits & Regulations
Apart from the area within Parque Nacional Tierra del Fuego, permits are not required to trek in the Argentine Fuegian Andes. Please note the Montes Martial and the Sierra Valdivieso circuits start and/or finish by crossing private land where trekkers must be on their best behaviour.

When to Trek
Treks in the Argentine Fuegian Andes are best from December to March. April is often also very mild, but any breakdown in the weather so late in the season is likely to bring snowfalls down to at least 300m. Even in summer the weather can be highly erratic, with sudden southerly storms in the mountains. Trekkers should always be alert to changes in the weather, as these mountains are exposed to sudden storms from the south.

Sierra Valdivieso Circuit

Duration 3 days minimum
Distance 51km
Standard Hard
Start/Finish Turbera Valle Carabajal (15 km from Ushuaia on Río Grande road)
Entry Free, no permit needed
Season December-March
Summary A pass-hopping route through rugged Fuegian-Andean wilderness suitable for experienced trekkers only.

Extending eastwards along the southern side of Lago Kami (Lago Fagnano) from the boundary of Parque Nacional Tierra del Fuego to the landmark summit of Monte Carabajal, the Sierra Valdivieso arguably offers the most scenic wilderness walking in the Argentine Fuegian Andes. The numerous (now mostly quite small) glaciers and névés of this jagged range are remnants of far larger glaciers that reshaped this landscape during past ice ages, gouging out countless alpine lakes and tarns. Connecting many of its tiny valleys are gentle passes that serve as convenient crossing routes between the raw ice-clad peaks.

The Sierra Valdivieso is seriously challenging country, however, and therefore the exclusive domain of trekkers confident of finding their own way through largely trackless terrain.

MAPS
At the time of research the Argentine IGM had still not published topographical maps of the area at a scale of any use to trekkers. One accurate and up-to-date map that is currently available is an uncontoured, large-format blueprint covering all of the Argentine Fuegian Andes between Lago Kami (Lago Fagnano) and the Beagle Channel at an approximate scale of 1:50,000. This sheet is produced by the Dirección de Topografía y Geodesía and is available for US$10 from the Instituto Fuegino de Turismo at Avenida

TIERRA DEL FUEGO

Maipú 505 (or its office on the wharf just across the road).

An old Chilean IGM map of the 1:250,000 Carta Preliminar series, *Canal Beagle* (No 5468), also covers much of the Argentine Fuegian Andes, but all detail on this sheet should be considered very approximate!

DAYS REQUIRED
Trekkers should reckon on taking a minimum of three long days to do the circuit, but it would be prudent to take supplies for at least two extra days. The area has interesting off-route features that are worth spending extra time to explore.

TREKKING STANDARD
The Sierra Valdivieso Circuit follows a largely unmarked and little-trodden route through rugged and challenging country. Most of the circuit is off-track, and suitable only to very fit and self-reliant parties with very good navigational skills. This is mainly open walking – through clearings, mallín country or above the tree line – though in places minor bush-bashing may be necessary.

Although this high-level route largely avoids the boggy country in the lower valleys, there is much waterlogged ground (caused in part by the vandalous work of introduced North American beavers). Note that the circuit crosses several exposed passes which may be snow-covered early or late in the season, and that particularly before December and after March snowfalls on the ranges are very common. Trekkers should also be mindful that the Río Carabajal – which is otherwise an easy wade – can quickly become dangerously difficult to cross after rain. Be prepared to wait a day or more for the water level to go down.

This trek is not for the inexperienced and is rated *hard*. The total walking distance is about 51km.

ACCOMMODATION & CAMPING
There are no huts or any other reliable shelter along the route of the trek, and it is essential to carry a good tent. Where possible, avoid camping above the tree line or in exposed areas.

For suggestions of places to stay in Ushuaia see the Trekking Bases heading earlier in this chapter.

SUPPLIES
Ushuaia is the only logical base for all trips into the Argentine Fuegian Andes. The city has a good number of middle range hotels. Cheaper range hiking equipment is available in Ushuaia and all other basic supplies can be bought in the modern supermarket at the western end of town.

GETTING TO/FROM THE TREK
The trek begins and ends at the Turbera Valle Carabajal, a peat-cutting operation near an old Gendarmería Nacional post, about 15km from the centre of Ushuaia on Ruta 3, the main road north to Río Grande. The best way of getting there is simply to hire a taxi *(remise)* from Ushuaia, which will cost around US$12 per vehicle in either direction. Taking public transport to the start of the trek is not much of an option. Bus No 3 goes to Ushuaia's eastern industrial outskirts, 6km from the town centre but still 9km (downhill) from the start of the trek. Longer-distance buses pass the Gendarmería en route, but the fare is likely to be higher than what a taxi would charge. Traffic is busy enough to make hitchhiking a reasonable possibility.

THE TREK
Stage 1: Ruta 3 to 'Laguna Paso Beban'
10km, 3½ to 4½ hours

The turn-off leaves the Ushuaia-Río Grande road near the old Gendarmería Nacional post (still recognisable by its high radio mast and Argentine flag), several kilometres north of the Reserva Natural de Tierra del Fuego entrance gate at the foot of the 1335m Monte Olivia.

Follow this short access road across the **Río Olivia** and past the **Turbera Valle Carabajal**, a modern peat-cutting operation. Rising up abruptly to the north, beyond the expanse of beautiful rusty-red moorland dotted with little ponds stretching along the broad valley mouth, are the impressive glaciated ranges of the Sierra Valdivieso, at

Argentine Fuegian Andes
(Sierra Valdivieso Circuit & Montes Martial Circuit)

1:180,000
Contour Interval 250m

0   2   4 km

Lago Kami
(Lago Fagnano)

Isla Chica

Laguna de la Yegua

Bahía Torito

'Laguna Mariposa'

Sierra Valdivieso

'Laguna Azul'

Monte Carabajal (1250m)

'Paso Valdivieso'

'Laguna Paso Valdivieso'

Paso Beban

PARQUE NACIONAL

Río

Valle Carabajal

'Laguna Paso Beban'

Laguna Arco Iris

Río Beban

Cerro Vinciguerra (1450m)

Cerro Portillo

To Paso Garibaldi

Cordón Vinciguerra

Laguna Encantada Superior

Cerro Esfinge

TIERRA DEL FUEGO

Laguna de los Témpanos

Laguna Encantada

Turbera Valle Carabajal

Monte Olivia (1370m)

Valle Andorra

Andorra (Grande)

START FINISH

Gendarmería Nacional

Lago del Caminante

Arroyo

'Paso del Caminante'

Cerro del Medio

Cerro Roy

Cerro Dos Banderas

Cerro Cortés

Montes Martial

Cerro Godoy

Laguna Margot

Cascada de la Novia

Cerro Martial

Chorrillo Este

Arroyo Grande

Glaciar Martial

Cerro Según

Cerro Bridges

Chair Lift

FINISH

Arroyo de la Oveja

Ushuaia

Ruta 3

Punta Observatorio

Bahía Ushuaia

Río Pipo

START

To Lapataia

Ruta 3

Puente Arroyo de la Oveja

whose eastern end stands the distinctive peak of Monte Carabajal (1250m).

The road proceeds into the **Valle Carabajal**, gradually going over into a foot track as it skirts along the edge of the lenga forest to reach a tiny meadow by the meandering **Río Carabajal** after 1½ to two hours.

Wade the shallow river and make your way across the open spongy valley floor around the western side of **Laguna Arco Iris**, then head north up into an obvious side valley. Climb through narrow strips of heath between stands of evergreen coigüe de Magallanes (a species more commonly known as guindo in Argentina) on the western side of the small stream, moving up briefly left into the damp, mossy forest as the gradient steepens. The vague route continues up across soggy streamside lawns and past small beaver dams to reach '**Laguna Paso Beban**' after two to 2½ hours. This deep alpine lake lies just above the tree line in a typical glacial trough surrounded by talus slopes. the slopes are partially colonised by prostrate lenga scrub and hardy Fuegian cushion plants.

Camp Sites There are reasonable camping options along the lower Valle Carabajal (especially near where Stage 1 crosses the river), and more scenic sites higher up below 'Laguna Paso Beban'.

Stage 2: 'Laguna Paso Beban' to 'Laguna Mariposa'
18km, 5½ to 7 hours
Sidle around the eastern side of 'Laguna Paso Beban', then head into the rocky inlet gully towards a small névé on the peak at the valley head. It's worth making a short side trip rightwards (ie east) to a saddle overlooking the beaver-infested valley of the Río Beban, before you continue up left (northwest) over a small snowdrift to reach **Paso Beban** after 50 minutes to 1¼ hours. Apart from a large cairn (and some distasteful rightwing graffiti painted on rocks) you can't see much from the pass itself, but a few paces on an attractive new valley reveals itself.

Drop gently down past rock spires high above you to the right, following occasional red streamer markings (mostly along the right side of the tumbling stream) on through boggy clearings in the stunted lenga to the first beaver dam. Make your way left through trees killed by inundation, then take a low ridge down through more beaver-disturbed areas to where a large side stream spills down in a waterfall on your left, 80 to 100 minutes on.

Walk on about 1km downstream, then find your way up south over steep slopes of coigüe forest and carpet-like heath. Move leftwards via rock shelves and low open ridges looking down along the marshy lower valley to Bahía Torito on Lago Kami (Lago Fagnano) to re-encounter the side stream at a small grassy plateau. Follow the banks of this now gently meandering stream to a tiny cascade, from where a short climb over a minor crest brings you to '**Laguna Azul**', a blue lake in a raw basin below rugged glaciated peaks, after 1¼ to 1½ hours.

Head on south-west beside a tiny mossy inlet stream, following a broad rock rib up through the middle of this bare gully to a ridge top giving a fine panorama of the surrounding Argentine Fuegian Andes. Descend directly west over steep slopes of loose frost-shattered shale past an elongated lake to reach '**Laguna Mariposa**', a larger and more beautiful lake, 1½ to two hours from 'Laguna Azul'. Cut up steeply left over a tiny peninsular ridge (with more good views down to Lago Kami), before dropping back down into a little bay and tracing the shoreline to meet the inlet, a final 30 to 40 minutes on.

Camp Sites Despite extensive beaver activity in the valleys and exposed terrain higher up, trekkers will find repeated camping possibilities along Stage 2. Most recommended are the camp sites around 'Laguna Mariposa, particularly on moist lawns near the lake's inlet stream.

Stage 3: 'Laguna Mariposa' to Upper Valle Carabajal
5.5km, 1½ to 2¼ hours
A vague path leads up along the streamside through the scrub, skirting around the left-

hand side of a smaller lake then on past tarns among the alpine tundra to arrive at **'Paso Valdivieso'** (also known as 'Paso de las Cinco Lagunas') after 30 to 40 minutes. This scenic spot lies directly below a long shelf glacier whose tumbling meltwater streamlets flow both north and south of the watershed. Just below the pass lies **'Laguna Paso Valdivieso'**, another highland lake bordered by a wet mallín, beyond which ice fields are visible on the upper slopes of the Cordón Vinciguerra.

Descend leftwards to 'Laguna Paso Valdivieso', then follow a well-defined trail around the eastern shore of the lake. Make your way down beside the cascading outlet stream, crossing to the right bank when you come to the first patches of scrub before dipping down into the forest to re-encounter the Río Carabajal, one to 1½ hours from 'Paso Valdivieso'.

Camp Sites Camping is very good in sheltered areas along the small streams on both sides of 'Paso Valdivieso', although the usual problem of finding suitably dry and level sites exists.

Stage 4: Upper Valle Carabajal to Ruta 3
17km, 5 to 6½ hours

Begin the long stretch down through the lovely wild Valle Carabajal. Avoiding occasional areas of beaver activity, follow rough animal trails through the lenga forest (with abundant chauras and the native Magellan strawberry) along the northern bank of the meandering river. The route leads into the increasingly extensive belt of open moors towards the valley mouth, crossing five larger side streams (which often meet the main valley in high waterfalls as they gush down from 'hanging' side valleys up to your left), before it finally cuts leftwards over the moorland to reach an obvious forested lateral moraine after three to four hours.

Pick up a good animal trail leading along this low ridge until it peters out at the familiar large peaty pond of Laguna Arco Iris, from where you can backtrack to the Ruta 3 road in a final two to 2½ hours. There is no public transport this far out of town (see Getting to/from the Trek), but the traffic is busy enough to make hitching a reasonable proposition. The 15km walk back to Ushuaia takes around three hours.

Camp Sites Numerous good camp sites can be found in forested riverflats virtually all the way along the Río Carabajal.

Montes Martial Circuit

Duration 3 days
Distance 26km (38km directly to/from Ushuaia)
Standard Hard
Start Puente Arroyo de la Oveja (on the Lapataia road)
Finish Ushuaia-Río Grande road (4km from centre of Ushuaia)
Entry Free, no permit needed
Season December-March
Summary This short but difficult route circumnavigates the mountains behind Ushuaia by way of a pass that grants some excellent views of the Cordón Vinciguerra.

Rising abruptly from the Beagle Channel directly behind Ushuaia, the short range known as the Montes Martial remains an undisturbed wilderness despite its proximity to the booming city. This trek circumnavigates the Montes Martial Range, leading through idyllic valleys covered by light beech forest and areas of Fuegian turbal.

MAPS

A large-format 1:25,000 blueprint produced by the local Dirección de Topografía y Geodesía in Ushuaia is the only available map accurate enough for use in serious navigation, although it is uncontoured. It is available for US$10 from the Instituto Fuegino de Turismo at Avenida Maipú 505 (or its office on the wharf just across the road).

An old Chilean IGM map of the 1:250,000 Carta Preliminar series, *Canal Beagle* (No 5468), also covers much of the Argentine

Fuegian Andes, but all detail on this sheet should be considered very approximate! Also refer to the Argentine Fuegian Andes map in this chapter.

DAYS REQUIRED

The Montes Martial can be done in two long days, but the ideal walking time is three days.

TREKKING STANDARD

Despite its relatively short distance and straightforward route, which crosses one low pass ('Paso del Caminante'), the Montes Martial Circuit will test trekkers' physical and route-finding abilities. The trail is often very vague – at times non-existent – with some sections of bush-bashing through forest or scrub. Route markings are few.

Although a ban on overnight trekking in Parque Nacional Tierra del Fuego otherwise applies, the described route has been tacitly allowed (until now) as it only briefly transits the eastern fringe of the park. Trekkers should be particularly mindful of the minimum-impact code when passing through this area.

The circuit route is more easily followed if walked in a clockwise direction, as there are various diverging roads to confuse those coming the other way. The trek is graded *medium to hard* and has a total distance of 26km (or around 38km if walking from and back to the centre of Ushuaia).

GETTING TO/FROM THE TREK

The trek starts from a road bridge passed on the way to Parque Nacional Tierra del Fuego, 8km west of Ushuaia. The travel agency *Akawaia* (☎ 21123), at San Martín 542 in Ushuaia, runs a minibus service out to Lapataia in the national park, with departures from near its office at 9.30 am and 12.30, 4.30 and 7 pm. The minibus returns from Lapataia at 10.30 and 1.30, 5.30 and 8 pm.

From Ushuaia the walk out to the start of the trek takes two to three hours. This trek ends at the Río Grande-Ushuaia road (Ruta 3), just 4km from the centre of town.

THE TREK

Stage 1: Puente Arroyo de la Oveja to Upper Arroyo de la Oveja
5.5km, 2½ to 3½ hours

If setting out from Ushuaia, follow the Lapataia road for 8km west to the **Puente Arroyo de la Oveja**, the first bridge you come to. Head for 15 to 20 minutes up the grassy slopes (past a small speedway circuit 500m over to your right) to the start of a tiny forested valley. Cross a wire fence here and follow an increasingly indistinct trail upvalley, climbing gently above the small gorge known as the **Cañadón de la Oveja**.

The route continues high along the forested slopes on the eastern side of the valley, crossing the base of two screeslides before dropping down to meet the Arroyo de la Oveja again at an impressive beaver dam. From here find your own way through open woodland along the banks of the stream, until you come out onto grassy meadows in the upper valley after two to three hours.

Camp Sites Although it is possible to camp in the damp forest lower down the valley, the small grassy clearings found on both sides of the upper Cañadón de la Oveja are more attractive.

Stage 2: Upper Arroyo de la Oveja to Upper Valle Andorra
6km, 3½ to 4½ hours

Continue up the valley through the thinning vegetation, crossing the small stream where necessary. Pick up guanaco trails that lead towards the head of the valley around to the right (north-east). These provide an ascent over grassy green slopes before you reach the **'Paso del Caminante'**, a stony open pass marked with a rock cairn, after one to two hours. The pass offers some good views north towards the mountains of the Cordón Vinciguerra. Condors can sometimes be observed gliding around these ranges.

Following this natural path, drop down rapidly to the tree line alongside a stream which originates at the pass. (A route alternative from this point steers away left from the gully, heading on north-north-west up over grassy slopes then through open forest to reach **Laguna del Caminante**.) Otherwise, make your way down through the wet forest along the steep true right side of the cascading stream to intersect with a horse track coming up the **Arroyo Andorra** (or Grande), the outlet of Laguna del Caminante, 50 minutes to 1¼ hours from the pass.

Turn right along the steep south side of the side stream. The track rises and dips many times, and in places diverging cattle pads lead off. After 2km the stream leads out into the much broader **Valle Andorra**, where the path becomes more distinct. To the north this valley is bounded by the glaciated range whose highest summit is **Cerro Vinciguerra** (1450m).

Camp Sites After leaving the upper part of the cañadón the camping is poor until the valley opens out after reaching the Arroyo Grande (or Andorra). At Laguna del Caminante, good camp sites can be found in the open forest above the outlet stream.

Stage 3: Upper Valle Andorra to Ruta 3
14km, 4½ to 6 hours
Head roughly east along the southern side of the Arroyo Grande, mostly keeping some distance from the river. The path leads through attractive beech forests occasionally interrupted by small areas of mallín. (Look out for occasional route markings, as often no definite route exists until the trail reenters the forest.) Continue until the route merges into an old 4WD track.

You can either follow this gradually improving road or continue along the trail beside the river to reach a peat cutting operation. The road continues past isolated farms and holiday houses to connect with the **Ruta 3** at the north-eastern outskirts of Ushuaia. From here you can walk back into town in one to 1½ hours.

Camp Sites On the first part of this section excellent camp sites can be found anywhere the land is dry enough and close enough to water, including excellent riverside camping by the river on the final section.

Parque Nacional Tierra del Fuego

Parque Nacional Tierra del Fuego forms a 630 sq km strip of rugged mountainous country stretching northwards along the Chilean frontier from the Beagle Channel to well beyond Lago Kami. The national park begins just 10km west of Ushuaia, and is surrounded by even more expansive areas of Fuegian-Andean wilderness.

PERMITS & REGULATIONS
Apart from the park's southernmost Lapataia sector, where relatively short day walks are possible, overnight and off-track walking – unless you are accompanied by a park-approved guide – is prohibited in Parque Nacional Tierra del Fuego.

The park entrance fee is US$5 (only payable from 1 November until 31 March).

MAPS
The simple maps of Parque Nacional Tierra del Fuego, available free of charge from Ushuaia's tourist office or the APN, show the location of the trails fairly accurately. Most visitors will find them detailed enough for the short and easy routes described below.

An uncontoured 1:25,000 blueprint covering the southern area of Parque Nacional Tierra del Fuego is available from the Instituto Fuegino de Turismo at Avenida Maipú 505 in Ushuaia. The Chilean IGM 1:50,000 sheet, *Puerto Navarino* (Section L, No 188), whose coverage includes the Lapataia sector, is currently the only good contoured topographical map available.

Also refer to the map of the Parque Nacional Tierra del Fuego (Sector Lapataia) in this guidebook.

CAMPING
Visitors are only allowed to camp at six park-authorised sites.

Camping La Roca, at the southern shore of Lago Roca (20km from Ushuaia), is an organised camping ground with fireplaces,

Parque Nacional Tierra del Fuego (Sector Lapataia)

1:130,000
Contour Interval 250m

0   2   4 km

hot showers, store and a confitería; tent sites cost US$5 per night.

Three other camping areas around Lapataia are free (but without facilities): Los Bandurrias, Los Cauquenes and Laguna Verde. You can also pitch your tent for free at the APN camping areas at Río Pipo and Bahía Ensenada.

ACCESS TO THE PARK

The travel agency Akawaia (☎ 21123), at San Martín 542 in Ushuaia, runs a minibus service out to Lapataia with departures from near its office at 9.30 am and 12.30, 4.30 and 7 pm. The minibus returns from Lapataia at 10.30 am and 1.30, 5.30 and 8 pm.

TREKS IN THE LAPATAIA SECTOR
Bahía Ensenada to Lapataia

Bahía Ensenada, a free APN camping area on a small bay sheltered from the southerlies by Isla Redonda and Isla Estorbo, is 14km by road from Ushuaia. A short day walk from Bahía Ensenada follows a path eastwards to a disused copper mine.

A longer and somewhat more demanding day trek leads along the coastline past old middens (archaeologically important mounds of shells left by the indigenous inhabitants) to the western end of Bahía Lapataia. From here you must find your way north through the forest to the park administration centre at Lapataia. The route is scrubby in places, often requiring some minor bush-bashing. The few streams en route rarely run in summer, so trekkers must carry water. Do not eat shellfish found along the seashore, as they may have been contaminated by blooms of the extremely toxic algae known as red tide (*marea roja* in Spanish).

Lago Roca

The arbitrary north-south international border through Tierra del Fuego (which divides the great island into Chilean and Argentine sections) also cuts through Lago

Roca, leaving two thirds of this beautiful lake within Chile. From the camping ground at the southern end of Lago Roca, a popular 6km path leads around the lake's northeastern shore as far as Hito XXIV – that's *veinticuatro* in Spanish – which marks the Argentina-Chile frontier. You are not permitted to cross the frontier, which is regularly patrolled, so you will have to backtrack to Lapataia.

Cerro Pampa Alta
The low heights of Cerro Pampa Alta grant some long views across the Beagle Channel to Isla Navarino and Isla Hoste. This lookout point is reached via a 3km path that leaves the Ushuaia-Lapataia road 1.5km west of the Río Pipo and Bahía Ensenada road turn-offs.

Laguna Negra & Isla El Salmón
From the road 2km south-east of Lapataia, a trail leads north along the western side of Lago Lapataia to a fishing spot opposite Isla El Salmón. Laguna Negra, a lovely lake in the forest, is easily accessible via a 1km circuit loop at a signpost 200m past the trail to Isla El Salmón.

Cañadón del Toro
From the camping area at the road head on the Río Pipo, a 2km trail leads to a small waterfall.

Other Treks in the Argentine Fuegian Andes

All the following treks are covered by the maps listed under the Sierra Valdivieso Circuit and/or the Montes Martial Circuit routes.

GLACIAR MARTIAL
This popular half-day outing to a small glacier on the upper northern slopes of the Montes Martial is reached via a minibus service (five times daily) from Ushuaia. From a winter ski field 7km from Ushuaia you can climb or ride the chair lift to the snout of the Glaciar Martial. The treeless upper slopes offer excellent views across the Beagle Channel to Isla Navarino. The trek can be lengthened into an overnight trip by continuing over the saddle and dropping down to intersect with the route through the Arroyo Grande (or Andorra) valley, described in the Montes Martial Circuit.

ESTANCIA TÚNEL & ESTANCIA LA SEGUNDA
This pleasant walk to isolated ranches on the shores of the Beagle Channel east of Ushuaia is an easy to medium trek of up to four days. First take the Ruta 3 (highway) south-east to the trout hatchery (*estación de piscicultura*), 6km from the centre of town, then cross the Río Olivia and continue past the Estancia

Río Olivia. A trail leads on for 11km around the steep-sided coastline to the Estancia Túnel, from where it is possible to continue a further 7km to the Estancia La Segunda.

Less experienced trekkers should backtrack along the coast; a more difficult and interesting route leads up the Río Encajonado via a pass in the Sierra Sorondo to connect with the Ruta 3 in the Valle Larsiparsahk (or Lashifasha) to the north.

LAGUNA PERDIDA
Laguna Perdida, a small lake on the southern side of the Cordón Alvear, can be visited in a return day trek. The route starts from the hostería (for information ☎ 23240) below the 1425m Cerro Alvear in the Valle de Tierra Mayor, 21km north of Ushuaia along the Ruta 3, and leads north-west through an area of mallín on the northern bank of the Río Larsiparsahk (also called the Río Lashifasha).

Transporte Los Carlos (☎ 22337), at Rosas 85 in Ushuaia, runs buses to Río Grande which pass the hostería en route. There are also transfers from Ushuaia to Lago Escondido (ask at the tourist office in Ushuaia about transport by other carriers).

MONTE OLIVIA CIRCUIT

Rising to a sharp 1335m pyramid virtually in Ushuaia's backyard, the remarkable form of Monte Olivia is one of the Argentine Fuegian Andes' major landmarks. A difficult two to three-day trek leads around Monte Olivia from the Cascada Velo de Novia on the Ruta 3, roughly 11km from the centre of Ushuaia. The route first crosses a small bridge over the Río Olivia then follows a trail north-east through a tiny side valley to an obvious snow covered pass between Monte Olivia and Cerro Cinco Hermanos. After a very steep descent along a rough route it leads northwards via a gully to meet the Ruta 3 again.

Isla Navarino

Isla Navarino lies on the Beagle Channel just to the south of the Fuegian 'mainland'. This large island is a superb subantarctic wilderness of rugged windswept ranges and alpine moors, and offers the most southerly trekking in the world.

GENERAL INFORMATION
Geographical Features

Isla Navarino is roughly 100km long and 40km wide. The Cordón de los Dientes, whose highest peaks rise to well over 1000m, forms the backbone of the island. This extremely craggy range stretches west to east through the northern part of Isla Navarino, and – as on the adjacent Fuegian mainland – is dotted with numerous remnant glaciers and small, deep glacial lakes. The Cordón de los Dientes divides Isla Navarino into two (not quite equal) halves and shelters the island's narrow northern coastal strip from southerly storms. About halfway along this northern coast is the tiny town of Puerto Williams, a strategic naval base and the remotest settlement – with the possible exception of Puerto Eden on Isla Wellington – anywhere in Chile. A road runs along Navarino's northern coast, connecting Puerto Williams with Puerto Navarino at the north-western tip of the island and with Puerto Toro on its eastern side. The larger southern half of Isla Navarino is an open expanse of subantarctic tundra, dotted with hundreds of moor ponds and a number of larger, relatively shallow lakes, the biggest of which are Lago Windhound and Lago Navarino.

Natural History

Physical isolation and severe climatic conditions on Navarino have affected the island's wildlife. The only true forests are found on the more sheltered north-facing slopes of the ranges. There is less diversity of tree species compared to areas further north, with deciduous lenga and the evergreen coigüe de Magallanes predominating. Where exposure to the elements becomes extreme, vegetation is reduced to beautiful stunted forms. Waterlogged peat bogs and attractive mossy lawns compete with the forest at all elevations.

There are no land-dwelling predators on Navarino. As a consequence, the flightless steamer duck is relatively common. Small flocks of this large bird can sometimes be encountered roaming through the brush or foraging around streams, well away from the protection of any sizable body of water. The caiquén, a common native goose, also lives and nests on the island in open areas close to water. The male caiquén has white and grey plumage, while the female is coffee-black. Isla Navarino's open alpine scrublands also provide a favourable summer habitat for the diucón *(Pyrope pyrope)*, an uncommon small grey-breasted bird with blackish-brown wings and red eyes, and the yal cordillerano austral *(Melanodera xanthogramma)*, an endemic southern subspecies of the yellow-bridled finch.

Isla Navarino also has a large population of guanacos. Without the threat from pumas, the animals are much less shy than their cousins on the mainland, and can often be observed in their wild state from close range. As on Tierra del Fuego, introduced North American beavers have caused major damage to the forests and river systems of Isla Navarino. Beavers gnaw down trees alongside the streams, building often enormous dams to create their favoured habitat. These industrious rodents will block even the smallest watercourse right up to the tree line, inundating large parts of valleys. As on the main island of Tierra del Fuego, from where the beavers migrated in the early 1950s, the absence of predators means there is no biological mechanism to control their numbers.

Climate

Isla Navarino has a stark subantarctic climate similar to the adjacent Argentine Fuegian Andes, though its mountains are somewhat more exposed to the fierce gales that frequently sweep in from the moody seas immediately south of the island. The Cordón de los Dientes shelters the northern coast of Isla Navarino from these southerlies. Navarino winters are cold, bringing heavy snowfalls right down to sea level, but temperatures are not as extreme as might be expected this far from the equator.

Places Names

Around Navarino's coast the nomenclature is of Spanish and indigenous Yaghan origin, but in back country areas of the island most land features still have no official name. In order to make the track notes easier for readers to follow, however, I have given key landmarks (mainly en route passes and lakes) tentative place names. These appear in inverted commas (eg 'Laguna Martillo') to emphasise that the name is not official.

PRACTICAL INFORMATION
Information Sources

The nearest CONAF office is in Punta Arenas, but staff at the town's excellent museum or the small tourist office may be able to provide limited information on conditions.

Permits & Regulations

Since Isla Navarino is a military zone, anyone planning an overnight trek must obtain permission from the police station in Puerto Williams. In practice this is a mere formality and all you have to do is leave the details of your trekking itinerary including the names of each member of your party.

When to Trek

Because of the southern latitude the trekking season is at its shortest, and treks should only be considered between December and late March. Always watch for possible signs of an impending deterioration in the weather.

Dientes Circuit

> **Duration** 4 days minimum
> **Distance** 53km
> **Standard** Medium-Hard
> **Start/Finish** Puerto Willians
> **Entry** Free, permit needed
> **Season** December-March
> **Summary** A highly rewarding trek through a remote subantarctic wilderness of rugged windswept ranges and alpine moors.

The little-visited interior of Navarino is a superb wilderness of many hundreds of lakes and craggy mountain ranges. A spectacular range of jagged pinnacles known as Los Dientes de Navarino are the highest peaks on the island. In fine weather the Dientes can be seen directly from Puerto Williams and are a key landmark for boats on the Beagle Channel.

MAPS

The central ranges of Isla Navarino are covered by two Chilean IGM sheets scaled at 1: 50,000: *Puerto Williams* (Section L, No 190) and *Lago Windhound* (Section L, No 203). Although relatively new, these maps fail to show many lakes and have other major topographic inaccuracies (such as incorrect vegetation). They do not indicate the circuit route. These attractive sheets are nevertheless of considerable use to walkers.

DAYS REQUIRED

The Dientes Circuit is best done in four or five relatively short days. The trekking stages given below are suggestions only. As good camp sites can be found along much of the route, parties can move at their own pace. The ranges of the island's interior are easily accessible and invite further exploration. The numerous possible off-route side trips would lengthen the trek by many days.

TREKKING STANDARD

The interior of Navarino is wild country, and this trek should not be taken lightly. Although somewhat protected by the mountains further to the west, the island often experiences savage weather, with strong winds and snowfalls even in summer. The trek is best done from early December to the end of March, though – provided the weather cooperates – more experienced and well prepared parties can go at least a month earlier or later.

The circuit follows an approximate route only. Most of the hiking route goes through relatively exposed terrain above the tree line, and in the central area of the Dientes there is no vegetation whatsoever. The advantage of this is that there is open walking for much of the way. In many places rough guanaco trails indicate the best route and can be easily followed. Beavers, however, have flooded large parts of the forested valleys with their (usually shallow) dams, making the going harder. On some sections peaty bogs must be crossed and in these areas the ground is waterlogged. The route is variously marked with tree blazings, cairns, coloured tape and paint splotches. Nevertheless, careful navigation and route-finding is required.

The Dientes Circuit has been rated as *medium to hard* and covers a total distance of about 53km.

ACCOMMODATION & CAMPING

There are no refugios (or any other buildings) along the route and it is essential that parties carry a good tent. See Trekking Bases

for a few suggestions of places to stay in Puerto Williams.

SUPPLIES

Essential trekking provisions can be bought at the general store in Puerto Williams, although the range is limited. Considering the town's isolation, however, prices are not unreasonable. Puerto Williams also has a small bakery.

GETTING TO/FROM THE TREK

The trek begins and ends in Puerto Williams, the only settlement of any importance on Isla Navarino. Puerto Williams is accessible only by aircraft or boat (see Trekking Bases).

THE TREK
Stage 1: Puerto Williams to 'Laguna El Salto'
12km, 4 to 5 hours

The first section of the walk takes a cleared track up to Cerro Bandera. This is a popular day walk for locals. With light daypacks, the trip to Cerro Bandera can be done in around 4 hours return.

There is a statue of the Virgin Mary at a road intersection that marks a turn-off heading inland, 1km west of Puerto Williams. Follow this road for 30 to 40 minutes, turning right at a fork. The road leads up beside the **Río Ukika** to a small dam (the water supply for the town) and carpark, from where two marked paths depart. The left path has tree blazings dabbed with red paint and eventually leads back to town.

Take the right track, following the east bank of the stream for 10 to 15 minutes. Watch carefully for where the foot track turns away to the left and continues steeply uphill in a series of switchbacks through the Magellanic lenga forest. One to 1½ hours on, the tree line suddenly gives way to wind-battered beech brush. A short stretch straight up the grassy slope leads to the now fallen sheet-metal Chilean flag on **Cerro Bandera**. When standing, the flag is clearly visible from Puerto Williams, and was originally erected here in the early 1980s during the tense period of military confrontation with

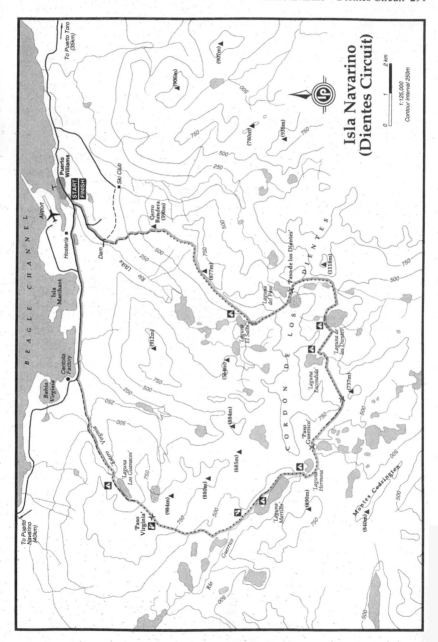

Isla Navarino
(Dientes Circuit)

1:125,000
Contour Interval 250m

0   1   2 km

Argentina. Magnificent views from Cerro Bandera stretch out along the Beagle Channel to Ushuaia and beyond.

Cerro Bandera is actually part of an exposed, stony plateau that extends to the south. In fine weather it is possible to continue along the ridge-line, but the route follows cairns over to the right. There are nice views of numerous lakes in the forested valley with the Dientes behind. Pick up a good guanaco trail that skirts above the irregular line of weathered shrubbery. When you reach a slope of loose, coarse talus coming down across the trail, descend right to reach the shore of 'Laguna El Salto' after two to 2½ hours.

Side Trips An interesting area of lakes, set in a barren landscape north-east of 'Laguna El Salto' and below the Dientes Range, is easily accessible. The area can be explored from 'Laguna El Salto' by following the route to the tiny shallow lake (see the following description) and heading over the lateral ridges. In places there are guanaco trails which indicate the easiest routes. It is also possible to climb the steep, lichen-covered ridges near to the summits of some of the Dientes peaks. The rock is crumbly and heavily fractured. A marked route leads up a rubble-filled couloir from a cairn on the first col. Other ascent possibilities exist in the range.

Camp Sites There is good camping in the picnic area by the Río Ukika dam. At 'Laguna El Salto' there are pleasant camp sites on moist cushion-plant lawns around the lakeside. Below 'Laguna El Salto' are more good sites, but higher up the terrain is very exposed and there is little firewood.

Stage 2: 'Laguna El Salto' to 'Laguna Escondida'
9.5km, 3 to 4 hours
Continue around the shore of 'Laguna El Salto' to the inlet cascade. Head up the side of the steep stabilised rubble chute on the right. The route follows the small stream, soon crossing the vegetation line. Only sparse lichen grows up here, so it is all open walking. Approaching the **Cordón de los Dientes** you pass a tiny shallow tarn and the stream soon disappears. Swing around left (eastwards) towards the ridge to reach a large rock cairn after 60 to 80 minutes. This ridge top overlooks **'Laguna del Paso'**, a lake filling in a barren glacial trough on your left, while a slightly lower gap is visible at the head of the lake. Do not descend the whole way to the shore of 'Laguna del Paso', but walk around on rock ledges above the lake. Some scrambling might be necessary, but you'll gain the **'Paso de los Dientes'** easily after a further 30 to 40 minutes.

Head down into the tiny attractive valley, passing a small glacier at the right. Take the east bank of an elongated lake and descend to another smaller lake. Pass this via its eastern side. The valley opens out just below the lake's outlet stream. The south coast becomes visible behind a multitude of lakes on the low-lying waterlogged land in the south of the island. Immediately before this, look out for route markings leading off to the right. Guanaco trails head east over a low ridge through stunted vegetation to the sizable **'Laguna de los Dientes'**, 60 to 80 minutes from the last pass.

From the upper side of 'Laguna de Los Dientes' head north-west up a gentle but distinct side valley. An interesting ridge of rock needles running off the Cordón de los Dientes will be on your right. Another big lake, **'Laguna Escondida'**, appears after 30 to 40 minutes. Set in stark surroundings, the lake is enclosed on three sides by steep craggy peaks.

Camp Sites The elevated route section above 'Laguna El Salto' is very exposed and unsuitable for camping. The scrub line is not reached again until 'Laguna de los Dientes'. The thinly wooded slopes above this and 'Laguna Escondida' are the best places to pitch tents.

Stage 3: 'Laguna Escondida' to 'Laguna Martillo'
8km, 3 to 4¼ hours
Sidle to the left around the beaver-cleared lakeside to cross the outlet stream and move

immediately onto the rise of low beech thickets. Continue across a short section of rock rubble before heading directly towards the obvious pass in the ridge to the south-west. Guanaco trails lead up to the crest of the pass, one to 1½ hours from 'Laguna Escondida'. This pass is marked by a high rock cairn, and offers a new panorama of lakes, forest and jagged peaks.

Do not head directly down the slope, but follow trails that contour to the right along the ridge. The route ahead – another low, easy pass – to the north-west soon becomes clear. Gradually descend the broken rock slopes to the tree line, circling around the higher ground to your right to avoid the more difficult terrain of boggy beaver dams and beech thickets. The route heads up to cross over the **'Paso Guerrico'** to reach **'Laguna Hermosa'** after one to 1½ hours.

This lovely liver-shaped lake with a tiny island on its left side is the source of the **Río Guerrico**, which drains into the Beagle Channel. Pick up trails that go well above the impenetrable scrub growing around the lake's southern shore. Where the vegetation thins out ahead, move down to cross the cascading outlet stream and make your way down along its true right bank to **'Laguna Martillo'**, 50 minutes to 1¼ hours on.

Camp Sites There are many potential camp sites along the route, though low vegetation generally provides poor shelter. The ground is often soggy, so choose your site carefully. The best camp sites are above 'Laguna Hermosa' and on the north-eastern shore of 'Laguna Martillo'.

Stage 4: 'Laguna Martillo' to 'Laguna Los Guanacos'
9km, 3½ to 4½ hours
Continue around the north-eastern side of the long and in places very narrow 'Laguna Martillo'. The route first stays close to the shore, but moves up at about halfway to cut off the broad peninsula near the northern end of the lake. Proceed downvalley on the northern side of the Río Guerrico, avoiding the waterlogged ground close to the river. A range of

spectacular spiked peaks rises abruptly on the left. To the right, a lower and more gently contoured range can be seen. At about 345° on the lower end of this range is a slight depression. This is the fourth and final pass.

Two km from 'Laguna Martillo', make your way up from the river through the narrow clearing along a small stream. Move diagonally upwards to above the tree line until you come to a sloping terrace. Rough trails up a tiny ridge covered with green cushion plants lead the way onto the range. There are superb views over the stony slopes to Ushuaia, the western Cordillera Darwin and other peaks. Peaks on the neighbouring Isla Hoste also stand out.

Head north-east across the barren plateau of **'Paso Virginia'**, passing two icy tarns. After 20 minutes you come to the edge of the flat area where the land falls away abruptly into a classic glacial lake, **'Laguna Los Guanacos'**. Large snowdrifts and loose scree cover the precipitous slopes enclosing the lake. Follow markings and cairns for a short way around to the right, where scree slides allow a rapid 200m descent to 'Laguna Los Guanacos'. Avoid occasional snowdrifts, which are dangerously icy.

Camp Sites There is good camping by the Río Guerrico downstream of 'Laguna Martillo', but to find dry, flat ground you may have to look hard. The scenic 'Laguna Los Guanacos' lies partially sheltered in a deep glacial trough, and camp sites can be found around the shores of the lake. Less exposed sites exist just below the outlet stream.

Stage 5: 'Laguna Los Guanacos' to Puerto Williams
14km, 4½ to 6 hours
A guanaco trail, so good in places that it seems it was deliberately constructed by humans, traverses the rocky western side of 'Laguna Los Guanacos'. The trail continues past the lake outlet and down below the tree line. The going becomes hard here as the forest is thick and there is no real path; just stay close to the **'Estero Virginia'**, crossing if necessary but generally keeping to the

TIERRA DE

right bank. After descending for 1½ to two hours through the valley of the 'Estero Virginia', you come onto fire-cleared hillsides on your right. Cut down rightwards over these open slopes to arrive at a centolla (king crab) processing plant on the Navarino's northern coast road. You can walk the 8km stretch back to Puerto Williams in around two hours. Occasional vehicles usually stop for hitchhikers.

Glossary

aduana – border (or customs) post (Spanish)

aerosilla – chair lift

Aisén – also spelt Aysén; Chile's wild and thinly-settled XI Region in Central Patagonia

alerce – a large conifer *(Fitzroya cupressoides)* mainly found in wet areas of the Lake District

alerzal – stand of alerces (Spanish)

amphitheatre – rounded glacial *cirque* enclosed by high rock walls

Andean – pertaining to the Andes, the world's longest and second highest mountain range

andinist – an Andean mountaineer

APN – Administración de Parques Nacionales, the national park authority of Argentina

Araucanía – the northernmost region of Patagonia, and the (former) territory of the Mapuche (Araucarian) Indian peoples

araucaria – a beautiful tree *(Araucaria araucana)*, whose umbrella-like form graces the forests and ridge tops throughout the Araucanía; known in Argentina by the Mapuche word pehuén and in English as the monkey puzzle tree

Araucarian – see *Mapuche*

arrayán – a native myrtle *(Myrceugenella apiculata)* with orange-red bark, usually found growing on waterlogged sites

arroyo – stream or creek (especially Argentine Spanish)

bahía – bay (Spanish)

bandurria – ibis often seen on pastures or wetlands throughout Patagonia

biota – flora and fauna of a national park or other area (Spanish and English)

bush-bashing – trekking off-tracks through (dense) forest

CAB – Club Andino Bariloche, the largest mountain club in South America

cabalgata – horse-riding trip (Spanish)

calafate – thorny bush of the *Berberis* genus, very common in southern Patagonia

caldera – a large crater that may arise from several smaller craters coalescing, a collapse or repeated explosions

caminata – trek or hiking trip (Spanish)

camino – road, but locally sometimes also used to mean 'foot track' (Spanish)

camping ground – a term used in this guidebook to mean places offering organised camping; camping grounds generally have at least basic facilities such as toilets and showers, and may charge a fee

camping libre – a free camping area without facilities (used mainly in Argentine national parks)

camp site – used in each trekking stage of this guidebook for any suitable place where camping is allowed; a camp site may be *wild* (if local regulations permit this), at a camping area designated by the park authority, or at a camping ground

CAP – Club Andino Piltriquitrón (the local mountain club in El Bolsón)

Carabineros (de Chile) – Chilean police force (also responsible for patrolling the frontier and for immigration control)

Carretera Austral – the 1137km unsurfaced 'Southern Highway' that runs south from Puerto Montt to Villa O'Higgins in southern Aisén

casa de familia – private household that takes in paying guests

cerro – summit (Spanish)

chaura – species of low shrub that produces edible berries

chilco – native Patagonian fuchsia *(Fuchsia magellanica)*

Chilote – inhabitant of the island of Chiloé

Chubut – Argentina's Central Patagonian province, centred around the Río Chubut

chucao – small ground-dwelling bird often heard (sometimes seen), mainly in the forests of the Lake District and Central Patagonia

cirque – high rounded precipice, formed by the weathering action of ice and snow, typically found at the head of a small alpine valley

club andino – mountain club (literally 'Andean club') (Spanish)

Codeff – Comité Nacional por Defensa de la Fauna y Flora, a conservation organisation based in Santiago de Chile

coigüe – group of three evergreen species of southern beech *(see also Nothofagus)*; known as coihue in Argentina

col – a mountain pass

colectivo – in Argentina, a public bus; in Chile, a shuttle taxi that stops to pick up passengers

colihue – native bamboo

Comarca Andina del Paralelo 42 – Andean region centred around the Argentine town of El Bolsón

CONAF – Corporación Nacional Forestal, the Chilean forestry and national park authority

confitería – small café-restaurant (Spanish)

contour – to move along a slope without climbing or descending appreciably

Cordillera – the long chain of the Andes (Spanish)

Cordillera de la Costa – a range of lower mountains running between the Andean Cordillera and the Pacific coast

couloir – a steep narrow gully filled with rubble

crevasse – deep fissure in a glacier

downclimbing – a descent that is steep enough to require trekkers to use their hands for support and/or safety

estancia – large cattle or sheep property

estero – stream or creek (especially Chilean Spanish)

filo – ridge or spur (Spanish)

4WD track – rough road suitable only for four-wheel drive vehicles

Fuegian – pertaining to Tierra del Fuego, eg the Fuegian Andes

fumarole – vent near or on volcano from which gases and steam are emitted

gaucho – Argentine cowboy

Gendarmería Nacional – Argentine equivalent of the Chilean Carabineros

geyser – a vent emitting hot water and steam, can sometimes erupt violently

glaciar – glacier (Spanish)

glissade – a snow-sliding technique used to descend snow slopes

GPS – Global Positioning System; a device that calculates position and elevation by reading and decoding signals from satellites

gringo – (not necessarily disrespectful) term for a foreigner of northern European descent

guanaco – Patagonian cameloid species (related to the llama)

guardaparque – national park ranger (Spanish)

guardería – national park ranger station (Spanish)

guindo – Argentine word for the coigüe de Magallanes *(Nothofagus betuloides)*

Hielo Norte – northern continental icecap, which lies entirely within the Aisén region of Chile

Hielo Sur – larger southern continental icecap

hito – natural or artificial surveying point that marks the international border (Spanish)

hospedaje – small (usually family-run) hotel

hostería – similar to a hospedaje

huaso – Chilean cowboy; in its wider sense, huaso simply means a country person

huemul – rare species of native Andean deer

icecap, ice sheet – vast dome-shaped glacier covering a mountain range in high-precipitation regions *(see Hielo Norte, Hielo Sur)*

icefall – very steep broken-up section of a glacier

IGM – Instituto Geográfico Militar, the military cartographic institutes in both Chile and Argentina

intendencia – Argentine term for the administration centre of a national park

lago/laguna – lake (Spanish)

lahar – landslide of volcanic debris and mud (of Javanese origin)

lenga – most common deciduous species of southern beech

llaca – small marsupial that inhabits the

forests of the Araucanía and Lake District; also called monito del monte

mahuén – plants of the genus *Mahuenia*, a rather atypical member of the cactus family
Magallanes – Chile's southernmost XII Region, which includes Chilean Tierra del Fuego
Magellanic forest – southern Patagonian forest (composed mainly of lenga and ñirre)
mallín – area periodically inundated, and typically covered by open swamp vegetation
Mapuche – group of ethnically related tribes that inhabited both sides of the Andes of northern Patagonia
mara – Patagonian hare
mirador – a lookout or viewing point (Spanish)
mochilero – backpacker (as in English, the word doesn't tell you whether the person concerned is trekking or simply using a backpack as convenient travel luggage) (Spanish)
mogote – species *(Mulinum spinosum)* of 'tumbleweed' found in dry areas of eastern Patagonia; also known as mata spinosum.
monito del monte – see *llaca*
monte – term used in Argentina to describe the scrub-covered hill country fringing the eastern Patagonian Precordillera; also used more generally to mean 'mountain summit', when it is synonymous with the Spanish word *cerro*
moraine – rock debris carried by glaciers and dumped as the ice melts
msnm – *metros sobre el nivel del mar*, or 'metres above sea level'

ñandú – native ostrich of the Patagonian steppes
névé – permanent snowfield in the high alpine zone
ñirre – a small deciduous southern beech species *(Nothofagus antarctica)*; spelt ñire in Argentina
Nothofagus – botanical name of the southern (literally 'false') beech genus, the most dominant trees of the Patagonian Andes
notro – also called ciruelillo, a common shrub *(Embothrium coccineum)* that produces flamboyant red flowers

nunatak – mass of rock projecting through an ice sheet, often found at the edge where the ice is thinnest

off-tracks – trekking route not following any real walking track
outlet – the place where a stream flows out of a lake

pampa – field or meadow; also used in Chile and Argentina to describe the vast steppes of eastern Patagonia (Spanish)
parque nacional – national park (Spanish)
party – used in this guidebook to mean a group of two or more trekkers
Patagonia – trekker's paradise
pehuén – see *araucaria*
pensión – boarding house or guest house
picada – usually less well-defined foot track (mainly Argentine Spanish)
playa – beach (Spanish)
portada – national park entrance gate (Argentine Spanish)
portería – national park entrance gate (Chilean Spanish)
Precordillera – Andean foothills that fringe both sides of the main range (Cordillera) (Spanish)
proveeduría – canteen or small store (such as at a camping ground or refugio) that sells basic provisions
puente – bridge (Spanish)
puesto – a small hut or primitive shelter, usually on a remoter part of an estancia *(see above)*, where the ranch workers can sleep a night or two
puma – the South American mountain lion (related to the cougar of North America)

quila – the collective term (of Mapuche origin) for about half a dozen species of vigorous native bamboo of the *Chusquea* genus

reducción – Indian reservation (Argentine Spanish)
refugio – mountain hut or 'refuge' (pronounced 'ref-oo-he-o') (Spanish)
rhea – *ñandú* (English)
río – river (Spanish)

ruca – traditional thatched house of the Mapuche people

SAEC – South American Explorers Club, a non-profit organisation for anyone with a general interest in South and Central America

scat – an animal dropping

scree – pile of weathered rocks at the foot of a cliff or hill

screeslide – slope of loose rock (known as scree or talus), below steep rocky mountainsides prone to weathering

scrub line – low, weather-beaten brush (usually *lenga*) on a high mountainside

seccional – guardería subordinate to the main APN intendencia (Argentine Spanish)

sendero – path or foot track (Spanish)

serac – large, prominent block of ice typically seen on steep glaciers or icefalls

SERNAP – Servicio Nacional de Pesca, the Chilean authority responsible for regulating commercial and recreational fishing

SERNATUR – Servicio Nacional de Turismo, the organisation which runs tourist offices in Chile

sidle – to move along a slope at right-angles

sierra – mountain range (literally 'saw') (Spanish)

southern beech – see *Nothofagus*

stage – an individual section of a longer trek

switchbacks – sharp bends in a path that takes a winding route directly up or down a steep slope

tábano – collective term for two or more kinds of blood-sucking horseflies that infest forested areas in the Araucanía and Lake District from early to midsummer

talus – synonym of scree

tarn – a small highland lake

tectonic – movements and processes in the earth's crust

Tehuelche – indigenous people who inhabited the steppes of south-eastern Patagonia

trail head – point from which a trekking route begins (eg a car park, roadside, or national park ranger station)

trans-Andean – leading across the main range of the Andes

tree line – altitude (which drops steadily from north to south) above which trees can no longer survive due to the severity of the climate; synonymous with 'timber line'

true left/true right – 'true' indicates the side of a river (or valley) from the perspective of a trekker facing downstream (or down-valley); for example, the northern bank of a stream that flows directly east-to-west must be its true right side

Valdivian forest – derived from the local Spanish term *bosque valdiviano*, this is the species-rich temperate rainforest that grows in the wettest areas of Andean foothills of the Lake District and the north of central Patagonia

ventisquero – alternative word for glacier (Spanish)

volcandinist – humorous contraction of the two words 'volcano' and 'andinist', meaning an amateur mountaineer who specialises in climbing Andean volcanoes

walking pad – indistinct path

wild camping – pitching a tent outside a camping ground or a national park-authorised camping area

yerba mate – green native South American 'tea', that is universally consumed by Argentinians and is popular in southern Chile

Index

MAPS

TEXT

TREKS

LONELY PLANET JOURNEYS

JOURNEYS is a unique collection of travel writing – published by the company that understands travel better than anyone else. It is a series for anyone who has ever experienced – or dreamed of – the magical moment when they encountered a strange culture or saw a place for the first time. They are tales to read while you're planning a trip, while you're on the road or while you're in an armchair, in front of a fire.

JOURNEYS books catch the spirit of a place, illuminate a culture, recount a crazy adventure, or introduce a fascinating way of life. They always entertain, and always enrich the experience of travel.

'Idiosyncratic, entertainingly diverse and unexpected . . . from an international writership'
– The Australian

'Books which offer a closer look at the people and culture of a destination, and enrich travel experiences'
– American Bookseller

FULL CIRCLE
A South American Journey
Luis Sepúlveda
Translated by Chris Andrews

Full Circle invites us to accompany Chilean writer Luis Sepúlveda on 'a journey without a fixed itinerary'. Whatever his subject – brutalities suffered under Pinochet's dictatorship, sleepy tropical towns visited in exile, or the landscapes of legendary Patagonia – Sepúlveda is an unflinchingly honest yet lyrical storyteller. Extravagant characters and extraordinary situations are memorably evoked: gauchos organising a tournament of lies, a scheming heiress on the lookout for a husband, a pilot with a corpse on board his plane . . . Part autobiography, part travel memoir, *Full Circle* brings us the distinctive voice of one of South America's most compelling writers.

Luis Sepúlveda was born in Chile in 1949. Imprisoned by the Pinochet dictatorship for his socialist beliefs, he was for many years a political exile. He has written novels, short stories, plays and essays. His work has attracted many awards and has been translated into numerous languages.

'Detachment, humour and vibrant prose' – **El País**

'an absolute cracker' – **The Bookseller**

Australia Council
for the Arts

This project has been assisted by the Commonwealth Government through the Australia Council, its arts funding and advisory body.

LONELY PLANET PHRASEBOOKS

Nepali phrasebook

Ethiopian Amharic phrasebook

Latin American Spanish phrasebook

Ukrainian phrasebook

Greek phrasebook

Vietnamese phrasebook

Listen for the gems

Speak your own words

Ask your own questions

Master of your own image

Building bridges,
Breaking barriers,
Beyond babble-on

- handy pocket-sized books
- easy to understand Pronunciation chapter
- clear and comprehensive Grammar chapter
- romanisation alongside script to allow ease of pronunciation
- script throughout so users can point to phrases
- extensive vocabulary sections, words and phrases for every situations
- full of cultural information and tips for the traveller

'...vital for a real DIY spirit and attitude in language learning' – Backpacker

'the phrasebooks have good cultural backgrounders and offer solid advice for challenging situations in remote locations' – San Francisco Examiner

'...they are unbeatable for their coverage of the world's more obscure languages' – The Geographical Magazine

Arabic (Egyptian)
Arabic (Moroccan)
Australia
  Australian English, Aboriginal and Torres Strait languages
Baltic States
  Estonian, Latvian, Lithuanian
Bengali
Burmese
Brazilian
Cantonese
Central Europe
  Czech, French, German, Hungarian, Italian and Slovak
Eastern Europe
  Bulgarian, Czech, Hungarian, Polish, Romanian and Slovak
Egyptian Arabic
Ethiopian (Amharic)
Fijian
French
German
Greek

Hindi/Urdu
Indonesian
Italian
Japanese
Korean
Lao
Latin American Spanish
Malay
Mandarin
Mediterranean Europe
  Albanian, Croatian, Greek, Italian, Macedonian, Maltese, Serbian, Slovene
Mongolian
Moroccan Arabic
Nepali
Papua New Guinea
Pilipino (Tagalog)
Quechua
Russian
Scandinavian Europe
  Danish, Finnish, Icelandic, Norwegian and Swedish

South-East Asia
  Burmese, Indonesian, Khmer, Lao, Malay, Tagalog (Pilipino), Thai and Vietnamese
Spanish
Sri Lanka
Swahili
Thai
Thai Hill Tribes
Tibetan
Turkish
Ukrainian
USA
  US English, Vernacular Talk, Native American languages and Hawaiian
Vietnamese
Western Europe
  Basque, Catalan, Dutch, French, German, Irish, Italian, Portuguese, Scottish Gaelic, Spanish (Castilian) and Welsh

LONELY PLANET TRAVEL ATLASES

Lonely Planet has long been famous for the number and quality of its guidebook maps. Now we've gone one step further and in conjunction with Steinhart Katzir Publishers produced a handy companion series: Lonely Planet travel atlases – maps of a country produced in book form.

Unlike other maps, which look good but lead travellers astray, our travel atlases have been researched on the road by Lonely Planet's experienced team of writers. All details are carefully checked to ensure the atlas corresponds with the equivalent Lonely Planet guidebook.

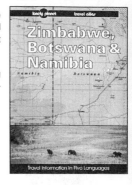

The handy atlas format means no holes, wrinkles, torn sections or constant folding and unfolding. These atlases can survive long periods on the road, unlike cumbersome fold-out maps. The comprehensive index ensures easy reference.

- full-colour throughout
- maps researched and checked by Lonely Planet authors
- place names correspond with Lonely Planet guidebooks
  – no confusing spelling differences
- legend and travelling information in English, French, German,
  Japanese and Spanish
- size: 230 x 160 mm

Available now:
Chile & Easter Island • Egypt • India & Bangladesh • Israel & the Palestinian Territories •Jordan, Syria & Lebanon • Kenya • Laos • Portugal • South Africa, Lesotho & Swaziland • Thailand • Turkey • Vietnam • Zimbabwe, Botswana & Namibia

---

LONELY PLANET TV SERIES & VIDEOS

Lonely Planet travel guides have been brought to life on television screens around the world. Like our guides, the programmes are based on the joy of independent travel, and look honestly at some of the most exciting, picturesque and frustrating places in the world. Each show is presented by one of three travellers from Australia, England or the USA and combines an innovative mixture of video, Super-8 film, atmospheric soundscapes and original music.

Videos of each episode – containing additional footage not shown on television – are available from good book and video shops, but the availability of individual videos varies with regional screening schedules.

Video destinations include: Alaska • American Rockies • Australia – The South-East • Baja California & the Copper Canyon • Brazil • Central Asia • Chile & Easter Island • Corsica, Sicily & Sardinia – The Mediterranean Islands • East Africa (Tanzania & Zanzibar) • Ecuador & the Galapagos Islands • Greenland & Iceland • Indonesia • Israel & the Sinai Desert • Jamaica • Japan • La Ruta Maya • Morocco • New York • North India • Pacific Islands (Fiji, Solomon Islands & Vanuatu) • South India • South West China • Turkey • Vietnam • West Africa • Zimbabwe, Botswana & Namibia

The Lonely Planet TV series is produced by:
Pilot Productions
The Old Studio
18 Middle Row
London W10 5AT UK

For video availability and ordering information contact your nearest Lonely Planet office.

Music from the TV series is available on CD & cassette.

PLANET TALK

Lonely Planet's FREE quarterly newsletter

We love hearing from you and think you'd like to hear from us.

When...is the right time to see reindeer in Finland?
Where...can you hear the best palm-wine music in Ghana?
How...do you get from Asunción to Areguá by steam train?
What...is the best way to see India?

For the answer to these and many other questions read PLANET TALK.

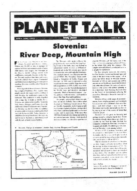

Every issue is packed with up-to-date travel news and advice including:

- a letter from Lonely Planet co-founders Tony and Maureen Wheeler
- go behind the scenes on the road with a Lonely Planet author
- feature article on an important and topical travel issue
- a selection of recent letters from travellers
- details on forthcoming Lonely Planet promotions
- complete list of Lonely Planet products

To join our mailing list contact any Lonely Planet office.

Also available: Lonely Planet T-shirts. 100% heavyweight cotton.

LONELY PLANET ONLINE

Get the latest travel information before you leave or while you're on the road

Whether you've just begun planning your next trip, or you're chasing down specific info on currency regulations or visa requirements, check out Lonely Planet Online for up-to-the minute travel information.

As well as travel profiles of your favourite destinations (including maps and photos), you'll find current reports from our researchers and other travellers, updates on health and visas, travel advisories, and discussion of the ecological and political issues you need to be aware of as you travel.

There's also an online travellers' forum where you can share your experience of life on the road, meet travel companions and ask other travellers for their recommendations and advice. We also have plenty of links to other online sites useful to independent travellers.

And of course we have a complete and up-to-date list of all Lonely Planet travel products including guides, phrasebooks, atlases, Journeys and videos and a simple online ordering facility if you can't find the book you want elsewhere.

www.lonelyplanet.com
or
AOL keyword: lp

LONELY PLANET PRODUCTS

Lonely Planet is known worldwide for publishing practical, reliable and no-nonsense travel information in our guides and on our web site. The Lonely Planet list covers just about every accessible part of the world. Currently there are eight series: *travel guides*, *shoestring guides*, *walking guides*, *city guides*, *phrasebooks*, *audio packs*, *travel atlases* and *Journeys* – a unique collection of travel writing.

EUROPE

Amsterdam • Austria • Baltic States phrasebook • Britain • Central Europe on a shoestring • Central Europe phrasebook • Czech & Slovak Republics • Denmark • Dublin • Eastern Europe on a shoestring • Eastern Europe phrasebook • Estonia, Latvia & Lithuania • Finland • France • French phrasebook • German phrasebook • Greece • Greek phrasebook • Hungary • Iceland, Greenland & the Faroe Islands • Ireland • Italian phrasebook • Italy • Mediterranean Europe on a shoestring • Mediterranean Europe phrasebook • Paris • Poland • Portugal • Portugal travel atlas • Prague • Russia, Ukraine & Belarus • Russian phrasebook • Scandinavian & Baltic Europe on a shoestring • Scandinavian Europe phrasebook • Slovenia • Spain • Spanish phrasebook • St Petersburg • Switzerland • Trekking in Greece • Trekking in Spain • Ukrainian phrasebook • Vienna • Walking in Britain • Walking in Switzerland • Western Europe on a shoestring • Western Europe phrasebook

Travel Literature: The Olive Grove: Travels in Greece

NORTH AMERICA

Alaska • Backpacking in Alaska • Baja California • California & Nevada • Canada • Florida • Hawaii • Honolulu • Los Angeles • Mexico • Miami • New England • New Orleans • New York City • New York, New Jersey & Pennsylvania • Pacific Northwest USA • Rocky Mountain States • San Francisco • Southwest USA • USA phrasebook • Washington, DC & the Capital Region

CENTRAL AMERICA & THE CARIBBEAN

Bermuda • Central America on a shoestring • Costa Rica • Cuba • Eastern Caribbean • Guatemala, Belize & Yucatán: La Ruta Maya • Jamaica

SOUTH AMERICA

Argentina, Uruguay & Paraguay • Bolivia • Brazil • Brazilian phrasebook • Buenos Aires • Chile & Easter Island • Chile & Easter Island travel atlas • Colombia • Ecuador & the Galápagos Islands • Latin American Spanish phrasebook • Peru • Quechua phrasebook • Rio de Janeiro • South America on a shoestring • Trekking in the Patagonian Andes • Venezuela

Travel Literature: Full Circle: A South American Journey

ANTARCTICA

Antarctica

ISLANDS OF THE INDIAN OCEAN

Madagascar & Comoros • Maldives• Mauritius, Réunion & Seychelles

AFRICA

Africa - the South • Africa on a shoestring • Arabic (Moroccan) phrasebook • Cape Town • Central Africa • East Africa • Egypt • Egypt travel atlas• Ethiopian (Amharic) phrasebook • Kenya • Kenya travel atlas • Malawi, Mozambique & Zambia • Morocco • North Africa • South Africa, Lesotho & Swaziland • South Africa, Lesotho & Swaziland travel atlas • Swahili phrasebook • Trekking in East Africa • West Africa • Zimbabwe, Botswana & Namibia • Zimbabwe, Botswana & Namibia travel atlas

Travel Literature: The Rainbird: A Central African Journey • Songs to an African Sunset: A Zimbabwean Story

MAIL ORDER

Lonely Planet products are distributed worldwide. They are also available by mail order from Lonely Planet, so if you have difficulty finding a title please write to us. North American and South American residents should write to Embarcadero West, 155 Filbert St, Suite 251, Oakland CA 94607, USA; European and African residents should write to 10 Barley Mow Passage, Chiswick, London W4 4PH; and residents of other countries to PO Box 617, Hawthorn, Victoria 3122, Australia.

NORTH-EAST ASIA

Beijing • Cantonese phrasebook • China • Hong Kong • Hong Kong, Macau & Guangzhou • Japan • Japanese phrasebook • Japanese audio pack • Korea • Korean phrasebook • Mandarin phrasebook • Mongolia • Mongolian phrasebook • North-East Asia on a shoestring • Seoul • Taiwan • Tibet • Tibet phrasebook • Tokyo

Travel Literature: Lost Japan

MIDDLE EAST & CENTRAL ASIA

Arab Gulf States • Arabic (Egyptian) phrasebook • Central Asia • Iran • Israel & the Palestinian Territories • Israel & the Palestinian Territories travel atlas • Istanbul • Jerusalem • Jordan & Syria • Jordan, Syria & Lebanon travel atlas • Lebanon • Middle East • Turkey • Turkish phrasebook • Turkey travel atlas • Yemen

Travel Literature: The Gates of Damascus • Kingdom of the Film Stars: Journey into Jordan

ALSO AVAILABLE:

Travel with Children • Traveller's Tales

INDIAN SUBCONTINENT

Bangladesh • Bengali phrasebook • Delhi • Hindi/Urdu phrasebook • India • India & Bangladesh travel atlas • Indian Himalaya • Karakoram Highway • Nepal • Nepali phrasebook • Pakistan • Rajasthan • Sri Lanka • Sri Lanka phrasebook • Trekking in the Indian Himalaya • Trekking in the Karakoram & Hindukush • Trekking in the Nepal Himalaya

Travel Literature: In Rajasthan • Shopping for Buddhas

SOUTH-EAST ASIA

Bali & Lombok • Bangkok • Burmese phrasebook • Cambodia • Ho Chi Minh City • Indonesia • Indonesian phrasebook • Indonesian audio pack • Jakarta • Java • Laos • Lao phrasebook • Laos travel atlas • Malay phrasebook • Malaysia, Singapore & Brunei • Myanmar (Burma) • Philippines • Pilipino phrasebook • Singapore • South-East Asia on a shoestring • South-East Asia phrasebook • Thailand • Thailand's Islands & Beaches • Thailand travel atlas • Thai phrasebook • Thai audio pack • Thai Hill Tribes phrasebook • Vietnam • Vietnamese phrasebook • Vietnam travel atlas

AUSTRALIA & THE PACIFIC

Australia • Australian phrasebook • Bushwalking in Australia • Bushwalking in Papua New Guinea • Fiji • Fijian phrasebook • Islands of Australia's Great Barrier Reef • Melbourne • Micronesia • New Caledonia • New South Wales & the ACT • New Zealand • Northern Territory • Outback Australia • Papua New Guinea • Papua New Guinea phrasebook • Queensland • Rarotonga & the Cook Islands • Samoa • Solomon Islands • South Australia • Sydney • Tahiti & French Polynesia • Tasmania • Tonga • Tramping in New Zealand • Vanuatu • Victoria • Western Australia

Travel Literature: Islands in the Clouds • Sean & David's Long Drive

THE LONELY PLANET STORY

Lonely Planet published its first book in 1973 in response to the numerous 'How did you do it?' questions Maureen and Tony Wheeler were asked after driving, bussing, hitching, sailing and railing their way from England to Australia.

Written at a kitchen table and hand collated, trimmed and stapled, *Across Asia on the Cheap* became an instant local bestseller, inspiring thoughts of another book.

Eighteen months in South-East Asia resulted in their second guide, *South-East Asia on a shoestring*, which they put together in a backstreet Chinese hotel in Singapore in 1975. The 'yellow bible', as it quickly became known to backpackers around the world, soon became *the* guide to the region. It has sold well over half a million copies and is now in its 9th edition, still retaining its familiar yellow cover.

Today there are over 240 titles, including travel guides, walking guides, language kits & phrasebooks, travel atlases and travel literature. The company is the largest independent travel publisher in the world. Although Lonely Planet initially specialised in guides to Asia, today there are few corners of the globe that have not been covered.

The emphasis continues to be on travel for independent travellers. Tony and Maureen still travel for several months of each year and play an active part in the writing, updating and quality control of Lonely Planet's guides.

They have been joined by over 70 authors and 170 staff at our offices in Melbourne (Australia), Oakland (USA), London (UK) and Paris (France). Travellers themselves also make a valuable contribution to the guides through the feedback we receive in thousands of letters each year and on our web site.

The people at Lonely Planet strongly believe that travellers can make a positive contribution to the countries they visit, both through their appreciation of the countries' culture, wildlife and natural features, and through the money they spend. In addition, the company makes a direct contribution to the countries and regions it covers. Since 1986 a percentage of the income from each book has been donated to ventures such as famine relief in Africa; aid projects in India; agricultural projects in Central America; Greenpeace's efforts to halt French nuclear testing in the Pacific; and Amnesty International.

'I hope we send people out with the right attitude about travel. You realise when you travel that there are so many different perspectives about the world, so we hope these books will make people more interested in what they see. Guidebooks can't really guide people. All you can do is point them in the right direction.'

– Tony Wheeler

LONELY PLANET PUBLICATIONS

Australia
PO Box 617, Hawthorn 3122, Victoria
tel: (03) 9819 1877 fax: (03) 9819 6459
e-mail: talk2us@lonelyplanet.com.au

USA
Embarcadero West, 155 Filbert St, Suite 251,
Oakland, CA 94607
tel: (510) 893 8555 TOLL FREE: 800 275-8555
fax: (510) 893 8563
e-mail: info@lonelyplanet.com

UK
10 Barley Mow Passage, Chiswick,
London W4 4PH
tel: (0181) 742 3161 fax: (0181) 742 2772
e-mail: lonelyplanetuk@compuserve.com

France:
71 bis rue du Cardinal Lemoine, 75005 Paris
tel: 1 44 32 06 20 fax: 1 46 34 72 55
e-mail: 100560.415@compuserve.com

World Wide Web: http://www.lonelyplanet.com
or *AOL* keyword: lp